Plutarco Elías Calles and the
Mexican Revolution

Plutarco Elías Calles and the Mexican Revolution

Jürgen Buchenau

ROWMAN & LITTLEFIELD PUBLISHERS, INC.
Lanham • Boulder • New York • Toronto • Plymouth, UK

ROWMAN & LITTLEFIELD PUBLISHERS, INC.

Published in the United States of America
by Rowman & Littlefield Publishers, Inc.
A wholly owned subsidary of The Rowman & Littlefield Publishing Group, Inc.
4501 Forbes Boulevard, Suite 200, Lanham, Maryland 20706
www.rowmanlittlefield.com

Estover Road
Plymouth PL6 7PY
United Kindom

British Library Cataloguing in Publication Information Available

Library of Congress Cataloging-in-Publication Data

Buchenau, Jürgen, 1964–
    Plutarco Elías Calles and the Mexican Revolution / Jürgen Buchenau.
    p. cm. — (Latin American silhouettes)
    Includes bibliographical references and index.
    ISBN-13: 978-0-7425-3748-4 (cloth : alk. paper)
    ISBN-10: 0-7425-3748-X (cloth : alk. paper)
    ISBN-13: 978-0-7425-3749-1 (pbk. : alk. paper)
    ISBN-10: 0-7425-3749-8 (pbk. : alk. paper)
    1. Calles, Plutarco Elías, 1877–1945. 2. Mexico—History—Revolution, 1910–1920.
3. Mexico—Politics and government—1910–1946. 4. Presidents—Mexico—
Biography. I. Title.
F1234.C192B83 2007
972.08'16092—dc22
                                                                    2006024488

Printed in the United States of America

∞™ The paper used in this publication meets the minimum requirements of
American National Standard for Information Sciences—Permanence of Paper for
Printed Library Materials, ANSI/NISO Z39.48-1992.

To Nicolas and Julia

Contents

Acknowledgments

Like many other inspirations, the idea for this book was born on a paper napkin in a hotel bar. Over a beer at the 1998 Latin American Studies Association (LASA) Congress in Chicago, Colin MacLachlan asked me whether I would be interested in writing a biography on Alvaro Obregón for Scholarly Resources. I was flattered by the suggestion and replied that in my opinion, the single greatest biographical lacuna in the Mexican Revolution was Plutarco Elías Calles, president from 1924 to 1928 and founder of the predecessor of the Partido Revolucionario Institucional (Institutional Revolutionary Party, or PRI), the party that ruled Mexico until the year 2000. The world has changed greatly since the turn of the millennium, including the PRI's fall from power and the acquisition of Scholarly Resources (SR) by Rowman & Littlefield, but the need for a study of Calles has remained.

This book would not have been possible without the help of numerous colleagues and friends. I am grateful for the help of the team of scholars who helped me launch the project: to Colin, for setting my sights on the genre of historical biography, and to Bill Beezley and Judy Ewell, the editors of the Silhouettes series at SR, for their guidance throughout the process. I also appreciate the encouragement of former SR editor Rick Hopper, who got this manuscript under advance contract. Ignacio Almada, Pedro Castro Martínez, Thomas Cole, Horacio Crespo, Greg Crider, Julian Dodson, Ben Fallaw, Carol Hartley, and Martha Loyo provided important suggestions for improving the manuscript. Carlos Carrillo, Timothy Henderson, Friedrich Schuler, and Paul Worley assisted me in finding sources. The history department at

UNC Charlotte provided a most congenial environment for my work, and I am particularly grateful for the friendship of my fellow Latin Americanists, Jerry Dávila and Lyman Johnson. I am very fortunate to have them as colleagues. Carlos Agüeros and the late Pablo Pellat gave me a home away from home in Mexico City.

This work also would have never come to fruition without the financial assistance provided by UNC Charlotte, the American Philosophical Society, and the Southern Regional Education Board. I also benefited from the cooperation of the custodians of Calles's private archive in Mexico City, the Fideicomiso Archivos Plutarco Elías Calles y Fernando Torreblanca. In particular, the director of the Fideicomiso, Norma Mereles de Ogarrio, provided valuable assistance and encouragement, as did Amalia Torreblanca. Patrick Jones of the UNC Charlotte Cartography Lab designed both of the maps used in this book.

Most importantly, I appreciate the help of Anabel, who has been an integral part of this project in more ways than one. Whether by listening to my ideas or by reading interminable drafts of my manuscript, the career of Plutarco Elías Calles has been a part of her life for the past five years just like it has been part of my own.

Charlotte, NC
February 2006

Glossary and Abbreviations

AFL	American Federation of Labor
Agrarista	Member of the Partido Nacional Agrarista, or political leader committed to land reform
bacanora	Potent liquor from the Sonoran sierra
cacique	Local boss
científicos	Positivist advisers of Porfirio Díaz who justified their political influence and corruption with their level of expertise
COM	Casa del Obrero Mundial (House of the World's Worker), an anarcho-syndicalist labor union in 1910s
comisario	Police chief or sheriff
Consejo de Ministros	Cabinet of president
CROM	Confederación Regional Obrera Mexicana (Mexican Regional Workers' Confederation), the largest confederation of labor unions in the 1920s and early 1930s
CTM	Confederación de Trabajadores Mexicanos (Mexican Workers' Confederation); national confederation of trade unions that replaced the CROM as the leading labor organization under Cárdenas administration
divisionarios	Generals of the highest rank (*general de división*)

ejido	Agricultural land redistributed to communal farms
Federales	Federal army under Porfirio Díaz, Francisco I. Madero, and Victoriano Huerta
hacendado	Owner of a great rural estate
jefe de operaciones	Regional military commander
Jefe Máximo	Supreme chief (of the Mexican Revolution); informal title given to Calles
JFCA	Junta Federal de Conciliación y Arbitraje (Federal Council for Reconciliation and Arbitration); mediation board for labor disputes
Laborista	Member of the Partido Laborista Mexicano
Maximato	Period from December 1928 to June 1935, during which Calles played an important informal political role
PAN	Partido Acción Nacional (National Action Party); Catholic opposition party founded in 1939
pequeña propiedad	Smallholding or family farm
PLC	Partido Liberal Constitucionalista (Liberal Constitutionalist Party); party founded in 1916 as alliance of Constitutionalist political leaders
PLM	Partido Laborista Mexicano (Mexican Labo Party); political wing of the CROM led by Luis N. Napoleón
PNA	Partido Nacional Agrarista (National Agrarian Party); party committed to land reform under the leadership of Antonio Díaz Soto y Gama
PNC	Partido Nacional Cooperatista (National Cooperatist Party); largest party in Congress after elections of 1922, supported Adolfo de la Huerta for president in 1923
PNR	Partido Nacional Revolucionario (National Revolutionary Party); ruling party founded by Calles at the beginning of Maximato
prefect	Political boss of a district in Sonora
PRI	Partido Revolucionario Institucional (Institutional Revolutionary Party); founded in 1946 as a reorganized version of the PRM
PRM	Partido de la Revolución Mexicana (Party of the Mexican Revolution); founded in 1938 as a reorganized version of the PNR

PSS	Partido Socialista del Sureste (Socialist Party of the Southeast); regional party allied with Calles founded by Felipe Carrillo Puerto
SEP	Secretaría de Educación Pública (Secretariat of Public Education)
Yoris	Term used by indigenous peoples of Sonora to denote Spanish-speaking people

Illustrations and Tables

Photographs

Maps

Tables

Chronology

1877	(September 25?)	Born Plutarco Elías Campuzano in Guaymas, Sonora
1880		After his mother's death, Plutarco moves in with his paternal uncle, Juan Bautista Calles
1883		Beginning of Plutarco's years in public school in Hermosillo, Sonora
1892		Plutarco graduates from Primera Escuela Municipal in Hermosillo after the ninth grade, the highest grade offered in the state of Sonora
1893		Calles begins his teaching career as a teacher's assistant
1897		Calles moves back to Guaymas
1898		Calles marries Natalia Chacón
1899		Birth of first child, Rodolfo Elías Calles Chacón
1902	(January)	Calles serves as manager of Hotel California; he is appointed to his first public position as treasurer of Guaymas

1903	(January)	Calles moves to northeastern Sonora to farmland owned by his father
1906		Failure of farm; Calles and partner establish flour mill in Fronteras
1910	(July)	Calles returns to Guaymas after failure of flour mill
	(November 20)	Outbreak of the Mexican Revolution after Francisco I. Madero proclaims the Plan de San Luis Potosí
1911	(May 25)	Dictator Porfirio Díaz resigns
	(August)	Calles moves to Agua Prieta
	(September 5)	Calles named *comisario* of Agua Prieta by Governor José María Maytorena
	(October 1)	Madero elected president
1912	(March)	Calles and Alvaro Obregón enter their military careers fighting against the Orozquista revolt
1913	(February 18)	Conspiracy led by General Victoriano Huerta overthrows Madero
	(March)	Constitutionalist coalition begins war against Huerta; Calles named lieutenant colonel
	(September–October)	First Chief Venustiano Carranza organizes provisional national government in Hermosillo, Sonora
1914	(July 14)	Huerta resigns
	(September)	Beginning of civil war in Sonora between the factions of Maytorena (allied with Pancho Villa) and Calles (allied with Carranza)
	(October)	Maytorenistas begin siege of Naco defended by Calles and General Benjamín Hill
	(November)	Beginning of war between the factions at the national level following the failure of the Convention of Aguascalientes
1915	(January)	Failure of the siege of Naco; Maytorenistas begin to lose ground

	(August)	Following Obregón's victory over Villa, Carranza names Calles military governor of Sonora
1917	(February 5)	Promulgation of Constitution of 1917
1919	(September)	Calles appointed secretary of industry and commerce
1920	(April)	Calles signs Plan of Agua Prieta that announces rebellion against Carranza
	(May–November)	Calles serves as secretary of war under Interim President Adolfo de la Huerta
	(December 1)	Calles named secretary of *gobernación* by President Alvaro Obregón
1923	(December)	Outbreak of de la Huerta rebellion
1924	(July)	Calles wins election as president of Mexico
	(August–November)	Calles on extended trip to Germany, France, and the United States
	(November 30)	Calles sworn in as president
1926	(August)	Outbreak of Cristero rebellion
1927	(June 2)	Death of his wife, Natalia Chacón de Elías Calles
1928	(July 17)	Assassination of president-elect Obregón leaves Calles as Mexico's foremost politician
	(September 1)	In last *informe* to Congress, Calles announces that he will not seek the presidency again
	(November 30)	Inauguration of Provisional President Emilio Portes Gil; beginning of Maximato
1929	(February)	Founding of Partido Nacional Revolucionario
	(May)	Escobar rebellion; Calles appointed secretary of war
1930	(August 2)	Calles marries Leonor Llorente
1932	(September 4)	Ortiz Rubio resigns; inauguration of Abelardo L. Rodríguez
	(November 25)	Death of Leonor Llorente

1934	(November 30)	Inauguration of President Lázaro Cárdenas
1935	(June)	Open break between Calles and Cárdenas; end of Maximato
1936	(April 10)	Forced into exile in the United States
1941	(May)	Returns from exile
1945	(October 19)	Dies in Mexico City

Introduction

Individuals must subordinate their will to their reason . . . [and] the
public must be taught to understand what they want.

—Jean-Jacques Rousseau, *The Social Contract*

On April 10, 1924, presidential candidate Plutarco Elías Calles gave a speech
at the tomb of Emiliano Zapata in Cuautla, a town in the southern Mexican
state of Morelos. It was the fifth anniversary of the assassination of the leg-
endary campesino leader who had fought for land and liberty since early 1911
shortly after the outbreak of the Mexican Revolution. The anniversary recalled
a heinous crime that had turned Zapata into the icon of the campesinos' struggle to regain land taken from them by great agricultural estates.[1] A tall, light-
skinned, and stern-looking man in a coat and tie, Calles looked out of place
among a crowd composed of friends and family of the slain hero. Yet he had
prepared words to win the campesinos over to his cause: "The forces of reaction must know," Calles announced, "that I will always stand on the side of the
most advanced principles of humankind. . . . The revolutionary program of Zapata, the *agrarista* program, is my own."[2] The presidential candidate assured the
crowd that they had nothing to worry about. He and all other "good revolutionaries," Calles declared, would continue Zapata's endeavors: "the hero rests
in peace, and his work is done."[3]

Although Calles won the election, he and the other "good revolutionaries"
did not live up to these lofty promises, and their claim that they represented
the revolution came back to haunt them. Exactly twelve years later, on April

10, 1936, Calles and several of his allies boarded a plane bound for their exile in the United States after a dozen years in the political spotlight. As word of their deportation spread, gleeful campesinos and workers inundated the office of President Lázaro Cárdenas with congratulatory telegrams. The missives referred to the exiles as "reactionaries," and to Cárdenas as the redeemer of the ideals of the revolution. They held particular venom for Calles, whom they portrayed as the root of many of the country's ills.[4]

This book tells the story of Calles, a complex and little-understood protagonist of the Mexican Revolution. Born in 1877, Calles hailed from the state of Sonora in northwestern Mexico. He was descended from a notable family fallen upon hard times, and he spent twenty years dabbling in various careers until the revolution afforded him the chance to rise to prominence in his state and, finally, the nation. Calles's ascent to the presidency followed that of his mentor, General Alvaro Obregón, the caudillo who emerged triumphant from ten years of warfare that had claimed more than a million lives. Along with Obregón and Cárdenas, he was one of the most important architects of the new state that emerged in the 1920s and 1930s. As president from 1924 to 1928, Calles embarked on an ambitious reform program, modernized the financial system, and defended national sovereignty against an interventionist U.S. government. Yet these reforms failed to eradicate underdevelopment, corruption, and social injustice. Moreover, his unyielding campaigns against the Catholic Church and his political enemies earned him the reputation of a repressive strongman. After Obregón's assassination in July 1928, Calles's adroit political maneuvering helped save his country from renewed civil war. Until Cárdenas took office, he continued to exert broad influence as the foremost political figure of his country while three weaker presidents succeeded each other in an atmosphere of constant political crisis. He played a significant role in founding a ruling party that reined in the destructive ambitions of leading army officers and promised to help campesinos and workers attain better living conditions. This party and its successors remained in power until 2000, and today's Partido Revolucionario Institucional (PRI, or Party of the Institutional Revolution) still celebrates Calles as its principal founding father. Many of the institutions and laws forged during the Calles era survived into the 1980s and, in some cases, to the present day.

Despite Calles's obvious significance, few historians have studied his career seriously. With the exception of several unpublished doctoral dissertations, there are no English-language studies.[5] Likewise, Mexican historians have only produced a handful of Calles biographies, and only one—Carlos Macías's study of Calles's early years and involvement in the revolution until 1920—mines the rich personal archive at the Fideicomiso Archivos Plutarco Elías Calles y Fernando Torreblanca in Mexico City.[6] Therefore, historian Alan Knight's call for a "good biography" of Calles as "one of the major lacunae in modern Mexican historiography" has remained unanswered for twenty years.[7]

This study fills the need for a book-length scholarly work on Calles and the Mexican Revolution. It portrays Calles as an authoritarian populist, the quintessential politician of an era dominated by generals, entrepreneurs, and educated professionals. Marked by his upbringing in a frontier society in rapid transition, his life was a quest for political survival, reforms, and order. Calles had great political acumen, he chose sides wisely, and he got lucky as well. He allied himself with the eventual winners of the revolution, and he survived a long series of revolts and assassinations that felled revolutionary leaders such as Francisco I. Madero (1913), Zapata (1919), Venustiano Carranza (1920), Pancho Villa (1923), and Obregón (1928), as well as hundreds of lesser-known figures. The lessons of his survival included support for reforms that benefited the campesinos and workers who had joined the revolution in order to find redress for landlessness, oppression, and low wages. Calles promoted a welfare system for workers, infrastructure improvements, the expansion of rural education, and (at least until 1927) a nationalist foreign policy. But what Mexican essayist Octavio Paz has called the "fiesta of bullets" also contributed to the use of repression in search of the political stability that had eluded Mexico for much of its existence as an independent country. Calles displayed little interest in representative democracy, which had failed in the nineteenth century and, again, in the revolution. He disdained popular participation in politics and regarded regional and local differences as evidence of chaos. He saw the Catholic Church as the root of many of his country's ills and a rival of the secular government that needed to be tightly controlled and monitored. And finally, Calles silenced his opponents through exile, jail, and death. His brand of populist politics was authoritarian, claiming to represent the interests of the people regardless of the popularity of his ideas and the means he chose to implement them.[8] A former schoolteacher, Calles believed that he knew best what his country needed, and he followed the eighteenth-century Swiss philosopher Jean-Jacques Rousseau's notion that "the public must be taught to understand what they want."[9]

Calles's career therefore reflects the contradictions of Mexican revolutionary populism. Populism is a political style rather than a specific program, an appeal to the masses that promises to support "the people" and "the nation" in their struggle with the elite and foreign powers.[10] Lacking a core value such as property, religion, liberty, or equality, populism has served as a tool of progressives and reactionaries, socialists and fascists alike. Latin American populism arose at the turn of the twentieth century as a reaction against the modernizing oligarchies of the nineteenth century. Early populist leaders such as Argentina's Hipólito Yrigoyen and Mexico's Madero were democratic populists, advocating the expansion of the suffrage and representative democracy. By the 1920s, however, Latin American populists such as Calles shifted their focus from political to economic and social reform, advocating national economic development, improvements in working conditions, unionization, and a discourse of economic nationalism that assailed the privileges of foreign investors.[11] As Argentine sociologist Torcuato di Tella has argued, Latin American populism after World War I shared many characteristics with social democracy in Western Europe; and indeed, Calles was a great admirer of labor parties in 1920s France and Germany.[12]

This analysis challenges earlier studies that have linked Mexican populism to the Cárdenas administration (1934–1940), which won widespread support by parceling out 42 million acres of land to campesinos and expropriating the foreign-owned oil industry.[13] Lacking ideological focus, the revolution was the ideal breeding ground for a populist political culture in which revolutionary leaders promised political and social change. As strongman of Sonora (1915–1919), Calles advocated improvements in public education, labor relations, and the general welfare of the working poor, and he limited the privileges of the U.S.-owned copper companies in his state. These reforms presaged the Constitution of 1917, the foremost manifesto of Mexican revolutionary populism. Calles entered national politics at a time when the revolutionary mobilization of radical intellectuals, workers, and campesinos had made populist rhetoric a prerequisite for political success. As he gained prominence, he honed a populist style that emphasized economic nationalism as well as better conditions for campesinos and workers under the watchful eye of the state. Like other populists of the 1920s such as Chile's Carlos Ibáñez, Calles was an architect of the politics of the masses, fueled by the advent of mass literacy, motion pictures, and the radio. He was the first presidential candidate in Mexican history to use radio and mass appearances in his campaign and should be viewed within the long tradition of Latin American populism. At the national level, the laws passed under his leadership paved the way for Cárdenas's own, more agrarian brand of populism. Calles's principal contribution to the development of this tradition was the creation of a state party purporting to represent "the revolution" and defend the *patria* against an array of putative enemies such as foreign investors, the U.S. government, and the Catholic Church. In reality, the party created in the

name of a revolution compromised with at least the first two of those enemies from the very beginning.

Not surprisingly, the Calles era (1924–1935) elicited strong opinions col-
ored by political passions. While Calles was president, allies such as Juan de
Dios Bojórquez applauded him for his reform program, and they panegyrically
praised his alliance with urban labor and his nationalist foreign policy.[14]
Meanwhile, the Catholic opposition called him a "Bolshevik" who had set
up a "reign of terror." These strong words referred to Calles's stringent 1926
laws regulating the church that led to the execution and exile of numerous
priests and the devastating Cristero rebellion, a grassroots campesino revolt
in central and western Mexico.[15] Political rivals criticized him as a power-
hungry dictator who had sacrificed both his principles and his friends in his
eagerness to rise to the top.[16] Opinions on Calles became even more sharply
divided during the following years, when Calles wielded considerable power
from behind the scenes as the so-called Jefe Máximo (supreme chief) of the
Mexican Revolution, a name that inspired the term "Maximato" for the years
1928–1935. His admirers praised him for bringing political stability to the
nation and for crafting a ruling party that would put an end to the civil wars,
coup d'états, and revolts that had marked the 1910s and 1920s.[17] As Calles
gave up much of his populist rhetoric in the course of the Maximato, his enemies multiplied. Worker and campesino leaders criticized him for forcing
workers into a pliant national union and failing to carry out land reform
mandated in the new constitution.[18]

As Calles's hold on power continued, the balance of these assessments
thus became more negative. In the words of Ramón Puente, the author of a
remarkably balanced portrait of the Jefe Máximo published in exile in 1933,
"he is the man who engenders the greatest amount of hatred . . . in the circle of the Revolution."[19] Calles's personality contributed to these largely negative opinions. Taciturn and highly intelligent, Calles did not elicit widespread popular admiration. He looked people straight in the eyes with a
severe, brooding, and mysterious gaze. U.S. journalist Carleton Beals, a former Calles admirer who became disenchanted with the Jefe Máximo in the
early 1930s, best summed up the prevailing perception of his public persona:
"a coarse, ruthless man of extraordinary intelligence and force and a glimmer
of idealism. [Calles] had a long, box-like face with cold, black, slit eyes, a
creased mouth, and a foundry jaw."[20]

Even more importantly, Calles had the misfortune of occupying chrono-
logical space between two more charismatic leaders. Obregón was the undefeated caudillo of the revolution, a personable and humorous general whose
leadership style entailed compromise. At the other end of the Calles era,

Cárdenas stands as an imposing figure who remains highly regarded in popular opinion due to his willingness to fulfill popular demands. Calles was neither an effective communicator and successful general like Obregón nor a hero of the masses like Cárdenas. More than any other issue, the Cristero rebellion illustrated his difficulties in understanding those who did not share his faith in reason and material progress. Moreover, a serious economic crisis overshadowed the second half of Calles's presidency, and the Maximato coincided with the Great Depression, a blow few leaders in the Western Hemisphere survived without damage to their reputation. Amidst this crisis, critics highlighted the fact that Calles and other leading figures of the Maximato lived luxurious lives while most Mexicans suffered. Frank Tannenbaum, a U.S. historian, longtime resident of Mexico, and confidant of Cárdenas, portrayed the Calles era as "debased and clouded years" and blasted the political leadership for their pursuit of "pelf and power."[21]

Following Tannenbaum's lead, many historians of twentieth-century Mexico have not treated Calles favorably. According to these historians, the revolution had stalled in the Calles era: idealism had yielded to pragmatism, revolutionary visions had turned into authoritarian policies, and a desire to redeem the working and middle classes had disappeared in selfish greed. A leading U.S. textbook still characterizes the Calles era as follows: "Something drastic had happened to the Revolution and its leaders. Honest, idealistic men . . . had been not only diverted from tasks of high priority, but corrupted as well."[22] Calles's historical memory also reflected an increasing critique of the repressive aspects of his rule. On October 2, 1968, government forces killed hundreds of student protesters in Tlatelolco, Mexico City, thereby unmasking the PRI state that Calles had helped build as an authoritarian regime. In the 1970s, a new generation of historians held Obregón, Calles, and even Cárdenas responsible for the crafting of the authoritarian system that had made the Tlatelolco massacre possible.[23] In the same vein, the recent democratization of Mexico has gone hand in hand with a reexamination of the Calles era. One recent scholarly current led by historians such as Carlos Macías, Edward Farmer, and Martha Loyo has sought to rehabilitate Calles as a reformer and modernizer.[24] Another group of historians including Ignacio Almada Bay and Pedro Castro has moved into the opposite direction by undertaking a sympathetic examination of leaders and movements opposed to Calles and his allies.[25]

Based primarily on archival sources—and particularly the holdings of Calles's personal archive—this book seeks to transcend these ongoing debates by examining Calles in his specific historical context. In many ways, the world in which he lived shaped Calles more so than the other way around. He bore the marks of the struggle for survival in a war-torn society, and these characteristics of a survivor informed both his reform agenda and his repressive political tactics. This focus on context avoids the pitfalls of traditional biographies. For example, many biographers attempt to plumb the psychological depth of their subject, a difficult endeavor in the best of circumstances and even more vexing when few sources have survived that elucidate emotion or motivation. Moreover, every biography runs the risk of overemphasizing the importance of its subject. With good reason, historian and cultural critic Claudio Lomnitz has warned against efforts to "anthropomorphize Mexican history"—that is, to identify the history of a diverse nation with the actions of its leaders.[26] Indeed, many traditional biographies overstate the impact of a given person on his or her environment and separate the self from that environment.[27]

To make this book accessible to a wide audience, I have avoided the temptation of writing an exhaustive, multivolume work. Instead, this study centers on the twenty-four years in which Calles was a public figure (1911–1935), using introductory and concluding chapters to frame the story. Although I have included aspects of Calles's personal and family life, his political career remains at the forefront throughout the narrative. Chapter 1 provides a sketch of his upbringing and early adulthood in the context of turn-of-the century Sonora (1877–1911). The next two chapters follow Calles in the violent phase of the revolution: Chapter 2 traces his emergence as a revolutionary leader allied with the Constitutionalist faction (1911–1915), and chapter 3 analyzes his years as strongman of Sonora (1915–1919). The following three chapters examine Calles's career on the national level: Chapter 4 treats his rise to prominence in the national government (1919–1924), chapter 5 provides an analysis of his presidency (1924–1928), and chapter 6 evaluates his role as Jefe Máximo until the inauguration of Cárdenas (1928–1934). Covering the years 1934 to 1945, chapter 7 reflects on the showdown between Calles and Cárdenas, his exile in San Diego, and his final years in retirement in Mexico City.

CHAPTER ONE

A Life Adrift

[My father] was an awful businessman. . . . He had ambition for power, but not for money.

—Interview with Alicia Calles, 1975

In the spring of 1895, a bright thirteen-year-old student enrolled in the Colegio de Sonora, a new school located in the state capital of Hermosillo. Adolfo de la Huerta Marcor was the son of a merchant from Guaymas, a port on the Gulf of California whose natives considered themselves bitter rivals of the inhabitants of Hermosillo. He was thus delighted when he met a fellow Guaymense, a teacher's assistant by the name of Plutarco Calles who was at the time no more than seventeen years old. The first thing that struck Adolfo was Plutarco's somber gaze. Unperturbed, the enthusiastic and outgoing Adolfo approached him and asked, "They tell me that you are from Guaymas. Is that so?"

"Yes," Plutarco replied, "I am from Guaymas."

Then Adolfo attempted to establish the familial and social contexts of the other teenager by asking the question "From what family?"

"From my own," Plutarco answered somewhat impolitely.[1] This exchange between two future friends and presidents of Mexico reveals one of Calles's enduring character traits: his sphinx-like refusal to let others pierce his soul.

Calles's first encounter with de la Huerta formed part of a long apprenticeship that lasted thirty-four years, or half of his entire life. Growing up in a middle-class household, Calles was descended from a family that had once

1

numbered among the most influential in Sonora. As a result, he embarked on a protracted search to reclaim that status, a search still unresolved by the time of the revolution. These decades forged the introverted and cunning personality that marked Calles's political career. Outside his family, who remembered him as a caring, warm individual, he did not permit himself to show emotion.[2] As he began his ascent to power thanks to a combination of luck and skill, he inspired admiration, respect, and fear—but seldom affection.

Background and Beginnings

On December 23, 1878, two well-to-do Sonorans, Alejandro and Dolores Elías Lucero, took a toddler to his baptism in a parish church in Guaymas. The child appeared too old for the ceremony: in an age of high infant mortality, Catholic baptisms occurred shortly after birth. Even stranger, the adults introduced themselves as the boy's paternal uncle and aunt, and neither of the boy's parents was present. The father, Plutarco Elías Lucero, was the progeny of a distinguished clan from northeastern Sonora, a drunk who was frittering away his family's money. His mistress, María Jesús Campuzano Noriega, was a native Guaymense of lower-middle-class origins. She had been married to a Francisco Calles and widowed shortly before her liaison with Elías. While we do not know the precise reasons for the parents' absence from the baptism, Elías had most likely disappeared from Guaymas, and Campuzano tended to the couple's younger daughter, María Dolores. Left to their own devices, the boy's uncle and aunt informed the priest that the child was born January 27, 1877, most likely overstating his age by eight months. The priest recorded his name as Francisco Plutarco Elías Campuzano, a child born out of wedlock.[3] Thus began the public record of a child who would always celebrate his birthday on September 25 and whom posterity would remember as Plutarco Elías Calles.

If the peculiar baptism appeared an ominous sign, things soon got worse for little Plutarco and María Dolores. Their father vanished from Guaymas to marry another woman, and their mother died in 1880, when the children were three and two years old, respectively. Neither their father nor his siblings offered to take in Plutarco and his younger sister. Finally, the children were farmed out among Campuzano's relatives, and Plutarco ended up in Hermosillo with his aunt, Josefa Campuzano, and her husband, Juan Bautista Calles, a dry goods merchant and the late Francisco's brother. Henceforth, the boy became known as "Plutarco Calles."[4]

Historians have often cited these difficult beginnings as the primary explanation for Calles's austere public persona. For example, Michael Monteón

Plutarco Elías Lucero
Source: FAPEC.

has argued that the multiple traumas of his early years forged an introverted, rigid, and suspicious nature exacerbated by a burning desire to be loved and admired, and Enrique Krauze maintains that Catholic values imparted the twin stigmas of an out-of-wedlock birth and belated baptism, setting the stage for his lifelong opposition to the Catholic Church.[5]

These explanations are too simplistic. Although Monteón is correct in pointing out the significance of the loss of Plutarco's mother in the forging of his personality, his psychoanalytical explanation does not mesh with

María Jesús Campuzano Noriega
Source: FAPEC.

Calles's own behavior as a father. Based on Plutarco's own life experience, a functional two-parent family served as his primary frame of reference, and he later duplicated this pattern as a father and grandfather deeply committed to the welfare of his offspring. Krauze's assertion that Plutarco grew up stigmatized measures the society of Sonora by the standards of central and southern Mexico. In that remote and sparsely populated state, births out of wedlock were common, and traditional nuclear families coexisted side by side with single-parent and unmarried households. In addition, there were only a handful of priests in the entire state, and many children went unbaptized. Thus, Plutarco did not feel the kind of stigma that would have attached to him in Mexico City or Guadalajara, cities with thousands of clergy.[6]

In addition to documenting a case of familial dysfunction, Plutarco's strange baptism therefore manifested some of the differences between the Mexican northwest and the country's heartland. With the exception of Baja California, no state is farther away from the national capital than Sonora; even today, the 1,200-mile trip from Hermosillo to Mexico City takes almost three hours by plane and more than a day by bus. At the time of Plutarco's birth, only 600 miles of railroad track existed in Mexico, compared to 40,000 in the United States, and none of it passed through Sonora. Overland travel was done by stagecoach, and the Sierra Madre Occidental mountain range posed a formidable obstacle to travel into the center. In addition, the Mexican northwest was sparsely populated. At the time of Plutarco's birth, the population of Sonora did not exceed 140,000, and Guaymas—its principal port and second-largest town—had approximately 4,000 inhabitants.[7] As Calles and his Sonoran allies would find out when they came to know the rest of their country, inhabitants of central Mexico regarded them as outsiders. Not surprisingly, the poet Federico Gamboa wrote in 1923, "[In] our national history, written in blood and tears, one will not find a single act [of Sonorans] . . . that would reveal the least solidarity with our many pains and our few pleasures. . . . They were never moved with us; they never cried with us."[8]

Indeed, Sonora's remoteness contributed to forging a society different in many ways from central Mexico. For example, Sonorans preferred wheat to corn tortillas, some of them twenty inches or more in diameter. Like other inhabitants of the north, they favored beef and other meats to the vegetables and turkey consumed in central Mexico.[9] Instead of tequila and mescal, Sonorans drank *bacanora,* a high-powered brandy that burned the throat and, according to Calles himself, produced hallucinations.[10] The Catholic Church played a small role in the Mexican northwest compared to the center and south; in 1830, there were only twenty-seven parishes and eighteen ordained priests in Sonora and Sinaloa combined.[11] Finally, after the U.S. annexation of the old Mexican northwest following the U.S.-Mexican War (1846–1848), a bicultural society began to emerge that enjoyed closer connections to the United States than with central Mexico. In 1853, the U.S. government purchased northern Sonora from Mexico in order to facilitate the construction of a railroad from Texas to the Pacific.

Just as Sonora was only one of what historian Lesley Byrd Simpson has called "many Mexicos," the state was itself geographically diverse, as Plutarco would find out in the course of his own migrations through central, southern, and northeastern Sonora.[12] The state was divided into nine districts, each named after its largest town: Altar and Magdalena in the northwest; Arizpe and Moctezuma in the northeast; Hermosillo, Ures, and Sahuaripa in the center; and Guaymas and Alamos in the south. The northwestern tip of Sonora, which borders the state of Baja California, is a parched region where the Colorado River provides the only source of irrigation. Moving eastward from that river, the terrain gradually slopes up and finally gives way to the jagged edges of the Sierra Madre. The peaks of this mountain range separate Sonora from Chihuahua. In the foothills of the Sierra Madre, northeastern Sonora features pastureland with modest rainfall. Toward the south, the mountains approach the coast as the state narrows, and the rain feeds rivers with increasing water volume. In particular, the waters of the Yaqui and Mayo Rivers give southern Sonora the potential of providing a veritable cornucopia of food. In the river valleys and in the coastal plain that continues southward into Sinaloa, Sonorans produce food for export to markets in the rest of Mexico and in the United States. In the southern tip, the colonial city of Alamos recalls an eighteenth-century silver boom (see map 1.1).[13]

In the words of historian Héctor Aguilar Camín, Sonora was a "nomadic frontier."[14] Migration and ethnic conflict shaped life in the Mexican northwest, and by extension, that of Calles as well. The state featured a variety of unassimilated indigenous civilizations such as the Apaches in the north and east, the Pimas and Seris, and the Mayos and Yaquis in the south. The nomadic Apaches roamed freely from their bases in the United States until the 1880s, when the Texas-Pacific Railroad facilitated the settlement and exploitation of the U.S. Southwest. The Spanish-speaking population, especially in northern Sonora, remained small in the face of the Apache threat. Most of this population, including the Elíases, had come to the area as military colonists during the eighteenth century. Taking advantage of a law that allowed them to keep as much land as they could defend, these colonists formed a class of notables in a remote outpost of the Spanish Empire. They lived in the vicinity of *presidios* (garrisons), where they mixed only to a limited degree with native society.[15] In the center and south, the nomadic frontier also witnessed intense struggles over land with the sedentary Mayos and Yaquis. In possession of the best farmland in the state, the Mayos and Yaquis resisted the encroachment of Spanish land grabbers, whom they dubbed *yoris*, a term that subsumed pure-blooded descendants of Spanish immigrants and mestizos, people of mixed ethnic descent. The Yoris, on the other hand, viewed the conflict with the indigenous peoples as an effort by *gente de razón* (people with reason) to bring civilization to *gente sin razón* (people without reason). This dichotomy between the supposedly civilized Yori and the al-

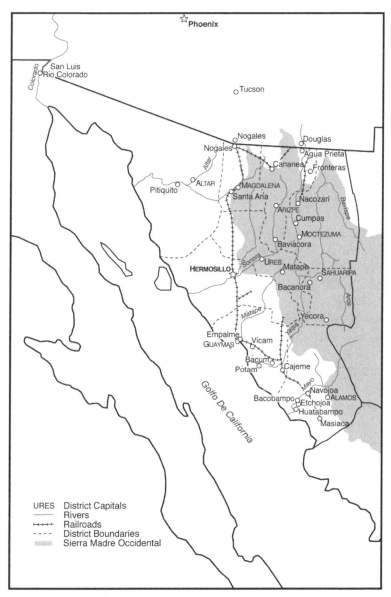

Map 1.1.   Sonora in 1910

legedly barbarian "Indian" belied a complex social reality. Some indigenous people acquired land and social status, and a few assimilated into Hispanic society. In addition, not all Yoris regarded indigenous communities as enemies. Many landowners required indigenous labor, and some Yori leaders cultivated the Yaquis and Mayos in particular as political allies. Finally, Franciscans and Jesuits maintained missions among the indigenous peoples. Nonetheless, the construction of a Yori identity in contrast with the indigenous "other" forged a high degree of cultural conformity among the notables, especially in the small urban centers.[16]

Because of the geographical isolation of Sonoran towns, political centralization remained elusive throughout much of the nineteenth century. After independence in 1821, the leaders of the largest towns—Alamos, Guaymas, Hermosillo, and Ures—jockeyed for which city would be the state capital, an issue that was not settled until 1879. Although the state governor appointed the district prefects, the towns successfully resisted their intervention in local political affairs.[17] These rivalries became part of a national conflict between Centralists and Federalists, factions that later became the Conservative and Liberal parties, respectively. Sonora first fell under the sway of a caudillo from Ures, Manuel María Gándara, who allied with the Yaquis and national Conservative politicians such as strongman Santa Anna. After the Liberals overthrew Santa Anna in 1854, Gándara lost influence to Ignacio Pesqueira, a native of the northeastern district of Arizpe and ally of Liberal leader Benito Juárez. Eight years later, Pesqueira made the prefectures elective offices in an effort to gain more widespread support.[18] As this coming and going of caudillos attested, political power rested less on the ballot box than on patron-client connections that sometimes reached across state borders all the way to Mexico City. Indeed, Sonora was not as isolated politically as Gamboa would have us believe. For instance, an enemy of Juárez, the Alamos native Félix Zuloaga Trillo, served as president from January 1858 to February 1859 during the civil war between the Conservatives and Liberals.[19]

Distant relatives of Pesqueira, the Elías clan numbered among the state's erstwhile notables. For decades, the family's origins were tied up in the controversy surrounding its famous descendant. For example, Catholic historians circulated the idea that the Elías family was of Jewish origins, and others identify its progenitor as a Sephardic immigrant.[20] Yet others claim that the Elíases were of Lebanese or Syrian descent.[21] So prevalent was the notion of the clan's Middle Eastern ancestry that Calles's enemies often called him "*el turco*," or the Arab.[22] As Carlos Macías has demonstrated, however, the founding father of this clan, Francisco Elías González, was an hidalgo, or poor noble, from the northern Castilian province of La Rioja in Spain. The noble status indicated that Elías professed to be of Catholic faith. Elías and his brother settled in the Arizpe region in the 1720s. Over the next three generations, the Elíases gradually expanded their holdings despite the constant threat of Apache attacks. In the early nineteenth century, they founded the hacienda San Pedro Palominas in the dry scrubland located west of the village of Fronteras. Over time, this hacienda grew to more than 30,000 acres, as the clan vastly increased its property through a combination of conquest and strategic marriages. The heyday of the clan came under the leadership of Plutarco's grandfather, José Juan Elías Pérez, who defeated a U.S. filibustering expedition in 1857. By 1865, Elías Pérez held more than 120,000 acres—most of it in northeastern Arizpe—and his relatives owned almost six times that much. However, Elías Pérez was to pay dearly for his allegiance to Juárez and Pesqueira. In 1864, Juárez's defeat at the hands of the Conservatives and their allies, the French occupation forces and the Austrian-born Emperor Maximilian, briefly returned Gándara to power. The following year, Elías Pérez died in battle against Gándara and his foreign allies. By the time Pesqueira vanquished Gándara in the course of Juárez's successful offensive against Maximilian, the Elías clan could not take advantage of the definitive triumph of the Liberals in the absence of a strong representative in Pesqueira's inner circle.[23]

Unfortunately, Elías Pérez's eldest son, Plutarco Elías Lucero, was not up to the task of serving as the new *pater familias* of a clan that included his mother, Bernardina Lucero, and eight younger siblings. Although he completed a law degree and at one time served as the prefect of Guaymas, his "true profession . . . was that of executor of a family estate diminished day after day by lack of attention, Apache attacks, and rustlers."[24] Elías Lucero developed a penchant for alcohol, and he lived a Bohemian lifestyle. While his brothers embarked on promising careers in commerce, the military, and politics, he turned into a drifter who never stayed too long in any one place. In 1872, one such stay in the town of Ures resulted in a short-term liaison that produced his oldest son, Arturo M. Elías Malvido, and another son, Plutarco, who died at two years of age. Soon afterward, Elías Lucero moved to Guaymas, where he accepted a job in city government and began his affair with María Jesús Campuzano that led to the births of Plutarco and María Dolores Elías Campuzano (see table 1.1).[25]

Growing up in Hermosillo, far away from the lands of the Elías clan, Plutarco Jr. initially knew little about the illustrious past of his paternal family. As Juan Bautista Calles's adoptive son, the boy known as Plutarco Calles lived the middle-class life of a merchant household. Juan Bautista, whose store went through some difficult times during Plutarco's childhood, did not

Table 1.1. The Immediate Family of Plutarco Elías Campuzano

Parents in **bold**, half-siblings in *italics*

Plutarco Elías Lucero (1848–1917) + Juana Lidia Malvido (?–1907)
1. *Arturo M. Elías Malvido (1872–1955)*
2. *Plutarco Elías Malvido (1874–1876)*

Francisco Calles Araujo (n.d.–1872) ∞ **María Jesús Campuzano Noriega (1844–1880)**
1. *Francisco Calles Campuzano (n.d.)*
2. *Aquila Calles Campuzano (n.d.)*

Plutarco Elías Lucero (1848–1917) + María Jesús Campuzano Noriega (1844–1880)
1. Francisco Plutarco Elías Campuzano (1877–1945)
2. Dolores Elías Campuzano (1878–?)

Source: Macías, *Vida y temperamento*, 32–36.

exactly coddle his adoptive son. Like the other Calles children, Plutarco was required to help out in the store when he was home from school. According to one source, he grew up barefoot and in hand-me-down clothes, an appalling state of dress in a society wont to judge social status by clothes and footwear.[26] In the minds of the Yoris, bare feet signified *gente sin razón*. Yet the boy grew up as one of the more fortunate members of society. Calles had enough money to send the children to school, and according to Plutarco's daughter Alicia, he treated his adoptive son well enough that his own children envied the newcomer to the family.[27]

Not surprisingly, Plutarco identified with the family that had taken him in. For years, he assumed the identity of an adopted child. When he eventually reclaimed Elías as his paternal family name, he continued to use the name Calles: he thus became known as Plutarco Elías Calles. The incorporation of his uncle's family name into his own indicates that Plutarco recognized the contributions of his adoptive family to his rearing and education. Indeed, most Mexicans knew Plutarco simply as "Calles," and his children's birth certificates listed Elías Calles as the paternal family name. Despite this act of recognition, however, the adult Plutarco ignored the Calles family while maintaining close relations with the Elías. Most likely, the reasons for this subsequent preference for his father's relatives were the notable past of the Elíases as well as the fact that Plutarco would spend most of his early adulthood in close vicinity to that clan.[28] He appeared to have high aspirations even as a child; legend has it that he predicted that he would become president someday.[29]

As a member of the Calles household, Plutarco gained the opportunity to pursue an education in one of the best school districts in Sonora, as Hermosillo benefited from its recent elevation to state capital. The distinction was a relative one. Although the state boasted the country's highest per capita expenditures for education, in 1874, it weighed in at a mere thirty-eight centavos. Literacy remained below 30 percent overall and less than 20 percent for women.[30] Teachers were sorely underpaid. In 1884, when Calles attended first grade in a school that enrolled sixty-six boys, the director and sole full-time teacher of that school only earned seventy-five pesos a year.[31] Teachers enjoyed little social prestige and found themselves obligated to look for other sources of income; next to their classroom duties, most of them kept busy as scribes, booksellers, and even smugglers.[32]

Young Plutarco did not exactly distinguish himself in the classroom. During his first three years at the Segunda Escuela Municipal, he was a lazy and inattentive pupil. In first grade, his teacher gave him a grade of *mala* (bad) for conduct, the second-lowest grade possible, and a grade of *poca* (little) for effort, also the second-lowest grade. According to the grade sheet preserved in the Sonora state archive, Calles fared poorly in large part because of his habitual absences from class.[33] These absences had three reasons: the child hated school; his duties helping out in his adoptive father's store sapped his energy; and in his first year, his family often kept him home due to the yellow fever epidemic. By the fourth grade, Plutarco also displayed a rebellious attitude. In July 1887, he only took one out of five final examinations. When Juan Bautista Calles found his adoptive son smoking a cigarette with two of his own children on an examination day, Plutarco received a severe beating.[34] Over the next months, Calles worked in the family store, seemingly destined to join the legions of Sonorans who had dropped out before completing elementary school. Very few students indeed reached ninth grade, the highest grade offered in Sonora, and only a handful went on to finish their studies at high schools such as the famous Escuela Nacional Preparatoria (ENP) in Mexico City.[35]

It turned out, however, that Plutarco had learned his lesson. He reenrolled in school and cut down on his missed classes. In 1889, he received good grades and transferred to the Primera Escuela Municipal, the largest school in Hermosillo.[36] There, he had the fortune of studying under Benigno López y Sierra, a reputable instructor from the central state of Jalisco. Although old habits reappeared in the form of missed classes and a rebellious attitude, Calles graduated with average to high grades in 1892. The following year, he was one of three members of his class who passed the teacher's exam.[37]

Trial and Error in the Porfiriato

Plutarco's student days coincided with the incipient modernization of Sonora under Porfirio Díaz, Mexico's preeminent strongman from 1876 to 1911 and

president for all but four of those years. A political outsider from the southern state of Oaxaca, Díaz succeeded in bringing political stability by forging
a compromise between the Liberal quest for foreign investment capital and
the Conservative penchant for political order.[38] The Díaz regime considered
the economic development of Sonora of crucial importance for its project of
political centralization. The northwest was where central political authority
remained weakest; it held great promise due to its mineral wealth; and the
proximity of the United States exposed the area to the specter of annexation.
U.S. investors and travelers discovered Sonora, and Sonorans began to work
on farms and mines across the border in the territory of Arizona. Small towns
such as Nogales emerged on the border, encouraging the mix of people and
cultures.[39] Beginning in 1877, the Texas-Pacific Railroad opened Arizona to
intensive settlement and exploitation. Consequently, the Díaz regime attempted to tie Sonora more closely to the center at the same time that the
state came into much closer contact with U.S. economy. Between 1880 and
1910, Sonora and the other states along the border emerged as the crucial
nexus between the U.S. and Mexican economies. During what would be
dubbed the Porfiriato, the remote north truly became "the border," an area
that connected the burgeoning U.S. economy with that of central Mexico.[40]
The influx of foreign investment created one of the country's most dynamic
export economies, an economy based on copper mining and commercial
agriculture.

To pave the way for modernization and strengthen their political influence
in a distant state divided by conflict among the notable clans, the Porfirians
engineered a political realignment. In 1875, Pesqueira had attempted to install his own nephew as governor in an attempt to keep his clan in power. The
ploy elicited widespread outrage among the Liberal notables who had thus far
supported Pesqueira, and they forced the old caudillo to retire. Nine years
later, the elections of 1884—the last relatively free elections until the revolution—ushered in a triumvirate of young leaders with close connections to
Díaz but few ties to the political elite in Hermosillo: Luis Torres, Rafael Izábal,
and Ramón Corral. Among these leaders, only Corral was a native Sonoran.
Over the next decades, this triumvirate took turns in the governor's office and
kept out the political opposition much as Pesqueira had. Backed by Díaz, they
throttled municipal autonomy, reinstated the sweeping powers that the governor had enjoyed until 1862, negotiated crucial deals with foreign investors,
and represented Sonoran interests in Mexico City. The realignment left the
Pesqueira family in the opposition along with their allies such as the Maytorena clan, wealthy landowners from the Guaymas area.[41]

Map 1.2. Mexico in 1910

Infrastructure improvements, and particularly the building of a railroad connecting Guaymas and Hermosillo to the U.S. border as well as to central Mexico, went hand in hand with political centralization. This project required a significant infusion of foreign capital. By 1882, the Sonora Railway connected Guaymas with the U.S. border at Nogales, and two decades later, what was now the Southern Pacific Railroad reached Mazatlán and Tepic. Railroad access to Mexico City, however, did not come until the completion of the final link between Tepic and Orendaín in 1926 (see map 1.2).[42]

The native peoples of Sonora stood in the way of Porfirian modernization. In the 1880s, the Yaquis and Mayos revolted under the leadership of José María Leyva, also known as Cajeme. The government forces prevailed in a protracted war that resulted in the execution of Cajeme in April 1887. However, the Yaquis retreated and waged guerrilla warfare from their base in the Sierra de Bacatete, a virtually impregnable mountain range east of Guaymas. The war took on a cyclical nature, ebbing and flowing with Yori resolve to take land and Yaqui ability to strike back. The Yaquis raided Yori settlements within one hundred miles of the sierra, only to give up their attacks once their provisions were exhausted. After several years spent living peacefully in the valleys gathering food and stockpiling weapons, the cycle began anew.

...c ioris confronted these guerrilla campaigns with escalating brutality.[43] In the early 1900s, the Porfirians resorted to ethnic cleansing and deported eight thousand Yaquis to the southeastern state of Yucatán, where they worked on henequen plantations as virtual slaves.[44]

The construction of the railroad and the offensive against the indigenous communities allowed the Porfirians to grant generous concessions to foreign investors. With the railroad in place, U.S. entrepreneurs targeted the agricultural potential of southern Sonora and, in particular, the Mayo and Yaqui rivers. In 1890, one investor obtained the rights to two-thirds of the waters of these rivers, long-term tax exemptions, and five million acres of land in exchange for the promise to develop a regionwide irrigation system. Almost two decades later, the Compañía Constructora Richardson (hereafter Richardson) acquired this concession.[45] This concession, however, paled in comparison to those awarded to U.S. copper companies in the northeast. In 1897, the Phelps-Dodge Corporation of Boston began to develop a mine near the town of Nacozari, and two years later, William E. Greene purchased from the Pesqueira clan the rights to a site near Cananea, located just south of the U.S. border. Thus was born the Cananea Consolidated Copper Company (CCCC) that turned a hamlet of two hundred inhabitants into the state's largest town in a matter of a decade. At fifteen thousand inhabitants, Cananea symbolized the copper boom; its workers hailed from all of northern Mexico and several foreign countries. The mining companies benefited from significant tax breaks and other incentives to exploit the copper deposits, which, together with those in neighboring Arizona, constituted the richest in all of North America.[46]

Therefore, Calles's native state changed rapidly between 1880 and 1900. The population in the northeast skyrocketed as landless laborers, migrants from other parts of Mexico, and Chinese immigrants all flocked to the mining towns in search of new opportunities. The south produced a cornucopia of food for export to other states and to the United States. Despite the tax breaks for foreign investors, the Porfirian economic model produced a balance sheet for the state government that looked impressive in macroeconomic terms, as the jobs created in the copper mines generated significant tax income. Between 1888 and 1907, state revenue increased from 3.67 to 6.56 pesos per capita at a time when the population grew by approximately 60 percent.[47] Although modernization entailed drawbacks, such as a federal military presence, authoritarian rule, and the loss of local political autonomy, it yielded material benefits. Hermosillo in particular became a prosperous city due to its location. Electricity illuminated the city at night, the railroad brought commerce and export opportunities for the area's orange growers, and a growing middle class patronized the stores of Juan Bautista Calles and other merchants. The railroad also brought U.S. culture to the city; according to one historian, other Sonorans considered the Hermosillenses the "Yankees of Mexico" due to their "thrift, advancement and close relations with Americans."[48]

Not surprisingly, Calles's years in the public schools of Hermosillo imbued him with the optimistic ideology of the Díaz regime. In particular, Porfirian education exposed him to the idea of positivism, a European doctrine that held that positive knowledge (as opposed to metaphysical or theological knowledge) derived from natural phenomena and their properties as verified by scientific experimentation. Following the ideas of ENP founder Gabino Barreda, positivist education focused on knowledge that would enable students to fulfill their role in a modern society. Positivists scoffed at humanistic knowledge that furthered critical thinking skills, let alone the teaching of religious ideas favored by the Catholic Church.[49] In a region without institutions of higher learning, public education served as the beginning and end of human knowledge. As Krauze aptly states, "Public education was a kind of lay religion—clear, disciplinary, rational, and methodical—defending an abstract and almost literary scientism."[50] It was an approach to reality young Plutarco took to heart.

This positivist philosophy of education had only recently come to Hermosillo via the Colegio de Sonora, a school founded by Corral in 1889. Founded in part to counteract a new Catholic school, the *colegio* imparted to students a rational base for disdain for the church, and it stressed the superiority of North American and European ways.[51] Students learned that Mexicans needed "order" (i.e., political stability enforced by the central government) in order to emulate the "progress" of the United States and the nations of Western Europe. Díaz's positivist advisers espoused the formula "less politics, more administration," and they believed that political decisions were best left to educated professionals. After 1895, this group came to be dubbed the *Científicos* because of their belief in science and progress. The Científicos arrogantly concluded that their level of education and professional expertise made them uniquely suited to shape the future of their country. They considered themselves an elite chosen by Darwinian natural selection. Disdainful of democratic procedures, they took the old practice of using political connections to enrich themselves to new heights. The Científicos concurred in the need for political and social reforms, so long as these reforms came from above.[52] Plutarco's education instilled in him what historian

William Beezley has labeled the "Porfirian persuasion"—the belief in progress and efficiency as attributes of a modern society.[53]

Calles's authoritarian populism of his later years therefore has its roots in his positivist education. To him—as to the Científicos—politics was a set of problems to be solved rather than the expression of the popular will through democratic procedures. The racial thought of the Científicos also imprinted itself on his mind. Positivists believed that the indigenous population constituted a major obstacle to national development; they proposed drastic remedies for this problem, ranging from the eradication of the native populations to their complete assimilation. Later on, the work of Justo Sierra would prove particularly influential in Plutarco's thinking. Sierra's *Political Evolution of the Mexican People* (1909) stressed the need to educate the indigenous population in order to create a racially mixed, Hispanicized society that combined the best characteristics of its Indian and Spanish origins. Indeed, such an amalgamated society in which Mayos and Yaquis disappeared was the Yori dream.[54]

Impressed by what he had learned and perhaps following the precedent of several of his adoptive father's relatives, Calles decided to become a teacher, someone who would pass this philosophy on to future generations. In 1895, he became an intern at the Colegio de Sonora with a monthly salary of thirty pesos, or five pesos more than the janitor. It was in that capacity as intern (the only teacher-training method available in Sonora, which did not have a normal school) that he met Adolfo de la Huerta, probably his closest friend during his years in Sonora. Calles proved a successful teacher—and one dangerous to the authorities "because of the spirit of independence which he fostered in his pupils."[55] Associated with an institution regarded as the pinnacle of progress in the state, he found the door wide open for a successful teaching career. In 1896, this career began in earnest with his appointment as an assistant teacher in the school where he had finished his studies. It was a career that remained in Calles's memory in a most positive way; many years later, he told his daughter Alicia that teaching was his favorite activity in his entire life.[56]

Calles's experience as a teacher proved important for his future career. His years in the classroom taught him the importance of molding minds, as well as to use force as he deemed appropriate. Calles the reformer remained a teacher at heart, albeit one trained in the nineteenth century when corporal punishment of wayward students remained the norm. In the words of his biographer Puente, "He never lost the psychological [traits] of the school teacher, who has seen men grow up since they were children, and who knows

Plutarco Elías Calles in the classroom
Source: FAPEC.

. . . that the most efficient way to direct adults is often a firm crack of the whip."[57]

His employment allowed Calles to set his sights on beginning a family. At barely twenty years of age, he got engaged to the nineteen-year-old Francisca Bernal. Francisca came from a prominent Liberal family in Hermosillo, a notable clan allied with the Pesqueiras. On August 9, 1897, the couple presented themselves to the magistrate in Hermosillo for the wedding ceremony. Before the wedding could proceed, however, the magistrate decreed that the intent to marry be publicly posted for fifteen days.[58] The document recording this event is the only surviving piece of evidence regarding Calles's liaison with Bernal. Aguilar Camín's work and two biographical reference works list Francisca as Plutarco's first wife and according to all three of these secondary sources, Francisca died soon thereafter.[59] Interestingly, Macías's exhaustive study of Calles's early years does not mention Bernal at all.[60] Most likely in response to Francisca's death, Calles decided to leave Hermosillo. On October 1, 1897, he resigned from his position because, as he stated in his resignation letter, "it does not meet my interests."[61] He moved to his native city of Guaymas, where he accepted an assistant teacher position at a monthly salary of fifty pesos, or 60 percent more than what he had earned in his former job. To supplement his income, he became director of a night school for artisans, and he wrote editorials and poetry for local newspapers such as *El Correo de Sonora, La Razón Social,* and *La Revista Escolar.* His editorials reveal his effort to apply the lessons from his own past by stressing the significance of two-parent families and public education in order to mold productive, contented citizens. They also demonstrate the fact that Calles had become an avid reader who surpassed those around him in his knowledge of the outside world.[62]

His poems, on the other hand, reflected a tormented state of mind. Published in February 1898 in a Guaymas newspaper, his poem "Duda" (Doubt) contained lines such as these:

> . . . The clarity
> Of my soul and my conscience
> You have converted nightly
> Into a terrifying specter
> And you leave my brain
> Converted into chaos
> And you leave my soul
> In the center of pain.[63]

In all likelihood, this poem reflected his worries over his professional future and his sorrow over Francisca's death rather than, as Krauze asserts, anxieties over his "illegitimate" origins.[64]

Indeed, the ghosts from his past returned to haunt Calles in his native city. Most importantly, he encountered his father, who had ignored him all of his life, and thereupon inserted the "Elías" into his name. Over the years, his uncle Alejandro Elías and his grandmother Bernardina Lucero de Elías had occasionally traveled to Hermosillo to see him. During those visits, they had informed him of his father's distinguished family history, but it was not until the reunion with his father that Plutarco embraced the familial tradition. Plutarco Sr. disapproved of his progeny becoming a lowly public schoolteacher. He knew that his son could not depend on income from family lands to survive, and teachers were poorly paid in comparison with other public servants. He also resented his son's love affair with Josefina Bonfiglio, a young woman of Italian descent who was to discover soon thereafter that she was pregnant with Calles's child, only to vanish forever from his life. Believing that his son spent too much time in love, and that he was not ready for a long-term commitment, Plutarco Sr. took his son to Arizpe for several months, where he introduced him to heavy drinking. This binge sent Calles on his way to repeating his father's mistakes.[65]

However, Calles managed to settle down again to continue the career that he had chosen. In 1899, he became the director of the second-largest school in Guaymas, a position that doubled his salary to one hundred pesos a month.[66] His future as a teacher appeared bright, and his personal life stabilized as well. On August 24 of that same year, he married Natalia Chacón, the daughter of the customs inspector of Guaymas, in a civil ceremony. A clan well connected to Porfirian political circles, his bride's family hailed from the port town of Mazatlán, Sinaloa. Plutarco soon found himself obliged to feed a growing family. In 1900, the couple's first son, Rodolfo, saw the light of day, and five more children followed in the next six years.[67]

The financial exigencies of Calles's growing household drove home his father's point that the salary of a teacher was not sufficient to live the comfortable lifestyle he desired, let alone achieve the notable status of his forebears. Although Calles claimed later on that his decision to give up his teaching career owed to his colleagues' conservatism—a statement designed to reinvent himself as a lifelong progressive—financial reasons likely played the most important role, as his second son, Plutarco, was already on his way. At the end of the 1901 school year, he resigned his teaching position and began a long search for a more lucrative profession.[68]

His half-brother, Arturo M. Elías Malvido, afforded Plutarco the first chance to make a better living by entrusting him with the management of the new Hotel California in January 1902. Designed as a fancy hotel for tourists and visiting entrepreneurs, the hotel was the most modern in town, featuring a French receptionist who spoke English, French, and Italian. It also sold firewood taken from the forests in the Yaqui Valley. In February, Calles gained his first position in public administration as treasurer of Guaymas, courtesy of Alberto Cubillas, a godson of Juan Bautista Calles and a close ally of the Porfirian triumvirate in Sonora. Four months thereafter, however, Calles resigned amidst allegations of embezzlement, as the treasury showed a shortage of 125 pesos. But the loss of this job proved only a small worry compared to the disaster that befell the Hotel California. In January 1903, the hotel burned down to the ground. The circumstances of the fire remain unknown to this day, but Plutarco's detractors later claimed that he himself had set fire to the hotel in order to collect insurance money.[69]

This misfortune and the death of his grandmother encouraged Plutarco to leave Guaymas for the village of Fronteras in the Arizpe district. Thirty miles south of the U.S. border, Fronteras was close to the home base of the Elías clan, where his uncles Manuel and Rafael administered the remaining family land. The area was then in the throes of the monumental transformation brought upon by the recent arrival of the copper mining companies. Known as the Moctezuma Copper Co., the Phelps-Dodge operation near Nacozari had built a railroad to the U.S. border town of Douglas. This railroad ran through Fronteras, a village of only eight hundred inhabitants sixty miles north of Nacozari. Even more significantly, Cananea lay only twenty miles to the northwest. One particular tentacle of the CCCC, the Cananea Cattle Company (or CCC) had spread far beyond that company town to grasp much of the surrounding land in an effort to provision the mine with lumber and food.[70]

Calles's move to Fronteras in 1903 constituted a desperate attempt to save from the clutches of the CCC what was left of the family's land. Over the past two decades, the Elíases had faced the adverse consequences of the Baldíos Law of 1883, which declared fallow land public property, to acquire new landholdings from owners who were unable to sustain intensive agriculture on their estate. The Baldíos Law provided legal cover for expropriation of this land as a public good subject to sale to private investors. Such was the case in much of the arid north, and especially Chihuahua and Sonora, where land surveyors alienated vast plots for the benefit of mining corporations and cattle ranchers.[71] As early as 1884, the family had lost half of its remaining 160,000 acres under the guise of this law, and less than two decades later, the CCC acquired 50,000 acres in San Pedro Palominas, the homestead of the family. The younger Plutarco decided to try his hand at agriculture as part of the family's endeavor to save the paltry remains of what had once been a formidable fortune.[72] The Elías strategy to defend the family patrimony sought to counteract a progressive concentration of landed wealth that contrasted with the stated Porfirian goal to make land available to a large class of yeoman farmers. According to one estimate, at the turn of the century only 4 percent of the population owned land privately in Sonora.[73]

For Calles, this move signified a change to a most unlikely profession. In April 1903, he took over the Hacienda Santa Rosa, a ranch of 7,500 acres, only about 500 of which could be irrigated. For a married couple that had always lived in urban settings, the move amounted to culture shock. Isolated from modern life and its amenities, Santa Rosa was located about twenty-five miles west of Fronteras, the nearest village with a store. The trip to Fronteras took the better part of a day on a dirt road. Even worse, Santa Rosa did not have a house for the family to live in. Employing two Yaqui laborers, Plutarco and Natalia built a primitive but spacious adobe residence for their growing family (between 1902 and 1905, the couple had three daughters, one of whom died in infancy). Calles dreamed of provisioning the nearby mines with food produced on his hacienda. Despite the help of his uncles, he could not win his battle against an unforgiving environment, and the deportation of his Yaqui laborers, coupled with the exodus of workers to Cananea, left him without a sufficient workforce. When a frost in January 1906 wiped out what had looked like a good harvest, Calles gave up farming forever.[74]

A few months later, he helped establish a new flour mill named Excélsior in Fronteras as a partner of Santiago (James) Smithers, an agent for Smithers, Nordenholt, and Co. of New York City. Santiago's company furnished the capital, while Calles, the manager of the mill, provided the local political connections. If the Sonoran initially had reservations of teaming up with a foreign investor, Santiago's marriage to his Aunt Dolores dispersed any doubts. Initially, the operation was a great success. By 1907, the mill was the largest of its kind in northern Sonora, producing 200,000 pounds of flour per year. Amidst the other Elíases, Plutarco had apparently found both a home and professional success. With a salary of 300 pesos, he settled into a comfortable life and increased his consumption of alcohol and tobacco products. He also let his duties slide: only three months after the opening of the mill, he was assessed a fine for his failure to keep proper business records.[75]

By that time, Calles was almost thirty years old, and he must have pondered whether he had made the right decisions in life. He was a reasonably well-educated man, a paterfamilias whose family pedigree opened many doors. But he had aspired to more than middle-class status when he gave up his teaching career. His endeavors as an entrepreneur had not met with success thus far; as hotel manager, farmer, and mill operator, Calles had failed to rejoin the elite from which he was descended.

Calles and the Coming of the Revolution

Nonetheless, for Calles, life in the northeast amounted to a training ground for his eventual political career. While in Fronteras, he professed an increasing interest in the national political scene. Beginning in 1905, he read an anarchist newspaper, *Regeneración*, a publication of the Partido Liberal Mexicano (Mexican Liberal Party). Printed in San Antonio, Texas, and distributed secretly in Mexico, *Regeneración* was the mouthpiece of the anarcho-syndicalist Flores Magón brothers, who encouraged opposition to Díaz from their exile in the United States. The fact that Calles read this newspaper by no means suggests that he was a Floresmagonista sympathizer, as the publication encountered a wide readership among the literate middle class of northern Mexico. Unlike de la Huerta, who briefly joined the Flores Magón movement, Calles remained aloof from the opposition.[76]

However, *Regeneración* introduced him to a new and radical perspective. The Floresmagonista critique represented the increasing difficulties of the

Porfiriato as it entered its fourth decade in power. The Baldíos Law had led to the concentration of land in fewer hands rather than the creation of a yeoman class of farmers. Foreign companies showcased a significant disparity in wages between foreign-born and Mexican workers. Aspirants to political office were increasingly impatient with the rule of a clique, many of whose members were approaching their eightieth birthdays. The newspaper decried the costs of Porfirian modernization in both the city and the countryside. Issues discussed in the newspaper included, among others, the system of debt peonage on the great haciendas, the miserable wages and lack of protection of industrial and mine workers, the favorable treatment of foreign employees, and the existence of child labor.[77]

Regeneración might have been idle reading if not for the unrest in nearby Cananea, where the 1905 collapse of the price of copper on the world market wreaked havoc with the balance sheet of the CCCC. The company passed its shortfall on to its workers. In June 1906, the miners protested against falling real wages in the wake of a 50 percent drop in the value of the silver peso against the gold-denominated dollar, which increased the prices of imported goods in the company store. Although the wage ranked among the highest in all of Mexico, it was a pittance compared to the earnings of the employees from the United States, who made up almost 25 percent of the workforce and continued to be paid in dollars. Influenced ideologically by the Western Federation of Miners and Floresmagonistas, the miners displayed a high degree of political consciousness. Not only did they see their company rake in millions of dollars while they worked twelve-hour days, but they also knew that they made just a fraction of the wages of their U.S. colleagues. After failed appeals to the governor and legislature to improve working conditions, the miners went on strike, only to be brutally repressed by government forces and Arizona Rangers. This bloodbath highlighted the overweening power of foreign-owned companies.[78] The Cananea strike was also the breeding ground for a generation of rebels who went on to play significant roles in the revolution, including Salvador Alvarado, Juan Cabral, and strike leader Manuel M. Diéguez, who served a term in federal prison.[79]

The trouble in Cananea, however, by no means touched off a chain reaction. Quite the contrary: The violence reminded Calles and other entrepreneurs who lived near the mines of their personal stake in the status quo. As a man of property, Calles viewed the strike with great concern, and he feared that the trouble would spill over into Fronteras. In addition, he had become involved in the local politics of the Fronteras region, the mechanism that determined access to land and water. He served various terms as *comisario* (police chief, or sheriff) and as a *regidor* (member of the municipal council) of

Santa Rosa and Fronteras. At one point, he even served a brief stint as interim *presidente municipal* (mayor).[80]

In this capacity as a local businessman in political office, Calles could ill afford to antagonize authorities, as he faced a growing controversy over land and water rights. In Fronteras, Mayor José Gómez Meza, a shop owner and friend of Calles, faced off against an opponent who accused the mayor of giving his friends privileged access to water from the only public well. Indeed, the Excélsior mill was the subject of several complaints about illegal use of water. These complaints intensified when Juan Bautista Calles's godson, Alberto Cubillas, became vice governor and intervened in the water dispute in favor of Excélsior.[81] Therefore, Calles's commercial success depended in part on his local political connections. Just like his reading of *Regeneración* did not make Calles an anarcho-syndicalist, one cannot infer from his involvement in local politics that he was an enthusiastic Díaz supporter. Rather, he played the political game in order to further his business interests. As late as 1909, he and his relatives wrote to the prefect of Arizpe, "We are people of property and work, unconditional friends of the government, and we only wish to avoid . . . difficulties and to protect our interests."[82] Later that year, Cubillas became governor, making a stance against the Porfirian regime even less likely.[83]

However, the Cananea strike proved a harbinger of greater trouble. Beginning with the global recession of 1907, Calles and Smithers experienced the flip side of modernization firsthand. As foreign demand for exports slumped and the price of silver and other commodities declined, this recession ushered in the most serious economic crisis of the Porfirian years. By 1908, the mining companies had laid off hundreds of workers in nearby Cananea and Nacozari, leading to the collapse of the regional market for flour. At the same time, the vicissitudes of local politics got the better of Calles after one of his political enemies replaced Gómez Meza in the mayor's office. Citing public complaints about Excélsior's excessive water usage, the new mayor curtailed the amount of water apportioned to the mill despite Cubillas's intervention on its behalf. In addition, Calles fell out with Gómez Meza, now judge of Fronteras, after the judge reportedly caught Calles in a furtive affair with his married daughter. Whether this story is true or not, the Elíases petitioned the prefect of Arizpe for Gómez Meza's removal. At a time when the prefects infringed upon municipal autonomy, the judge resigned within a matter of days. This was the first of several instances in which Calles turned on his own friends; combined with the financial troubles of the flour mill, the incident convinced him to move on. Calles and Smithers declared bankruptcy, and in the summer of 1910, they moved to Guaymas to open a business that sold flour, animal feed, seeds, and other farm supplies.[84]

Unlike Calles's other two failed ventures as a hotel manager and farmer, which one could blame on bad luck and poor soil and climate, respectively, the bankruptcy of the flour mill illustrated the shortcomings of the Porfiriato. As he and Smithers had witnessed, modernization had increased the country's vulnerability to global economic trends.[85] Equally as important, he had learned that political ties to the Porfirians helped little in the sordid political spectacle of Fronteras.

Therefore, Calles returned to his native city at an important inflection point in both his life and the history of Sonora. Whereas northeastern Sonora had introduced him to one important group of Díaz opponents—the mine workers influenced by the Floresmagonistas—Guaymas featured an anti-Porfirian faction based among the elite and middle classes. Disappointed in the process of modernization, many Guaymenses manifested a growing discontent with the Díaz regime. Although the railroad had brought prosperity to the city, it had also created an even more favorably endowed company town east of Guaymas that looked more like a U.S. town than a Mexican one. With its cookie-cutter houses and lawns as well as street names such as "Calle Willard," what foreigners called Junction City and Mexicans called Empalme was a visible reminder of the U.S. presence. Even more importantly, the oligarchs of Guaymas had lost influence during the Porfiriato.[86] In 1886, the notable José María Maytorena, an ally of the Pesqueira clan, had launched an unsuccessful bid for the governorship that amounted to the last electoral challenge to the triumvirate of Corral, Izábal, and Torres.[87] Since then, his family had numbered among the political "outs" but had survived by living off its considerable landholdings in the Guaymas area.[88] In the early 1900s, however, the deportation of the Yaquis cost the Maytorenas and other *hacendados* thousands of low-cost workers. After several failed appeals, Maytorena's son, also named José María (or Don Pepe), organized an opposition movement. Educated at Santa Clara College in California, Don Pepe gave shelter to fugitive Yaquis and sought to restore the municipal autonomy that the triumvirate had destroyed over the previous decades. An 1892 law had given the governor the power to appoint district prefects and judges of first instance, and Governor Corral routinely bypassed the notables of Guaymas in favor of cronies without any ties to the area. Worse yet, the prefects and judges selected by Corral frequently meddled in local politics and engaged in underhanded dealings with foreign companies, often cutting out local entrepreneurs.[89] When Corral became vice president of Mexico in 1904, the Guaymense elite were glad to be rid of him.[90]

As Corral was only one step away from succeeding the aging Díaz, state politics got increasingly tied up with the national political scene. In a 1908 interview with the U.S. journalist James Creelman, Díaz had declared that he would not run for another term as president in the next elections, scheduled for June 1910. The Creelman interview caused great excitement and helped spawn a movement in favor of General Bernardo Reyes, a career military officer from the northern industrial city of Monterrey. Believing that Reyes would give them a fresh chance at winning political office, Maytorena and other Guaymenses supported him. When Díaz reneged on his statements and announced his intention to run for yet another term, Reyes and his retainers set their sights on the vice presidential position. Díaz, however, decided to stick with Corral, and Reyes went to Madrid on a diplomatic mission. Nevertheless, he had awakened the provincial power brokers, who had been alienated by the heavy-handed maneuvers of the Porfirians. Reyes's withdrawal opened the door for another opposition candidate: Francisco I. Madero, a landowner from the northeastern state of Coahuila. Educated in Paris and Berkeley, Madero had returned to Mexico incensed at the lack of political opportunity for the opposition. Published in 1909, his treatise *La sucesión presidencial* (The Presidential Succession) blamed his country's problems on Díaz's desire to remain in office and on the aging and corrupt clique that supported him.[91] The publication of this book launched an anti-reelectionist movement opposed to Díaz's effort to seek yet another presidential term, and Madero toured the country to test the waters for a possible candidacy of his own. In January 1910, Madero visited Guaymas and other towns in southern Sonora. The enthusiastic reception he received revealed the groundswell of political disaffection in that region. In April, an anti-reelectionist convention in Mexico City nominated Madero for the presidency. Predictably, Díaz did not accept this challenge, and he had his opponent jailed on the eve of the elections.[92]

Once in Guaymas, Calles realized the need to build up ties to the opposition movement. After Díaz's predictable election victory, upon which Madero was released from prison, Calles allowed Maytorena to use the offices of "Elías, Smithers y Cía" for clandestine meetings of the Guaymas anti-reelectionist club. To be sure, this was a small gesture, as Maytorena owned the building that housed the company. Calles also moved his family out of harm's way, installing them in the house of his father-in-law, Andrés Chacón in Nogales, from where they could easily cross into Arizona if the situation demanded it. He would not do more; as he reminded de la Huerta, he owed much to Governor Cubillas, Juan Bautista Calles's godson who had given him his first public post as municipal treasurer of Guaymas eight years before.[93]

On November 20, 1910, Calles's days of hedging came to an end when Madero raised the specter of rebellion with his Plan of San Luis Potosí. Proclaimed from exile in Texas, this plan called for Díaz's removal as well as free, democratic elections, and it promised to redress the grievances of campesinos, workers, the middle classes, and regional elites. Both the social rebels of Cananea and what one historian has called the "affluent malcontents" of Guaymas supported Madero's cause.[94] But while the Sonorans applauded, others put their lives on the line. In Chihuahua and the southern state of Morelos, campesinos such as Pascual Orozco and Emiliano Zapata interpreted Madero's manifesto as a call to insurrection. A former mule skinner, Orozco made Madero's cause his own, ambushing a federal convoy in early January 1911. Later that month, Orozco's forces carried the revolution from Chihuahua into the mountainous eastern districts of Sonora. Concerned about outside interference in Sonoran affairs, Maytorena ordered two of his lieutenants, Salvador Alvarado and Juan Cabral, to participate in the campaign. Ultimately, the two lieutenants and their troops played a minor role in the victory of the rebels. In May 1911, Orozco captured the border town of Ciudad Juárez, and Díaz resigned from office. Soon thereafter, interim president Francisco León de la Barra scheduled nationwide free elections, clearing the way for Madero to run for the presidency Díaz had denied him the previous year. A revolution that followed the banner "effective suffrage, no reelection" had swept away a national oligarchy that had sustained itself in office indefinitely. In October, Madero won an easy victory at the polls.[95]

Sonora had not played a great role in the revolution of 1910. Instead, most elite and middle-class Sonorans, including Calles, had cooperated with the Porfirian regime in foiling popular challenges to political stability. Even Maytorena, an inveterate Díaz opponent, hoped that the presidential transition would prove but a brief episode of bloodshed and leave intact political hierarchies and social structures. With the exception of Cabral, who called for a land reform to break up the largest estates, Don Pepe and his followers shared Madero's focus on democracy rather than social change. In an era when Zapata and Orozco kept their men armed, the Yoris knew that the Yaquis might take advantage of unrest to reclaim land by violent means.[96]

The Sonoran pattern contrasted with the revolutionary process in neighboring states such as Sinaloa and Chihuahua. Sinaloa witnessed a large agrarian movement that merged with rancheros from the sierra and members of the landed elite to produce a multiclass coalition.[97] In Chihuahua, Orozco's grassroots movement had sought to overthrow not only Díaz but also the state's foremost *hacendado*, Luis Terrazas, who owned land with a combined acreage equal to that of the U.S. state of South Carolina. In addition, a former cattle rustler from Durango known as Pancho Villa commanded a campesino army. As a result, the revolution triumphed in Chihuahua as a popular movement. Conscious of grassroots power, Governor Abraham González proposed an ambitious program of social reform, only to depart for an extended leave of absence when new president Madero named him secretary of internal affairs (*gobernación*). Chihuahuans thus lived an uneasy compromise between elite rule and popular demands.[98]

At the very least, however, the revolution had shuffled the political deck in Sonora, and Calles attempted to take advantage of the new opportunities in the July 1911 state elections. He ran for one of two congressional seats allotted to the Guaymas district; de la Huerta was a candidate for the other seat. However, Elías, Smithers y Cía followed the familiar path of his other business ventures into failure, and Calles pulled out shortly before the vote. By contrast, de la Huerta stood an excellent chance of winning, as he had negotiated a peace agreement with Yaqui commanders just weeks before Díaz's surrender. On July 30, Maytorena triumphed in the gubernatorial elections and de la Huerta won election to the state Congress. By then, Calles had moved back to the northeast to start over yet again.[99]

Growing up in Sonora during the Porfirian era had shaped the young Plutarco Elías Calles in important ways. He had been unable to shake the long shadow of his bohemian and irresponsible father. His drift in search of the social status of his forebears took him across Sonora and into a variety of failed undertakings. Calles had learned a lot about his home state as a result of his meanderings that followed nine years of formal education. He had seen the virtually anarchic freedom of the frontier congeal into the machine politics of the Porfiriato. He had witnessed a significant mining boom that had relegated the traditional mainstays of the region's economy, ranching and farming, to a secondary position. He had watched foreigners assume a great degree of control over the economy, and he had observed the suffering of his fellow Sonorans when his state's high degree of exposure to the world economy brought about a serious economic crisis. And he had grown up in a world in which the conquest of native societies was still in full swing. In this world, middle-class Sonorans felt threatened by the Catholic Church, the United States, the Yaquis, and, most recently, the central government.

Calles's experiences as a petty capitalist and local officeholder during the Porfiriato influenced his future political outlook. His multiple failures as an entrepreneur and his inability to assert himself in the municipal politics of Fronteras and Guaymas taught him two important lessons. Most importantly, he understood the cynical nature of politics in the world in which he lived. As he found out, clientelist politics opened and closed doors for personal wealth. Rather than an exercise of civic responsibility, to him the contest of political forces served as an arena of competing material interests. As a consequence, Calles deprecated representative democracy as a naïve sham. Like the Científicos whose positivist philosophy had educated him, he viewed politics as administration, and he was far more interested in the outcome than in the process of politics. Calles therefore judged the Porfiriato by its material performance. Like many other middle-class Sonorans, he had no reason to oppose the regime until such time as it failed to advance his interests. Therefore, Calles was an opportunistic and lukewarm revolutionary, a latecomer to Madero's revolution.

At thirty-three years of age, Calles appeared doomed to a life in obscurity. With a growing family to support, he had left a teaching profession that could not sustain the lifestyle he desired, only to fail as a hotel manager, farmer, and entrepreneur. He had joined the revolutionary movement too late to gain political capital from its triumph, and he did not display any leadership abilities or political ideology that would have distinguished him from the other hangers-on who hoped to rise to prominence on Madero's coattails. If the triumph of Madero had put a definitive end to the fighting, Calles might have been destined to continue his dabbling in business and politics with inconclusive results.

Calles's struggles in Porfirian Sonora played a crucial role in forming his political outlook and personality, more so than a supposed stigma derived from his origins as an orphan born out of wedlock cited by historians influenced by psychoanalytical approaches.[100] Life in northwestern Mexico had proven a school of hard knocks that left a lasting legacy in his perception of his environment

CHAPTER TWO

Seeking Order in Chaos

One is either [Calles's] friend or his enemy.

—Djed Bórquez [pseud.], *Hombres de México*

On July 30, 1911, Calles and two other partners opened a small store in Agua Prieta. Among other items, Elías, Fuentes y Cía sold hardware, machinery, and wine. Plutarco was still looking for a venture that would allow his growing family to live a lifestyle that fit its notable background. A small, unattractive, and dirty town on the railroad line that connected the copper mines of Nacozari to the U.S. border, Agua Prieta appeared an unlikely place for such an endeavor. Its name, which translates into "black water," seemed appropriate: In Agua Prieta, the water turned black due to soot particles that floated in the air. These particles emanated from a giant copper smelter just across the border in Douglas, Arizona, a town named after a copper baron. Just like other border communities that had grown rapidly during the last decade of the Porfiriato, Agua Prieta manifested the ugly side of the integration into the North American economy. On one side of the border, Douglas featured a large smelter that processed the ore from Nacozari and other mines. By 1910, it had become a prosperous town of thirteen thousand people. On the other side, Agua Prieta was a seedy town of broken dreams, a place where *El Norte* beckoned with promises of a better life unfulfilled for those who lived there. Its three thousand inhabitants included the lowest-paid workers of the smelter, often migrants driven off their land by greedy *hacendados*, failed harvests, or lack of water. The adobe, one-story houses gave a drab appearance. There was no sewage, and the town's water came from Douglas. Prosperity, which had found a permanent home in Arizona, had made but a pit stop in Agua Prieta. Well protected by local authorities, its saloons, brothels, and gambling parlors served not only Mexican customers but also visitors from dry areas in Arizona.[1]

Calles could not have known just how fateful his decision to try his luck in Agua Prieta was to be. The burg lay in a strategically significant area for the control of the northwest. The border facilitated the procurement of arms, ammunition, and information, and Chihuahua was only a day's ride away. Whereas the peaks of the Sierra Madre made access difficult elsewhere along the long border between the two states, Agua Prieta lay in a gap separating the Sierra Madre from the Rocky Mountains. In 1853, that same gap had inspired the U.S. government to purchase a slice of northern Sonora in order to build a railroad through the newly acquired territory. Since then, the Paso del Púlpito, located some thirty miles southeast of Agua Prieta, has provided Sonora's only direct access to Chihuahua.[2] As both states became focal points of revolutionary violence, Agua Prieta's strategic location provided unexpected opportunities for Calles. Over the next four years, he would experience a rough apprenticeship that gave focus to a new career goal: that of a political leader.

Cacique of Agua Prieta

Calles's years in Agua Prieta began with a stroke of good luck. On September 5, 1911, four days after assuming office as governor of Sonora, Maytorena named him *comisario* of Agua Prieta.[3] Recently redefined by law, the office of *comisario* combined those of police chief, justice of the peace, and magistrate. In the absence of a mayor, Calles was also the chief executive of the small town. The *comisario* enjoyed powers exceeding those of the famed sheriffs on the western frontier of the United States: he answered only to Maytorena and Benjamín Hill, the prefect of Arizpe. Maytorena had good reasons for picking Calles for the post. Having met Calles during the days of the Maderista opposition movement in Guaymas, he trusted him as a political ally. He also believed that Plutarco's family ties in the Arizpe district would help him establish good relations with the cattle ranchers and *hacendados* of the area, an important factor in the border region. Finally, Calles had reportedly asked de la Huerta to intercede on his behalf for this position in a "region that will be developed soon."[4]

The new position offered Calles a fresh start as a cacique, a local boss who interpreted and applied the law to his own liking. In particular, the growing

traffic across the border provided great opportunities for smuggling to an aspiring merchant with political leverage. As de la Huerta asserted, Calles took
advantage of these opportunities by means of a joint venture with his ac-
quaintance J. S. Williams, general director of the Moctezuma Copper Co. in
Nacozari, in which the *comisario* combined the orders from his store with the
duty-free imports of the copper mine. In reselling the smuggled items, which
were far cheaper than those that had cleared the border legally, Calles
achieved a considerable profit margin.[5] He also knew that his extensive family connections would help him both in his business and in the new political
post. Combining roles as a merchant, smuggler, and the enforcer of law and
order, Calles became a "border broker"—a member of a small group whose
access to credit and arms in the United States would confer upon it a crucial
role in the civil wars ahead.[6]

Calles had at last begun to turn the corner. His family found material comfort in Agua Prieta; for the first time, they enjoyed the benefits of electricity
and plumbing. Instead of the outhouses and petroleum lamps of their resi-
dences in Santa Rosa, Fronteras, and Guaymas, their home had a bathroom
with running water, and electricity in the kitchen and living room. Since
winters in Agua Prieta are among the coldest in Mexico, the newfound
amenities provided welcome relief. However, the rented house was too small
for a family of seven, which revealed the fact that Calles was still by no
means a wealthy man. For his part, Calles found additional comfort in the
person of Alice Gatliff, the owner of the Curio Café, a restaurant and cu-
riosity shop.[7] The woman dubbed *la gringa de las curiosidades* was rumored to
be his mistress. In future years, Calles would stay at her house whenever he
returned to Agua Prieta.[8]

Yet Calles did not face an easy task in his new position. Only a few days
after his appointment, he wrote a letter to Maytorena outlining the deplorable situation in Agua Prieta. He informed the governor that there were
only four police officers in the border town. According to Calles, the local
school director received a regular salary but did not have a school building,
let alone furniture or supplies. There were no chairs in his office, and the
prison was a miserable adobe hut from which prisoners escaped easily and
regularly.[9]

Appalled at the situation, Calles espoused a set of goals—political order,
morality, and public education—that provided a first glimpse of the reformist
and authoritarian leader that he would become. Consistent with his positivist education, he launched a campaign for public morality that included
antialcohol measures. Within two weeks of taking office, he had signed a decree prohibiting the consumption of alcohol during the local Independence

Day celebrations. He also banned children from bars and dismissed local officials known for their lack of discipline and venality. *San Lunes* (Saint Monday)—the practice of skipping work on Mondays—was out with Calles in charge. To exert a greater degree of control over his subordinates, he forced municipal employees who resided in Douglas to move back to Agua Prieta. In addition, the *comisario* sought social and material improvements. He opened two new schools, and he recommended the opening of a school for adults seeking to complete at least their primary education. He began a series of public works projects, including a permanent office for the *comisario* (which later doubled as a hospital) and the rebuilding of the town jail. It helped his reputation that his store, bolstered by the new political connections, sold on credit.[10] Finally, Calles used a heavy dose of repression. According to one of his critics, he ordered the hanging of a worker who, in a state of inebriation, had insulted President Madero.[11]

True or not, the anecdote illustrated the curious tension between a new democratic political culture and old-style tactics of ensuring order pursued by local authorities. The new political culture represented one of the most significant legacies of the Madero movement, which had allowed a new generation of politicians to win power by the ballot box. With the theoretical achievement of liberal democracy, this generation learned that people expected their voices to be heard and their vote to count. Even officials like Calles who held appointive rather than elective office needed to pay lip service to the idea of popular sovereignty. Therefore, the triumph of Madero led to an important shift in expectations across the entire spectrum of society.[12]

However, the president could not fulfill these expectations. Madero was a timid leader hampered by the terms of his armistice with the Porfirians. During the months before Madero's election and inauguration, Interim President León de la Barra allowed the adherents of the old regime to fortify their positions. In particular, most of the army officers were loyal Díaz supporters who remained opposed to the new political order. They were delighted when the armistice left the federal army (the *Federales*) in charge of national security and stipulated the disarmament of the rebel forces. Madero fulfilled his part of the bargain and called upon the revolutionary forces that had rebelled in his name to deliver their arms. This move earned the new president the enmity of some of his erstwhile supporters, and bands of armed campesinos defied his order and contributed to a wave of riots and banditry not seen in more than four decades. Moreover, Madero did little to address his country's social problems. Besieged by political instability, his government did not return hacienda land to campesinos, and the abysmal working conditions in many factories, mines, plantations, and sweat shops continued as if Díaz still ruled.[13]

Maytorena's government in Sonora typified the new national political order. Don Pepe was in an enviable position compared to several other governors, as Sonora had not witnessed much fighting. However, the state government faced financial difficulties that constrained its ability to address economic and social problems. Maytorena inherited a debt that amounted to one-third of the annual state budget, as the unrest had aggravated an existing shortfall in tax collections. Therefore, the governor limited himself to a small number of political, judicial, and educational reforms. He attempted to restore the impartiality of the justice system, he initiated an electoral reform, he vainly proposed to move the state administration from Hermosillo to his hometown of Guaymas, and he launched a literacy program in a state in which two-thirds of all adults could not read and write. Overall, however, Don Pepe did not accomplish any more than Madero did at the national level. Like the president, he was often overwhelmed by events. He showed little interest in the welfare of campesinos and mine workers, and he authorized local leaders to suppress strikes by force. For example, when the Cananea workers struck for higher wages, more stringent safety standards, and shorter shifts in December 1912, Maytorena ordered the arrest of strike organizers. Although he maintained good relations with Yaqui leaders, he failed to implement a definitive land settlement with them.[14]

One reason for the modest track records of both President Madero and Governor Maytorena was the persistence of unrest. Even before Madero's inauguration on November 6, 1911, Zapata had concluded that the new president would never make good on his campaign promise of restoring hacienda lands to campesino villagers. Zapata's "Plan de Ayala" of November 25 sought the overthrow of Madero and the restitution of all land alienated under Porfirian legislation. Another rebel, General Bernardo Reyes, desired to bring back the old guard, albeit without Don Porfirio and his fellow octogenarians. In mid-December 1911, he left his self-imposed exile in San Antonio, Texas, to lead a revolt from northeastern Mexico. Having failed to garner much support due to his close association with the Díaz regime, Reyes surrendered on Christmas Day. Simultaneously, a third revolt broke out in Chihuahua led by Emilio Vázquez Gómez, whose brother had served as Madero's running mate in the 1910 elections.[15]

Sonorans could not remain immune from these developments. Maytorena's triumph had produced a new set of political "outs," the labor unrest in the Cananea copper mine continued to simmer five years after the 1906 massacre, and the Yaquis were fuming over the governor's failure to restore their ancestral lands. The national rebel movements linked up with this local discontent. In particular, Agua Prieta was host to a multitude of schemes

against Maytorena and Madero, from anarchists among the miners to partisans of Vázquez Gómez.[16] In late 1911, the region became the seat of rebellion against Vice Governor Eugenio Gayou, who had narrowly defeated a
northeastern candidate in the elections.[17] Both Maytorena and Gayou were
from Guaymas, and encouraged by the Vazquistas, the northeasterners
charged that Don Pepe had resorted to fraud in ensuring Gayou's victory. As
tensions simmered, Isidro Escobosa, a self-proclaimed defender of his region's
interests, began guerrilla activities in the Cananea area.[18]

The unrest gave Calles his first opportunity to showcase his value to Maytorena. In early October, Escobosa's troops infiltrated Agua Prieta and killed
one soldier. Following Calles's recommendations, Maytorena stationed a garrison in Agua Prieta and meted out capital punishment to captured rebel
leaders.[19] In December, Calles led his very first military campaign against a
contingent of Escobosa supporters and clamped down on the rebels with an
iron fist.[20]

In March 1912, the situation became even worse when General Pascual
Orozco from neighboring Chihuahua rebelled against the government. Once
Madero's most significant ally, Orozco was disgusted with the president's
nepotistic penchant for rewarding his own family members with lucrative
government posts. He was further spurred to action by Zapata's Plan de Ayala that recognized Orozco as the head of the rebellion against Madero.
Dated March 25, the "Plan Orozquista" assailed the Madero family for occupying numerous posts in the federal and state governments, and it called for
a ten-hour workday and higher wages. The plan also demanded agrarian reform and the expropriation of the foreign-owned railroad system. Inspired by
anarcho-syndicalism, this plan found admirers among the miners of Cananea
and Nacozari. Not a man of political principle, Orozco also obtained the
backing of the Vazquistas and members of the landed oligarchy. By August, a
few thousand Orozquistas were in northeastern Sonora, and Escobosa and
other rebels joined their cause.[21] Far away from their base of operations in
Chihuahua, these rebels resorted to banditry by looting haciendas, farms, and
stores; stealing livestock and valuables; and raiding the villages through
which they passed. Sonoran leaders viewed the roaming bandits as a threat
to the sovereignty of their state. Maytorena, for example, portrayed the
Orozquista challenge as "anarchy and destruction launched from the mountains of Chihuahua."[22] He was concerned enough about this revolt that he
allowed U.S. citizens to receive arms and ammunition through the conduct
of their consulates in Cananea and Nogales.[23]

The Orozquista rebellion embroiled Calles in controversy. During a visit
to Douglas, the Mexican consul in Laredo, Texas, heard a rumor that Calles

and his associates conspired with the rebels. The consul recommended send-
ing the offenders to Mexico City to make them talk or to kill them if they refused. The charges fell on deaf ears with Maytorena, who stressed Calles's
loyalty to the established authorities. Whether the allegations were true or
not, at least one Elías—Calles's half-brother Arturo M. Elías Malvido, a former Porfirian diplomat and opportunist par excellence—did turn his back on
the Madero government. Elías became a supporter of the Huerta regime the
following year.[24]

Maytorena's confidence was soon rewarded when Calles turned Agua Prieta into an important base of operations against the Orozquistas. As the
comisario reported, "The state can count on a great number of citizens in this
district who are ready to defend the legally constituted government."[25] Calles
gathered intelligence across the border, rounded up suspected rebels, and recruited volunteers for a military force of approximately one hundred men.
This force was a *batallón irregular:* an armed group that complemented the
Federales in enforcing order in the countryside. Although they received
funding from the federal and state governments, these battalions primarily
obeyed the man who had commissioned them—in this case, Comisario
Calles.[26]

His battalion then joined up with a larger battalion led by Alvaro Obregón
Salido, a young chickpea farmer who had just been elected mayor of Huatabampo in southern Sonora. Under Obregón's nominal command, this force
ultimately reached 1,300 troops. Calles himself did not see any military action
during this campaign; instead, he remained in Agua Prieta to serve as the
principal node of communication until the expeditionary force entered Chihuahua. Obregón was successful in this, his first campaign. He got as far as
Casas Grandes, Chihuahua, deep in Orozquista country.[27]

Thus began Calles's association with Obregón that would one day transform the national political landscape. Obregón was born in 1880 in the
southern district of Alamos as the youngest of eighteen children. Like those
of Calles, his ancestors spanned different sectors of Sonoran society. His
mother was a Salido, one of the most influential families in the Alamos district, and several of his older siblings had married into other notable clans.
His father, a farmer, came from a middle-class family. He died after a flood
and a Yaqui attack destroyed the family farm, and the Obregóns moved to
the town of Huatabampo near Navojoa. In contrast to Calles's exposure to
positivist thought in Hermosillo, Obregón received most of his education
from his older sisters; his learning was homespun and practical, centered on
basic literacy and survival skills in a rural environment. Unlike Calles,
Obregón appreciated native peoples: he spoke Mayo as well as Spanish, and

his contingent included hundreds of Mayo troops. In appreciation of the contributions of the Mayos under his command, he later named his youngest son Mayo. He received practical instruction in menial work and entrepreneurship as a mechanic, self-made tobacco farmer, cigarette producer, and shoe salesman. In contrast to Calles's failings as an entrepreneur, Obregón accumulated capital through these endeavors, and in 1906, he purchased 180 hectares of land in Huatabampo, a plot he baptized "La Quinta Chilla" (the penniless farm).[28]

The differences between the two men who would become the two most powerful leaders of the 1920s were striking indeed. Calles did not enjoy action on the battlefield. As Obregón once quipped, he was "the least general-like of the generals," comments that alluded to Calles's spotty military record and his preference for business suits over military uniforms.[29] Obregón, on the other hand, was a brilliant military strategist who felt more at home in the field of battle than in political office. As an entrepreneur, Calles imagined grand schemes for wealth and success, only to fail time and again; Obregón turned Quinta Chilla into a successful agribusiness. Calles was a thinker, Obregón was a doer; Calles was pensive and mysterious where Obregón was extroverted and humorous; Calles excelled by planning, Obregón, by executing; Calles's intellectual strength was theoretical where Obregón's lay in practical application; and Calles succeeded by dogged determination while Obregón triumphed by sleight of hand. In the words of his foe Martín Luis Guzmán, Obregón "did not live on the ground of everyday sincerities, but on a tableau: he was not a person . . . but an actor. His ideas, his beliefs, his sentiments were those of the . . . theater, to shine before an audience."[30] Calles, on the other hand, was a planner rather than an actor, and his brusqueness often stood in the way of communicating effectively with other people. This is not to say that the two leaders had nothing in common: they shared decisiveness, belief in material progress, and a disdain for democratic and decentralized political structures. For the moment, Calles and Obregón formed an alliance of convenience in which the former was dependent on the latter. By far the stronger partner, Obregón viewed Calles as a pawn on a chessboard of revolutionary politics.

Calles's time as *comisario* was the turning point of his career. The position itself was not so different from the other local posts Calles had occupied in Porfirian Sonora. In Agua Prieta, however, he had stepped into a power vacuum, and the absence of a mayor and functioning town council had made him a local boss who combined business and politics to his advantage. Equally importantly, the Orozco revolt had elevated him to the ranks of the self-made revolutionary military commanders. This new class of military leaders with strong local connections had gained much prestige during the revolt, and they stood to gain even more in case there was renewed revolutionary violence at the national level.[31]

Military Commander in the Constitutionalist Revolution

Such a scenario came to pass in February 1913, when Madero confronted a rebellion of Porfirian military officers led by Reyes and the old dictator's nephew, Félix Díaz. Both of these Porfiristas served prison terms in Mexico City after spearheading revolts against the Madero administration, and they plotted Madero's overthrow from their confinement. On February 9, rebel forces freed Reyes and Díaz. Reyes died during the escape, and after a failed attempt to attack the National Palace, Díaz's troops marched across town and occupied the armory (Ciudadela) west of the city center. Eager to end the rebellion, Madero ordered General Victoriano Huerta, a trusted federal commander who had distinguished himself in the campaigns against Orozco, to besiege the Ciudadela. However, Huerta kept his options open by negotiating with Díaz and allowing supplies to enter the armory. Thus began the *decena trágica,* the tragic ten days during which government and rebel troops staged battles that claimed hundreds of lives without bringing about the victory of either side. Finally, on February 18, Huerta switched sides and dispatched one of his aides to the National Palace to arrest Madero and Vice President José María Pino Suárez. U.S. Ambassador Henry Lane Wilson, a diplomat who had long considered Madero unfit to rule, brokered a formal agreement between Díaz and Huerta with the help of several European colleagues. At gunpoint, Madero and Pino Suárez wrote their resignations. The secretary of foreign relations, next in line for the presidency, spent just forty-three minutes in office before resigning, long enough to appoint Huerta secretary of the interior, the president-designate in the absence of the president, the vice president, and the secretary of foreign relations. An intimidated Congress confirmed Huerta as president before midnight. Three days later, one of his minions assassinated Madero and Pino Suárez, leaving the state governors with the choice of accepting the new regime or rejecting it in the name of the martyred president.[32]

Governor Maytorena considered this a difficult decision. On the one hand, Huerta had taken power by force, and Sonorans feared that the new federal government would impose a governor of its choice, who might terminate other elected officeholders in the state. Maytorena could not support a usurper backed by the Porfirian military, much less someone connected to the assassination of his political allies. In addition, news of the murders led to widespread popular indignation, especially in the urban centers and along the border.[33] On the other hand, Don Pepe stood much to lose from a challenge to Huerta. Madero had not guaranteed political stability, and the turmoil of the past six months had constituted the exact situation that Maytorena had sought to avoid in supporting him in 1910. The state Congress waffled, business interests lobbied for Huerta's recognition, and the federal government maintained heavily armed garrisons in the state. Defiance of Huerta entailed a possible seizure of Hermosillo and installation of a military governor. With the Yaquis on the warpath and scattered bands of Orozquistas still operating in eastern Sonora, such interference might easily have destroyed what remained of political stability. Compelled by similar considerations, most state governors except Abraham González of Chihuahua and Venustiano Carranza of Coahuila recognized the Huerta regime within a week. Maytorena temporized and sought to prevent bloodshed by pressuring protesters not to hold demonstrations near the federal garrisons.[34]

This waiting game undermined the governor's authority in favor of Calles and other caciques who had commanded irregular troops against the Orozco rebellion, and it began a long process that ultimately led to a split of the Sonoran revolutionaries into pro- and anti-Maytorena factions. While Maytorena waffled, Calles and Obregón took matters into their own hands. Calles marched south from Agua Prieta in order to gain distance between his forces and the federal garrison in the nearby border town of Naco. Eager to erase the stain of his nonparticipation in the revolution of 1910, Obregón rounded up his troops in southern Sonora, ready for battle. Most problematic for the governor was the fact that Alvarado and Cabral, his erstwhile military commanders during the revolution of 1910, prepared for war as well.[35] Alvarado in particular was disappointed at the governor's stance and accused him of "shameful womanly vacillations."[36] At an impasse, Maytorena decided to take a six-month leave of absence in Tucson, Arizona. He later justified his action by the argument that nonrecognition would have led to the confiscation of property, the imposition of forced loans, and the arrests of innocent people due to the mere fact "that they did not support our cause."[37] In other words, a war against Huerta would have entailed a wholesale attack on liberty and property rights that this privileged *hacendado* would not support.

Maytorena's departure tipped the scales in favor of Calles and the other hawks who were preparing for armed conflict with the Huerta regime. Initially, Interim Governor Ignacio L. Pesqueira—a member of the famous clan that had dominated Sonora until 1876—followed Maytorena's lead and attempted mediation through the offices of the U.S. consul in Hermosillo. In the course of these talks, he came close to recognizing Huerta. However, Cananea erupted in revolt, and the radical leaders of that mining town vociferously denounced the coup. Soon thereafter, Alvarado and several of his troops charged into the legislature and demanded an immediate break with the federal government. Finally, on March 5, 1913, Pesqueira and the state Congress decreed that Sonora would not recognize the Huerta regime. This declaration pitted the state government against the well-armed federal garrisons that remained loyal to Huerta.

The belated nonrecognition decree did not satisfy Calles and his allies in the northeast. On March 13, Calles and other officials from the districts of Arizpe and Moctezuma issued the "Manifiesto de Nacozari" on behalf of what the signatories declared were five thousand men under arms. The manifesto enjoined Sonorans to fight against the "absolutist" Huerta regime. It was a call for the defense of the autonomy of Sonora rather than a program for social change like the Plan Orozquista or the Plan de Ayala. Wrote the insurrectionists, "None of us ignores the urgent necessity of reestablishing peace . . . , even at great sacrifice; but . . . the storms provoked by a popular rebellion are preferable to a peace sustained by the guns of a military dictatorship."[38] The goals of Calles and the other Sonoran rebels were thus strictly political: to defend the sovereignty of the state. Nonetheless, Huerta's coup gave leaders like Obregón and Calles who had not participated in the fight against Díaz a second chance to claim the mantle of revolution.

Geography and an alliance with other northern movements helped the Sonoran rebels survive the crucial first months. The absence of a rail connection between Mexico City and Sonora impeded the reinforcement and provisioning of Federal garrisons in that distant state, and Pesqueira could still count on the battalions mobilized against the Orozquistas, especially in the northeastern districts of Arizpe and Moctezuma. These troops remained loyal to the caciques who had recruited them. Moreover, the U.S. border helped the rebels procure weapons and money, and Maytorena and other Sonorans in the United States served as agents on behalf of the Constitutionalists.[39] In addition, Pesqueira found support in other border states. A wealthy landowner and former senator with a patrician bearing, Coahuila governor Venustiano Carranza had seen his political ambitions thwarted by Díaz. As an ally of the Maderos, he refused to recognize Huerta.[40] The government of neighboring Chihuahua would have joined Carranza had Governor González not been assassinated on Huerta's orders. Instead, Pancho Villa assumed leadership over the Chihuahuan rebels and fought in the names of Madero and González, both commemorated on the paper currency issued by his faction.[41] The Monclova Convention of April 18 united these three northern factions in the Constitutionalist movement with Carranza as *primer jefe*, or first chief.[42] Separately, the Zapatistas continued to fight the Federales from their base in Morelos. From their perspective, the changes of government from Díaz to de la Barra to Madero to Huerta had not made any difference in the issue that concerned them the most: the return of hacienda lands to campesinos.[43]

However, the Constitutionalist chances at victory appeared remote, as Huerta's Federales controlled most of the nation. Government troops ran Carranza out of Coahuila, leaving the Constitutionalist movement scattered in pockets of resistance. Although these pockets bordered the United States, the U.S. government under new President Woodrow Wilson was initially of no great help to the rebel movement. Wilson neither recognized Huerta nor First Chief Carranza, and he forbade arms sales to either party under the Neutrality Laws. The diverse aims of the rebel coalition further dimmed the prospects of immediate victory. Both Zapata and Villa pursued social agendas, and the former continued to demand the restitution of campesino lands. Obregón and Carranza, on the other hand, advocated the reestablishment of political order in a constitutional framework that continued to guarantee private property. Reportedly, Obregón summed up this attitude by telling Carranza, "We have no *agraristas* here, thank God! All those of us who are involved in this effort are doing it for patriotism and to avenge the death of Mr. Madero."[44] This endeavor was difficult enough. To attack the well-defended Federal garrisons, Constitutionalist leaders could only count on their battalions established during the Orozco revolt. Calles and other military commanders understood that they needed to build a rebel army from scratch rather than relying on deserters.[45]

For Calles, the Constitutionalist cause required a full-time commitment to the war against Huerta. He entered that war as a newly commissioned officer: shortly before the beginning of hostilities, Pesqueira had awarded him his first military rank, that of lieutenant colonel.[46] As commander of the Constitutionalist forces of northeastern Sonora who reported directly to Pesqueira, Calles became a soldier of the revolution. He abandoned his post as *comisario* and his store, and he shipped his family to safety in Nogales, Arizona, where they moved in with Natalia's father, Andrés Chacón. Life in Arizona imprinted his children with a transnational orientation, and the Calles family began to measure Mexico by U.S. standards. But the temporary exile of the family also tore at its unity. Not only did Calles see his wife and children infrequently, but his family was also exposed to antirevolutionary sentiments. Whereas Chacón supported the Constitutionalists, his sisters viewed them as criminals and rapists. Moreover, Plutarco's and Natalia's daughters,

Resting on the battlefield
Source: FAPEC.

who attended the only Spanish-language school in Nogales, experienced the humiliation of having the die-hard Porfirista Brígido Caro as their teacher. Ten years later, Caro would write a scathing biography that still stands as one of the most negative portraits of Calles.[47]

With his family safe, Calles jumped into military action in a foolhardy fashion. Upon the publication of the Nacozari Manifesto, his six hundred troops attacked the federal garrison stationed in Naco. Engaged in a battle many miles away, Obregón, who had attempted to warn Calles against the undertaking by telegraph, could not come to his assistance. As a result, the Federales pushed the outnumbered Calles forces back to Agua Prieta. The leader of these forces, however, apparently kept his personal safety foremost in his mind. As Adolfo de la Huerta later claimed, he found Calles asleep, hidden under an automobile.[48] Only Obregón's intervention saved Calles from an early and ignominious end to his military career. After seizing Cananea and Nogales, Obregón's troops joined up with the remaining Calles forces, and the Naco garrison fell after a siege of fifteen days. Obregón took the opportunity to ridicule Calles's military leadership by baptizing him "the mill owner from Fronteras" in reference to his earlier career.[49] This label stuck as the chickpea grower from Huatabampo went on to become the most successful general of the revolution. Years later, U.S. military intelligence officers reported that Calles was "weak, vacillating, and not fond of fighting," and that "no one [has] ever accused him of being a good soldier."[50]

Calles henceforth lent administrative rather than military support to Obregón's offensive against the Federales as one of the primary procurement agents of the Constitutionalist movement. In violation of U.S. Neutrality Laws, he bought weapons, ammunition, and clothing in the United States, the funds from which often came from forced loans and cattle smuggling. In his new position as military commander of Nogales, Calles took advantage of his cross-border connections by confiscating cattle from ranchers loyal to Huerta and selling the animals in the United States for fifteen dollars a head. Of course, these activities favored his business interests as well.[51] Calles and Maytorena even coordinated the clandestine removal of a biplane from a warehouse in Arizona. The plane had been purchased by Maytorena's agents and impounded by U.S. authorities; several weeks later, it rained bombs on Guaymas. Finally, Calles recruited and trained troops for the revolution. In these capacities, he proved that he was more valuable as an administrator than as a military commander, and he expanded his own power base, as his activities provided opportunities for enrichment for local entrepreneurs and military leaders alike.[52] Calles thus played a significant part in Obregón's increasing success against the Federales. By June 1913, only the federal garrison in Guaymas remained under Huertista control.[53]

Ironically, however, Obregón's military success begat significant divisions among the Sonoran Constitutionalists. Pesqueira, a man close to the powerful foreign mining interests, not only represented civilian authority in Sonora, but First Chief Carranza had also given him nominal control over the state's military forces as head of the Division of the Northwest. With good reason, Obregón bitterly resented Carranza's preference for the interim governor.[54] But his rancor toward Pesqueira was only the tip of the iceberg. The Constitutionalists accumulated a mounting debt to the Yaquis, who had contributed a contingent of more than a thousand troops to their campaign. Yaqui commanders pressed Pesqueira to make good on Maytorena's old promise to restore some of their ancestral lands that had been seized by foreign and

Sonoran landowners. Pesqueira, however, stalled on the issue, and the Yaqui leaders began to plan for a new military conflict.[55]

In late July 1913, even deeper fissures appeared when Maytorena returned from Tucson to reclaim the governorship. Although a movement that called itself Constitutionalist could hardly block the governor from returning to office, many Sonoran leaders opposed his reinstallation, including Pesqueira and a majority of state legislators. In the northeast, Calles and Arizpe prefect Ignacio Bonillas regarded Maytorena's return as a potential threat to their authority. In the south, Alvarado—the leader responsible for besieging the Federal holdout in Guaymas—had never reconciled himself to what he regarded as the governor's cowardice. As Calles, Bonillas, and Alvarado saw it, Maytorena conjured the specter of a failed Maderista governor as a prominent figure in the Constitutionalist movement. Indeed, although Maytorena continued to benefit from his long-standing ties to Yaqui leaders, the Yaquis recalled his earlier failure to deliver on his promise to return land to them. In addition, the Cananea mine featured a well-organized labor union whose leaders were ready to press their demands by armed force; in fact, Cananea mayor Manuel Diéguez was a former activist and strike leader in that union. Like the Yaquis, mine workers remembered a governor who had not paid attention to their concerns.[56]

However, Maytorena found a temporary ally in Obregón, who pursued an agenda that sacrificed Alvarado's and Calles's interests to further his own ambitions. Eager to weaken Pesqueira, the caudillo brokered the governor's reinstallation. Incensed about the opposition he had faced, Maytorena dismissed Pesqueira as commander of the Division of the Northwest, Calles as military commander of Nogales, and Bonillas as prefect of Arizpe. Following the old strategy of "divide and conquer," Maytorena named Obregón the supreme military commander of the state on August 7. However, Calles refused to step down, and to give his position some weight, he seized a passenger train with one of Maytorena's closest collaborators aboard. In light of this situation, Obregón traveled to Nogales to negotiate with Calles and his allies. The resultant agreement between Obregón and the border brokers decreed the exile of Bonillas and Pesqueira but confirmed Calles in his post.[57]

Obregón henceforth played the role of peacemaker between Maytorena's group from the Guaymas area and the opposition, who found themselves divided in Calles's northeastern and Alvarado's southern factions. For his part, having failed to dislodge Calles, Maytorena attempted a different tack by an attempt to improve revenue collection. One of these decrees required state approval (and, presumably, the payment of a fee) for the sale of real estate other than mining properties to foreigners.[58] Another measure struck directly at the border brokers by establishing a statewide customs authority with the power to inspect border transactions and to punish wrongdoers.[59]

In this climate of mounting discord, a battered First Chief Carranza arrived in Sonora in mid-September after a march of seventy-nine days through a forbidding landscape. Having lost control over the state government of Coahuila, the first chief was eager to maintain unity in the only state largely controlled by the Constitutionalists. As he knew, the bickering among the Sonorans had brought Obregón's offensive against the Federales to a halt. He therefore resolved to forge a united Constitutionalist program that incorporated popular demands for social change. Shortly after his arrival, Carranza made Hermosillo the provisional capital of his movement and gave his first public address as first chief.[60] The speech demonstrated to what extent the war against Huerta had changed the aims of the Constitutionalists:

> At the moment when the armed struggle . . . has ended, the social struggle, the class struggle in all its power and its grandeur must begin. Whether they want it to happen or not, the new social ideas must win out among the masses against all opposition. It is not merely a question of dividing up the land and the natural resources, not merely a question of honest elections, not merely a question of opening new schools or of the equal distribution of the wealth of the land. Something much greater and much more sacred is at stake: the creation of justice, the pursuit of equality, the disappearance of the powerful, and the creation of equilibrium in our national economy.[61]

To resist the Huerta government successfully therefore required incorporating popular demands for social change. In fact, Huerta himself carried out a modest reform program in order to steal the thunder of the Constitutionalists.[62] This speech not only revealed the transition from the Maderista search for democratic rule to a broader agenda for socioeconomic change, but it also impressed upon Calles a model for his own public image in future years. Calles could never hope to become a caudillo like Obregón and Villa, someone who skillfully steered tens of thousands of troops with a leadership style marked by folksy charisma. Instead, Carranza projected an image Calles could hope to emulate: that of a well-bred, visionary national leader.

Despite his conciliatory words, Carranza ended up stoking the rivalry between Maytorena's and Calles's groups rather than mitigating it through compromise. Soon after his speech, he toured northeastern Sonora to meet with Calles and other border brokers. On that occasion, the first chief came away impressed with Calles's administrative talents, and he decided to support his faction. On October 20, 1913, he named a provisional national government that included Calles allies Bonillas and de la Huerta, but none of

Maytorena's collaborators. Carranza further antagonized the governor by asserting federal powers in the state. As Bonillas assumed oversight over customs collections, Carranza effectively negated Maytorena's earlier decree and returned control over customs revenue to the border brokers. Finally, the first chief significantly upgraded Calles's stature: on March 15, 1914, he appointed him chief of the *fuerzas fijas* (garrisoned troops) in Sonora. Predictably, Maytorena was incensed at Carranza's actions, viewing them as interference into the internal affairs of his government.[63]

Carranza's five-month stay in Sonora therefore exacerbated the divisions between Maytorena and his opponents. Thus far, Obregón had held the factions in equilibrium and prevented open conflict. In the winter of 1913–1914, however, the mounting successes of the Constitutionalist campaign outside Sonora drew the caudillo's attention away from his native state. By February 1914, Villa had conquered Ciudad Juárez and Chihuahua City, and Obregón had vanquished the Federales in Sinaloa. In March, the Division of the Northwest left Sonora to confront the Federales farther south, while Carranza moved to the strategically important border town of Ciudad Juárez, Chihuahua. Obregón took most of his military commanders with him, and he later asserted that he left Calles at the border "because I did not want [him] to teach my soldiers to run away."[64] This reference to Calles as an inept, cowardly military leader was far from the truth, as Carranza ordered Calles to remain as a safeguard against Maytorena.[65]

The Battle for Sonora

The absence of Obregón and his entourage constituted a great opportunity for Calles. Thus far, he had been a pawn on the chessboard of revolutionary politics, moved hither and fro by Obregón, the grand master of the Constitutionalist forces in Sonora. With Carranza's support, Calles suddenly stood a chance of playing a prominent role in his own right. As he knew, such a role would come at the expense of Governor Maytorena.

Thus, Carranza had hardly left Sonora when Calles attempted to use his new office as chief of the garrisoned troops to strip Maytorena of his personal escort.[66] However, Calles had underestimated Carranza's determination to uphold the elected state government at a time when the Federales still controlled most of the nation, and to his surprise, the First Chief reinstituted the escort. Maytorena denounced Calles for the "incursion of military authorities into the sphere of civilian government . . . restricting almost completely the powers of civilian authorities."[67] The governor also consolidated his position under the guise of respecting Carranza's dispositions. Among his first measures was an order to place tax collection in the hands of agents of the state rather than the federal government. As Calles knew, Maytorena's control of customs houses and tax collection agencies would place the border brokers at a serious disadvantage, as they depended on their share of receipts for supplying the revolutionary military and maintaining their clientelist networks. He therefore responded by bringing Carranza into the fray to keep his sources of revenue flowing. Upon his request, the first chief ordered the creation of a wartime fiscal committee under the leadership of a member of the Elías clan.[68] Two months later, Calles launched a second attempt at disarming Maytorena. This time, the governor jettisoned his guards, only to recruit a private army of one hundred troops. Calles's moves reminded many Sonorans of Huerta's tactics, and popular demonstrations in the capital supported Maytorena. Viewing Calles a liability in Sonora, Obregón ordered him to join him in his battles against the Federales in central Mexico. Although First Chief Carranza reinstituted Calles to his post, the incident had rendered Calles ineffective in Hermosillo, and he soon found out that Maytorena had gained the support of Yaqui leaders. In view of this turn of events, Calles evacuated Hermosillo and returned to his home base in Agua Prieta.[69]

The mounting Constitutionalist victories in the summer of 1914 gave Calles another opportunity. When Huerta's defeat appeared all but assured, the first chief withdrew recognition from Maytorena, whose waffling he had long resented. Emboldened, Calles again acted too rashly, marching to Hermosillo and besieging the governor's palace. Maytorena called on all Sonorans to defend the sovereignty of their state and proclaimed his sympathy with agrarian and labor causes. With the help of Yaqui troops, the governor pushed Calles back to Cananea and arrested all Calles supporters in the areas under his control. For his part, Calles purged the border area of Maytorena allies and even ordered the execution of a U.S. citizen who supported the governor. Alvarado, whose troops in southern Sonora represented a decisive third force, at first attempted to mediate between the two contenders. When Alvarado attempted to disarm Yaqui troops under his nominal command who had joined the governor's forces, however, Maytorena had him thrown into jail. By July 1914, just as Huerta was packing his bags for exile in Europe, Alvarado was gone forever from Sonora, leaving Maytorena as the apparent winner of the conflict.[70]

Calles's failure to dislodge Maytorena highlighted the difficulties of waging a war on political grounds alone, as well as the effectiveness of the governor's discourse that appealed to the common people of Sonora. Elsewhere in Mexico, agrarian factions such as the Zapatistas took what they considered rightfully theirs, and ideologically focused worker's organizations demanded better pay and greater bargaining rights. What historian Alan Knight has called the "logic of the Revolution" was beginning to shape the political outlook of the Sonorans. Building a new revolutionary army required popular participation in the war, which in turn forced elite and middle-class leaders to include campesino and worker demands in their program.[71] Aptly described in Mariano Azuela's novel *Los de abajo* (The Underdogs), this radicalizing logic engendered contradictions within the Constitutionalist coalition.[72]

Thus Calles watched as Maytorena forged alliances of convenience with Yaquis and workers—alliances at variance with his prior political record as governor. As Knight has put it, "Maytorena was a fat, rich, educated landowner; Calles, despite his paternal blood, a footloose parvenu, literate and talented, but lacking his rival's breeding and status."[73] Nonetheless, the *hacendado* Maytorena curried the allegiance of the Yaquis with promises of a land reform. Popular grievances percolated up to the leadership, and a governor who had once repressed union organizers emerged as a champion of the underdogs.[74] Conversely, Calles depended on the support of the mining companies in his effort to defend and expand the small slice of territory that he controlled in northeastern Sonora. Thus, he represented himself as an advocate for law, order, and the social status quo: in Obregón's words, a "whip to punish insurgent workers."[75] During his conflict with Maytorena, he also displayed a great willingness to accommodate foreign capital. U.S. citizens who lived in the northeastern districts admired him for his "spirit, confidence, and determination," and one of them concluded that Calles's control over all of Sonora would result in peace.[76] When the miners' union in Cananea struck to obtain higher wages and better working conditions, Calles declared martial law and jailed several strike leaders. Maytorena supported the strikers, and up to one-fifth of the Cananea miners joined his forces. In the process, Calles gained allies of his own: the U.S. mining companies, landowners, and many middle-class Sonorans tired of revolutionary warfare and the troops who marauded in Maytorena's name.[77]

After Huerta's long-awaited resignation on July 15, 1914, the growing conflict between Carranza and Villa subsumed this rivalry. At the top, this conflict involved personal ambitions as well as different political views. Villa recognized that his strengths lay in the numbers of his military force and in his numerous military exploits, which included a decisive victory over the Federales in the battle of Zacatecas in June 1914. He strove for local and state autonomy, and he was distrustful of centralized rule, which had threatened such autonomy since the Porfiriato. Therefore, Villa sought a weak president. Like Zapata, he also championed land reform, and he distrusted

Carranza's group as upper-class "men who sleep on soft pillows."[78] The first chief, on the other hand, favored a centralist approach and an emphasis on civilian government. He was afraid of the younger and more charismatic Villa. Another point of contention was the U.S. occupation of Veracruz in April 1914, ostensibly carried out to prevent a shipment of German weapons from reaching the Federales. In the aftermath of the occupation, Carranza issued a shrill note of protest to President Wilson, while Villa privately told U.S. diplomats that he supported the seizure of Veracruz.[79] At the grassroots level, the conflict between Carrancistas and Villistas was a clash of political tendencies rather than irreconcilable ideologies. While these tendencies provided a predictor of where members of both camps stood on a variety of issues, the quirks of cacique politics provided many exceptions at the local and regional levels. Taking into account these important qualifiers, the Villistas had a regional and rural outlook and favored regional autonomy, the prerogatives of local caciques, and agrarian reform. For that reason, Zapata was a natural ally for Villa. The Carrancistas, on the other hand, shared a nationalist and urban perspective and advocated central control, civilian rule, and commercial agriculture.[80]

Obregón, whose subordinates were generally of lower social origin than the Carrancistas, represented a third and decisive force. During his army's long trek south to the state of Jalisco, his forces demonstrated that they were just as adept at defeating the Federales as Villa's División del Norte. While their outlook was similar to that of the Carrancistas, they favored social reforms as a way of incorporating popular demands into an essentially capitalist platform. In particular, they increasingly made the concerns of urban workers their own and recognized the need for some land reform. However, Obregón—even more so than Carranza and Villa—remained essentially opportunistic. Enjoying neither the political legitimacy of Carranza nor the military stature of Villa, he saw his interests best served by the elimination of both of these leaders.[81]

As Carranza, Obregón, and Villa groped for a negotiated solution to their differences, all three considered Maytorena and Calles useful assets for their own schemes of national domination. Of the three, Carranza pursued the most consistent policy: he backed Calles. In August 1914, Carranza took up residence in Mexico City after the collapse of the Huerta regime, and he invited Calles to visit the national capital along with other supporters from northern Mexico. This first trip to the national capital reinforced Calles's allegiance to the first chief. By contrast, Obregón played both sides of the Sonoran conflict in order to limit Carranza's influence, and he offered up Calles to Villa as a political gambit. At a meeting in September 1914,

Obregón, Villa, and Maytorena agreed on a compromise that would have entailed the acceptance of Obregón as military commander in exchange for the subordination of Calles's forces to Maytorena's.[82] Upon Maytorena's return to Hermosillo, however, a handbill circulated in Sonora that accused Alvarado, Calles, and Obregón of crimes against the sovereignty of the state. Presuming it to be the work of Maytorena, Obregón resolved to get rid of the governor by cutting a different deal with Villa. During a second meeting, the two generals agreed to replace Maytorena with Cabral, the only Sonoran leader to have embraced agrarian aims from the beginning of the revolution. Reached only after acrimonious debate during which Villa repeatedly threatened to kill Obregón, the agreement further entailed the acceptance of Carranza as provisional president, which would have barred him from running in the subsequent national elections, and it sent Calles and his forces to Chihuahua. However, Carranza and Maytorena rejected the proposal, and Calles resolved to stay in Sonora until Cabral was installed in the governor's palace. On September 23, 1914, Maytorena narrowed Obregón's options further by declaring that he was an ally of Villa and a champion of land reform. The governor's action pushed Obregón to support Calles, as the caudillo would not tolerate a self-proclaimed Villista as the leader of his home state. At last, Calles enjoyed the backing of both Carranza and Obregón.[83]

The Sonoran imbroglio in which Calles played such a prominent role doomed any hope of a peaceful settlement of the differences among the revolutionary factions. As a result, the Convention of Aguascalientes of October 1914, a meeting of representatives from all Constitutionalist factions as well as Zapata's army, only served to confirm the battle lines for the upcoming conflict. Soon after the inauguration of the convention, the delegates witnessed an alliance of Villistas and Zapatistas against the Carrancistas, with Obregón's representatives in the middle. Dominated by Villistas due to their numerical superiority, the convention chose the colorless Eulalio Gutiérrez as provisional president. Obregón briefly saw realized his dream of eliminating Carranza and Villa, but he had underestimated both leaders. Before Obregón could tell Carranza that he had been removed from office, the first chief moved his cabinet to Córdoba, where he ordered his subordinates to withdraw from the convention. At the same time, Gutiérrez named Villa chief of military operations, and Villa's troops moved into combat position close to Aguascalientes. On November 12, 1914, Obregón reluctantly took sides on behalf of Carranza. Soon thereafter, the combined forces of Carranza and Obregón, still operating under the Constitutionalist banner, went to war with Villa's and Zapata's armies, which fought under the name of Conventionists.[84] Obregón's decision to support Carranza brought help to Calles in the form of the caudillo's nephew, Benjamín Hill, whom the first chief named provisional governor and commander of the Constitutionalist forces in Sonora. Just as Mexico had two heads of state—First Chief Carranza and Conventionist President Gutiérrez—Sonora had two governors in Hill and Maytorena: one appointed by the first chief, and the other one the last holdover from the democratic elections of 1911.

Initially, the Conventionists appeared to have the upper hand in this war, both nationally and in Sonora. Villa controlled most of the Mexican north; Zapata reigned supreme in Guerrero, Morelos, and parts of three other states; and Carranza abandoned the capital and took up residence in Veracruz, recently evacuated by the U.S. occupation forces. Things looked even bleaker for Calles in Sonora, where open warfare had erupted three weeks before the convention of Aguascalientes. Maytorena's populist platform gave him widespread popular support, his forces easily outnumbered the Constitutionalists, and he had armed Yaquis under his command. Hill and Calles only held the northeastern corner of the state, including Cananea and Agua Prieta. In view of Maytorena's military advantage, Carranza ordered them to abandon Cananea and move their headquarters to Naco, a small town on the U.S. border ten miles west of Agua Prieta. Naco gave the Constitutionalists access to the United States, from where they were able to procure money and arms. In addition, the border protected their northern flank. In possession of the latest military technology, Hill and Calles used machine guns, trenches, minefields, and barbed wire to construct a defensive perimeter.[85]

Equipped with modern weapons, this defensive perimeter saved the Constitutionalists from extinction in Sonora. On October 1, 1914, Maytorena sent 1,300 troops, including 600 Yaquis and 300 miners, to attack Naco.[86] Engaged in battles farther south against the bulk of Obregón's army, Villa left the governor to his own devices, and the attack bogged down at the perimeter Calles and Hill had constructed. The ensuing siege lasted until January 15, 1915, when the U.S. government, concerned about the accidental shootings of U.S. citizens, brokered an agreement between the warring factions. The agreement declared Naco a neutral zone and allowed the Constitutionalists to use U.S. territory to return to Agua Prieta.[87] Having been promoted to brigadier general in October 1914, Calles assumed the command of the Constitutionalist forces in Sonora after Hill departed to join Obregón in central Mexico.[88] For the first time, he was the top Constitutionalist officer of his state, the head of what he jokingly referred to as the "República de Agua Prieta." However, he was already far more than that. Before Obregón's major offensive of March 1915, his redoubt constituted one of only five areas controlled by the Constitutionalist army, along with the port cities of Tampico and Veracruz and parts of Jalisco and Yucatán.[89]

The defense of Naco amounted to Calles's breakthrough as a revolutionary leader. To survive the siege, Calles had sacrificed his health, as his exposure to 107 frigid nights spent in encampments during an unusually cold winter had left him with a rheumatic ailment that would torment him for the rest of his life. But he had also finally gained some prestige as a military leader. His endurance invited one of his supporters to make exaggerated comparisons to José María Morelos (1765–1815), martyred leader of the popular movement for independence and one of the greatest national heroes. As this admirer claimed thirteen years later, Calles, like Morelos, had "endured a siege of more than one hundred days, and like that caudillo who contributed so much to making independents of us, he broke the siege and won."[90] Hyperbole aside, this viewpoint overlooked the contributions of Hill, who deserved primary credit for the successful defense of Naco. It also ignored other defenders of Naco such as Max Joffre, a graduate of the military academy of Chile and veteran of South American wars.[91]

The failed siege of Naco was the turning point in the war between the factions in Sonora. By January, Maytorena found the state treasury empty, leaving him unable to pay his troops. As his deteriorating financial situation forced Don Pepe to requisition food and weapons without paying for them, the tide of public opinion turned in Calles's favor. The governor soon faced massive desertions from his ranks, chaos in Cananea, and the dissolution of his grand coalition. Meanwhile, a steady infusion of Carrancista cash and supplies via the United States kept Calles's men content and well equipped. As Villa continued to ignore Sonora, the cruel war of attrition favored the side that could still pay its troops over the one that could not. By March, the Maytorena administration had effectively collapsed amidst food riots, monetary devaluation, and low morale. An increasing number of military commanders joined Calles, among them one of Cabral's lieutenants, the twenty-year-old Lázaro Cárdenas. In the following weeks, the Callistas made several sorties from their base, defeating Maytorena's forces in four separate encounters.[92] Don Pepe's demoralized supporters abandoned him en masse, and in July, Calles's troops broke out of Agua Prieta and established control over northeastern Sonora, including the Cananea and Nacozari copper mines.[93]

By then, the Constitutionalists had triumphed on the national level as well. Obregón's decision to join Carranza had given the alliance a great boost, not only because the caudillo commanded a sizable army but also because he understood the logic of the revolution better than his ally did. After Obregón's forces occupied Mexico City following the collapse of the

Huerta regime, the caudillo treated the high society of the capital with disdain, even ordering those who resisted his orders to sweep the streets. On that occasion, Obregón courted the Casa del Obrero Mundial (COM, or House of the World's Worker), an anarcho-syndicalist organization affiliated with the Industrial Workers of the World that claimed more than fifty thousand members across the nation. As the war unfolded in 1914–1915, the Sonoran convinced Carranza of the necessity to craft a program that incorporated popular demands for land and social justice. On January 6, 1915, Carranza proclaimed an Agrarian Law that promised to restitute all campesino lands alienated illegally, and six weeks later, he formed an alliance with the COM that provided for their military support in return for the right to organize the workers in the areas under Constitutionalist control. Thus, COM-led Red Battalions participated in Obregón's campaign.[94] In addition, the Constitutionalists benefited from covert U.S. assistance. Not only could they—as Calles knew from personal experience—obtain U.S. arms and ammunition in violation of the Neutrality Laws, but the U.S. occupation forces also benefited them directly by leaving them several caches of weapons before evacuating Veracruz, where Carranza set up his provisional government in late 1914. With better equipment, a superior military strategy, and a national vision, the Constitutionalists prevailed; in April 1915, Obregón's forces scored a decisive victory over the Villistas at Celaya, Guanajuato.[95]

The Constitutionalist victory at the national level allowed Calles to lay claim to the highest post in his native state. On August 4, 1915, Carranza named Calles provisional governor and military commander of Sonora.[96] To be sure, the nomination initially meant little, as the Constitutionalists only controlled parts of the districts of Arizpe, Magdalena, and Moctezuma. Maytorena continued to rule over the rest of Sonora until the expiration of his term in late August, upon which he once again moved to Arizona. He left a weak interim governor in his place who never enjoyed any real authority, as fighting continued in many areas of the state. The war between the factions was by no means over.[97]

In the fall of 1915, Calles therefore confronted his greatest military challenge when Villa finally turned his attention toward Sonora after his defeats in central Mexico. Villa's troops arrived in mid-September, forcing Calles to withdraw behind his fortifications in Agua Prieta. With seventeen thousand Villistas bearing down on Agua Prieta, Calles called upon all Sonorans to display unity in the face of what he portrayed as an external threat. The speech is remarkable for the distinctions it constructs between Constitutionalists and Villistas, legality and banditry, and civilization and barbarism:

The Constitutionalist army . . . [represents] the realization of the revolutionary ideals that are the sentiment of the honorable Mexican people, a people that . . . demands . . . its liberty, its improvement, and its greatness. I have always believed that wars and revolutions that do not defend ideals and principles are crimes, and that the blood spilled as a result of these wars is like the blood drawn by an assassin's dagger. . . . Thus, Francisco Villa, whose movement . . . does not have motives other than the venting of personal passions, does not represent any principles that merit him respect; nor does he deserve any title other than that of *bandido máximo*. To confront the tremendous threat of this horde of defeated and criminal Villistas who intend to come to destroy lives and property, we need to unite in order to annihilate the traitor and to give the coup de grâce to the banditry that characterizes this faction.[98]

On the night of November 1, Villa's forces charged Agua Prieta, only to receive a rough welcome. An outnumbered but well-trained garrison of four thousand held off the Villistas, who experienced a replay of the disastrous campaigns against Obregón in central Mexico. In the intervening months, Calles had built trenches that formed a semicircle around Agua Prieta, covered the supply routes to these trenches, and mounted a search light that illuminated the terrain shortly after the attack began.[99] Moreover, U.S. de facto recognition of Carranza's government in October 1915—that is, the acceptance of his faction as the group in power in the absence of formal diplomatic relations—afforded Calles legal opportunities to purchase weapons across the U.S. border. Equipped with machine guns, the Constitutionalists mowed down the advancing Villista cavalry and scored the greatest military victory to date for Calles, who had just been promoted to "General de Brigada."[100] This victory gave the final impetus to the campaign to take over Hermosillo, and two weeks later, the Constitutionalists defeated the Villistas near the state capital. Only approximately three thousand Villistas made it to Chihuahua in a hasty retreat, and on December 16, Calles moved into the governor's palace.

Through a combination of skill and luck, Calles had arrived at the pinnacle of a state in revolutionary upheaval. Chief among his advantages were a formal education, considerable administrative ability, family networks, experience in various areas of Sonora, and an uncanny ability to pick the winning side. In addition, Calles also enjoyed an unusual share of good fortune, benefiting from the export to the national theater of the best military leaders. He was far from the greatest general the state had produced; apart from Obregón, a man who would come to be known as the "undefeated caudillo

of the revolution," Alvarado and Hill could also claim greater military accomplishments. Nor had Calles, like Maytorena, roused the state's underdogs to participation in the revolution with a populist platform. But he had
been at the right place at the right time, he had coordinated the Constitutionalist efforts to procure money and arms from the United States, and the
successful defense of Naco in the absence of Obregón and the bulk of his
army had given his forces the upper hand in Sonora.

Calles had learned important lessons for his future career from the chaos
of revolutionary politics in Sonora. Most importantly, he had learned the
utility of a platform that incorporated popular demands for land and justice.
If he intended to be successful in his new gubernatorial post, he needed to
follow the logic of the revolution to a far greater extent than his existence as
a cacique on the border had ever necessitated. As Calles knew, his political
program would need to resemble Maytorena's populist agenda, and the man
Obregón had reportedly considered his whip against the workers would need
to include popular demands for land and better pay. Finally, he had learned
that temporary alliances and friendship meant little in the theater of revolutionary politics.

CHAPTER THREE

Strongman of Sonora

The yoke of ignorance is the reason why our people have been the vic-
tims of exploitation by the bourgeoisie and the wealthy.

—Plutarco Elías Calles, Decreto No. 8 (1915)

In May 1917, Calles gave a rousing speech on the plaza of Nogales to rally
supporters around his political program. A former provisional governor and
military commander of Sonora, he was running for governor in the first
statewide elections since 1911. The speech declared his intention to install
a government "more radical than ever."[1] The proletariat supported him,
Calles declared, and he therefore had a mandate to carry out a socialist program. He promised that his government would eliminate the aristocracy (i.e.,
the notables) and represent the rule of the people, as opposed to that of the
privileged classes. The enemies of the government, Calles assured the crowd,
should expect no mercy from him.[2] Although bystanders might well have assumed that Calles was a socialist committed to the destruction of capitalism
in Sonora, those who knew the candidate had reason to hope that pragmatic
rule would follow his firebrand rhetoric. Indeed, Calles assured U.S. investors
and government officials that his speech was a mere "sop to the Mexicans,"
and that they could expect a much more conservative administration than
his oration suggested.[3]

Nonetheless, the speech highlighted the fact that Calles had reinvented
himself as an authoritarian populist who steered one of the most reform-
oriented state governments of the Carranza era. In fact, these years featured

the crafting of Calles's political personality. In a dress rehearsal for his later role as a national leader, the governor pursued a reform program focused on public morality, education, economic development, and improvements in the living conditions of the working poor. He also tapped nationalism as a unifying force. Calles believed he knew best what his people needed, and he used repression to achieve his goals. In particular, he waged a brutal campaign against those who stood in the way of what he believed to be the public interest of the Sonoran people, including his political enemies, the Church, and the Yaquis.

Thus, a close look at the Calles era in Sonora challenges the assertion of historian Adrian Bantjes that "it was not until the 1930s . . . that revolutionary change came to Sonora."[4] It also qualifies Ignacio Almada's broad condemnation of the Calles regime as one that came to power with the help of "military victory, sweeping repression, and the support of the U.S. government."[5] Under Calles, reform and repression were two sides of the same coin, an effort to confer legitimacy and authority to the Constitutionalist state government. His years as the dominant political figure in Sonora displayed the contradictions of the revolution between popular aspirations and elite agendas, between promises and betrayal, and between nationalist visions and the capitalist reality of a state in the immediate vicinity of the United States.[6]

"Land and Books for All"

Provisional Governor Calles found a state in shambles after thirty months of warfare. It was not until early 1916 that his government controlled all of Sonora, and the extended fighting had produced appalling conditions. The warring bands had sacked towns and villages, requisitioned food, raped women, and dragged young conscripts off into battle. The major U.S.-owned copper mines had suspended operations during the Calles-Maytorena conflict, and thousands of Sonorans had abandoned their land, work, and families to participate in the fighting. The fighting had exacted a heavy toll on those troops, and many of those who survived the war never returned home. Women played active roles to fill the vacuum left by those who had died or departed, giving them an important voice in the revolutionary process.[7] Many of them had even participated in the fighting as *soldaderas*, and a photo of one of the soldaderas under Calles's command has survived to this day.

Complicating Calles's task, Sonorans remembered the pledges made by the contending sides during the war between the factions. In particular, the copper miners had completed a process of political awakening that had be-

A *soldadera* in Calles's army
Source: FAPEC.

gun with the events leading up to the strike of 1906. Constitutionalist soldiers who had put their life on the line for Calles demanded their share of the
spoils of war. Facing continued water shortages, farmers in the Yaqui Valley
demanded the recision of the water rights given to the Richardson during the
Porfiriato. Thus, Aguilar Camín's stereotype of the Sonoran revolutionaries
as rugged individualists ignores the fact that Calles faced many of the same
popular demands as his comrades-in-arms Alvarado and Diéguez, who had
become governors of Yucatán and Jalisco, respectively: land for the landless,
more rights and better pay for workers, respect for municipal autonomy, and
Mexico for the Mexicans.[8]

Making his job even more difficult, Calles needed to avoid friction with foreign investors, and particularly the U.S.-owned copper companies, while taking steps to end the Porfirian tax exemptions that imposed severe limits on the state budget. Taxes on workers' wages and consumption constituted the state's greatest source of revenue, and the Constitutionalists desired to impose production taxes on foreign mining companies. The copper companies, however, relied on the diplomatic protection of the U.S. government for what they viewed as long-term contracts to extract minerals at minimal tax rates.

Adding to these difficulties were the ambitions of the provisional government of First Chief Carranza to centralize political authority. With Obregón sidelined after the loss of his right arm, sustained at the Battle of Trinidad on June 3, 1915, Carranza endeavored to restore the authority of the federal government in the states. He infringed upon state and local sovereignty and even toppled several governors who did not follow his lead. The first chief also attempted to rein in the influence of the Constitutionalist army by barring military commanders from serving in civilian posts, but Obregón successfully resisted Carranza's plans. Finally, Carranza promulgated decrees on the national level and expected his governors to apply them in their states. Federalism—a principle enshrined both in the 1857 constitution and in the 1917 document that was to supplant it—existed only in the degree to which a state could resist federal directives.[9]

Aware that he was more vulnerable to local demands than to those from Mexico City, Calles took a bold approach to this daunting array of contradictory pressures. On the day of his nomination as governor, he issued a populist manifesto, "To the Sonoran people," that reflected the logic of the revolution that had forced middle-class rebels to embrace the goals of campesinos and workers. His program, he declared, represented the national Constitutionalist program, "ideals that are already being consummated by the redemptive work of the great Constitutionalist revolution. . . . [It] is neither chimera nor deception, but the reality itself of a glorious people that has irrigated with its blood the soil on which the well-being and greatness of Mexico will thrive."[10] After these flowery phrases, Calles turned to the specific plans for his administration. He stated his commitment to public morality, human rights, effective suffrage, local autonomy, and an independent judiciary, all goals dating back to the Maytorena years. But unlike Maytorena, Calles did not stop at political reform. He emphasized the goal of public schooling in each community exceeding five hundred inhabitants, as well as his intention to require all mining and industrial companies to establish schools at their expense. He outlined his plans for the first teacher's college in Sonora. Calles called for the division of hacienda land among landless campesinos, the establishment of a rural credit institution, an equitable system of taxation, and "broad protection for workers." He closed his manifesto with the words "land and books for all"—a variation on Zapata's motto "land and liberty."[11] Promulgated while Calles and his allies were on the offensive against the Conventionists, this program was a smorgasbord of both elite and popular demands for change, suffused by the desire of forging campesinos and workers into Mexicans.

Issued four days after taking office, Decree No. 1, the *Ley Seca*, or Dry Law, indicated that Calles was serious about his program. Just as Arizona entered the Prohibition era, the decree proscribed the production, importation, and distribution of any amount of alcoholic beverages.[12] This law was not the first of its kind—Abraham González had issued a similar decree in Chihuahua three years before—but it was the most stringent in the nation. It elicited favorable commentary among Carrancistas near the U.S. border; in the opinion of the consul in El Paso, Texas, Calles's antialcohol efforts could serve as a model for Ciudad Juárez, the troubled town across the border.[13] Opponents ridiculed the Ley Seca, given their new governor's own proclivities for wine and hard liquor. As one famous story had it, Calles celebrated his very first decree as governor with a good swig of brandy, and the following year, he was reportedly found to be in possession of a bottle of *bacanora*, the highly potent liquor of the sierra.[14]

Whether these stories are true or not, the governor had personal experience with the devastating effects of alcoholism. His father slowly drank himself to a death that finally arrived in 1917 in the form of cirrhosis of the liver, and Plutarco Jr. had spent years immersed in drinking and carousing. After his father's death, he described his own experience with drunkenness thus: "it is . . . alarming . . . [to] see monkeys, express trains, blimps, [and] bears . . . an entire circus that passes through your brain."[15] In addition, Calles believed that his campaign against drinking addressed one of the root causes of poverty. In an August 1917 letter to the governor of Sinaloa, which had just abolished its own dry law, he vowed to "eliminate the disgusting vice of inebriation, the cause of the ruin and degeneration of our people."[16] No longer, Calles reasoned, would workers drink away their wages and let their families starve, and no longer would they miss work on San Lunes in order to cure their hangovers. Calles was also concerned about the secondary impact of drinking in the Prohibition era in the United States. As *comisario* of Agua Prieta, he had witnessed the ill effects of alcoholic tourism such as gambling, prostitution, and violent crime. Calles feared that the border area would become the cesspool of Arizona as Prohibition became increasingly widespread.

Indeed, Agua Prieta, Naco, and Nogales came to compare favorably to border towns in Baja California, where drinking and gambling continued unabated. Finally, the campaign against alcohol corresponded to an authoritarian quest against insubordination. To demonstrate that he meant business, Calles reportedly ordered the execution of a man arrested for drunkenness in Cananea, and other stories of the governor's cruelty against alcoholics abounded.[17] A good example of what Alan Knight has labeled the "Puritan streak" of the Constitutionalists, the Ley Seca set the tone for an energetic governorship.[18]

However, the decree was virtually unenforceable in a state where most liquor was distilled privately and where contraband easily crossed state and even national boundaries. It therefore restricted rather than prevented access to alcohol, and it drove up the price of liquor, beer, and wine. To do more would have antagonized First Chief Carranza, who informed Calles that he opposed the prohibition of beer and wine.[19]

The Ley Seca was only the first of a large number of reform decrees. For example, Decree No. 4 outlawed gambling, which Calles portrayed as a source of vice and social disintegration.[20] Over the next eight months, Calles also promulgated social reform legislation that placed him among the ranks of the most progressive Constitutionalist governors, together with Alvarado and Diéguez, who implemented similar decrees in Yucatán and Jalisco and conferred with Calles about appropriate legislation.[21] One Calles decree struck at large landowners by forbidding repurchase agreements. These agreements allowed *hacendados* to protect themselves from taxation and agrarian reform by holding large tracts of land that nominally remained the property of their former owners. Moreover, the prospect of repurchase also enticed sellers to part with their lands at less than a fair price. Other measures slapped new taxes on landowners and mining companies and required them to exploit the natural resources in their possession.[22] Directed primarily against *hacendados* who did not keep their land under cultivation, the land tax outlined in this decree was modest compared to Alvarado's in Yucatán.[23]

Indeed, Alvarado's governorship constitutes perhaps the best framework of comparison to Calles's administration. Like Sonora, Yucatán displayed a great degree of dependence on U.S. investment. The International Harvester Co. held a monopoly over the processing and distribution of henequen, or sisal hemp, the state's main export used for the production of binder twine for the North American wheat crop. A landed elite, the *casta divina* (divine caste), controlled most of the state's arable land and a poor majority of indigenous Maya, many of whom lived as debt peons on the henequen plantations. Fears of a Maya uprising of the kind that had produced the bloody

Caste War of the 1840s led to the formation of a coalition hostile to the re-
olution that kept control of the state until 1915, when Alvarado arrived with
an army of seven thousand troops to secure Constitutionalist control over
Yucatán. Alvarado had embarked on an ambitious reform drive similar to
that of Calles. Spurred on by burgeoning henequen prices, he had launched
an ambitious education program, passed agrarian and labor reform laws,
moved against the Catholic Church, outlawed drunkenness, and founded a
revolutionary party, the Partido Socialista de Yucatán. His governorship witnessed the founding of "Ligas de Resistencia" (Resistance Leagues), grassroots organizations that mobilized campesinos, urban workers, professionals,
and women to fight for better living conditions and a voice in the political
process. Alvarado also made a small dent in the International Harvester monopoly over henequen by establishing a statewide marketing agency. Like
Calles, however, Alvarado had no intention of breaking the backbone of his
state's economy. Thus, his agrarian law was aimed at ending debt peonage
and the establishment of small private plots of land for landless Mayas, but it
left intact the henequen-producing haciendas.[24]

Like Alvarado, Calles inaugurated a modest land reform program. The division of large estates into *ejidos,* or communal landholdings, had never been
a high priority for Sonoran revolutionaries with the exception of Cabral's
program and Maytorena's pitch to please his Yaqui allies. Moreover, Carranza, who had opportunistically called for the return of misappropriated
campesino land at the height of the war between the factions, had
backpedaled after his triumph over the Conventionists. Just like Alvarado,
Calles favored the *pequeña propiedad,* the family farm, as the basis of a U.S.-
style society of yeoman smallholders. As he knew well, a plot of irrigable land
could serve as a reward for lesser retainers. Therefore, he expropriated lands
of his political enemies (and particularly Porfirista landowners and the
Yaquis) by gubernatorial fiat and distributed them among his supporters. This
method allowed him to create a new group of politically loyal landowners,
many of whom were Constitutionalist troops dislocated from their place of
origin during the bloody war between the factions.[25] Ironically, then, Callista
land reform was directed *against* the indigenous population, or at least those
communities that had supported Maytorena.

An important area of reform where Calles followed precedents set by Carranza was the judiciary system. Decree No. 9 established an independent judiciary to replace one that had served as a mere arm of the executive branch
under a succession of different governments. Essentially a restatement of the
provisions of the federal constitution of 1857, the decree was designed to show
that the rule of law had returned. Unfortunately, much of the law remained a

dead letter in Sonora, just as similar attempts did in the rest of Mexico. Nonetheless, the statement of intent was significant for a movement that called itself Constitutionalist.[26]

In the area of gender relations and the family, Calles legalized divorce and moved to rein in the worst abuses committed by men against their wives, girlfriends, and mistresses. Decree No. 11 forbade husbands to hire out their wives for pay. Following a Carranza law on the national level, it also permitted divorce under certain circumstances. Unlike the national law, which remained broad and vague, the decree retained the gender discrimination typical of its times. According to Decree No. 11, a woman's adultery always constituted grounds for divorce, while a man's sexual transgressions only warranted divorce if he had behaved in ways that brought public scandal or "dishonor" upon his wife. Such behavior included cohabitation with a mistress and the commission of adultery in the married couple's house.[27]

Calles's most important initiatives focused on education. Both of the mainstays of the state's economy—cash crop agriculture and mining—drew workers into remote areas, where their children remained, in the governor's words, "without the elementary education that the law requires."[28] As a result, one decree authorized the establishment of municipal libraries and evening schools for adults; another established the state's first normal school for teachers; and yet another forced large estates and mining companies to establish schools to educate the workers' children.[29] A year later, the state budget committed more than 1.5 million pesos to public education, or almost 58 percent of total expenditures. This budget included funds for public libraries and adult education, another important Calles initiative.[30] In sum, while Calles could not eradicate the widespread illiteracy, he put in place an infrastructure for future improvements. By 1918, his policies had resulted in the construction of more than one hundred new schools, and student enrollment had doubled since 1910.[31]

Calles's greatest innovation in education, and the one that was most important to him personally, was the establishment of a school for orphans of the revolution. Established in Hermosillo under the name "Francisco Madero" and renamed "Cruz Gálvez" to honor a colonel killed in the war against Maytorena, this new institution of learning was a boarding school designed to impart practical skills as well as literacy and math at no cost to the students.[32] As Calles explained, "After the revolution, it became our duty to look after the orphans left by the war. . . . The idea has always appealed to me of establishing a great school . . . , which would not proportion purely intellectual instruction, but which would bring about a balance between mental work and physical work." Such a balance, Calles believed, "would equip children to become men and women of action in practical life."[33] The Cruz Gálvez school had three separate sections—for boys, girls, and a small "correctional" section for delinquents. The boys' section received the most funding, and education in the school followed strict gender lines: boys learned carpentry and other crafts while girls learned sewing and cooking.[34] Both private and public funds helped make these schools a success; in Calles's words, "there was not a town or a family which failed to give. As fast as the money came in, we began to build."[35] The state's commitment to Cruz Gálvez would continue to grow over the next several years, a remarkable feat in an era when continued fighting and the intermittent closure of the copper mines severely depressed revenues. In the 1917 state budget, the first that funded the school at full enrollment, Cruz Gálvez absorbed 7 percent of the allotment for education, an amount almost equal to the total expenditures for the school district of Hermosillo.[36] The expenditure repaid itself in more ways than by educating the young. Cruz Gálvez soon became an industrial venture, a wholly Mexican-owned institution that provided the state with locally manufactured products.

Calles played an integral role in the development of the Cruz Gálvez school. On his frequent visits, he informed pupils of his commitment to their institution, and he enrolled his daughters in the school. As the school grew to more than eight hundred students by 1918, this investment would pay political dividends in future years. The graduates of Cruz Gálvez, many of whom came to assume important positions in private and public life, displayed a filial loyalty to Calles, addressing him as "Papá" as late as the 1930s. There is no question that Calles's own upbringing played a role in making the school one of his priorities.[37]

This reform program cost money at a time when two years of fighting had left the state treasury virtually empty. The best target for refilling state coffers was the foreign-owned mining companies, which had realized millions of dollars in profits over the past decades. Unfortunately, these companies claimed to have suffered serious financial losses after the war between the factions. Indeed, the accounts presented by the CCCC and Moctezuma displayed a situation so dire that the copper companies even demanded an exemption from the decree mandating employer-sponsored schools in rural areas. Calles, however, was not so easily fooled. Like Carranza, the governor insisted that foreign companies should be treated on equal terms with Mexican ones, which implied full payment of all taxes and other obligations and an end to the privileges these firms had enjoyed in the Porfirian era. He knew that a production tax of a few cents on every dollar could fund all of his programs and restore the fiscal health of his state. Even as the foreign companies pointed to the multiyear concessions granted to them by the Porfirians as legally binding contracts, Decree No. 18 levied a 1.5 percent tax on all mining production.[38]

Calles handled this delicate situation with an approach that combined firmness on the general principle with flexibility on the terms of payment. The governor was lucky in the timing of his plan, as copper prices had soared during World War I. The managers of the copper companies knew the governor as a pragmatic politician who favored foreign investment. They had welcomed his triumph over Maytorena who, as we have seen, had incited the miners to strike against their bosses to further his own political ends. As a result, both sides understood that the implementation of Decree No. 18 would be a matter of negotiation between the state government and each of the individual firms. Although the managers of the copper companies opposed the new law as an infringement on their concessions, they also knew that they depended on the state government to rein in their workers. Thus, they made partial payment of the new tax under protest. In March 1916, Decree No. 39 abrogated all Porfirian concessions. The copper companies made further loans and payments while informing Calles that they reserved the right to take the state to court once conditions normalized. In exchange, the governor provided military protection to the copper mines. Both Calles and the copper barons had understood the symbiosis between foreign capital and Sonora: one could not survive without the other.[39]

The flip side of Calles's reform program was a fierce campaign against his political enemies. These enemies included Yaqui commanders, Conventionists, and Sonorans disenchanted with the new regime. Calles certainly had his detractors; as one resident of the border region wrote to Carranza, Calles was "the most hated man on the entire border due to his ineptitude, cowardice, and falsehood."[40] As Calles consolidated his power in the fall of 1915, he went on the offensive against enemies such as this one. He offered his rivals among the revolutionary leaders both the carrot and the stick. Signed during Villa's futile foray into Sonora, Decree No. 7 granted amnesty to all deserters who abandoned the "felon Francisco Villa."[41] After the Constitutionalist victory, however, Decree No. 32 confiscated the holdings of all political enemies, including Porfiristas, Orozquistas, Huertistas, Maytorenistas, and Villistas.[42]

The state's indigenous population, and especially the Yaquis, bore the brunt of this campaign against the governor's opponents. For example, Decree No. 33 declared that "the nomadic tribes and those of the Yaqui and Mayo River will not enjoy the right of Sonoran citizenship as long as their farms and villages maintain their anomalous organization."[43] However, it offered an incentive for those who joined the Yori world: "the individuals from these tribes who live in the organized communities of the state will have the privilege of citizenship."[44] Implicit in the decree was the desire for land belonging to the indigenous people of Sonora, land to be distributed among the victorious Callista officers.

Calles also took action against the Catholic Church, which he accused of being in league with Porfirian and Huertista, or "reactionary," interests. Although the church was undoubtedly an element critical of the Constitutionalists, its influence in Sonora was not nearly as great as in other states, and certainly not significant enough to explain Calles's response. Carlos Macías has estimated that there were no more than thirty-five Catholic priests in Sonora, many of them Spanish nationals opposed to revolutionary nationalism.[45] On March 16, 1916, Calles ordered his military commanders to expel all priests from the state within forty-eight hours. In Calles's opinion, the priests were spies and enemies, "bad elements" who meddled in state politics.[46] An early example of the anticlericalism that would later give rise to the church-state conflict at the national level, the measure was a reflection of the governor's aversion to organized Catholicism. In a comparative context, however, Calles's anticlericalism was not unusual, as Diéguez demonstrated with his persecution of the church in Jalisco, one of the strongholds of Catholic authority. In Yucatán, Alvarado adopted similarly draconian measures.[47]

Finally, Calles tested the loyalty of those who held public office in his governorship by means of a questionnaire regarding their position in the past political conflicts. An unprecedented step, this questionnaire included items such as "What was your role in the political struggle initiated . . . by the Apostle Madero between 1909 and 1910? Explain if you were either a soldier or a civilian who worked on behalf of the Revolution of 1910, specifying concrete actions."[48] A latecomer to the revolution, the governor himself would have been hard pressed to answer this question in a satisfactory fashion. At that time, however, Calles did not have to answer to anyone except Carranza and Obregón. Although unrest continued, the Constitutionalist governor appeared firmly in the saddle.

The Sonoran Maximato

Just at the moment when Calles appeared to have consolidated his position, the specter of a large-scale U.S. military intervention forced him into a new role. The problem began in the wee hours of March 9, 1916, when Pancho Villa and his retinue arrived at the border near Columbus, New Mexico.

Villa reportedly rallied his troops with references to the lost battle of Agua Prieta, when Calles's Constitutionalists had obtained supplies and reinforcements via U.S. territory. At 4:45 AM, the Gold Shirts stormed Columbus and its garrison of five hundred soldiers to the shouts of "Viva Villa! Viva Mexico!" In the ensuing shooting, seventeen U.S. citizens and more than one hundred Mexicans lost their lives before Villa's men withdrew across the border.[49] The first foreign attack on the continental United States since the War of 1812, Villa's incursion produced outrage in the United States. Shortly thereafter, President Wilson sent a "Punitive Expedition" into Chihuahua to capture Villa. Led by General John Pershing, who would soon distinguish himself on the battlefront in France, the *Punitiva* revived Villismo, which appeared to the public eye as a patriotic movement to defend Mexico from U.S. imperialism. From a low of four hundred troops, Villa's following once again grew to one of the nation's largest armies, and the rebels not only carried out a successful guerrilla campaign against the invasion forces but also captured Chihuahua City. The popular support for Villa forced Carranza, who had initially acquiesced in the U.S. invasion, to adopt a more stringently nationalist rhetoric. Moreover, the Punitiva weakened Carranza's faction because the U.S. government declared an embargo on the shipment of arms and ammunitions. Finally, it raised the possibility of U.S. invasions elsewhere along the border, and it prompted Obregón to join Carranza's provisional government as secretary of war.[50]

The trouble in Chihuahua forced Calles to dedicate himself to military matters once again, as the revival of Villismo encouraged the Yaquis to rebel against the state government. On March 29, 1916, Obregón appointed Calles *jefe de operaciones militares* (chief of military operations) in Sonora to lead the campaign against the Yaquis.[51] In the latest installment of a perpetual Yori promise, Calles resolved to crush the Yaquis once and for all. As Calles soon found out, however, his troops could not dislodge the enemy from the impenetrable mountains of the Sierra de Bacatete, and the Yaquis carried out raids far beyond their tribal boundaries throughout summer and fall 1916.[52]

The new threats thrust Calles into a military rather than political role. Between April and July, the same General Calles who had just begun to demobilize the militias that had laid waste to Sonora toured the state in search of recruits to defend the government against the twin threats of Yaqui insurrection and U.S. intervention. The recruits served until July 28, 1916, when Calles disbanded the new militias in view of the decreasing likelihood of another U.S. incursion. At the same time, he oversaw the Yaqui campaign, and beginning in August, he dedicated himself full time to that endeavor.[53]

Calles's expanded military powers came at the price of relinquishing his position as provisional governor to Adolfo de la Huerta on May 16, 1916. According to de la Huerta, Calles was immensely displeased with having to give up the powerful position he had just obtained eight months before.[54] Therefore, Calles did not, as historian Edward Farmer states, resign the governorship out of a "disdain for routine office duties."[55] Instead, the change of governors was the work of Carranza, who feared the concentration of power in the hands of military leaders. As a result, one of his decrees had forbidden concurrent service as military governor and *jefe de operaciones*.[56] Moreover, the civilian de la Huerta was one of his closest collaborators, having served in his provisional national government since its inception in October 1913.[57] Finally, Carranza considered Calles too radical, and he particularly opposed the governor's antialcohol campaign and the expulsion of the priests.[58]

As Carranza found out soon enough, however, Calles's political strength did not depend on holding the position of governor. His injured vanity aside, Calles knew that de la Huerta's appointment constituted a best-case scenario for him, and he was confident that his friend would follow his lead. Indeed, U.S. intelligence agents described the new era as a bicephalous system with a "military" and a "civilian" governor. As one of these officers remarked shortly after the transition of power, "Sonora now [has] two governors. One, de la Huerta, has the name and absolutely no power. Calles, the 'deposed' governor, possesses all the pay, powers, and emoluments of the office."[59] Although hyperbolical, these remarks pointed to the fact that Calles continued to exert influence upon de la Huerta, a successful politician in his own right.

Thus began the Sonoran Maximato, the period during which Calles served as the arbiter of political life in his home state through clientelist networks. In particular, Calles relied upon his family ties in the northeast as well as his support among army officers, and especially those who had served at Naco and Agua Prieta in 1915. Many of these officers came from middle-class origins and admired Calles for his administrative skills and his reform program. They had not forgotten the fact that the national Constitutionalist movement had supplied them with food, clothing, and ammunition across the U.S. border while their adversaries withered in starvation and outdated weaponry. Since January 1915, the Callista officers had enjoyed a streak of victories that had given them ample opportunities for enrichment from the property of their defeated enemies. They continued to depend on Calles at a time when political stability had not yet been restored, and more so than ever in the crises of 1916. Calles's campaign against the Yaquis also offered a chance to reward Constitutionalist soldiers with land. Supported by a new rural credit bank and a favorable tax structure, troops turned into yeoman farmers were Calles's staunchest allies.[60]

The network that sustained Calles's informal power also rested upon his friendship with the new provisional governor. De la Huerta combined integrity with a sharp intellect, and unlike Calles and Obregón, he held a high school degree and had even attended university. As a civilian, he displayed an abiding respect for constitutional rather than military rule. De la Huerta had not yet built up an independent regional power base in the state; in Sonora, he was as dependent on Calles as the latter was on Carranza and Obregón nationally. Conversely, de la Huerta's service in the first chief's provisional government gave him significant influence in the national Constitutionalist movement, while Calles's national influence remained limited to his alliances with governors Alvarado and Diéguez. De la Huerta stressed his "intimate . . . friendship" with General Calles, whose "unconditional approval" had helped him assume the position.[61] Calles sometimes tired of the solicitude of his friend. As he put it, "I am disappointed that you are still being so childish, and that you are trying to give me explanations for your conduct that I do not need."[62] Such solicitude, however, should not be mistaken for submission. De la Huerta possessed negotiating skills that Calles lacked, and during his term of governor, he even negotiated a temporary truce with the Yaquis after the exhaustion of Calles's military efforts. The Sonoran Maximato was thus a system of shared governance, much as Calles later shared power with presidents and party leaders at the national level.[63]

First and foremost, Calles and de la Huerta needed to pay attention to the stormy international scene, and particularly the implications of World War I. The conflagration that had begun in Europe in August 1914 progressively drew in much of the rest of the world. The Wilson administration figured first as a creditor to the Western Allies, then as a mediator, and finally—after April 1917—as a belligerent that supported the Allies. For his part, Carranza, who had received assistance from both the United States and Germany during the war between the factions, left no doubt about his desire to keep Mexico out of the conflict. His government was concerned about its role in case the United States declared war on Germany and Austria. Would President Wilson attempt to force Mexico to follow suit? Worse yet, would he use the war as a pretext to expand the purview of the Punitive Expedition? From the vantage point of Calles and other leaders in the border region, the latter possibility evoked the specter of a permanent U.S. military presence.[64] Fueled in part by German involvement, the specter of a more general war with the United States lingered throughout the year following Villa's attack on Columbus. If U.S. troops had twice invaded Mexico in a span of three years, Carranza and his men feared, what would stop them from doing it yet again?[65]

Governing Sonora meant coming to terms with this stormy period between the United States and Mexico. For Sonorans, these relations were more than a matter of high politics or military strategy. As we have seen, the formidable U.S. economic influence, which exceeded that in most other states, bred resentment among Sonorans. During the war between the factions, Maytorena had attempted to tap into these sentiments by inciting the Cananea miners to paralyze the CCCC, and as provisional governor, Calles had gained political capital by confronting the copper companies. On another level, there were instances of popular xenophobia directed not only against U.S. citizens but also Chinese and Spaniards as well. Patriotism, economic nationalism (both primarily elite phenomena), and a smattering of popular xenophobia combined to produce a richly textured nationalist imaginary contested by different social groups.[66]

This crisis therefore constituted both a challenge and an opportunity for Calles and de la Huerta. As revolutionary politicians, they needed to respond to these nationalist expectations by calling for an end of all remaining privileges of foreigners, albeit without harming their vital relationship with foreign investors and arms suppliers. On the other hand, the threat of another U.S. invasion strengthened their hands in dealing with their adversaries and earned them popular support at a time of patriotic rallying behind the leaders. On the national level, Carranza applied this lesson by mixing nationalist rhetoric with pragmatic actions, and Calles and de la Huerta followed suit.[67]

This pragmatism primarily rested on the realization that the copper companies could resist compliance with any law by shutting down operations. These firms had never accepted Calles's decree that terminated the Porfirian concessions, and Calles was fortunate that rising copper prices in the World War I era had made them amenable to paying the new production tax. As military commander, Calles therefore adopted a cooperative approach toward U.S. investors while guarding a nationalist image. For example, he informed Obregón that the main purpose of his presence in the border region was to protect the copper mines, a message that most likely referred to the threat posed by the Punitiva.[68] Six months later, he demonstrated that such "protection" meant cracking down on labor organizers. When several pro-labor delegates of the town council in Cananea proposed to hold all U.S. residents in jail until Pershing withdrew from Chihuahua, Calles sent a contingent of soldiers and ordered the execution of five of the delegates.[69] In August 1916, the execution of radical labor leader Lázaro Gutiérrez de Lara in Cananea sent a message that independent labor activism would not be tolerated. The saber-rattling helped the CCCC and the other copper companies drastically increase earnings over the next year as the world war dragged on into its third year, and the production taxes paid by these firms finally stabilized the state treasury.[70]

Nonetheless, de la Huerta's most significant measure as governor—the establishment of the Cámara Obrera (Workers' Chamber) in October 1916—had the potential of upsetting this precarious balance between foreign capital and the state administration. Decree No. 71 targeted the "economic malaise of the working classes." Postulating that the redemption of these classes constituted an important revolutionary ideal, the decree set up a Cámara Obrera to study issues relating to workers and their relationship with their bosses. The decree also charged the new chamber, which primarily consisted of mine workers, with issuing compensation judgments for workers injured on the job. The Cámara Obrera practically became an arm of the state government, a legislature with distinct responsibilities. Its representatives received a monthly stipend, and they were enjoined to avoid strikes by means of mediating labor disputes. The objectives of the decree therefore consisted of avoiding class conflict and finding negotiated solutions to labor disputes. The foundation of the Cámara Obrera constituted the type of paternalistic measure that characterized the Sonorans' approach to organized labor at the national level.[71] In fact, its creation roughly coincided with Obregón's shutdown of the Casa del Obrero Mundial, which in late 1916 claimed more than a hundred thousand workers nationwide. The disappearance of the COM made the Cámara Obrera the primary mouthpiece for workers in Sonora, and one of the few government-sanctioned ones in all of Mexico. Protected by the state, the chamber successfully proposed several decrees that improved the conditions of workers in Sonora. These decrees established the right of collective bargaining, and they set up impartial boards of arbitration for labor disputes. They prescribed maximum daily and weekly work hours, minimum wages, and an obligatory day of rest per week; and they mandated employer-funded health care for workers as well as indemnities for workplace injuries.[72] As de la Huerta pointed out, the decrees resembled legislation designed for the protection and safety of workers in the United States.[73]

In February 1917, the Cámara Obrera's objectives received a great boost from the promulgation of a new federal constitution. Carranza had assembled a convention in the city of Querétaro to update the old Juárez-era constitution of 1857, which had failed to prevent the establishment of the Porfirian dictatorship. This convention consisted of representatives of Carranza's and Obregón's faction, with the latter dominant due to their greater numerical weight within the victorious coalition. The timing was most propitious, as the Wilson administration drifted toward war and gradually disengaged from the Mexican imbroglio. On February 5, 1917, the day the last U.S. soldier left Mexican soil, the delegates approved a document far more radical than what Carranza had envisioned. While most of the Carrancistas had merely desired small amendments to the old constitution, the Obregonista majority viewed the constitutional convention as an opportunity to enshrine their economic and social objectives as the supreme law of the land. Obregón's reform-minded delegates successfully pushed for a clause that kept the Catholic Church out of political life (Article 3). Another article (27) made land and the subsoil the patrimony of the Mexican nation, for private use only under government concession. This article limited the privileges of the foreign companies: one of its provisions stipulated that foreigners who owned land or subsoil resources apply for new government concessions. Yet another article (123) established the right of collective bargaining and unionization, as well as a six-day week, an eight-hour day, and the workers' right to indemnity payments in case of injury. Legislation that had existed in embryonic fashion in Sonora and other states thus became federal law as a part of the national constitution. Carranza did not like these radical aspects of the new constitution, but the document allowed him to become constitutional president, and that was enough for him at the moment.[74]

The new constitution both codified and circumscribed the Sonoran reform program. The document included provisions similar to many of Calles's reform initiatives and therefore eliminated many of the grounds on which Carranza had objected to Calles's policies. But Calles's antialcohol measures were not included in the document. Even more significantly, the constitution also ended the era in which social reforms had been formulated in the states rather than in the central legislature. As in the Porfiriato, the president would again expect compliance with dictates from Mexico City, and Carranza was not interested in enforcing what he considered the radical aspects of the constitution.

The rebuilding of federal authority also threatened to undermine a spoils system crucial to Calles's success. Officials loyal to him had long administered the customs and port authorities, and control of these institutions presented a great opportunity for corruption and smuggling, with Calles reportedly receiving a percentage of the proceeds. For example, in October 1916, de la Huerta imposed a prohibitive duty on cattle passing from Sonora to Arizona. When *Jefe de operaciones* Calles prohibited the grazing of cattle within twenty-five miles of the border, ostensibly to prevent smuggling, and rumors flew that he wanted the smuggling business to himself, and that ten dollars per head went to his bank in the United States.[75] The resultant cash flow mitigated his continued struggles as an entrepreneur evidenced by the failure of his various business ventures during these years—ventures that included a tannery and a bank.[76] A further element in the spoils system—the practice of parceling out land expropriated from political enemies among loyal subordinates—also foundered beginning in 1917. The formal establishment of a national government made the decisions of Calles and de la Huerta subject to federal review, and the two leaders saw several of their expropriations overturned. Even more significantly, federal officials began to purge customs offices of Calles's and de la Huerta's provisional appointees.

However, Calles's informal authority remained strong enough that he was able to weather a stern challenge to his power from Mexico City. Dissatisfied with the course of the Yaqui campaign, in October 1916 Obregón replaced him as *jefe de operaciones* with his undersecretary, General Francisco R. Serrano, and Carranza ordered de la Huerta and Calles to Mexico City for reassignment to other duties.[77] These steps were designed to clear the way for Obregón's brother José for the upcoming gubernatorial elections. Calles was consternated by this bald attempt to remove him from office. As Serrano reportedly told a Constitutionalist officer, he "gave every indication of being a whipped man. He was sullen and morose . . . [and] he asserted that he was at a loss to explain his recall."[78] On the strength of his clientelist networks, however, Calles outlasted this challenge to his bailiwick even in the absence of a formal post. He continued to correspond with his retainers by telegraph, and he was soon allowed to return to Sonora, while de la Huerta once again took a position in the national government. In January 1917, Calles announced his candidacy for the governorship, and his election was a foregone conclusion.[79] In the statewide elections of June 1917, Calles won an overwhelming triumph over José Obregón to become the first elected governor of Sonora under the new federal constitution. Obregón had received only lukewarm support from his brother once the caudillo realized the extent of Calles's political influence in his home state. In poor health and temporarily retired from politics in Huatabampo, Alvaro Obregón recognized Calles's political strength. The election made Calles constitutional governor, a post with a much greater cachet of authority than the provisional governorship he had begun in August 1915. He was never again seriously threatened in his hold over the state.[80]

Constitutional Governor

Calles's period as constitutional governor began with a most unwelcome surprise. On June 22, 1917, the managers of the CCCC halted production and took their movable equipment across the border. The measure was a bold step to force Calles to rescind the production taxes and rein in the labor agitation promoted by the Cámara Obrera. Without revenue from either the production taxes or workers' earnings, the managers reasoned, Calles would have to give in. Exacerbated when the El Tigre copper mine followed the step of the CCCC, the crisis tested Calles's mettle in dealing with powerful foreign investors and a suddenly desperate populace in Cananea. Within days, Cananea authorities reported a critical food shortage and recommended the transport of the town's six thousand miners to other areas. Calles faced a stark alternative: give in to the copper barons and lose face politically, or stand his ground and risk a fiscal and social crisis of enormous proportions. A third solution—government administration of the mines—was not a feasible option in light of the enormous costs involved in resuming operations at Cananea as well as the possibility of a U.S. boycott of imported copper. As his first act in office, Calles temporarily moved the state capital to nearby Magdalena to be able to keep an eye on developments and to aid the miners with food and supplies.[81]

The governor dealt with the crisis on two fronts. In public, he lambasted the copper companies and maintained that he would not change laws for their benefit. He also removed the miners from Cananea so that they would not cross into the United States in search of work, where they, as he believed, would "encounter a difficult situation shameful to our race."[82] Indeed, soon thereafter, Arizona authorities broke a strike at the Copper Queen mines in Bisbee, detaining twelve hundred miners, including many Mexican immigrants, in inhumane conditions.[83] Behind the scenes, Calles was more conciliatory. He sought mediation through the services of a former lobbyist for the copper companies who entertained good relations with J. S. Williams, the manager of the Moctezuma Copper Co. in Nacozari. Williams was not only a friend of Calles's but also the manager of the only major foreign-owned mine that remained in operation.[84]

However, Calles realized that the CCCC would not be so easily swayed. To coordinate his strategy with Carranza, the governor took a fifteen-day leave of absence and traveled to Mexico City in what was only his second trip to the capital. Compared to de la Huerta, interim governor Cesáreo Soriano was a much weaker figure, dependent on Calles politically. Soriano and Calles had business dealings going back to the latter's tenure as comisario of Agua Prieta; at that time, Soriano had served as the customs accountant at the border, and he had played an important role facilitating Calles's smuggling operations. Nonetheless, as Calles did not return from his leave of absence until July 1918, Soriano and another interim governor, Miguel H. Piña, came to serve almost half of the governor's two-year term.[85]

Conveniently for Calles, it fell to Soriano to take the unpopular steps needed to come to a negotiated solution with the copper barons. On Calles's instructions, Soriano held firm in the matter of the reform laws. But his first act as governor—the closure of the Cámara Obrera—amounted to a significant concession to the CCCC. To justify this step to the public, Soriano argued that the promulgation of Article 123 made the Cámara a superfluous institution. In fact, however, closing the Cámara was in the interest of both the copper companies and the state government. Not only was the Cámara a useful gambit in the negotiations with the CCCC, but Calles also regarded it as a thorn in his side, as the workers' delegates demanded far-reaching reforms that included a fair profit-sharing arrangement.[86] Ultimately, the removal of the Cámara induced the CCCC to acquiesce in the remainder of Sonoran revolutionary legislation and cleared the way for the company to resume operations on November 17, 1917, just in time to enjoy the last halcyon year of the copper boom. A year later, the end of World War I sent demand for copper, and hence prices, back to the prewar level.[87]

By that time, Calles had once again attempted to crush the Yaquis, the one enemy that had thwarted him thus far.[88] After the failure of Calles's 1916 campaign, de la Huerta had negotiated an armistice, under the terms of which the Yaquis agreed to live in concentrated villages in the valleys in exchange for food and a promise that they could keep their arms. Over time, however, the Yaquis realized that they had been placed into a Sonoran version of concentration camps. In May 1917, between 1,000 and 1,500 Yaquis broke out of the villages, leaving behind a trail of destruction.[89] Calles was livid at what he viewed as the "treachery" of the Yaquis, and once the summer heat had abated, he petitioned Carranza for the reinforcements required to resume the campaign. After obtaining the president's assent, he declared war on the Yaquis.[90] In the "Manifesto to the people of Sonora" of October 24, 1917, Calles, as *jefe de operaciones*, and Soriano, as interim governor, vowed to pursue an "energetic, definitive, and, if necessary, terrible campaign against that relatively insignificant group of individuals who are hostile to any civilizing influence." The only solution to the problem, they believed, was extermination.[91] However, this campaign failed just as the previous one had. Unsuccessful on the battlefield, Calles created a distraction by removing Soriano from office, claiming that the interim governor had accepted a bribe from a gambling house in Navojoa as a reward for ignoring the Yaqui activities in that region. However, not everybody believed this version. According to one of Calles's enemies, the Porfirista Brígido Caro, Soriano lost his job because Calles was incensed that the interim governor had not shared the bribe with him. Whatever the case, in August 1918, Calles abandoned the Yaqui campaign and returned to Hermosillo to finish out the term as governor.[92]

By contrast, Calles softened his position regarding the church. In a small concession, he allowed priests to enter Sonora temporarily to administer baptisms and last rites to the dying. Ultimately, the governor recognized the enormous political cost of his anticlerical policies, which had antagonized not only Carranza but also many of his own supporters. In April 1919, Calles signed a new law that allowed one priest for every ten thousand inhabitants—a total of twenty-six priests for the entire state. Encouraged by this compromise, the clergy returned to Sonora.[93]

Likewise, Calles and his cohorts displayed an ambivalent attitude toward the large Chinese population of their state. Many of the Sonoran Chinese had originally arrived in the United States, where they had worked as coolies in railroad construction. As California and other U.S. states adopted xenophobic legislation, some of these workers followed the railroad south across the border. In Sonora, they were joined by others who arrived directly by boat, diverted by increasing U.S. strictures against Chinese immigration. By 1910, Sonora was the home of almost five thousand Chinese, a third of the Chinese population in the entire country. The overwhelming majority of these immigrants were male.[94] The Chinese originally settled along the border and in the coastal areas, and from there fanned out to Hermosillo and Cananea. As the largest foreign community in the state, the Chinese played the role enjoyed by European communities elsewhere in Mexico. Almost two-thirds engaged in commercial and money-lending activities. These petty merchants built familial support systems that spread financial risks and rewards over a number of different ventures.[95]

Sonoran nationalists targeted the Chinese as an undesirable ethnic group. Unlike U.S. investors, the Chinese competed with native capitalists and found themselves the target of envy and racist stereotypes at every level of society. In Cananea, for example, the Chinese population of some eight hundred residents virtually dominated local commerce. As immigrant nonwhites, the Chinese became "pariah capitalists" in a society that grew increasingly xenophobic throughout the revolution.[96] Many Sonorans also portrayed the Chinese, some of whom peddled opium and ran illegal gambling parlors, as harbingers of vice. In 1916, a schoolteacher and entrepreneur from Magdalena, José María Arana, led a movement to rid Sonora of the Chinese. As Arana stated, "When the first Chinese came to Mexico they were humble and miserable; but now they have enriched themselves, and we can stand them no longer."[97] In response, the Chinese founded the Chinese Fraternal Union, which became the largest mutualist organization in the state.

This controversy placed the state administration in a predicament. On the one hand, joining the anti-Chinese fray would have enhanced Calles's populist credentials. On the other hand, a campaign against the Chinese would have harmed a sector of society that paid its taxes and conducted its business exactly as Calles desired of all Sonorans. Moreover, Calles desired to show foreigners in Sonora that if they were expected to follow Mexican law, they would also be protected by it. As Soriano instructed local authorities in December 1917, "The truly democratic character of our institutions . . . absolutely rejects any type of persecution against individuals, groups, or classes." The interim governor ordered all *presidentes municipales* to inform leaders of anti-Chinese demonstrations that they were required to respect the rights of all foreigners.[98] Four weeks later, Calles told the *presidente municipal* of Magdalena, "You, as the authority, are required to give protection to those foreigners [or] you will suffer the consequences."[99] Nonetheless, he also suppressed further Chinese immigration into Sonora and pressured Chinese merchants to employ Mexicans rather than their own relatives.

A similar ambivalence marked Calles's approach to World War I, and particularly the issue of German activities. As U.S. military intelligence records illustrate, Calles was friendly to German interests. He admired Germany for reasons ranging from that country's well-organized military to its experience with social security and medical insurance for all workers. Calles allowed German espionage free rein, his military trainer was also a German imperial agent, and the governor furnished another agent with money and a firearm.[100] However, the limits of this cooperation were quite clear to Calles. He knew that Carranza had rejected the overtures for a German-Mexican alliance contained in the infamous Zimmermann telegram, the publication of which had contributed decisively to the U.S. entry into the war in April 1917. Like his superiors, Calles would not embroil Mexico in a conflict with the United States that held no benefits for either the central government or his own ambitions. Cited by the historian Friedrich Katz, the testimony of German agent Anton Dilger to the effect that he and Calles prepared an attack on the United States in July 1918 must therefore be regarded as implausible.[101] Neither U.S. military intelligence sources nor Mexican documents corroborate Dilger's boast to German diplomats that he could provoke a war between the United States and Mexico "by having General Calles attack the United States."[102] Mindful of his need to procure supplies and weapons from the United States, Calles took pains to assure U.S. officials of his friendly attitude toward the United States.[103] Soon thereafter, the war ended with the defeat of the Central Powers, and Calles once again turned his attention to his reform program.

Indeed, Calles's last year as strongman of Sonora was probably the most productive one in terms of social reform. It witnessed the issuance of three major reform laws: the "Ley de Gobierno" (Government Law); the "Ley de Trabajo" (Work Law); and the "Ley Agraria" (Agrarian Law). These laws codified many of the decrees of the previous four years and exceeded them in many cases. The Ley de Gobierno defined the responsibilities of the governor and the state legislature and affirmed the principle of the *municipio libre* (free municipality). The Ley de Trabajo ensconced the right of collective bargaining, the right to strike, and the above-mentioned laws regarding boards of arbitration and workers' compensation. It also outlawed debt service beyond one month's worth of wages and the *tienda de raya*, the infamous company store in which workers could exchange scrip for goods at inflated prices. Finally, the Ley Agraria sought to foster smallholding, entitling agricultural workers to their own parcels of land and fixing the upper limits of landownership depending on the quality and use of the land. If carried out to the letter, the Agrarian Law would have eliminated most large estates in Sonora.[104]

All of these laws based themselves on the Constitution of 1917, and they resembled it in that the government applied them inconsistently. For example, Calles never intended to break up all large estates; instead, his main goal was to promote food production. He believed that the future of Sonora lay in farmers such as the ones organized in Obregón's Garbanzo League, an alliance of chickpea producers who farmed small to midsize plots. He envisioned a use of the law against the remaining political enemies of the government, and, in particular, the Richardson. Calles and Carranza had canceled the Richardson concession in 1916 because of the company's failure to develop and irrigate land in the Yaqui Valley as promised, and the governor continued to fight legal battles about this matter. From the governor's point of view, the Ley Agraria could be used to transfer the vast landholdings and water rights of the Richardson to small producers that could be just as successful as the Garbanzo League. He also settled a small military colony composed of German-speaking émigrés from the United States in sparsely populated northwestern Sonora.[105]

There are few sources on Calles's personal life during these turbulent years. Until 1917, Natalia and the children remained in Nogales, Arizona, far away from the paterfamilias. After Calles's triumph in the gubernatorial elections, the family moved to Hermosillo, only to lose him to the Yaqui campaign. On his sojourns away, Calles found comfort with others than those of his closest kin. In 1918, while in Agua Prieta, Calles got seventeen-year-old Amanda Ruiz pregnant with what would be (at least) his fourteenth child, counting one with Josefina Bonfiglio and twelve with Natalia. Kept a secret from Natalia's family, Manuel Elías Calles Ruiz grew up assured of his father's financial support. Calles had repeated his own history with the extramarital liaison, but his support for Manuelito demonstrated that he was determined to be a better father than Plutarco *padre*. In July 1928, after Natalia's death, he invited Manuelito and his mother to Mexico City, and only the chaos following Obregón's assassination prevented a face-to-face meeting with his "other" family. During the 1940s, Manuel even lived with his father.[106]

Calles neared the conclusion of his term on September 1, 1919, aware of the fact that a provision in the new constitution prohibited the reelection of presidents and state governors. In May 1919, he accepted Carranza's nomination as secretary of industry, commerce, and labor. Calles spent his last months in office with an eye on national developments, limiting himself to ensuring the passage of the reform laws and helping de la Huerta succeed him as constitutional governor. To that end, Calles formed a party exclusively dedicated to working for his friend's election, and on September 1, he rejoiced when de la Huerta took office as governor.[107]

When Calles left for Mexico City, he looked back on four years in which his state government had stood at the forefront of social reform. Callista Sonora was one of the early "laboratories of the revolution,"[108] where the victorious Constitutionalists tested a variety of social and political reforms for eventual use at the national level. By 1919, his state had achieved advances in elementary school enrollment and the working conditions in the copper mines. Calles and de la Huerta had also set a legal framework for land reform, and they had reversed two decades of generous Porfirian concessions to force the U.S.-owned mining companies to share some of its revenue with the state.

But these advances came at a high price. Yaquis and Maytorenistas paid for their opposition with their lives and their lands; the Chinese community found itself attacked by xenophobic mobs and restrictive legislation; Catholic priests were expelled from the state, only to be readmitted briefly before the end of the Callista government; Calles reined in labor protests that did not suit his interests; and liberal democracy—the goal of the revolution of 1910—remained elusive. In particular, the bloody campaigns against the Yaquis constituted an early sign of Calles's authoritarianism.

From Calles's perspective, the years in which he dominated Sonoran politics comprised three distinct phases. The first of these phases was his time as provisional governor (August 4, 1915–May 16, 1916), during which Calles ruled by decree. This first governorship witnessed the formulation of some of the most important reform decrees and the extension of Constitutionalist au-

thority over the state. The second phase consisted of the provisional governorship of Adolfo de la Huerta (May 1916–June 1917). During this period,
Calles continued to exert influence through his ties to de la Huerta and other
allies who shared his political agenda. The year was marked by the threat of
a U.S. invasion, another war against the Yaquis, and the promulgation of a
new national constitution that codified several of Calles's and de la Huerta's
initiatives. Amidst conflicts with Yaquis, the CCCC, and the central government, the third phase (July 1917–August 1919) featured Calles as elected
governor. Ruling alternately through interim governors and directly as
elected governor, Calles codified the most important reform measures during
those years, yet failed to subdue the enemies he had been fighting for almost
a decade.

CHAPTER FOUR

In the Shadow of the Caudillo

Friendship does not subsist . . . in the arena of politics. From the bottom up, there may be convenience, support, and loyalty; or from the top down, affectionate protection or utilitarian appreciation. But simple friendship, an affective sentiment that unites two equals, is impossible. . . . In politics, the most intimate friends will often become the fiercest of enemies.

—Martín Luis Guzmán, *La sombra del caudillo*

In September 1919, Calles embarked on the long journey to Mexico City to begin a term as secretary of industry, commerce, and labor in Carranza's government. This trip, which involved travel by train as well as by boat, was his fourth overall to the national capital. It was a voyage into a different world. With a population more than twenty times that of Hermosillo, Mexico City had more inhabitants than all of Sonora. Here was the seat of power from pre-Columbian times to the present day, a world-class city with cosmopolitan flair, and the place where most of the important political decisions were made. The elite of Mexico City exuded arrogance and a sense that their city was the host of civilization in an underdeveloped nation. With reference to one squalid village south of the capital, *capitalinos* claimed that "outside Mexico [City], everything is Cuautitlán."[1] Overlooked by two impressive snow-capped volcanoes, the Popocatépetl and the Ixtaccíhuatl, the city boasted broad boulevards, bombastic architecture, and fancy department stores that awed and intimidated visitors from the rest of the country. Calles was no exception, regarding Mexico City as a metropolis of perversion unsuitable for young people of sound mind.[2] The capital was also located at the epicenter of "Spanish oppression and Catholic obscurantism," in Calles's mind the root causes for poverty and underdevelopment in Mexico.[3] As biographer Puente put it, "the courteous atmosphere" of high politics was "something new for Calles, who [had] not yet lost his provincial simplicity. It bothered him to . . . subject himself on a daily basis to the rigors of etiquette."[4] Initially, Calles left his family in Hermosillo in the hope that he would return soon.[5]

However, this journey inaugurated a new phase in Calles's life, as he found himself thrust into national politics. Calles, Obregón, and de la Huerta (hereafter referred to as the Sonoran Triangle) made their mark on the new state that slowly emerged from a decade of violence. The Sonorans expanded their wealth and power by entering into an uneasy alliance with the Mexico City elite, an alliance that involved political agreements and participation in joint business ventures. Thus, the strangers from the north became integral political and economic players on a national scale.[6] This period witnessed the emergence of Obregón, the undefeated caudillo from the revolutionary wars, as Mexico's foremost leader. Although Calles lived these years in the shadow of this caudillo, he began to make his own mark on national politics even before he became a presidential candidate.

Calles's road to the presidency offers important insights into Mexican politics in the 1920s. Revisionist historians have portrayed these years as a period of consolidation during which the winners of the revolution cemented their power and even as a time when the Sonoran leaders betrayed the "ideals" of the revolution.[7] However, the new revolutionary state remained weak, and the meaning of the revolution was hotly contested until the early 1940s. In what Antonio Gramsci would have labeled a "catastrophic equilibrium" in which "the old is dying and the new cannot yet be born," a fragile compromise between contending forces in a society in upheaval, the Sonorans needed to pay attention to popular demands for social change.[8]

The Revolution Devours Its Own

When Calles arrived in the capital, Mexico remained in turmoil after nine years of revolution. Although the Constitutionalists had established control over most of the country, enemies abounded both outside and within the government. For example, in southern Mexico, Don Porfirio's nephew Félix Díaz continued to wreak havoc, and in distant Baja California, Colonel Esteban Cantú defied the central government, boosted by the proceeds from U.S. "vice tourism," especially his brothels and gambling houses near the border.[9]

Pancho Villa also remained a threat, although his troops failed to take the border town of Ciudad Juárez in his last major offensive in June 1919.[10] Finally, Zapatista guerrillas remained at large in Morelos and surrounding states. Apart from the persistent trouble in the Yaqui region, Sonora seemed to Calles a model of stability compared to the rest of Mexico.

Still more worrisome were the ambitions of the country's victorious generals. Obregón had withdrawn from the Carranza administration and returned to his farm, La Quinta Chilla, to prepare for his bid for president in the 1920 elections. During the constitutional convention of 1917, he had struck a gentleman's agreement with Carranza, in which Carranza agreed to support Obregón in 1920 in exchange for the caudillo's backing of his bid to be named president of Mexico by the Constituyente for the 1917–1920 period. As time went by, however, Obregón realized that Carranza intended to renege on his promise and support a civilian candidate. Other generals such as Pablo González harbored presidential aspirations as well. Further down the chain of command, local caciques disobeyed orders to subordinate themselves to the federal government. Private armies beholden to these warlords controlled vast areas, sometimes seizing hacienda land in the name of *agrarismo*, other times plundering for no apparent reason. The military commanders sent out to rein in these private armies were either powerless to stop the caciques, or they ended up colluding with them.[11]

The greatest issue Calles faced as the new secretary of industry, commerce, and labor was the national economy. The economy had bottomed out at the height of the factional fighting in 1915, and mining and agricultural production had declined to less than half their 1910 levels.[12] The network of railroads had suffered great damage, as troops had ripped up track and blown up bridges and depots. The currency was in even worse shape. During the war between the factions, both sides had printed large amounts of paper money to finance their campaigns. After the collapse of these currencies, Mexicans used U.S. dollars, government paper notes, and IOUs signed by revolutionary leaders. Those who owned gold and silver coins hoarded these valuables in the hope of awaiting better times. The inflation of paper money depreciated wages and wiped out savings accounts, and the shortage of bullion depressed commerce. Although these conditions improved with the consolidation of the revolutionary state, most Mexicans still felt the material consequences of war, hunger, and disease. For example, the destruction in the countryside had impaired food production, and more and more pesos chased a diminishing food supply. The endemic graft in the revolutionary armies compounded the problem of feeding a population, a large part of which had abandoned the countryside for the cities during the preceding decade. As a result of widespread malnourishment, typhus and other diseases swept the nation, including the worldwide Spanish influenza epidemic of 1918.[13] Finally, Calles and his colleagues confronted an acute financial crisis, as the decline in worldwide demand for mineral exports following the end of World War I in November 1918 had plunged the country into a recession. Against a backdrop of devastation and poverty, this crisis made a mockery of the revolutionary slogans that had stoked the hopes of ordinary Mexicans.

Carranza also confronted a revolution too radical for his taste that interacted with other social movements throughout the world. The carnage of World War I had discredited the so-called West—the guiding light of the positivist ideology of the Porfirians, and to an extent, that of Carranza and Calles. In Russia, the October Revolution of 1917 had ushered in the world's first socialist state. Vladimir I. Lenin, the leader of what would soon be called the Soviet Union, expropriated industries, mines, and large estates. In Germany, the military collapse at the end of the world war ushered in the democratic revolution of November 1918 that found itself besieged by enemies from the far left and right from the first day. Even in the United States, a bastion of liberal capitalism, the Red Summer of 1919 manifested the appeal of socialism to industrial workers.

In this atmosphere, the promises for social reform in the 1917 constitution became pressing issues for the Carranza government. Although Carranza himself would have preferred to ignore most of these promises campesino movements insisted on the redistribution of hacienda land, and labor pushed for the right to strike and better working conditions. Separated by widely divergent cultural practices as well as the differences between food producers and consumers, these two sectors never formed an alliance. However, both found help from representatives of the middle classes. As Calles's and Obregón's careers attested, the revolution had provided new opportunities for the middle classes. Most military and civilian leaders from this group advocated capitalist development with safeguards for campesinos and workers, and a considerable minority of middle-class intellectuals such as Marte Gómez, Juan de Dios Bojórquez, and Rafael Nieto even advocated socialism. As these radical intellectuals saw it, the Soviet Union resembled Mexico as a largely agrarian society with a legacy of authoritarianism and great inequality of income.[14] Despite this radical strain within the ruling coalition, one does well to recall Carleton Beals's observation that "the Mexican revolution had no prophet and no body of positive theory; it was obliged to formulate its own ideology and own program as it went along, a halting, fumbling misdirected series of experiments that have brought the masses little but a sense of freedom—a freedom not too easily demonstrable."[15]

Not surprisingly, the revolution continued to devour its own, and months before Calles's arrival in Mexico City, Carranza had already eliminated Zapata, the living symbol of land reform in Mexico. Unable to defeat the guerrilla tactics of the agrarian leader, Carranza turned to a former Zapata supporter, General Pablo González. González laid a carefully conceived trap. In early April 1919, he commissioned a deserter he had captured, Jesús Guajardo, to approach Zapata with an offer to surrender his weapons to him. To gain Zapata's trust, Guajardo waged a staged battle against government troops. Although still suspicious, Zapata agreed to meet with him at the abandoned hacienda of Chinameca. After saluting Zapata upon his approach to the hacienda, Guajardo's men leveled their weapons and killed him. The treacherous way in which González had planned Zapata's death served notice to all revolutionary leaders that Carranza's methods to silence opponents resembled those of former dictator Victoriano Huerta.[16] The assassination of Zapata left Calles with no illusions regarding the political methods of Carranza, a man whom he had once admired.

The Carranza regime also faced great difficulties with the United States and Great Britain. The Allied victory in World War I left the governments of both nations free to turn their attention to supporting foreign business interests in Mexico. After President Wilson suffered a stroke while attending the 1919 peace convention in Versailles, France, the formulation of U.S. foreign policy fell to Albert B. Fall, Republican senator from New Mexico and chair of the senate's Foreign Relations Committee. Well connected to oil interests, Fall threatened the Carranza administration with military intervention in case it did not repeal the nationalist provisions of Article 27 of the new constitution. Declaring land and subsoil the patrimony of the nation, this article had repealed Porfirian legislation that had allowed foreign ownership of land and mineral resources. While military intervention was an empty threat, Carranza and other leaders knew that Senator Fall was powerful enough to bring about a rupture of diplomatic relations, a step that would have deprived the government of access to both credit and weapons in the United States. In July 1919, U.S. officials sent menacing notes to Carranza that demanded the annulment of Article 27. In addition, the Carranza regime was heavily in debt to U.S. and British banks, and the fighting had emptied the national treasury. Finally, foreign nationals claimed millions of dollars in losses as a result of the revolution, and the U.S. and British governments resolved to press these claims.[17]

The pending question of implementation of Article 27 therefore made Calles's post in the national government a stern test for an aspiring leader. His position had remained vacant for ten months, ever since the resignation of his predecessor, Alberto J. Pani. During his tenure, Pani had addressed issues such as the reconstruction of commerce in a country plagued by banditry and continued revolutionary violence. He had convened Mexico's first merchant congress and established a dialogue among the country's chambers of commerce on how to revive the exchange of goods, money, and services. To discuss draft legislation regarding the implementation of Article 27, Pani had held a meeting of representatives of industry, mining, and oil; predictably, the industrialists rejected his plans, and his effort to impose a new tax on oil production got stalled in court.[18] Ordinarily, Calles would have vigorously pursued new negotiations of the kind that he had successfully concluded with the copper companies in Sonora.

However, Calles soon learned that his position held no such prospects of shaping important policies. Instead, his appointment placed him in a holding pattern, as Carranza's primary motive for bringing him to Mexico City had been to keep him away from de la Huerta and Obregón. The president had always been jealous of the role of the Sonorans in the fight against Huerta. He had not forgotten that the state had held out against the dictatorship even as the Federales chased Carranza all the way to Sonora. As president, Carranza impinged on Sonoran sovereignty by means of a decree that established federal jurisdiction over the Río Sonora, a stream dependent on seasonal rainfall that did not empty into the ocean. This effort alienated Governor de la Huerta and put him firmly into Obregón's camp. In addition, Carranza resented the idea of a military leader occupying the presidential chair and looked for a civilian to succeed him.[19] Caught between his two mentors, Calles could therefore not achieve much in his five-month term.

Nonetheless, a large-scale strike in Orizaba, Veracruz, gave Calles an opportunity to lay important groundwork for his future national role. Apart from Cananea, Orizaba was probably the one city most famous for labor activism; in 1908, nearby Río Blanco had featured the second great strike of the Porfirian era—a strike suppressed (like that of Cananea) with brutal force. Orizaba not only boasted one of the two largest breweries in Mexico but also the sweatshops of the country's foremost textile producers. Taking the lead of the Casa del Obrero Mundial (COM), the workers in those companies had affiliated with Carranza. After the Constitutionalist victory, they had won the right of collective bargaining in exchange for their service in the Red Battalions that had proven effective in the campaigns against Villa. However, Obregón's closure of the COM in late 1916 had left the workers without the protection of a national labor movement. In November 1919, the industrialists of the Orizaba region launched a concerted attempt to abrogate the contracts with the new, local labor unions, and to reimpose a labor system based on individual contracts. Workers from all major industries went on strike, and by the time Calles intervened in the dispute, the stoppage threatened to engulf the region. Although he did not succeed in brokering an agreement, he earned himself the support of the workers, who viewed him as their advocate.[20] As Calles stated in an interview with the newspaper *El Universal,* the "individual contract . . . signifies the death of the labor unions, which would mean that workers are at the mercy of the industrialists."[21] Indeed, the labor laws in Sonora, laws that had guaranteed collective bargaining and workers' rights, had placed Calles and de la Huerta among the vanguard of the Constitutionalist leadership as far as support for urban labor was concerned. Impressions such as these gave the Sonorans political capital among labor organizations.

Calles also got firsthand experience with the oil controversy, the single greatest problem in U.S.-Mexican relations at a time when Senator Fall held sway over U.S. foreign policy. The late 1910s and early 1920s had witnessed a dramatic increase in oil production, and Article 27 threatened to nationalize this growing sector of the economy. Facing a severe budget shortfall, Carranza used the provisions of this article to raise taxes on new oil drillings. The refusal of the oil companies to pay these taxes led Carranza to assume a more strident stance, and he canceled all future drilling concessions and sent the army out to the oil fields to interrupt operations. However, the oil magnates defied this legislation by forging documents and bribing government officials. Calles did not think Carranza's response went far enough. He opposed the president's half-hearted proposal for a petroleum law that would have imposed but minimal restrictions on the oil companies, and he helped defeat it in Congress.[22] Moreover, when one of his close friends, the agronomist Luis L. León, informed him that he had discovered oil in Hermosillo, he realized that the cancellation of drilling concessions affected Mexicans as well as foreigners. As he noticed to his chagrin, the oil magnates had found a way around the law, while León would have to wait until Carranza lifted his decree.[23]

Meanwhile, Calles got caught in the clash between Carranza and Obregón regarding the presidential succession in 1920. Carranza made it clear that he desired to turn over power to a civilian after his term expired. His choice was the colorless Ignacio Bonillas, the Mexican ambassador to the United States and formerly an ally of Calles during the war between the factions. The Elías family had known the U.S.-trained engineer from Magdalena, Sonora, for decades, as he had once measured *ejido* land in the vicinity of Fronteras.[24] The nomination of Bonillas was a slap in the face of Obregón, who had expected Carranza to reward him for winning the revolution on the battlefield.

It also threw Congress into turmoil, where an alliance in support of Obregón's candidacy held the majority. Although Calles had no problems with Bonillas personally, he threw his weight behind Obregón. On February 1, 1920, he resigned from his post, citing his political ideas and the commitments that bound him to one of the "contending parties."[25] He was less diplomatic in a note sent to de la Huerta that same day, in which he lambasted the "small circle that surrounds Don Venustiano, . . . the most corrupt people in the country."[26] Soon thereafter, he returned to Sonora after a stop in Zacatecas, where he addressed a convention of labor representatives. After a last-ditch effort to dissuade Bonillas from his candidacy, the stage was set for a conflict of Obregón supporters with the national government.[27] A third candidate for president, General Pablo González, waited in the wings in Monterrey.

Afraid that Obregón might seek help from his home base, Carranza made the mistake of threatening Sonoran governor de la Huerta. In late March 1920, the president ordered General Manuel Diéguez and a contingent of federal troops to Sonora under flimsy excuses, and de la Huerta protested in the strongest terms possible. Not only did the governor view the move as unnecessary, but he also worried that the presence of Diéguez, a veteran of the Yaqui wars of the mid-1910s, might incite the Yaquis to another rebellion.[28] In a letter, Calles warned Diéguez not to follow Carranza's orders: "If troops march on this state, there will be a civil war that will perhaps be the bloodiest ever, and you will be one of those responsible for that war."[29] As Diéguez's troops continued to proceed toward Sonora, and Carranza declared the dissolution of powers in that state, de la Huerta realized that Carranza intended to depose him and decided to confront the federal government. On April 9, 1920, the Sonoran legislature decreed that it no longer recognized the Carranza administration, and de la Huerta appointed Calles military commander of the state.[30]

Thirteen days later, Calles was the first of 107 military officers to sign the "Plan of Agua Prieta." Authored by former interim governor Gilberto Valenzuela, the document rejected Carranza as president on the grounds that he had violated the sovereignty of the state and mocked the popular vote, and it announced the creation of a Liberal Constitutionalist Army headed by de la Huerta. This proclamation had originally borne the name of "Plan de Hermosillo," a name changed due to Calles's desire to memorialize the name of the town where he had begun his career as a revolutionary almost eight years before.[31] Just as in March 1913, the government of Sonora stood against the federal government.

This time, however, there would be a quick end to the regime in Mexico City rather than a drawn-out struggle followed by factional conflict. One key to this rapid success was the attitude of González, who withdrew his support from Carranza although he did not recognize the Plan of Agua Prieta. Other military leaders joined González in what amounted to a strike of the generals. On May 7, 1920, González's troops entered Mexico City, and Carranza and more than eight thousand men, women, and children left the capital in a convoy of trains that reportedly measured eight miles in length. The president intended to escape to Veracruz, where he would set up a national government just as he had done in late 1914. But there would be no reprise of Carranza's triumphs during the war between the factions. None other than Zapata's assassin, General Guajardo, held up half of the convoy shortly after its departure, and the remainder of the trains ran into torn-up tracks in the state of Puebla. Fleeing from Obregón's armies, Carranza and a small entourage rode north into the mountains on horseback. While Obregón made a triumphant entry into Mexico City, Carranza and his men soldiered on until May 20, when they reached a small village in northeastern Puebla. There, the military commander of the region introduced the president to a General Rodolfo Herrero, who led the group to the isolated hamlet of San Antonio de Tlaxcalantongo. In the early hours of May 21, 1920, Herrero's small party assaulted the hut in which Carranza slept, and the president died during the attack.[32] Although the circumstances of Carranza's death have never been conclusively elucidated, it served Obregón's purposes. Reportedly, the caudillo expressed great satisfaction at the news of the passing of his former ally.[33]

Indeed, Carranza's death opened the door for the triumph of the Sonoran Triangle. On May 24, Congress approved de la Huerta as interim president and delayed the upcoming presidential elections until September 5. On June 1, 1920, de la Huerta took the oath of office and named Calles secretary of war and navy. In November, he also awarded Calles the highest military rank, that of "General de División."[34] Meanwhile, Obregón was free to run for the presidency with the support of the federal government. These events demonstrated again that the revolution had not brought democracy to Mexico as Madero had desired. The use of force had determined Carranza's successor. Just as in Sonora, Calles had participated in a political system in which elections served as a mere cover for individual ambitions. As one of his political opponents, Martín Luis Guzmán, put it, "Suffrage does not exist in Mexico. What does exist is the violent conflict of groups contending for power, supported occasionally by public opinion. That is the true Mexican constitution; the rest is a mere farce."[35]

Politics and Kinship in the Sonoran Triangle

The demise of Carranza made Obregón the most powerful man in Mexico. While the caudillo shared power with de la Huerta and Calles, this alliance was based on unequal power relationships. Obregón's influence in the military leadership made him the preeminent leader in national political life. In the words of Guzmán, the caudillo was the "grand master in the political game and judge of the ambitions of others."[36] Interim President de la Huerta's power base was in Mexico City, and especially in Congress and the government bureaucracy.[37] Enjoying neither the benefit of clientelist relationships with military leaders on the national level nor the support afforded by a network of friends in the federal government, Calles appeared the weakest of the three Sonorans.

A closer glance, however, shows Calles in a strong position as the crucial intermediary in the triangular relationship. In the words of biographer Ramón Puente, "Obregón [was] the military caudillo; de la Huerta, the civilian representative; and Calles, more than either military or civilian: a politician."[38] As we have seen, Calles and de la Huerta had been friends since the early 1890s. After the Plan of Agua Prieta, Calles built up a close personal friendship with Obregón as well, a friendship that surpassed what Guzmán would call the "convenience" and "utilitarian appreciation" that marked the relationship of de la Huerta and Obregón. According to Calles's daughter Alicia, Obregón was a frequent guest in the family residence. Calles provided the glue that held the triangle together for more than three years.[39]

Calles also benefited from his increasing understanding of Obregón's political personality. Puente has provided the best explanation of this advantage vis-à-vis Obregón:

> In Obregón, one finds a plethora of life, of self-confidence that makes him as powerful as a tidal wave . . . Calles exudes less vitality, an energy that one might call passive, and an intimate confidence that results in a quiet character. When Obregón comes with the momentum of an unstoppable wave, he finds Calles impassive. The wave clashes as if it hit a jetty, and the equilibrium reestablishes itself between the two.

Puente genders Calles's psychological edge as "male" characteristics of penetration and domination. "Calles fundamentally understands Obregón's soul. He seems to have dedicated all of his . . . pedagogical practice to probe this spirit. He understands it like that of a child; he penetrates and dominates it like a man. . . . Obregón never comes to understand Calles. Probing souls is not his specialty."[40]

De la Huerta was the first member of the triangle to occupy the presidential office. His presidency came at a difficult time, as the U.S. government had broken diplomatic relations after what Wilson considered a coup d'état against an elected government. The future appeared ominous. In November 1920, the presidential elections in the United States brought Republican Warren G. Harding to power, a man who enjoyed close ties to Senator Fall. Eighteen months into what had turned into a full-fledged postwar economic crisis, U.S. nonrecognition deprived Mexico of loans as well as access to weapons and ammunition. Not surprisingly, de la Huerta dedicated himself to national reconciliation, and the interim president showed clemency toward the enemies of his government unprecedented in the era of revolutionary violence. Over Obregón's objections, he negotiated Pancho Villa's surrender in exchange for a grant of a large ranch in Canutillo, Durango. Villa's remaining followers received other rural properties. The deal not only earned de la Huerta the friendship of Villa but also Obregón's distrust.[41] De la Huerta also allowed Félix Díaz—Don Porfirio's nephew and Victoriano Huerta's coconspirator, who had long defied the Constitutionalist government from his power base in the southern state of Oaxaca—to go into exile. Yet another example is the president's treatment of Pablo González, who was implicated in a revolt against the government, apprehended, and sentenced to death. In light of insufficient evidence, de la Huerta ordered González's release. Articulate, artistic, and unostentatious, de la Huerta found admirers throughout Mexico. The goodwill created by his tenure helped Obregón win election as president for the term 1920–1924 without serious challenges.[42]

As secretary of war, Calles played an important role in the de la Huerta administration. Most importantly, he initiated a process of professionalization of the military that would continue for the next twenty years. As we have seen, the rebellion against Huerta had swept away the Federales, the old professional army built up over the preceding five decades, and ushered in a ragtag, impromptu force in which raw power rather than hierarchy and seniority determined status. At over 200,000 troops, this revolutionary army constituted a tremendous burden on the federal budget, and the independent ambitions of many of its leaders concerned the civilian de la Huerta. Having found the War Secretariat in disarray, Calles launched a program to reduce the army in size and to establish clear and consistent personnel procedures. His ambitious goal was a well-trained army of 50,000 loyal to the national government.[43] Predictably, his endeavors produced fierce opposition, and in July, the specter of a mutiny against Calles almost induced Obregón to leave his ranch for Mexico City several months before he was scheduled to begin his term as president. Nonetheless, at the end of Calles's five-month tenure as secretary of war, 120,000 soldiers remained on the federal payroll, and mutinies had begun to diminish.[44]

Calles was also involved in all of de la Huerta's major decisions regarding negotiations with Villa as well as Félix Díaz's exile and González's amnesty. In all three cases, he consistently advocated a harder line but ultimately deferred to the interim president. He also helped rein in the remaining regional caudillos. The one strongman who enjoyed perhaps the greatest degree of autonomy was Baja California's Cantú, who had used his state's geographical isolation—an isolation even greater than that of Sonora—to remain neutral in the war between the factions. After the Constitutionalist victory, Cantú had irked the central government by defying federal decrees and running an operation dedicated to smuggling, gambling, and prostitution based in the border towns. Upon Carranza's death, he proclaimed that he did not recognize the de la Huerta administration, and that he would remain loyal to a regime that no longer existed. De la Huerta and Calles sent an expedition to Baja California under the leadership of a fellow Sonoran, General Abelardo L. Rodríguez, a former commander in the Yaqui campaign. By September, Cantú was in exile in Los Angeles. As military commander of Baja California, Rodríguez became an important Calles ally in national politics.[45] Finally, Calles developed a reputation as a friend of agrarian movements by organizing rural civil defense groups against armed landowners who defied federal decrees. This stance earned him the support of *agrarista* leaders such as Antonio Díaz Soto y Gama. A former Zapatista delegate at the Convention of Aguascalientes, Soto y Gama was the head of the Partido Nacional Agrarista (PNA, or National Agrarian Party) and a staunch Obregón ally.[46]

With the Obregón presidency on the horizon, Calles knew that his second appointment in the national government would result in a far longer stay. Therefore, he moved his family to a house in Mexico City, not far from the presidential residence in Chapultepec Castle. Since 1913, they had spent four years in Nogales, Arizona, with Natalia's father and another three years in Hermosillo. Only during the brief periods when Calles served as constitutional governor of Sonora had the family lived together. Plutarco's occasional visits had produced more children, and Gustavo, the twelfth and youngest child, was born in 1918. However, the separation had produced estrangement. While Natalia worried about her husband's safety, her letters preserved in Calles's personal archive do not show great intimacy, let alone hints that Calles consulted his wife on political matters.[47] As Natalia's health declined over the course of the next five years, two other women became political advisers to Calles: his private secretary, Soledad "Cholita" González, and his daughter Hortensia, or "Tencha."[48]

The move reunited Calles with seven of his nine surviving children, as his two oldest sons had already left the home. Rodolfo and Plutarco were both educated in the United States, establishing a pattern that demonstrated Calles's attraction to Mexico's northern neighbor. Rodolfo, the eldest, attended military academies in San Francisco and New York before obtaining a baccalaureate degree in accounting from Columbia University, likely the first university degree in the Elías family. Known as "Aco" to friends and family, Plutarco also attended a military boarding school in California and then enrolled at New York University, having missed the deadline to apply to West Point. Unlike his brother, Aco did not earn a college degree.[49]

These two sons—and particularly Rodolfo—played important roles in the building of their father's career. Both contributed to the family patrimony and the building of networks on the national level. With his college degree in accounting, Rodolfo helped his father reverse more than forty years of unsuccessful business ventures. The two men teamed up with Aarón Sáenz Garza, Aco's brother-in-law and close friend of Obregón's, to found the "Compañía Industrial y Colonizadora de El Mante" (hereafter El Mante). Located in a sparsely populated region of the northeastern state of Tamaulipas, this 50,000-acre estate became one of the nation's largest sugar producers, thanks to irrigation provided by the reservoir of the same name constructed during the Calles presidency. For his part, Aco found his calling as the owner of the hacienda "Soledad de la Mota" in the northern state of Nuevo León, a gift from his father. Once again, political power translated into business success and vice versa, as his father ensured the construction of a road into that remote region that allowed Aco to produce citrus on his hacienda. Aco proved a capable administrator of Soledad de la Mota, which became his father's favorite place of refuge from the hustle and bustle of Mexico City.[50] Political power and kinship ties hence afforded the family increasing opportunities for enrichment.

The other seven children accompanied Natalia to Mexico City and, for the most part, followed Rodolfo's and Aco's path to success. Over time, the family came to treasure the capital as the country's center of power despite the concerns of the paterfamilias. In 1922, Hortensia married a native of Mexico City, Obregón's private secretary Fernando Torreblanca Contreras. In a gesture that showed that anticlericalism trumped family loyalties, at least in highly public ceremonies, Calles—unlike Obregón—did not attend the church wedding. Soon thereafter, Plutarco's eldest daughter, Natalia, married another *capitalino*, Carlos Herrera. Yet another daughter, Alicia, wed Jorge Almada, a landowner from Sinaloa. Of all the daughters, Ernestina was the only one to marry a Sonoran, the Guaymas native Tomás Robinson.[51] The three youngest children, Alfredo, Artemisa, and Gustavo, married toward the end of their father's career. Whereas Gustavo would further the interests of the clan just as his elder siblings had done, Alfredo and Artemisa caused their father more headaches than the other children combined: the former, for his reckless and irresponsible spending habits, and the latter, for her unhappy marriage to Joseph Eller, a physician from New York City.[52] In Calles's personal and professional life, his family's move to Mexico City therefore constitutes a watershed date. As this provincial Sonoran politician emerged as a national leader, his family made significant contributions to and benefited from Plutarco's ascent (see table 4.1).

From Mexico City, the family observed the taming of the revolution under President Obregón. True to his nature as what one historian has labeled the "great compromiser of Mexico's time of troubles,"[53] Obregón forsook ideology for pragmatism. He recognized the fact that his country remained in turmoil after a decade of war. Facing the lack of U.S. diplomatic recognition, he adroitly moved to implement some of the promises of the new constitution to campesinos and workers while reassuring foreign investors and those landowners who would cooperate with him. He established a rural education program, selectively parceled out hacienda land to campesinos, and promoted the growth of labor unions. However, he avoided tackling the thorny issue of the foreign domination of the oil industry, and his land reform stopped well short of satisfying demands. The result of Obregón's opportunism was an array of contradictory policies. For example, his alliance with Soto y Gama led the president to support land redistribution in Morelos and adjoining states. This stance brought an international outcry when campesinos assassinated the widowed *hacendada* Rosalie Evans, an outspoken target of land reform in the state of Puebla.[54] Nonetheless, Obregón also allowed the Terrazas clan to reclaim most of its vast holdings in Chihuahua, and he confronted armed agrarian movements elsewhere in the north. These contradictions demonstrate Obregón's strength as a political operator in a weak state. Just as the governing elite and ordinary Mexicans negotiated rule in a complex process that a recent scholarly work terms "everyday forms of state formation,"[55] so did elite participation in state formation proceed through *pactos*, or informal agreements among leaders. Thus, Obregón's effort to centralize authority after a decade of war entailed cultural as well as political aspects. Under Obregón, the government in Mexico City promoted a national culture and consolidated federal authority in the states, many of which remained under the control of caudillos who had gained power and wealth during the revolution.

Table 4.1. The Elías Calles-Chacón Clan

Plutarco Elías Calles (1877–1945) + Natalia Chacón (1879–1927)

1. Rodolfo Elías Calles Chacón — 1900–1965
   - Emilia Lacy
   Grandchildren: Natalia, Alejandro, Rodolfo, and Emilia Elías Calles Lacy
2. Plutarco Elías Calles Chacón, a.k.a. "Aco" — 1901–1976
   - Elisa Sáenz
   Grandchildren: Alicia, Plutarco, Fernando, Alvaro, Enrique, Irma, and Héctor Elías Calles Sáenz
3. Bernardina Elías Calles Chacón — 1902–1902
4. Natalia Elías Calles Chacón , a.k.a. "Chona" — 1904–1998
   - Carlos Herrera
   Grandchildren: Natalia, Carlos, and Jorge Herrera Elías Calles
5. Hortensia Elías Calles Chacón, a.k.a. "Tencha" — 1905–1996
   - Fernando Torreblanca
   Grandchildren: Norma, Hortensia, and Myrna Torreblanca Elías Calles
6. Ernestina Elías Calles Chacón, a.k.a. "Tinina" — 1906–1984
   - Tomás G. Robinson
   Grandchildren: Ernestina and Eugenia Robinson Elías Calles
   - Jorge Pasquel
   - Miguel Aranda Díaz
7. Elodia Elías Calles Chacón — 1908–1908
8. María Josefina Elías Calles Chacón — 1910–1910
9. Alicia Elías Calles Chacón — 1911–1988
   - Jorge Almada
   Grandchildren: Alicia, Marcela, Gabriela, and Jesús Almada Elías Calles
10. Alfredo Elías Calles Chacón — 1913–1988
    - Elena Alvarez Murphy
    Grandchildren: Alfredo, Fernando, Santiago, Jorge, and Alberto Elías Calles Alvarez
    - Sara Riveroll
    Grandchildren: Sara and Roberto Elías Calles Riveroll
11. Artemisa Elías Calles Chacón a.k.a. "Micha" — 1915–1998
    - Joseph Jordan Eller
    Grandchild: Adriana Eller
    - Rodolfo Ogarrio
    Grandchildren: Eugenia and Francisco Ogarrio Elías Calles
    - Augusto Bouras
12. Gustavo Elías Calles Chacón — 1918–1990
    - Gabriela Peláez
    Grandchildren: Gabriela and Susana Elías Calles Peláez
    - Guillermina Guajardo

Sources: Macías, *Vida y temperamento*, 32; information provided to author by Norma Mereles de Ogarrio; FPEC, serie 011400, exp. 27, leg. 1 "Homenajes 1971," "Lista de hijos, yernos, nietos y cuñados del General de División Plutarco Elías Calles."

Despite his background as a teacher, Calles did not play a significant role in cultural state formation, which consisted of a campaign to expand public education in rural areas as well as the sponsorship of artistic production. The aim of the education campaign was to forge campesinos into Mexicans by increasing literacy and civic consciousness in the countryside. In 1921, Obregón established a new cabinet-level agency, the Secretaría de Educación Pública (Secretariat of Public Education, or SEP) and nominated the rector of the National University, José Vasconcelos, to head the new agency. The SEP not only federalized rural education, but it also launched an ambitious program to open new schools in the countryside. Nor was Calles involved in the symbiosis between the Obregón administration and mural artists such as Diego Rivera, José Clemente Orozco, and David Alfaro Siqueiros, whose radical interpretations of Mexican history came to adorn the interior of government buildings. Although Obregón and his aides did not agree with these interpretations, they realized that the murals educated Mexicans from all regions about their common national history, and that their existence advertised tolerance of differing viewpoints.[56] Most importantly, the murals advertised the rich historical legacy of the country's indigenous peoples. They played an important role in an *indigenismo* movement that joined the efforts of the SEP to incorporate the "Indian" population into Mexican society by validating and celebrating their cultural heritage.[57]

Instead, Calles contributed decisively to Obregón's effort at political centralization as secretary of *gobernación* (interior affairs). Although the new position removed Calles from direct influence over the military, it invested him with great influence in national politics. In control of the federal police, *gobernación* not only played an important role in internal security, but it also monitored electoral disputes at the state level. In 1920s Mexico, where those who were the first to arrive at a voting booth often ended up overseeing the voting and counting the ballots at the end of the day, such disputes were inevitable, and many states featured shadow governors and legislators claiming fraud in rigged elections that had shown them as the losers. *Gobernación* did not have the final say in the matter, but its opinion weighed heavily in Congress, the body in charge of declaring the winners of state elections. Within the Consejo de Ministros, or Council of Ministers, only Hacienda (Finance) Secretary de la Huerta equaled Calles's power. On New Year's Day 1922, the newspaper *El Universal* published an informal poll that anointed de la Huerta as the country's most popular political leader behind Obregón.[58]

Calles used his authority as secretary of *gobernación* to build a network of loyal governors and military commanders. Some state governments had been in the Sonoran column since the Plan of Agua Prieta. For example, the conservative agrarian caudillo of San Luis Potosí, Saturnino Cedillo, had served Obregón's interests from the beginning, and Sonora itself remained under leadership friendly to the central government.[59] In Baja California, Abelardo Rodríguez continued to hold sway as military commander. By 1921, Rodríguez had closed most casinos and bars in Tijuana and claimed victory over Cantú's "immoral" legacy.[60] However, this friend and associate of Calles built a business empire of his own during the next decade, and his holdings included at least one casino.[61] In states like Veracruz, where two or more warlords jockeyed for supremacy, Calles supported the one most akin to his political program. Thus, he allied himself with Governor Adalberto Tejeda, a self-proclaimed socialist who favored land reform, the full application of the anticlerical provisions of the constitution, national control over the oil industry, and housing reform. Calles's support helped Tejeda win out over the conservative General Guadalupe Sánchez as well as another cacique, Manuel Peláez, who was allied with the foreign-owned oil companies operating in the Huasteca region.[62]

The flip side of this centralizing strategy consisted in subduing military leaders who continued to defy central authority. To bring recalcitrant strongmen under control, Calles and Obregón resorted to the time-tested method of the carrot and the stick: bribes and offers of government positions contrasted with the use of military force. The president himself considered corruption accepted practice; in his inimitable words, "no general can resist a cannon shot of fifty thousand pesos."[63] He also joked about the fact that he had lost an arm during the campaign against the Villistas by claiming that he was only half as corrupt as the other generals because he had only one hand with which to steal.[64] Although coercion proved far more difficult, Calles made an important beginning by enhancing a small intelligence division, the Servicio Confidencial, originally founded by Carranza. Under the leadership of Gilberto Valenzuela, the author of the Plan of Agua Prieta, the renamed "Oficina de Servicios Confidenciales" monitored the activities of prominent generals suspected of plotting an uprising.[65] By the time Calles left his post in September 1923, the national government enjoyed a level of control over its territory not seen since 1910, although some pockets of resistance continued.

Calles also helped strengthen the power of the executive branch at the expense of Congress. In particular, the secretary of *gobernación* assisted in undermining the most powerful party, the Partido Liberal Constitucionalista (Liberal Constitutionalist Party, or PLC). Founded in 1916, the PLC counted both Obregón and his nephew, General Benjamín Hill, among its founding members. Composed primarily of urban intellectuals and a smattering of lesser military leaders, the party's congressional delegation formed the bedrock of Obregón's support. The PLC held three posts in the Consejo de Ministros, including the War Secretariat under the direction of Hill, Calles's former comrade-in-arms. However, the relationship between party and president went sour even before Obregón's inauguration. Obregón mistrusted the party, and he resented the fact that a Congress composed primarily of civilians held more authority under the constitution than the military leaders who had—as he believed—risked their lives for the underdogs. For its part, the PLC demanded that the independence of the legislative branch be respected. Shortly after Obregón's inauguration, the party suffered its first blow following a banquet given in honor of Calles, Hill, and José Inés Novelo, a prominent PLC member. Hill and Novelo became very ill immediately after the banquet, and the former died a few days later. Since no one could imagine that Obregón had poisoned his own nephew, rumors held Calles responsible for what some observers called the "feast of the Borgias."[66] Hill's death augured the demise of the PLC. In the elections of 1922, a coalition of four small opposition parties supported by the Sonoran Triangle swept the PLC from power in Congress.[67]

In the process of helping this coalition defeat the PLC, Calles established significant linkages with labor and campesino organizations—ties that would serve as building blocks of his presidential bid in 1924. He established a good working relationship with Soto y Gama's PNA, the largest agrarian party in Congress and one of the four parties in the anti-PLC coalition. Even more importantly, he became the primary liaison in the executive branch for two other parties that had allied with the PNA in the 1922 elections: the Partido Laborista Mexicano (PLM, or Mexican Labor Party), and the Partido Socialista del Sureste, (PSS, or Socialist Party of the Southeast). The leaders of these parties, Luis Napoleón Morones and Felipe Carrillo Puerto, became Calles's most significant allies on the national level and helped him develop a populist image as a radical within the Sonoran coalition who was genuinely committed to the welfare of the working poor.[68]

Because of his connections to national and international labor organizations, Morones was a particularly valuable ally. Born into a working-class family in Tlalpan, Mexico City, he worked as an electrician before joining the revolution as a member of the COM. Later that year, he founded the union of the Mexican Telegraph and Telephone Company. After the dissolution of the COM, Morones attempted to organize a Socialist Party before contributing to efforts to create a central labor union that would coordinate the efforts of the various company unions across the country. That organization became the Confederación Regional Obrera Mexicana (CROM, or Re-

gional Confederation of Mexican Workers), a union committed to se
collective bargaining, higher wages, shorter work hours, workers' comp
tion, and profit sharing for all workers. During a trip to France, Italy, ...
Spain to study workers' organizations in countries with long-established labor movements, Morones came to understand the importance of worker solidarity across borders. He coordinated the creation of the Pan-American
Workers Confederation headed by American Federation of Labor (AFL)
leader Samuel Gompers as president and Morones as vice president. In 1919,
he helped found the PLM, which soon thereafter declared its support for
Obregón in exchange for a promise to back the CROM.[69]

Although Morones had thus begun his career as an Obregón loyalist, he
gravitated toward Calles, as the CROM's efforts to incorporate rural laborers
antagonized the staunchly Obregonista PNA. As federal deputy from the
PLM, Morones displayed firebrand rhetoric that led outsiders to believe that
he was an admirer of the Soviet Union. In fact, however, he was a reformist
rather than an anarcho-syndicalist or a Marxist committed to radical
change.[70] Widely considered more amenable than Obregón to workers' issues,
Calles began to cultivate Morones soon after meeting him in the Obregonista
campaign headquarters. In January 1921, when the Pan-American Workers
Confederation met in Mexico City, the secretary of *gobernación* announced to
a crowd that included Gompers and Morones that his government supported
"the struggle of the proletariat of the world."[71] Four months later, a throng of
150 workers organized by Morones seized Congress to the shouts of "Long live
the Russian Revolution" and placed a red-and-black banner on the rostrum.
Unimpeded by Calles, whose job it would have been to disperse the demon-
strators, this show of strength prompted leading PLC representatives to draft
a futile memorandum of protest against Morones and other Laboristas.[72]

The Yucatecan leader Carrillo Puerto, on the other hand, helped Calles
reach out to campesinos. Fluent in Yucatec Maya, the middle-class Carrillo
Puerto identified himself as a socialist early on in the revolution. He served
in Zapata's army before working as a stevedore in New Orleans. As the president of Alvarado's Partido Socialista de Yucatán (Socialist Party of Yucatán,
or PSY), he used his knowledge of Maya to mobilize campesinos in Ligas de
Resistencia (Resistance Leagues) loyal to the party. In 1919, Carranza dis-
mantled the PSY and forced Carrillo Puerto to seek refuge in Mexico City,
where he met both Calles and Morones. Upon the triumph of the Sonoran
Triangle, Carrillo Puerto returned to Yucatán, founded the more broadly
based Partido Socialista del Sureste (PSS), and oversaw the rebuilding of the
Ligas de Resistencia. The 1920 elections made him a federal deputy, and two
years later, he became governor of Yucatán.[73]

Gompers visits Obregón and Calles
From left: Plutarco Elías Calles, Samuel Gompers, Alvaro Obregón, Luis Morones, and unidentified person
Source: FAPEC.

Calles realized that an alliance with the Yucatecan leader would give him an independent power base. Furthermore, he was concerned about the grassroots nature of the Ligas, fearing that unbridled political mobilization would provoke fresh political unrest. When the PSS was rumored to entertain the notion of joining the Moscow-led Comintern, Obregón ordered Calles to visit Yucatán in February 1921 to remind Carrillo Puerto that Yucatán could not conduct its own foreign policy. While in Yucatán, however, Calles overstepped his mandate by showing his support for Carrillo Puerto and encouraging the Ligas to follow the direction of the state government. In the state capital of Mérida, the *gobernación* secretary identified himself as a socialist, painting Mexico City as a nest of reaction in which he and Obregón served as guarantors of the revolution.[74] A week later, he lectured an assembly of the Ligas de Resistencia on the virtues of the revolution. He professed "great respect and affection for our primitive races," and announced his dedication to a campaign of morality, democracy, and land reform. He exhorted the audience to eradicate alcoholism as a cause of poverty and domestic violence, and to follow the law under Carrillo Puerto's direction.[75] A year later, Carrillo Puerto became governor, and the realization that his state's budget depended on the continued export of henequen soon tempered his socialist zeal. For Calles, the governor of Yucatán was a significant ally because he remained independent of the Obregonista PNA.

However, these allies remained in a minority position in Congress. The 1922 elections brought the ascendancy of yet another party, the Partido Nacional Cooperatista (PNC, or National Cooperatist Party). Unlike the other parties such as Soto y Gama's PNA, Morones's PLM, and Carrillo Puerto's PSS, the PNC did not claim to represent a social grouping. Its most prominent members included regional warlords such as Guadalupe Sánchez of Veracruz as well as civilian professionals such as Martín Luis Guzmán and the young party president, Jorge Prieto Laurens. In Congress, the party controlled the powerful Permanent Commission in the Chamber of Deputies, where the PNC held an absolute majority. This emergence of a new dominant party made Obregón's job more difficult, as the PNC (like the PLC before it) demanded the active law making role that Congress enjoyed under the constitution. The middle-class professionals in the PNC such as Guzmán and Prieto Laurens, mistrusted caudillo rule and longed for the return of civilian leadership.[76]

Apart from the emergence of the PNC as a legislative counterweight to executive rule, the absence of diplomatic relations with the United States and Great Britain constituted another ongoing problem for the Sonoran triangle. Without diplomatic recognition, foreign financial institutions, which held millions of dollars of defaulted Mexican debts, balked at extending new credit to the Obregón administration. In late May 1922, de la Huerta traveled to New York City to negotiate with New York banker Thomas Lamont, the representative of the foreign banks. Eager to come to a speedy agreement, de la Huerta recognized 1 billion dollars' worth of foreign debt—much of which had originated in the Huertista period of 1913–1914—without obtaining a firm commitment to two specific loans that Obregón had requested. To de la Huerta's consternation, Lamont and the other bankers continued to make new credit contingent upon U.S. diplomatic recognition despite his acceptance of the old debt. Nationalists roundly criticized the deal as an act of surrender to Uncle Sam. While Calles continued to stick by his ally, Obregón, influenced by de la Huerta foe Alberto Pani, expressed his disapproval of the outcome of the negotiations. Although relations between de la Huerta and Obregón remained cordial, the finance secretary resented what he saw as a cynical attempt to discredit him.[77]

By contrast, Calles's new friends, and particularly Morones, furthered the goal of U.S. diplomatic recognition in ways that reflected positively on the secretary of *gobernación*. Most significantly, Calles and Morones launched a propaganda campaign within the United States that drew on Morones's ties to U.S. labor organizations. The linchpin of this campaign was Samuel Gompers, who regarded Calles as his closest ideological kin among the revolutionary leaders. Gompers and the Rumanian-born socialist Roberto Haberman, a friend of Carrillo Puerto's, became propagandists for the diplomatic recognition of Mexico. Aided by the Mexican Financial Agency in New York City, they mobilized AFL chapters to demand the recognition of a regime that, as they saw it, defended the interests of workers rather than foreign capitalists.[78]

Thus, Calles was well positioned for a presidential bid in the 1924 elections. He had served a successful stint as *gobernación* secretary supported by small, but significant, labor and campesino organizations. Most significantly, he enjoyed de la Huerta's friendship and Obregón's backing to take his turn as the third member of the Sonoran triangle to lead the nation.

To Be President at Any Cost

However, the presidential campaign would not pass without acrimony and tragedy. On the morning of July 20, 1923, General Pancho Villa set out to return to the hacienda of Canutillo, Durango, that he had received from President de la Huerta three years before. He had attended a baptism in which he became the godfather of a child in a distant village. In the city of Parral, he approached an intersection where a man raised his hand and shouted "Viva Villa!" in salute to the hero of the División del Norte. Slowing down to make a turn, Villa was an easy target for the assassins commanded by the shout to open fire on his automobile. Nine bullets killed him within seconds.[79]

It did not take long for Calles to become implicated in Villa's assassination. Over the past year, Villa had toyed with a political career, and he frequently expressed his admiration of de la Huerta, for whom, as he had stated, he would even return to the battlefield. Even though de la Huerta had never declared his intention to run in the 1924 elections, the generous terms of Villa's amnesty created the impression that he had struck a secret deal with de la Huerta. Villa's death focused suspicion upon Calles and Obregón, who had much to gain from breaking up the presumptive de la Huerta-Villa alliance. Thus, when the secretary of the Chamber of Deputies asked aloud, "Who killed Villa?" the reply "Calles" spontaneously came from the assembly. The acerbic humor on the street agreed: as one joke had it, the answer to the question "Who killed Villa?" was "Cálles-e," or "shut your mouth."[80] Foreign diplomats concurred with this assessment, and speculation mounted until a member of the state legislature of Durango, Jesús Salas Barraza, signed a confession that he had ordered Villa's assassination. The confession quelled what would have been a damaging political firestorm for Calles. Only recently, the work of historian Friedrich Katz has corroborated an earlier published interview with Salas that pointed to a conspiracy involving General Joaquín Amaro, one of Calles's closest associates. According to Katz, Salas assumed personal responsibility for the murder in order to take the heat off Calles and Obregón.[81]

Indeed, Villa's assassination formed part of a larger political crisis regarding the upcoming presidential campaign. It was no secret that Calles aspired to the presidency, and that Obregón supported his candidacy, considering him a pliant understudy who could easily be controlled from behind the scenes. Calles had positioned himself well within the president's orbit, and de la Huerta showed no interest in running for president.[82] Ineligible for reelection, Obregón remained by far the country's strongest political figure based on his control over most of the military leadership. He rotated his supporters in the military among regional commander posts, never allowing them to build up an independent power base in any one of those positions. In addition, the president enjoyed close ties to regional caudillos such as Saturnino Cedillo of San Luis Potosí and Tomás Garrido Canabal of Tabasco.[83] Calles realized that his own alliances with de la Huerta, Morones, and Carrillo Puerto would not win him enough freedom of action to escape the shadow of his mentor.

Nonetheless, Calles declared his candidacy on September 6, 1923, and resigned from his post as required by the constitution. Formulated in Soledad de la Mota, where Calles spent time recuperating from a bout of the rheumatic ailment that had first afflicted him during the siege of Naco, his inaugural declaration placed his policies in a worldwide context. Calles portrayed his campaign as part of a global quest (undertaken in many different countries by a variety of political actors) to redeem the less fortunate. According to Calles, this quest held particular importance in Mexico, a country of stark differences in income and wealth. He therefore affirmed his support for Article 27 and other nationalist and social reformist provisions of the constitution, and he portrayed himself as an advocate for the "humble classes."[84]

Calles's campaign was the first populist presidential campaign in Mexican history. It rested on his reputation of a radical politician allied with the labor leader Morones and the agrarian Carrillo Puerto and followed up on the rhetoric that had served him well during his campaign for the elected governorship of Sonora seven years before. His campaign relied on five basic promises: an effort to provide for public primary education; the division of hacienda land into *pequeñas propiedades*, or smallholdings; the implementation of the

labor provisions of the 1917 Constitution; the defense of Mexican sovereignty vis-à-vis the United States, and an end to cacique rule. Appealing to
campesinos, workers, and the middle class, this program was typical of populist platforms in Latin America of the 1920s. According to Calles, the middle class was to play a particularly crucial role:

> In the class struggle of the modern world, there is a third class that should play
> a great role: the middle class. Always repressed, the middle class has been put
> down and exploited by those above, without achieving a sufficient degree of
> understanding by those below. . . . I would be very pleased if I could achieve
> . . . that the middle class take its place in the fight, organize, rise up from the
> depression in which it finds itself and by its efforts, come to occupy its rightful
> place, balancing the other two classes [labor and campesinos] for the benefit of
> the Republic.[85]

Calles also mixed radical appeals to workers and campesinos with efforts to
seek the middle ground. As he declared, his program neither promised "mir-
acles nor chimerical transformations. . . . I only promise to sustain . . . our
Constitution and its revolutionary postulates."[86]

Two influential groups opposed Calles's presidential bid. Most importantly, a faction of disgruntled generals impervious to Obregón's bribes
banded together to stop Calles from becoming president. In allusion to the
fact that neither Obregón nor Calles had participated in the revolution of
1910, the group called itself "Unión de Militares de Origen Revolucionario
1910–1913" (Association of Military Leaders of the Origins of the Revolution, 1910–1913). Quite possibly, Obregón and Calles decided to kill Villa to
preclude an open rebellion of these generals, many of whom had seen their
influence decline over the last three years. Members of this group of "has-
beens" included Calles's old comrades-in-arms, Salvador Alvarado and
Manuel Diéguez, as well as Carranza's son-in-law, Cándido Aguilar, former
Secretary of War Enrique Estrada, and Guadalupe Sánchez, Governor
Tejeda's rival in Veracruz. These generals not only blamed their declining
fortunes on Calles's ascendancy, but they also regarded the candidate as an
inferior military leader and radical firebrand who had not earned the right to
be president. Estrada and Sánchez were particularly opposed to his anticlericalism, viewing him as a *come cura*, or "priest eater" who sought to extirpate
the church.[87]

The other group consisted of civilians such as Education Secretary Vasconcelos and PNC leaders Prieto Laurens and Guzmán. Vasconcelos held a
personal dislike for Calles; years later, he attacked his masculinity by baptizing him "la Plutarca" in an allusion to his neat appearance.[88] Prieto Laurens

had seen an earlier overture to Calles rebuffed, and Guzmán opposed Calles's candidacy as an imposition by Obregón. Some Cooperatistas also resented Calles for what they viewed as his radicalism and his affiliation with campesino and labor parties. A hotly contested and fraudulent gubernatorial election in San Luis Potosí further incensed Prieto Laurens and his allies. In this election, Prieto Laurens faced off with PNA candidate Aurelio Manrique, like regional strongman Cedillo a supporter of Calles's candidacy. After violence forced the early closing of voting booths across the state, both sides claimed victory. Upon the recommendation of the sitting governor, Obregón and Calles ordered new elections and set up a provisional government. While the matter dragged on for several weeks before Manrique won out, Prieto Laurens accused the Gobernación Secretariat of federal interference in a state election.[89]

This opposition would not have caused major problems for Calles if the Sonoran Triangle had continued to operate in unison. As it was, however, relations between Obregón and de la Huerta deteriorated throughout the summer of 1923 due to the finance secretary's increasing misgivings about the president's policies. In particular, he held Obregón responsible for Villa's assassination, and he opposed the Bucareli Accords of August 1923, which awarded U.S. recognition in exchange for a commitment not to apply Article 27 retroactively to foreign investors. Stung by having taken the fall for Obregón in his negotiations with Lamont, de la Huerta saw the president agree to far more sweeping concessions than those he had offered the U.S. bankers the previous year. After studying the minutes of the Bucareli conference, de la Huerta became incensed at what he viewed as surrender to U.S. economic interests. In September, the events in San Luis Potosí, which he regarded as an instance of federal intervention in state affairs, prompted de la Huerta to offer his resignation as finance secretary. Before Obregón and de la Huerta could make a final attempt to patch up their differences, Guzmán's newspaper, El Mundo, publicized the full text of the resignation letter. Calles's comment on de la Huerta's action was terse and revealing: "I have lost a friend forever."[90] As he saw it, the spat forced him to choose between his friend and his mentor. Unable to speak to either Obregón or de la Huerta from distant Nuevo León, he chose power over friendship.

The breakup of the Sonoran Triangle prompted de la Huerta to reconsider his decision not to run for president. While he initially pondered a withdrawal from politics, a public scandal over his tenure as finance secretary convinced him of the need to salvage his honor by means of a presidential bid. Within two days of de la Huerta's resignation, the new finance secretary, Alberto Pani, one of de la Huerta's personal enemies, accused him of financial mismanagement. The charge was an unfair one; while de la Huerta had spent money in an attempt at pacifying Mexico through federal largesse, he had not enriched himself in the process. After this attack on his integrity, there was no turning back from the collision course. On October 14, a large demonstration on the Zócalo clamored for him to declare his candidacy, and five days later, de la Huerta obliged. On November 23, he accepted the presidential nomination of the PNC, leaving Calles with the support of the PNA, PLM, and PPS.[91] Within a week, de la Huerta's candidacy encouraged armed revolts.

Thus began what history remembers as the de la Huerta rebellion, an amorphous uprising with little political focus. De la Huerta had nominal leadership over the rebellion as candidate for president, and his Plan of Veracruz gave the rebellion a common platform on December 7, 1923. Yet he did not have an effective voice in the coordination of the campaign, and the manifesto contained little of substance beyond a commitment to institute women's suffrage.[92] The leaders of the rebellion shared nothing more than their opposition against Obregón's imposition of political candidates at the federal and state levels. With reason, a contemporary author dubbed the war *la rebelión sin cabeza*, the "headless rebellion," in reference to the lack of a unified leadership.[93] One could also call it the *rebelión cualquierista*, or the Rebellion in Favor of Whoever Can Beat Obregón and Calles.

Indeed, a regional analysis reveals a wide diversity of motives and objectives. In Veracruz, it was a revolt by the state's military commander, Guadalupe Sánchez, against his long-time nemesis, Governor Tejeda. A wealthy *hacendado*, Sánchez faced off with Tejeda over the issue of land reform. Predictably, Tejeda's agrarian stance implied a strategic alliance with Calles and Obregón, whereas Sánchez and the landed elites backed de la Huerta. In the central states of Jalisco and Michoacán, the followers of Enrique Estrada, an Obregonista disaffected with the imposition of Calles, constituted the backbone of a rebellion that proceeded without clear political purpose. While Estrada maintained close ties to the landowners, his ally, former Michoacán governor Francisco Múgica, had participated in the *Constituyente* of 1917 as one of the authors of Articles 27 and 123. In the southern theater, and particularly in Oaxaca, rebels fought a battle for states rights informed by widespread resentment of *norteño* rule. Finally, Yucatán featured a rebellion designed to overthrow Carrillo Puerto.[94]

It was in Yucatán that Calles, who took an active part in leading government troops into battle, suffered the most sensitive casualty of the rebellion. On December 21, rebel officers overthrew the state government and captured Governor Carrillo Puerto. Less than two weeks later, a court martial ordered the execution of Carrillo Puerto and his associates. Calles's reaction promised swift retribution; those responsible for the crime, as he commented to Morones and Obregón, "have signed their own [death] warrant."[95]

Yet Calles's loss was small compared to the bloodletting on the opposite side. According to official figures, more than 100 officers, 23,000 troops, and 24,000 "civilians" (most of them former soldiers who had been dropped from the payroll) joined the de la Huerta rebellion. These same figures only showed 35,000 soldiers under the government's command.[96] Obregón, however, once again led his troops to victory at the decisive Battle of Ocotlán, Jalisco. With U.S. arms and financial assistance flowing freely to his government after the reestablishment of diplomatic relations, the rebellion ended in disastrous defeat. Despite efforts to mediate the conflict by enjoining Obregón to drop Calles, the president stood fast by his ally, demonstrating not only his resolve to impose his successor but also Calles's political strength. After the smoke had cleared, the list of the dead rebels included Alvarado and Diéguez as well as prominent governors such as García Vigil. In Congress, Morones carried out a purge of Delahuertistas accentuated by the January 1924 murder of Senator Field Jurado, a politician who had led a filibuster of the ratification of the Bucareli Agreements. For his part, de la Huerta went into a prolonged exile in the United States.[97]

The de la Huerta rebellion left a significant legacy for Calles's political future. It was the first of three conflicts that weeded out the caciques who had formed independent fiefdoms during the revolution. In doing so, it strengthened Calles's influence in national politics by eliminating adversaries in the military. However, the rebellion also increased his dependence on Obregón: not only did it demonstrate Calles's need for the military protection of his mentor, but it also gave Obregón a chance to elevate officers loyal to him to a general's rank. Finally, the civil war changed the tone of Calles's campaign rhetoric, which now drew a line between himself and what Calles called the "redoubts of reaction."[98] Singling out rebel leaders Sánchez and Estrada for their pro-*hacendado* policies, Calles painted himself as a representative of the "true" revolution.[99] In March 1924, Calles resumed his political campaign full time upon the triumph of the government forces over the bulk of the rebel armies. He knew that de la Huerta's defeat left him as the frontrunner for the elections, although he would have to ward off an electoral challenge from several candidates with regional power bases. The most important of these candidates was the Sinaloan general Angel Flores, who enjoyed the support of many of the former de la Huerta supporters.

In light of these challenges, Calles emerged as what historian Georgette José Valenzuela has labeled the "worker-campesino candidate."[100] His boldest declaration may have come on April 10, 1924, when he gave his famous speech at Zapata's tomb. Flanked by Soto y Gama and other agrarista leaders, he declared that Zapata's program was his own.[101] Two days later, Calles toned down this rhetoric in the first-ever radio address by a Mexican political leader. On that occasion, he struck a conciliatory tone, pointing out that his program did not seek the "ruin" of the propertied classes. To uplift the proletariat from its misery and ignorance, he argued, would lead to the betterment of all Mexicans.[102] He spent the rest of the spring campaigning with promises of land reform and implementation of labor rights. Calles even appealed to women, whom he called "half of the fatherland"—albeit without proposing any concrete steps to ameliorate gender inequality in a country that would not award the franchise to women for another thirty years.[103]

Then, suddenly, Calles had reached his ultimate goal. In July 1924, election day came without additional political unrest, and official returns from the election showed Calles with 1,340,634 votes, compared with 250,500 for Flores.[104] The cost of reaching this prize, however, had been immense in political and personal terms. Calles had lost the best friend he ever had, an ally who had helped him counterbalance Obregón's power. Following a war in which Obregón had once again shown his superior military abilities, the incoming president was also more at the mercy of the caudillo than ever before. The results for Congress revealed that Calles would face an uphill struggle, as a conglomeration of regional parties allied with Obregón dwarfed the delegations of the pro-Calles parties. After the elections, many Mexicans wondered whether Calles would serve a similar role to that of President Manuel González in 1880—a weak president who was never able to shake the shadow of Porfirio Díaz, his mentor and predecessor, and whose presidency entered the history books as a brief interlude in a long period of one-man rule.

Calles's rise to president was a tale of war, corruption, and betrayal. On the heels of a governorship in which he had made his native state into a laboratory for social reform, he had entered national politics seeking to develop a political base among organized labor and the official campesino organizations. His success in this endeavor had made him into an essential cog in the Obregonista political machine, which first swept aside President Carranza and then, together with de la Huerta, claimed national prominence for itself. Meanwhile, his family had followed the paterfamilias to Mexico City, taking advantage of the new opportunities provided by Calles's rise to power. Finally, the Sonoran Triangle imploded in a clash of personal differences and rivaling political ambitions. As his best friend went on a collision course with his most valuable political ally, Calles abandoned friendship for the quest for power. With Obregón immensely strengthened from the successful conclusion of the war against the Delahuertistas, Calles became president in the shadow of the caudillo, or by the grace of Obregón.

This story affords insights into the genesis of populist leadership in Mexico. Uniquely among all Latin American nations, revolutionary Mexico had formulated a constitution that reflected populist demands, and all revolutionary leaders needed to pay lip service to this constitution. In his effort to build a power base among campesinos and workers, Calles was the one member of the Sonoran Triangle most committed to the new document. His alliances with Morones and Carrillo Puerto and his track record as governor of Sonora made him the preferred candidate of the labor and campesino parties in Congress. Although the depth of his support for what he viewed as the proletariat had yet to be demonstrated, he entered his presidency as a populist leader who claimed that his time in office would be devoted to helping and redeeming the underdog. He began his term as someone who did not inspire much love among his followers but who had proven the ultimate value of recognizing political opportunity.

CHAPTER FIVE

El Señor Presidente

Injuries ought to be done all at one time, so that, being tasted less, they offend less; benefits ought to be given little by little, so that the flavor of them may last longer.

—Niccolò Machiavelli, *The Prince*

In August 1924, Calles embarked on an extended trip abroad that took him to Germany, France, and New York City. He spent two weeks in a clinic in the leafy Berlin suburb of Grünewald to treat the rheumatic ailment in his leg that had been a constant companion for almost ten years and remained in Berlin for several additional weeks resting and recuperating.[1] He took time to study the social conditions in interwar Germany, a country rife with political polarization, but a model for Calles so far as its society was concerned. With some justification, a nationalist German citizens' association in Mexico had even advertised Calles to their fellow Germans as a "gushing adorer of all things German."[2]

During Calles's sojourn in Germany and France, the president-elect engaged in constant comparisons between his country's revolutionary experience and European social democracy. In late nineteenth-century Germany, industrialization and population growth had produced a strong labor movement with a powerful political wing, the Social Democratic Party (SPD). Over time, this labor movement and the SPD had won significant concessions from employers, backed by state legislation similar to that of revolutionary Sonora. Calles particularly marveled at the country's infrastructure and industry, as well as a social safety net that shielded workers from the worst consequences of layoffs, sickness, and workplace injuries. In Germany, he saw realized many of the objectives of his and de la Huerta's own decrees in Sonora and the new constitution. He also admired the country's literacy rate that approached 100 percent. To try to learn from the German example, Calles collected informational literature on the German agricultural cooperatives, or *Genossenschaften*, as well as on the chemical and steel industries. Equally importantly, he found what he saw as the ideal qualities of a social democratic leader embodied in President Friedrich Ebert (1871–1925), a Social Democrat from a working-class family who appeared to represent a clean break from the Prussian aristocrats who had governed the country up to the end of World War I. Only six years younger than the German president, Calles considered himself to be a kindred spirit of Ebert's. Ebert was a moderate within the SPD who advocated democracy and better working conditions at the same time that he authorized the use of military force against those further to the left, such as the famous Rosa Luxemburg. When he learned of the riots, starvation, and violence in the chaotic German winter of 1919, Spartacist demonstrations in major cities, and the general economic collapse and hyperinflation that followed the 1923 French occupation of the Rhineland, Calles drew parallels between the recent histories of the two nations.[3]

The trip is an apt starting point for an analysis of Calles's presidency. Most historians have analyzed his tenure solely in comparison with those Mexican leaders who preceded or followed him, that is, Carranza, Obregón, and Cárdenas. Focusing narrowly on the Mexican national political trajectory, this approach ignores the multiple ways in which Calles reflected on and drew lessons from other countries. In Germany and in France, where he spent a few weeks after his sojourn in Berlin, he noted the worldwide power of populist rhetoric. As he told a cheering crowd composed of French trade unionists, "I was elected president of my fatherland by the workers, and I am proud to have in my hand . . . the strong hand of the Mexican proletariat. . . . If I cannot accomplish my mission, I will wrap myself in the flag of the proletariat and throw myself into the abyss."[4] This populist rhetoric was a powerful prop for Calles and helped him escape from Obregón's shadow until economic crisis and the church-state conflict endangered the survival of his government.

The Reform Program

On November 30, 1924, Calles took the oath of office in the newly built Estadio Nacional in Mexico City, a stadium designed by Education Secretary

José Vasconcelos. Standing on Calles's left, conspicuous to all, was General Obregón. The outgoing president remained his country's most powerful leader even as he left the presidency in the hands of his protégé to return to growing chickpeas in Sonora. It was the first time that the inauguration of a new president was a great state affair, and the first time since 1884 that the office had passed peacefully from one elected president to the next. Whereas Obregón had been sworn in during a relatively small ceremony in the Chamber of Deputies, Calles's inauguration, broadcast by radio to remote corners of the republic, manifested the advent of mass politics. Fifty thousand spectators holding banners from the PLM, the CROM, and other progovernment parties and organizations crowded the stands of the stadium. The banners proclaimed Calles to be the president of the workers and campesinos, the man who would realize the promises of the revolution for the poor majority. Confetti and balloons filled the air, and after Calles swore his oath, organizers released hundreds of pigeons.[5] Forgotten for the moment were the deaths of Madero, Zapata, Carranza, and Villa, the revolutionaries slain in the fratricidal conflict that had consumed Mexico since 1910. Ignored also was the de la Huerta rebellion that had resulted in the elimination of almost 40 percent of the army's leading officers.

Calles came to power in an enviable situation compared to that of his predecessors. The defeat of the rebellion nominally headed by de la Huerta had eliminated many of the anti-Calles officers, and the country enjoyed a degree of political stability unknown since the days of Porfirio Díaz. The president entered office in a peaceful transfer of power and with the diplomatic recognition of the United States. He presided over a country that had begun to emerge from the post–World War I economic doldrums, with its tropical and mineral exports bolstered by increasing demand from the United States and Europe. His alliance with Morones gave him access to organized labor. The lone holdover from the Obregón administration, Finance Secretary Alberto Pani, had overseen a reduction in the budget deficit throughout 1924, and he even projected modest surpluses for the coming two years. Though no fan of Calles, whose anticlericalism he resented, the Obregonista Pani steadfastly served the new president until his resignation in 1927.[6]

Calles's greatest problem at the outset of his rule was the ubiquitous presence of Obregón's supporters among the military leadership, state governors, and Congress. The ex-president remained popular in the military; he enjoyed the loyalty of Pani, Gobernación Secretary Gilberto Valenzuela, Education Secretary José Manuel Puig Casauranc, and Foreign Secretary Aarón Sáenz; and Obregonistas such as the Agrarista leader Soto y Gama controlled Congress. Among the state governors and regional bosses, Jalisco's

The presidential inauguration
Source: FAPEC.

José Guadalupe Zuno Hernández remained a steadfast Obregonista. On the day of Calles's inauguration, the new president angrily accused Obregón and Zuno of conspiring against him.[7] Although friendly to Calles, Cedillo and Tejeda and their armed campesinos remained, first and foremost, Obregón allies. Finally, the public image of Calles, an image of an inscrutable, ill-tempered, and melancholy leader, further accentuated his political weakness with regard to his jovial and charismatic predecessor. To many, Calles appeared Obregón's creation, a caretaker president who would return power to the caudillo upon the conclusion of his term. Whereas Obregón could count on the support of the generals since the failure of the de la Huerta rebellion, Calles could not claim such allegiance among the civilians in the government, many of whom had favored de la Huerta. In a sense, he appeared too "civilian" to the generals and too "military" to the civilians.

To escape from Obregón's shadow, Calles launched an energetic reform program, consolidating public opinion behind him within two months of taking office in what a U.S. military intelligence report classified as a "miracle."[8] This program resembled that of his years as governor of Sonora, blending measures designed to improve the fiscal situation of the state with the professionalization of the army, nationalist efforts to control natural resources, and the promotion of economic development, education, and social welfare. Like the Sonoran copper companies in 1915–1918, Mexican exporters of the mid-1920s benefited from increasing demand for raw materials at a time of robust economic growth in Europe and the United States. In both cases, Calles took advantage of this windfall by imposing higher taxation and by launching social reform legislation designed to benefit worker and campesino organizations allied with the state. As governor and as president, he had to contend with Obregón's hold over the military. Finally, neither the leaders of 1910s Sonora nor those of 1920s Mexico could ignore the political implications of U.S. economic influence. Herein, however, lay a significant difference between the two periods. Whereas U.S. participation in World War I drew resources away from addressing economic nationalism during Calles's tenure as governor, his presidency would have to deal with a meddlesome U.S. government. Moreover, the issue of governing all of Mexico would prove to be far more complicated than ruling over Sonora. Although clientelist arrangements remained at the heart of political power, these arrangements were difficult to sustain across a far-flung and diverse nation.[9] As a result, Calles needed to rely on the leaders of the incipient mass movements that had supported his candidacy.

Therefore, Calles's most important step at the outset of his rule was to elevate Morones to a position in the cabinet. In 1923, both leaders had reportedly signed a secret pact that committed Calles to assist the CROM labor union in exchange for Morones's support of his presidential campaign.[10] The new president brought Morones into the national government as secretary of industry, commerce, and labor, and members of the CROM's political wing, the PLM (Partido Laborista Mexicano), served as governors and in the federal and state legislatures. The CROM leader used his new position to win Calles's support for wage increases and further steps toward enforcement of the provisions of the revolutionary constitution, which mandated a workday of eight hours, overtime pay, sick and vacation leave, workers' compensation, and a host of other benefits for wage earners. In the cotton textile industry, for example, nominal wages for male workers rose 34 percent between 1925 and 1929, a period of low inflation and (in the latter two years) even commodity price deflation.[11] Calles and Morones also strengthened the Junta Federal de Conciliación y Arbitraje (JFCA, or Federal Board of Conciliation and Arbitration). Like its predecessors in Sonora and other states, the JFCA was staffed by an equal number of representatives from business and organized labor, along with one government official. Yet the Calles presidency brought out a dark side of Morones as well. With the president's protection, he persuaded, bribed, and forced hundreds of independent labor unions into the CROM, which in 1926 improbably claimed a membership of two million, or more than 10 percent of the entire population.[12] Among the independent labor unions, most of which were more radical than the CROM, the largest had twenty thousand members. In the process, the CROM became an instrument of corruption; as critics remarked, its acronym stood for *cómo roba oro Morones*, or "how Morones steals gold."[13] Obese and decked in expensive diamond jewelry, the CROM leader turned into the venal cacique that Katherine Anne Porter caricatured as Braggioni in her short story "Flowering Judas."[14] Thus, the precipitous decline in the number of strikes from 136 in 1924 to just 7 in 1928 owed to the alliance of the CROM with the state, rather than a greater degree of contentment among the workers. For example, in the summer of 1926, Morones sent scabs to end a railroad workers' strike in the Isthmus of Tehuantepec.[15]

Perhaps Morones's greatest contribution came in government policy toward the foreign-owned oil companies. As we have seen, Article 27 of the Constitution of 1917 contained provisions providing for the nationalization of the oil industry. The article had spawned a controversy between the U.S. and Mexican governments that had contributed to delaying U.S. diplomatic recognition of the Obregón regime. In the early 1920s, the oil issue appeared of paramount significance for the country's economic future: in 1921, oil production had peaked at 193 million barrels, then the highest output of any single country in the world. Over the next four years, however, the deposits showed signs of exhaustion, and output steadily declined. By 1924, annual production had decreased to 140 million barrels, and lower revenues translated into a series of labor disputes in the oil industry. In this atmosphere, the newly elected Congress opened its sessions a month after Calles's inauguration and began to debate a set of regulatory petroleum laws designed to increase tax revenue and to establish national oversight over oil production. Since any regulation of the oil industry fell within the purview of his agency, Morones, a staunch supporter of petroleum regulation, emerged as the driving force behind the deliberations. Although Calles's campaign speeches had seldom addressed the oil question, the president threw his support behind Morones. He knew that successful regulatory legislation would portray him as a nationalist who had managed to rescind Obregón's concessions to the United States at the 1923 Bucareli meetings.[16]

This move against the oil companies provoked a showdown with the administration of U.S. President Calvin Coolidge, whom Calles had met during his October 1924 sojourn in the United States. On that occasion, the two leaders had exchanged diplomatic pleasantries, although U.S. journalist Carleton Beals later reported that the president had given Calles a cool reception. As Beals asserted, Calles took this slight just as personally as he did all other imagined and real assaults on his persona.[17] His stance regarding the Bucareli Accords—a treaty that Coolidge considered a prerequisite for continued U.S. diplomatic recognition—complicated relations with the U.S. government that were already strained by the failure of the Mexican treasury to make payments on the foreign debt. On June 12, 1925, Secretary of State Frank B. Kellogg suddenly dragged the simmering conflict out in the open, suggesting in a press release that the Calles administration might soon face another rebellion. In a thinly veiled reference to the de la Huerta rebellion, in which the Obregón administration had benefited from U.S. assistance, Kellogg declared that Calles could expect his support only if he protected U.S. lives and property. He announced that Mexico was "on trial before the world."[18]

Kellogg's surprising offensive reflected the influence of the U.S. ambassador to Mexico, James R. Sheffield. This Yale-educated lawyer enjoyed close personal ties to the oil interests. In an early manifestation of U.S. political discourse during the Cold War, Sheffield railed against what he portrayed as a Bolshevik government allied with the Soviet Union, with which Obregón had inaugurated diplomatic relations in August 1924. The myopic ambassador played up the activities of a few small Marxist organizations in order to show that Mexico was turning into a Bolshevik country. The ambassador also labeled Morones a "Bolshevist" and saw the Soviet legation as the prime agent of communist agitation.[19] He deeply loathed both Calles and Morones, and enjoyed racial stereotyping of a people he considered lazy and backward: "There is very little white blood in the cabinet," Sheffield stated in a letter to the president of Columbia University. "Calles is Armenian and Indian; . . . Saenz [sic] the Foreign Minister is Jew and Indian; Morones more white blood but not the better for it; Amaro, Secretary of War, a pure blooded Indian and very cruel."[20] Or, as he stated more generally,

> The Mexican official with his Latin-Indian inheritance is no mean antagonist in the matching of wits. He is resourceful in argument, a master of sophistry, skilled in deceit and quick to play upon the weakness of others, whether through flattery, corruption or threat. Having moral standards utterly at variance with our own, all sense of obligation . . . rests lightly on his conscience. It is quite useless to continue to appeal . . . to a mind unwilling to admit truth or acknowledge error. . . . It requires extreme patience and much tact to meet the studied indifference and even hostility so constantly exhibited toward the interest of the United States and sometimes even myself.[21]

Although Kellogg did not share Sheffield's exaggerated views, the dispatches did influence him to take a hard-line stance toward the Calles administration. Documents forged by William Randolph Hearst's "Yellow Press" that alleged the existence of a Mexican Red Army fueled anticommunist fervor in the United States, as did boastful comments of a Soviet official to the effect that the establishment of diplomatic relations with Mexico gave the Soviet Union a base in the Americas. Finally, Kellogg likely overestimated the existing rivalry between Obregonistas and Callistas as fissures that could be exploited by a firm U.S. stance.[22]

In response to Kellogg's statement, Calles cast himself as a nationalist defender of Mexican sovereignty. In a public reply, the president declared that the words of the secretary of state amounted to blackmail.[23] In a letter to the *New York World*, he also accused Kellogg of following the dictates of "selfish interests" and defended his "patriotic and humanitarian" program to improve the living conditions of all Mexicans.[24] The attack therefore gave a leader in need of popular support a unique opportunity to assert a nationalist and populist stature. As a result, a general rejection of the Bucareli Agreements turned into specific policy to subject U.S. investors to Mexican sovereignty. Soon thereafter, Morones drafted a regulatory petroleum law that was much more stringent than the versions debated in Congress during the first half of the year. Approved in December 1925, this piece of legislation required foreign oil companies to forgo outright ownership of their wells and apply for confirmatory concessions valid for fifty years.[25] Congress also passed an Alien

Land Law that same month that restricted foreign ownership of land and the subsoil, especially near the coasts and the country's international borders. For the moment, Calles and Morones had translated international difficulties into success in domestic politics. But the crisis had not passed, and it was to gain a much more menacing dimension over the next eighteen months.

Despite Morones's influence, other aspects of Callista policies smacked of classical liberalism. Indeed, a financial reform designed to inspire confidence in the economy, increase tax revenue, and stabilize government finances over the long haul demonstrated the president's commitment to a capitalist economy. The most significant aspect of the reform was the creation of the country's first official bank of issue, the Banco de México, which opened its doors on August 31, 1925. The Banco de México replaced a system in which a select number of large banks printed official bank notes with the authorization of the federal government. With a cash infusion of 55.7 million pesos from the government, this bank guaranteed its notes in gold up to half of their value. Initially, the new bank also served as a commercial institution and competed with the older banks of issue; within six years, however, it had displaced its competitors, and a change in the law had eliminated its commercial transactions to make the Banco de México a central bank similar in some ways to the U.S. Federal Reserve. The creation of the official bank of issue ended the last vestiges of the irresponsible printing of paper money that had marked the first years of the Constitutionalist government.[26]

A second important goal was to address the financial obligations of the government. These obligations consisted of a budget deficit exceeding 40 million dollars, as well as almost 1.6 billion dollars worth of U.S. claims recognized in the de la Huerta-Lamont Agreement. Finance Minister Pani had spent the last year of the Obregón administration tackling the budget deficit, which had reached 59 million dollars under de la Huerta's tenure. In March 1925, Pani introduced the nation's first income tax, a tax ranging from 2 to 8 percent. Taking advantage of the favorable economic climate, the finance secretary accomplished his goal of eliminating the deficit by the end of 1925 despite increased expenditures in the federal budget. At the end of that year, the treasury reported a surplus of 24 million pesos, as compared to a deficit of 100 million pesos during 1922.[27] Pani used the opposite approach on the financially more significant question of the claims of U.S. bankers and bondholders. Blaming his archenemy de la Huerta for negotiating ruinous terms and for heading a rebellion that made the repayment of these claims impossible, he had not made any payment on this debt since December 1923. Payment in full would have severely crimped the nation's economy. Fortunately, in the favorable economic climate of the 1920s, the

International Committee of Bankers proved amenable to compromise, and in September 1925 they began discussions with Pani on the subject of revising the de la Huerta-Lamont Agreement. The resultant Pani Amendment reduced the debt to the still considerable sum of 890 million dollars and stipulated low interest rates for its payment.[28] The bankers had also acquiesced, albeit under protest, in the creation of the Banco de México with gold that could have been used for the repayment of this debt. As the main concession of his government, Pani promised the privatization of the railroads.[29]

Calles also launched a strong effort to professionalize the military—an effort that not only helped put government finances on a solid footing but also promised to increase political stability. As we have seen, the revolutionary military had remained top heavy, with 153 generals in an army of 53,000, or six times as many generals per 10,000 soldiers as in the United States. This surplus of generals had endured through the de la Huerta rebellion, after which Obregón had rewarded his loyalists with the positions vacated by rebel leaders. Some generals among the twenty-one *divisionarios* that remained as the highest-ranking officers in the military saw themselves as future presidential candidates who could come to power either on Obregón's coattails or through a military coup. In addition, the military continued to absorb more than one-third of the federal budget. It fell to the secretary of war, the Zacatecas native Joaquín Amaro, to tackle these problems. Of indigenous background, this *divisionario* was a veteran of the battle against Pancho Villa, and he had distinguished himself during the de la Huerta rebellion. As his most significant asset from the perspective of Obregón and Calles, Amaro did not have a strong home base, and he thus displayed no personal loyalties beyond that to the two remaining chiefs of the Mexican Revolution. He also had strong organizational and administrative talents, and he was not afraid to take tough measures. Amaro imposed a draconian austerity program; for example, he declared a moratorium on all promotions and discharged many lower-ranking officers. By late 1925, Amaro had reduced the army's share of the budget to 25 percent.[30]

In 1926, Amaro sponsored several major legislative initiatives regarding the army. The first of these laws was a new Organic Law that supplanted an old one dating from the Porfiriato. The Organic Law defined the role of the army as the defender of nation, constitution, and public order, and it put in place regular inspections of army units. A few months later, the Law of Promotions ended (at least in theory) the irregular promotions that had made generals out of privates during the decade of fighting and required professional training and active duty for advancement in rank. The Law of Discipline severely penalized corruption in the army, and the Law of Retirement and Pensions set up a reward system and a mandatory retirement age for career officers and troops. As was to be expected, the generals initially scoffed at these laws, seeing them as government rhetoric with which they did not have to comply. And, in fact, many of the provisions of these four laws, and particularly those contained in the Law of Discipline, were unenforceable. After his initial failure to make the laws respected, Amaro resorted to bribery, allowing the *divisionarios* to enrich themselves in exchange for enforcing the new provisions among their own subordinates.[31] If Amaro had therefore decided that the *divisionarios* could only be held at bay by means of co-optation, he zealously realized the more idealistic aspects of his program in a reorganization of the Colegio Militar (Military College). As he hoped, the Colegio Militar would produce an honest and patriotic military leadership to replace the *divisionarios* who had risen through the ranks in the course of the revolution.[32]

Together, financial and military reform set the stage for the improvement of Mexico's infrastructure. The privatization of the railroad led to new investments into the rail network, and in 1927, the completion of the last missing link between the Pacific and central Mexican railroads finally established a land connection between Sonora and Mexico City. With a view to ending challenges to the central government as well as to the purposes of economic development, the Calles government gave an even greater impetus to road building, a project planned by the Obregón administration but scuttled after the outbreak of the de la Huerta rebellion. Shortly after his inauguration, Calles convened several governors in the nation's capital to survey and prioritize all existing plans for road building projects. He publicly announced an ambitious goal to construct 6,100 miles of new roads in Mexico, and in February 1925, he handed over the project to a new National Roadways Commission. By late 1927, the commission reported the completion or work in progress on 610 miles, a rate of progress that made the stated goal of completing the work in seven years sound highly unlikely. Nonetheless, the commission inaugurated work on several important highways, including Mexico City-Acapulco and segments of the Pan-American Highway that ultimately connected Nuevo Laredo on the Texas border with Tapachula on the border with Guatemala. The government paid for road building exclusively with funds generated by new taxes, and particularly a gasoline tax of three centavos per liter.[33]

Calles hoped that these improvements would boost both the export economy and its industrial production, and he recognized the crucial importance of lessening his country's dependence on imported manufactured items. The

Porfiriato had witnessed the beginnings of a modest steel industry in the vicinity of Monterrey. Led by the famous Garza-Sada clan, the Monterrey industrialists produced beer and glassware along with steel, and investors in Mexico City, Puebla, and Veracruz operated textile mills and cigarette factories, among other ventures. After the decade of revolutionary violence interrupted the building of new industries, Obregón and Calles prioritized the revival of a sector of the economy that had the potential of employing thousands of Mexicans and lessening their country's dependence on imports. In particular, Foreign Secretary Sáenz held a personal stake in the matter as an ally and distant relative of the Garza-Sadas.[34] During the period 1917–1924, investors had feared the influence of organized labor and took their capital to other countries, resulting in a process of disinvestment in industry. To offset this trend, Calles invited foreign companies to establish industrial plants in Mexico with the help of tax and other incentives.[35] In 1925, Ford Motor Co. began plans for an assembly plant, and other companies such as Bayer, DuPont, Hoechst, and Palmolive soon followed.[36]

Calles's agricultural policies revealed his desire to increase the productivity of farmers, an objective that required the privileging of commercial over campesino concerns. The president provided small farmers with access to credit guaranteed by the federal government by means of the new Banco Nacional de Crédito Agrícola, or National Farm Credit Bank. The federal government earmarked 18 million pesos for this bank, which made loans to local credit institutions engaged in lending money to farmers for the purchase of seeds and equipment, or for the construction of warehouses, dams, or irrigation systems. Therefore, the infrastructural improvements promoted by the government sought to increase agricultural output. The product of a semiarid state, Calles considered the issue of irrigation particularly important for increasing his country's agricultural potential.[37] During the same February 1925 meeting that produced the National Roadways Commission, Calles and the governors agreed to construct seven hydroelectric dams that provided parched regions with electricity and water. One of these dams provided water to the El Mante sugar company, of which he was one of the principal shareholders. Calles therefore revealed himself to be an agrarian engineer who was primarily concerned with increasing agricultural output.

However, his dependence on caudillos such as San Luis Potosí's Saturnino Cedillo and Veracruz's Adalberto Tejeda, who in turn relied on campesino mobilization, led to a commitment to land reform greater than Calles himself would have liked. Of course, these caudillos were hardly orthodox followers of Agrarista principles. Cedillo supported land reform primarily when it suited his purposes, and above all to benefit himself and his close followers.[38] In four years, the Calles regime distributed 3 million acres of land to over 300,000 campesino families, or twice as much as Obregón. The lion's share of the redistributions occurred in Agrarista hotbeds such as Morelos, San Luis Potosí, and Veracruz. To be sure, much of this land offered little potential for cash-crop agriculture. Moreover, for the most part, the government left intact the large estates that supplied food to urban centers and/or exported commodities. Nor did the Calles government restore much land to indigenous villages: as in Sonora, his vision remained that of the *pequeña propiedad*.[39]

Calles gave much more heartfelt support to rural education, a crucial effort in a country with a literacy rate below 25 percent. As he stated in a speech, "The happiness, the glory, and the greatness of the fatherland depend on the preparation given to [future] generations. Smiling and full of activity, they arise from distinct social circles, and like tender butterflies, they extend their wings over all areas of social life."[40] During Obregón's presidency, Vasconcelos had established approximately one thousand new, federally funded rural schools. Buoyed by higher federal revenues, the Calles government added two thousand additional primary schools.[41] True to Calles's Yori vision, this expansion of state education sought to achieve the assimilation of the indigenous population. The new schools therefore stressed Spanish-language instruction in heavily indigenous areas. Even more importantly, public instruction was designed to transform rebellious campesinos into loyal citizens. Education Secretary José Manuel Puig Casauranc developed Vasconcelos's civics curriculum that emphasized the accomplishments of the Sonoran Triangle as the heirs of the revolution. Thus, despite an official commitment to advertise the nation's cultural diversity, educational policy sought the elimination of indigenous culture by turning "Indians" into Mexicans. As neither teachers nor students could be controlled from Mexico City, however, the results of this nationalist education campaign confounded expectations. Over time, the teachers turned the Education Secretariat, an agency dominated by urban intellectuals loyal to the state, into a seat of socialist thought within the government. As historian Mary Kay Vaughan has demonstrated, rural schools constituted a field of negotiation in which the state, teachers, and campesinos all contended in shaping the daily practice of education.[42]

Finally, the Calles government made a considerable effort to improve health and hygiene. Five decades after the onset of modernization, sanitary conditions remained deplorable throughout Mexico. Untreated water and milk as well as open sewers spread disease, inoculations against contagious diseases were virtually unknown, and most rural areas did not have running water, let alone interior plumbing. To address these problems, Calles created a new cabinet-level agency for public health, the Departamento de Salud Pública (Public Health Department). With a modest budget, the new agency issued the nation's first health and hygiene guidelines, enforced by regular inspections of restaurants, canteens, markets, and butcher shops. Although this effort looked better on paper than in practice, as overworked and poorly paid inspectors willingly accepted bribes from violators, it constituted the first concerted effort to address a serious problem that had claimed millions of lives and retarded economic growth. In addition, the Departamento de Salud Pública launched a major campaign against smallpox, inoculating several million Mexicans against that dangerous disease, and in 1926, a comprehensive decree required the registration of prostitutes. Calles also toyed with the idea of prohibiting the consumption of alcohol—a goal he had announced shortly after his election—but ultimately discarded the plan as unworkable. While all these initiatives contributed to bettering public health and hygiene, they also provided new opportunities for corruption. Moreover, the progressive rhetoric that underlay these decrees could not mask the effort of the state to intrude into the daily lives of countless Mexicans and, above all, women working as market vendors, bakers, and prostitutes.[43]

Repression and Crisis

Just like in Sonora, the Callista program at the national level entailed the repression of the political opposition and elements deemed undesirable or unproductive. For example, the federal government launched an all-out war on the Yaquis. As governor, Calles had not succeeded in dislodging the Yaquis from their redoubt in the Sierra de Bacatete, a mountain range almost impossible to conquer with a land-based attack. Following the stoppage of a train with Obregón on board by a Yaqui contingent, airplanes strafed the Yaqui camps in the mountains and finally bombed them into submission. Similarly, the federal government helped the governors of Baja California and Sonora to expel those states' sizable Chinese populations, an effort that intensified after the onset of economic crisis in the second half of 1926. As a result, by the end of his term as president, Calles was known as *el hombre de hierro*, the man of iron.

To the disappointment of many of their working-class supporters, Calles and Morones also suppressed radical labor movements such as the Confederación de Sociedades Ferrocarrileras (CSF, or Confederation of Railroad Societies). Affiliated with the Industrial Workers of the World, this umbrella organization of the independent railroad workers' unions totaled seventy-five thousand members. Throughout the mid-1920s, anarcho-syndicalists gained influence within the CSF who rightfully considered the CROM an instrument of an essentially capitalist government. The CSF had a strong incentive to remain independent of the CROM, as an agreement between the government and the new private management of the railroad to reduce a surplus in personnel threatened its existence. When the workers protested against the impending layoffs, Calles announced that they were federal employees who did not have the right to strike. Subsequently, the government not only purged four thousand workers from the payroll but also reduced wages by an average of 25 percent. Throughout 1926, the conflict escalated, as the union stopped trains and paralyzed vital shipping routes. When the union declared a nationwide strike in February 1927, an event followed by the payment of a one-time subsidy from the Soviet legation the following month, the government retaliated with soldiers and additional layoffs. Morones, the supposed agent of Moscow, accused the railroad workers of being in the pay of the Soviet government. Finally, in September 1927, the federal arbitration board declared the strike an illegal walkout. Using both force and strikebreakers, Calles and Morones ultimately prevailed, and the CROM gobbled up the independent railroad workers' union.[44]

By far the most significant example of Callista repression was the campaign against the Catholic Church. As governor, Calles had expelled all Catholic priests from Sonora, and he had alienated many of his Constitutionalist allies over the expulsion of a small group of clergy that did not pose a threat to him. Likewise, President Calles's campaign against the Catholic Church drew criticism from among his staunchest supporters with the exception of Morones and a handful of anticlerical regional bosses such as Tabasco's Tomás Garrido Canabal and Veracruz's Tejeda. In states like Jalisco and Puebla, which included more than a thousand parishes, the church could not be shoved aside as easily as in Sonora. For most Mexicans, Catholicism was not just "high religion," the teachings of a religious corporation that gave them hope for redemption in the afterlife; it was also a popular religion, a means of cultural expression of the subaltern. Through open-air processions and other popular celebrations such as Carnival, Holy Week, and the Day of the Dead, Mexicans gave expression to their own way of life. Catholicism was therefore a field of negotiation in which citizens contested culture and power, and when Calles attacked the church, he challenged a lifestyle. Infatuated with progress and the force of reason, the president set out to weaken both official and popular religion and, in doing so, prompted widespread opposition to his government.

For Calles, the conflict with the church was a personal quest; one that dated back to his childhood. As he once related, "When I was an altar boy . . . I stole alms in order to buy candy."[45] Indeed, many observers who interacted with the president during his conflict with the church point to the deep-seated and even irrational nature of his opposition to organized Catholicism. Calles's hatred of the church ran so deep that it defied structuralist explanations of his behavior, confounding historical analyses to the present day. A comparative framework that places Calles's behavior in the context of other "statists" around the world, whether of the populist, fascist, or communist variety, cannot account for his single-minded determination to weaken the church, although it does explain his desire to centralize education under the tutelage of the state. Nor can we understand the full extent of his anticlericalism with reference to his efforts to sponsor the emergence of a national bourgeoisie loyal to his government, or even as an essential part of his reform program. The historian must therefore conceive of Calles's attitude toward the church as behavior that can only be fully appreciated in the idiosyncratic context of his own personal life. Scholars have hypothesized that Calles's early years served as catalysts for his opposition to the church. In particular, his origins as illegitimate child, physical abuse by his adoptive father, his positivist schooling in Hermosillo, and the association between Catholicism and Yaqui resistance all offer possible explanations for Calles's virulent opposition to the Catholic Church.[46]

In addition, Calles saw himself as an heir to Juárez and other nineteenth-century Liberals who had waged a long, bloody, and only partially successful struggle to separate church and state. The Liberals had long attempted to put an end to the wealth and extralegal privileges, or *fueros,* of the church. The Bourbon Reforms of the late eighteenth century had already included an attack on the *fueros,* which exempted the clergy from secular courts. After independence, the church still enjoyed considerable economic power as the owner of almost half of the arable land in Mexico. Not surprisingly, the constitution of 1857 outlawed church ownership of land and mandated civil marriages and secular education.[47] After the Porfirians struck a deal with the church that included official neglect of most of the anticlerical articles in this constitution, the revolutionary Constitution of 1917 had reaffirmed these Liberal tenets. Under Articles 3 and 130, the church could not own any land, nor could its priests teach children or run for political office. The articles also outlawed outdoor religious ceremonies, as well as those directed by foreign-born priests.

Anticlericalism therefore formed part of the Callista struggle with the Old Mexico: the attempt by secular, middle-class nationalists influenced by Anglo-Saxon, Protestant ideas to impose their vision on the Catholic campesinos of the center and south. Of course, implementation of these provisions was another matter. Personally opposed to anticlericalism despite the leanings of several of his governors such as Alvarado, Calles, and Diéguez, Carranza had opposed a regulatory law that would have put the constitutional provisions into practice. Although Obregón had supported the inclusion of Articles 3 and 130 in the constitution, he remained a pragmatist mindful of the need to cultivate Catholic supporters such as Cedillo and Vasconcelos. This policy of toleration continued until January 11, 1923, when the Apostolic Delegate consecrated a shrine to Christ the King on Cubilete Mountain in the state of Guanajuato. Obregón considered this open-air celebration on a mountain generally regarded as the geographic center of Mexico a public challenge of his government, and he expelled the Apostolic Delegate from the country with seventy-two hours' notice. Later that year, the de la Huerta rebellion exacerbated this conflict when insurgent commander Guadalupe Sánchez drew on Catholic support in Veracruz.[48] Catholic opposition to the revolution therefore factored into Calles's position as well. In particular, Calles and his supporters feared the possibility that the church might harbor a movement to overthrow the government.[49] Indeed, a Catholic resistance movement was well organized in many areas of Mexico, and especially in the central states of Guanajuato, Jalisco, and Michoacán.

Calles brought the conflict between church and state to a new high. During his presidential campaign, he had announced his opposition to the Catholic Church, an opposition that he contrasted with a tolerant attitude toward religion in general.

> My enemies say that I am an enemy of the religions and cults, and that I do not respect religious beliefs. I . . . understand and approve all religious beliefs because I consider them beneficial for the moral program they encompass. I am an enemy of the caste of priests that sees in its position a privilege rather than an evangelical mission. I am the enemy of the political priest, the scheming priest, the priest as exploiter, the priest who intends to keep our people in ignorance, the priest who allies with the hacendado to exploit the campesino, and the priest allied with the industrialist to exploit the worker.[50]

Calles therefore justified his anticlericalism as part of a populist agenda to redeem his country's oppressed masses. As he believed, the poor majority needed immediate help in *this* life rather than the promise of a place in heaven in the afterlife. Indeed, the church had done all it could to derail revolutionary reforms. From exile in San Antonio, Texas, Archbishop José Mora y del Río had stated his opposition to the new constitution immediately after its promulgation in 1917. Calles also noted that his social agenda applied Jesus Christ's teachings to society, while the church desired to maintain the majority of Mexicans in ignorance and poverty. In addition, anticlericalism was an important vehicle of creating a national bourgeoisie loyal to the new leadership rather than to local allegiances or to the global reach of the papacy. His opposition to the church focused on organized Catholicism, and Calles was supportive of Protestant missionaries as well as efforts to form a national Mexican Catholic Church that would break away from the Vatican just as the Church of England had done in the late 1500s. Among the members of the national government, Secretary of Foreign Relations Aarón Sáenz was a Protestant.[51]

Indeed, one of Calles's early efforts as president was to help the founding of a schismatic church. On February 22, 1925, a group of CROM members that included the secretary general entered the Iglesia Soledad de Santa Cruz in eastern Mexico City and drove out the priests in that church under the threat of violence. After the priests had departed, a former Catholic clergyman, Joaquín Pérez Burdar, installed himself in the church as patriarch of the "Mexican Apostolic Church," accompanied by Manuel Monge, a Spanishborn priest. The following Monday, Monge attempted to celebrate the Eucharist in this church, but his service was interrupted by a riot that included more than one thousand protesters. When Pérez appealed to the government to guarantee the freedom of his church to practice its faith, Gobernación Secretary Valenzuela censured him for his forcible takeover of government property entrusted to the Catholic Church. However, Valenzuela encouraged the patriarch to seek through legal means what he had obtained by force. Strikingly, the secretary made no reference to the fact that the constitution forbade the foreigner Monge from administering religious services. A few days later, Calles ordered both churches out of Soledad, and he awarded to Pérez the small, unoccupied Corpus Christi church in downtown Mexico City. Rather than remaining above the fray, the president had taken sides in favor of a schismatic church.[52] Although only five or six parishes declared their adherence to Pérez, this incident had widespread repercussions. Government support for the schismatic church, however disguised, incensed Catholics who rallied around the parishioners of La Soledad who had fought to protect their priest and faith.[53] It prompted Obregón to send Calles a strongly worded missive from Sonora that warned him of supporting a movement that could only divide the ruling coalition and undermine the work of the revolutionary government.[54]

Open conflict erupted early in the following year. On January 27, 1926, a number of bishops strongly denounced the anticlerical policies of the government. One week later, a reporter for the newspaper *El Universal* asked Mora y del Río to state his position regarding the constitution on the occasion of an article commemorating the ninth anniversary of that document. The archbishop referred the reporter to his 1917 statements that were highly critical of the constitution. The reporter printed the archbishop's old diatribe without explaining the fact that his quotes were nine years old. As Mora y del Río had criticized specific provisions of the constitution, the government interpreted these quotes as an open challenge to the revolutionary state, and the archbishop did not ask *El Universal* to publish an explanation of the source of the quotes. After a few days had passed without further comment from the archbishop, the new Gobernación Secretary Tejeda declared the statement an act of rebellion.[55]

Calles seized this opportunity for cracking down on the Catholic Church. He called upon Congress to grant him extraordinary powers to suppress worship illegal under the constitution, as well as the passage of regulatory laws to implement Articles 3 and 130 of the constitution. In response, the church organized the Liga Nacional de la Defensa de la Libertad Religiosa (National League for the Defense of Religious Liberty, hereafter Liga). Regardless of Liga protests, what would be known as the Calles Law reformed the penal code to include teaching activities by priests and religious services (such as outdoor ceremonies) forbidden by the constitution. The law also required the registration of all priests with the government. By the time of the publication of the Calles Law on July 2, 1926, the president and Tejeda had ordered the closure of all monasteries and convents, the government seizure of numerous church buildings, and the expulsion of more than two hundred foreign nuns and priests. The Liga immediately mounted a fierce counterattack, declaring an economic boycott on the government and enjoining parishioners to refrain from paying taxes. The bishops issued a pastoral letter threatening to suspend masses beginning July 31, 1926, the effective date of the new law.[56] At first glance, nothing could have pleased Calles more than this prospect. As he boasted to a French diplomat, "Each week without religious ceremonies will cost the Catholic religion 2 percent of its faithful."[57]

Upon further reflection, however, Calles understood that the church strike could lead to a widespread popular rebellion. Yielding to pressure by Obregón, Calles therefore agreed to meet with representatives of the clergy. On August 21, 1926, he held talks with the bishop of Michoacán, Leopoldo Ruiz y Flores, and the bishop of Tabasco, Pascual Díaz, who was also secretary general of the Mexican episcopate. Ruiz and Díaz approached the president with a conciliatory tone, hoping for a face-saving compromise. Although Calles refused to amend the provisions requiring the registration of priests and capping their number at one for each ten thousand Mexicans, he offered the priests the opportunity to seek remedy in Congress. He also promised them that his government would use the data obtained through the registration of priests for statistical purposes only.[58] Only two days later, another El Universal article, which quoted Calles as stating that he had not come to an agreement with the church, shattered this fragile understanding. The bishops, who had been on the verge of announcing the suspension of the strike, voted to continue their stance toward the Calles Law.[59]

A few weeks later, devout Catholics of western and central Mexico rose in arms to the shouts of "¡Viva Cristo Rey!" or "Long live Christ the King!" Thus began the second major revolt on the watch of the Sonorans, a revolt that would come to be known as the Cristero rebellion. Within months, the rebellion included twenty-five thousand mostly campesino troops in the states of Colima, Jalisco, and Michoacán. Ably commanded by the Porfirian general Enrique Gorostieta, it eventually grew to fifty thousand soldiers, or a force almost as large as the federal army. The Cristero rebellion was further proof of the strength of grassroots politics: the campesinos defended their church and their priest as a way of fighting for their way of life. In the process, they destroyed many of the new public schools established during the past five years—schools that imparted a rationalist curriculum hostile to the church.[60] The war dragged on for three years and wreaked more havoc on the war-torn society. It created martyrs for the Cristero cause such as Father Miguel Pro Juárez, executed without due process for his alleged role in an attempt on Obregón's life. The conflict not only claimed the lives of more than seventy thousand people, but the fighting in the Bajío also led to the devastation of this grain-producing area. As a result, the country's production of cereals plummeted by almost 40 percent between 1926 and 1929.[61]

The Cristero rebellion contributed to the premature end of Calles's reform project. Combined with declining fiscal revenues and a serious crisis in U.S.-Mexican relations, it imposed daunting obstacles to the Callista dream of a secular, nationalist society managed by a new entrepreneurial class of landowners and industrialists. In the process, the authoritarian aspects of Callista rule prevailed over the reform drive and contributed to a legacy that would make Mexicans remember the repressive man of iron rather than the auspicious beginning of his presidency.

The second half of the Calles presidency witnessed the beginnings of a serious economic slowdown three years before the onset of the Great Depression. National product and income, which had increased 14 percent during Calles's first two years in office, declined 4 percent over the next three years. Government receipts, which had reached a high of 322 million pesos in 1925, dropped to 300 million pesos three years later, forcing the Calles government to reduce expenditures from 325 million pesos in 1926 to just 288 million pesos in 1928.[62] By late 1927, the Calles government faced a massive fiscal crisis, as it could not finance expenditures bloated by its ambitious infrastructural and education projects. New Finance Secretary Luis Montes de Oca responded to this crisis by slashing government spending. Following the precepts of classical liberal economics, this move brought the books closer to balance but aggravated the economic downturn. Further exacerbating the problem, Montes de Oca attempted to counteract the slide of the peso by reducing the money supply. When combined with the effects of the Great Depression, the overall impact of this slowdown ultimately proved staggering: between 1926 and 1932, per capita gross domestic product (GDP) fell 30.9 percent.[63]

What had happened to the boom of the early Calles years? Along with a decline of commodity prices, and particularly that of silver, capital flight and the dislocations wrought by the Cristero rebellion constituted the most important factors in the early onset of economic crisis. The disinvestment in the oil industry of the early 1920s had been an early harbinger of the effect of populist policies on foreign capital. Regardless of the capitalist orientation of the Mexican government and the CROM leadership, the oilmen shunned Mexico for fear of government regulation of their industry and the close association between Calles and organized labor. In the absence of new exploration, oil production dropped from 140 million barrels in 1924 to 50 million barrels in 1928. As a result, export revenue dropped from 192.6 million dollars in 1925 to 172.1 million dollars in 1928.[64]

Both the Cristero rebellion and the economic crisis formed the backdrop to a high-stakes conflict with the U.S. government. The reform period had witnessed a confrontation with Ambassador Sheffield and Secretary of State Kellogg. In this conflict, Calles and Morones confidently sought to renegotiate the privileges of foreign investors. As this conflict dragged on throughout 1926 and the first half of 1927, the degree to which he needed to tend to the Cristero rebellion and economic matters increasingly shaped Calles's approach to the United States. Therefore, an assertive and independent posture gave way to more conciliatory policies as the resources of the government to support such a posture declined.

Throughout 1926, the controversy with the Coolidge administration drew ever wider circles. Taken by itself, the oil controversy would not have resulted in a significant spat. Petroleum output continued to decline steadily throughout this period, and no one in Washington held the illusion that Calles could be pressured into liberal concessions. But the Coolidge administration feared that Calles would use the precedent to seize other U.S.-owned properties. Equally importantly, a Catholic lobby led by the Knights of Columbus pushed for the withdrawal of U.S. diplomatic recognition and other measures designed to force Calles to back off his attacks on the church.

In August 1926, Mexican involvement in a civil war in Nicaragua stoked the controversy. From 1912 to 1925, the U.S. government had stationed Marines in Nicaragua in order to maintain in power a pro-U.S. regime headed by the Conservative Party. In August 1925, Coolidge withdrew the Marines a year after elections had produced a coalition government that appeared to guarantee political stability. To expand its power base in anticipation of the U.S. withdrawal, this new government permitted the organizing of the small urban workforce with the help of the AFL and the CROM.[65] Shortly after the departure of the Marines, the loser of the elections, former president Emiliano Chamorro, launched a revolt.[66] In November 1925, he forced Vice President Juan B. Sacasa, the leader of the Liberal contingent within the former coalition government, into exile; and two months later, a pliant Nicaraguan Congress installed Chamorro in the presidency. Recalling the fact that Chamorro was a staunch U.S. ally who shared responsibility in a long military occupation, Foreign Secretary Sáenz recalled the Mexican minister. Sáenz and Calles offered assistance to Sacasa, and beginning in August 1926, Mexican weapons shipments bolstered a Liberal uprising that soon controlled most of Nicaragua. The two leaders had miscalculated, however, as Kellogg considered Sacasa unacceptable in light of the assistance he received from Calles. Ultimately, the Coolidge administration decided to support a compromise candidate from the Conservative Party, former president Adolfo Díaz. On December 24, 1926, U.S. Marines returned to Nicaragua to prevent further Mexican assistance to Sacasa.[67]

Kellogg took advantage of the Nicaragua imbroglio to launch another offensive against the Calles government. In December 1926, he leaked information to the press that alleged Soviet support for Mexican influence in Nicaragua.[68] The press also played up the impending arrival of the new Soviet minister Alexandra Kollontai—the first woman ever in the diplomatic corps in Mexico City—as evidence of a Soviet offensive. This allegation could not have been more misplaced. Slandered for her reputedly loose morals and ridiculed for her risqué wardrobe, Kollontai appeared an easy target in a male-dominated political culture, and she lasted just seven months.[69] A month after her arrival, Kellogg stepped up the pressure on Calles. In a meeting with the Senate Foreign Relations Committee, Kellogg accused Calles of spreading Bolshevism to Latin America and asserted that the State Department would not tolerate an export of radical ideologies. The statement linked Mexican support for Sacasa and the pending oil question as evidence of a Bolshevik plot against U.S. interests.[70]

This attempt to portray the Calles government as Bolshevik sought to shore up domestic support for Kellogg's aggressive stance. At that time, the State Department confronted Republicans who advocated a more conciliatory approach, such as Commerce Secretary Herbert Hoover, as well as progressive Midwestern senators, such as William Borah and Burton Wheeler. Press opinion was sharply divided: while the Hearst press and Catholic newspapers supported the Secretary of State, many of the mainstream publications were highly critical of his Mexico policy. Thus, Kellogg saw his charge that Mexico exported "Bolshevism" to Nicaragua as the best way to convince a recalcitrant U.S. Congress and public that he needed to take action.[71]

Calles realized the significance of congressional and public opinion in the United States as much as Kellogg did. He launched a concerted campaign to portray the actions of his government as acts of self-defense against a coalition of avaricious oil interests and interventionist politicians. This campaign was directed by none other than his half-brother Arturo M. Elías, the Mexican consul in New York City. In particular, Calles and Elías could count on the assistance of "Carlos" (Carleton Beals) and "Ernesto" (Ernest Gruening). Self-proclaimed socialists, these two intellectuals provided a staunch defense of the Calles administration on all three fronts: the oil question, the religious conflict, and the civil war in Nicaragua. After Kellogg's statement, Calles stepped up his own rhetoric. In response to the charges of Bolshevism, he declared that Mexico had "no use for such exotic doctrines."[72] He denied that Mexico had provided military assistance to the Sacasa faction but asserted that in any event, his country had the same right to support a friendly government as the United States.[73]

To resolve the diplomatic crisis, Calles therefore took advantage of his ties to foreign-born progressives. As historian Mauricio Tenorio has put it, Mexico had entered its "cosmopolitan summer:" a period of thirty years in which leftist foreign visitors came to visit the revolution up close.[74] A cohort that included journalists Beals and Gruening along with historian Frank Tannenbaum, novelists Katherine Anne Porter and B. Traven, and others, many of these foreign visitors became effective propagandists for the revolutionary state. Gruening was particularly partial to Calles, and he remained his most steadfast defender long after his death.[75] Likewise, the German-U.S. novelist B. Traven expressed a favorable opinion in his only nonfiction work, *Land des Frühlings* (Land of Spring): "Neither . . . Obregón nor . . . Calles are socialists the way the term is understood in Europe. . . . The people elected by the workers, however, . . . keep the promises they made to the workers before the elections. In many cases, and, I want to say, in most cases, they even exceed these promises once they are in office."[76]

Despite the efforts of his friends, however, Calles saw U.S.-Mexican relations sink to a low point after Kellogg's statements in the U.S. Senate of January 1927, leading to widespread speculation about a U.S. invasion. In particular, Calles worried that U.S. troops would attempt to seize the disputed
oil fields, which lay close to the Gulf Coast.[77] Most historians have long dismissed the likelihood of such an invasion. After a review of State Department correspondence, for example, historian James Horn concluded that
neither Coolidge nor Kellogg planned a military intervention.[78] However,
new documentation available in the Calles archive shows that the Calles administration was in possession of U.S. confidential documents that raised le-
gitimate fear of a war with the United States regardless of Kellogg's intentions. The source of these apprehensions was a spy in the U.S. embassy, an
alcoholic who went by the code name 10-B. Beginning in the late 1910s, this
unique agent purloined sensitive documents of the military attaché for pe-
rusal by Mexican government officials. By 1926, this correspondence revealed that the U.S. War Department had drawn up a number of invasion
plans. Although these plans were contingency operations, they greatly
alarmed Calles, who instructed his military commander in the Gulf region,
General Lázaro Cárdenas, to set fire to the oil fields in case of a U.S. invasion so that the flames could be seen as far away as New Orleans. Calles and
his aides also learned of U.S. plans to suspend the Neutrality Laws, which
forbade the export of weapons and ammunition to Mexican opposition
groups, and the documents revealed a number of plots against the Calles administration, including one hatched by a commander in the de la Huerta rebellion.[79] According to one source, Calles threatened Coolidge with the publication of these documents in case he did not employ a more conciliatory
approach.[80]

By the summer of 1927, both sides neared exhaustion. Kellogg found himself the subject of intense criticism and even ridicule in the Senate. Incensed
about the leak at the U.S. embassy, Kellogg at last recalled Sheffield and replaced him with Dwight Morrow, a career diplomat sent to his new assign-
ment with Coolidge's admonition to keep the United States out of war with
Mexico. For his part, Calles had begun to feel the twin impact of recession
and the Cristero rebellion. He had abandoned his support of the Nicaraguan
Liberals, and he was ready for a face-saving compromise on both the religious
and oil fronts. He allowed Morrow to play a part in the mediation of the
church-state conflict, and he influenced a Supreme Court judgment favorable to the oil companies in December 1927. Although the Calles, Petroleum, and Alien Land Laws all remained on the books, the court conceded a
grandfather clause to existing interests that placated Coolidge and Kellogg.[81]

Calles had arrived at the nadir of his presidency. The Cristero rebellion, the slumping economy, and the conflict with the Coolidge administration annihilated many of the gains made in the first two years of his rule.

These were turbulent months in Calles's family life as well. Plutarco, Natalia, and their unmarried children lived near the presidential residence in Chapultepec Castle, which sits on an imposing hill in western Mexico City surrounded by the park of the same name. The family did not find the castle suitable as a residence, as its architectural layout allowed little privacy. Instead, they moved into a smaller home a short distance from the castle.[82] Surrounded by legions of servants, the family lived in a degree of luxury that sharply contrasted with their modest abodes in Hermosillo and Santa Rosa in the early 1900s. On June 2, 1927, however, Natalia died unexpectedly of pulmonary embolism following gall bladder surgery in Los Angeles. As was both her and her husband's wish, she did not receive last rites.[83] Not surprisingly, the latter half of 1927 saw Calles more somber and melancholy than ever, and indeed, familial tragedy may have contributed to the president's retrenchment from two years of reform. Yet just as Calles went through one of the darkest periods of his life in the months following Natalia's death, the demands of the presidency—and in particular, the question of his own succession—soon reclaimed him for his difficult job for one final year.

The Return of the Caudillo

In hindsight, it might appear that Obregón's return to the presidency was inevitable from the outset. The caudillo had backed Calles's candidacy in 1924 expecting to regain power four years later. Although Morones and high-ranking generals such as Arnulfo Gómez and Francisco R. Serrano had presidential designs of their own, many observers believed that Calles was prepared to fulfill his commitment to Obregón at whatever price, hoping that his reward would be another term in 1934. As early as December 1924, one cartoon published in a Mexico City newspaper captured this image of Obregón's dominant role. In the cartoon, Obregón departs the capital by train, leaving a bawling Calles with somewhat feminine features behind. The caption announces, "Don't cry, Plutarco, I will be back within four years."[84]

A closer look at Calles's role in the selection of his successor, however, reveals a more complex story. Indeed, Gómez, Morones, and Serrano all had reason to hope for Calles's backing until the summer of 1927. Unlike Obregón, his three contenders were close to the center of power, and they represented a combination that Calles could not ignore. In addition, many

The Elías Calles-Chacón family in 1926
Standing, from left: Artemisa Elías Calles Chacón, Alicia Elías Calles Chacón, Plutarco Elías Calles Chacón, Natalia Elías Calles Chacón, Fernando Torreblanca Contreras, Rodolfo Elías Calles Chacón, Ernestina Elías Calles Chacón, and Alfredo Elías Calles Chacón
Sitting, from left: Hortensia Elías Calles de Torreblanca (with daughter Norma), Natalia Chacón de Elías Calles, Plutarco Elías Calles, Elisa Sáenz de Elías Calles (with daughter Alicia), Emilia Lacy de Elías Calles (with daughter Natalia), and Gustavo Elías Calles Chacón
Source: FAPEC.

Obregonistas were uncomfortable with the idea of violating the principle of no reelection, the single most cherished tenet of the revolution of 1910. In the words of a former congressional deputy, "On the one hand, we were personal friends of [Obregón's]; but on the other hand, we did not think he could legally be elected to the presidency again."[85] As a result, new evidence confirms historian Jean Meyer's hypothesis that Obregón became the inevitable candidate only after he shrewdly took advantage of the difficulties of the Calles regime in its last years.[86]

During the first eighteen months of the Calles presidency, Obregón exerted only limited influence in national politics. Although he had his loyalists well positioned, other revolutionary politicians—and particularly Morones—more than offset this influence. The CROM moved into the position of a virtual partner in government, financial and fiscal reform pleased native capitalists, land distribution kept the agraristas reasonably happy, and the petroleum conflict earned both Calles and Morones the support of middle-class nationalists. In this context, Obregón limited himself to giving advice, as when he counseled Calles to desist from backing the schismatic church. As Calles's subsequent actions in the church-state conflict show, the president heeded not Obregón but Morones and anticlerical governors such as Garrido, whose persecution of the church in Tabasco later induced the Catholic novelist Graham Greene to pen one of the most famous novels of the revolution, *The Power and the Glory*.[87] Likewise, Calles engineered a much more assertive policy toward the United States than what Obregón would have advised. Finally, and most importantly for the succession issue, Obregón loyalists initially failed in their efforts to reform Article 83 of the Constitution, an article that forbade individuals who had served as president to occupy this post again for any reason and under any circumstance. Obregón enjoyed much more success in regional politics; his status as the foremost landowner of southern Sonora not only influenced the nationalization of the Richardson land development company in 1926 but also the campaign against the Yaquis the following year.[88]

As a result, Obregón initially put his plans for reelection on the back burner and publicly announced that he would not be a candidate in the elections slated for July 1928.[89] During the first sixteen months of the Calles presidency, he did not visit Mexico City even once, electing instead to influence the political scene by means of letters and a never-ending procession of his supporters to his home in Cajeme. These visits informed the caudillo of the strength of his opponents, as manifested in the failure of the constitutional amendment. According to one striking document, Obregón endeavored to outmaneuver rather than confront his opponents. Preserved as a copy in Calles's personal archive, the document witnesses a provisional agreement between Obregón and a Morones agent in February 1926. Through this pact, both presidential hopefuls agreed to forsake a presidential bid in 1928 in favor of General Serrano, a former Obregón protégé who had served as the caudillo's chief of staff during his campaign against the Conventionists.[90] If this striking document, knowledge of which reached Calles through the leak in the U.S. embassy, is not apocryphal, the most likely interpretation is that Obregón might have desired to block the ambitions of Morones, the man he considered the gravest threat to his ambitions. Aware of the fact that his influence in the military would facilitate a return to power in spite of this pact, Obregón knew that his primary objective was the elimination of a rival who was then at the peak of his popularity and, unlike Obregón, eligible to serve as president. At the time, the caudillo considered Serrano a far lesser threat.[91]

Early in Calles's presidency, Obregonismo thus became identified with opposition to Calles (and, of course, Morones) even as the two Sonorans maintained amicable relations. The best example of this dynamic was the attitude of Jalisco governor Zuno, who used his affiliation with Obregón as a strategy to defend the autonomy of his state. As the above-mentioned episode relating to Calles's inauguration attests, Zuno and Calles disliked each other, and Zuno particularly resented the effort of the CROM to incorporate the labor unions of his state. As a result, he formed a coalition of parties that controlled the governorship of Jalisco during the rest of the 1920s, as well as an independent umbrella organization of labor unions that competed with the CROM. Zuno's challenge to Calles and Morones did not go unanswered; in March 1926, the federal Congress began proceedings designed to strip him of his gubernatorial post. To keep his camarilla in power, the governor resigned from his post and allowed one of his supporters to take his place. Until August 1929, the Zuno faction governed Jalisco, opposing Calles on matters ranging from the religious conflict to infrastructure projects. Other Obregonistas such as Soto y Gama and Cedillo opposed Morones for the continuous efforts of the CROM to speak for campesinos under the guise of defending the interests of the proletariat.[92]

Until the summer of 1926, Calles played a passive role in the succession question, awaiting a political shift that would force his hand. Although he had apparently promised his support to Obregón prior to his candidacy, he remained mindful of the political strength of Morones. His attitude in the succession question therefore was one of expediency rather than principle. Like Morones and Obregón, the president had no compunction about supporting whomever best suited his interests.[93] The three most powerful men all understood the Machiavellian character of political alliances in revolutionary Mexico, and all of them had shown on more than one occasion that self-interest overrode loyalty and even friendship. Following the political tide, Calles therefore initially sympathized with a Morones candidacy. In 1925, the failure of the constitutional amendments in Congress and the resignation of the Obregonista Valenzuela gave the appearance that the president favored Morones. As late as January 1927, the Obregonista Pani alluded to the existence of a strong Moronista camarilla in the national government.[94] Over time, however, Morones appears to have tallied the significant opposition to his candidacy. In the end, he never made himself an official candidate.

Beginning in the spring of 1926, the Obregón campaign thus gathered steam. The caudillo himself took an increasingly active role in events in Mexico City, visiting the capital several times in an effort to sway legislators to amend the constitution. To the measure that Morones's rise to power engendered criticism, Obregón's arguments began to carry the day in the legislature. On November 19, 1926, Congress passed laws allowing nonconsecutive reelection and lengthening the presidential term from four to six years.[95] The key to congressional approval was the attitude of PNA leader Soto y Gama, who stated that "political means are simple means: if they are useful to us, we accept them, and if they are not, we reject them . . . when reelection helps us by bringing to power a man who has demonstrated that he is an Agrarista, we [favor it]."[96]

Recognizing these trends, Calles gravitated toward Obregón. Although the president never openly supported the campaign of his predecessor, he knew that the deepening crisis of his government made him increasingly dependent on the caudillo. In particular, the Cristero rebellion required Calles to rely once again on the Obregonista military. The escalation of the conflict with the United States also played into Obregón's hands, as the war scare with the United States called upon the help of the army rather than that of the CROM. Governors such as Garrido, one of Calles's principal allies in the conflict with the church, pushed Calles to endorse Obregón. It is therefore impossible to separate Obregón's ascendancy from the crisis that befell the Calles administration. Indeed, the difficult historical moment aided Obregón's ambitions, and the caudillo used the crises in order to further his own goals. He repeatedly offered his services as a mediator in the church-state conflict. Likewise, the war of extermination against the Yaquis not only augmented Obregón's landholdings in southern Sonora, but it also served as an opportunity to demonstrate his value to the government.[97]

As Calles threw his weight behind Obregón, the presidential contest turned into a quite unequal race among three *norteño* generals. Generals

Gómez and Serrano were two of the most influential military commanders and subordinates of Calles and Obregón, respectively. Of the two, Gómez, a native of Navojoa, Sonora, was by far the superior politician. On June 23, 1927, a new party, the Partido Antireeleccionista, the name of which recalled Madero's opposition movement in the waning days of the Porfiriato, chose Gómez as its candidate in the presidential elections. A short while later, a newly formed Partido Nacional Revolucionario (not to be confused with the Callista creation of 1929) anointed the Sinaloa native Serrano, a childhood friend of Obregón's. Serrano's primary vehicle of political mobility had been his loyalty to Obregón, and he enjoyed an unsavory reputation for his nighttime escapades with women and alcohol.[98] Two days later, Obregón formally launched his presidency, mocking the divided opposition for its inability to set aside personal ambitions to launch a unified candidate. He also portrayed Gómez and Serrano as reactionaries bent on destroying the social achievements of the revolutionary government.[99] This dare produced predictable effects; on July 1, 1927, the two rival generals agreed to campaign jointly for Obregón's defeat, albeit without giving up their individual presidential bids. For its part, Morones's PLM meekly supported Obregón even though the caudillo implicitly criticized the party by announcing that "very little has been done among the urban working elements because the whole of our legislation on that subject has a political rather than a social character."[100]

Although the Antireeleccionistas could not triumph against Obregón's political machine, Gómez and Serrano's presidential bids amounted to direct challenges of a political system that sought to predetermine the outcome of presidential elections. As the last dispute among the Sonoran leaders had ended in the devastating de la Huerta rebellion of 1923, Calles and Obregón were determined to quash such challenges at whatever cost, including the lives of their former protégés. On October 1, 1927, Calles seized upon a weak pretext to order the arrest of Serrano and that of his closest associates. Two days later, government troops mowed down Serrano and a dozen supporters in Huitzilac, Morelos. It was the most visible instance of a nationwide crackdown on Obregón opponents, and a U.S. intelligence report estimated the total casualties at no fewer than five hundred.[101] One month later, a firing squad executed Gómez in Coatepec, Veracruz.

The deaths of Serrano, Gómez, and other high-ranking military leaders had a chilling effect. The bloodshed further reduced the number of generals capable of overthrowing the national government, and the failure of the Antireeleccionistas therefore marked another step in the road toward political centralization. Yet the Serrano-Gómez movement, which wrapped itself in the cause for which Madero had lost his life, also manifested the enduring opposition to Obregón and Calles.[102] Obregón approached the presidential campaign fully identified with repression, and he and Calles had the blood of their opponents on their hands. The massacre elicited outrage throughout Mexico, and rumors of assassination attempts against Obregón and Calles abounded. In May 1928, bombs exploded in the Chamber of Deputies and at Obregón's campaign headquarters.[103]

Nonetheless, the deaths of Serrano and Gómez precluded an effective challenge to Obregón, the only remaining candidate in the 1928 elections. In the first half of that year, he toured the country to rally supporters around his candidacy. In March, he visited the Bajío, the heartland of the Cristeros, and urged the insurgents to exercise patience until he returned to the presidency. Obregón cast himself as someone called back into service to the nation by popular demand. In his campaign speeches, he took pains to portray his candidacy as a continuation of the past eight years. "No more promises," he exclaimed in Orizaba, Veracruz, in April 1928. "The nation already knows our [Calles's and Obregón's] points of view."[104] In early July, Obregón was elected to a second term. Calles anticipated with great relief the transfer of power, which was to take place December 1, 1928. Little did he know that his greatest challenge as a political leader still lay ahead.

Posterity judges political leaders more often by the way they conclude their terms than by their first few years in power. Calles is no exception to this trend, as his detractors recall the Cristeros, the bloody suppression of the railroad strike, and the bodies of Father Pro, Gómez, and Serrano rather than the creation of the Banco de México, his early stand on oil, and his ambitious project to bring education and infrastructure to rural areas. Criticized by Catholics for his persecution of the church, by democrats for his authoritarian leadership style and his repressive methods, and by socialists for making labor into a pliant instrument of the state, *el señor presidente* Calles does not enjoy the historiographical cachet of revolutionary icons such as Madero, Zapata, and Villa, or fellow Latin American populists such as Brazil's Getúlio Vargas or Argentina's Juan and Evita Perón.

This discussion has suggested that the Calles presidency consisted of populist (1924–1926) and repressive (1926–1928) phases that belie the generalizations that mark most scholarship on Calles. In the words of historian Alan Knight, a populist has a "limited shelf life; and, over time, tends either to lose momentum or fail, or, in a few cases, to undergo 'routinization,' whereby the initial populist surge is eventually diverted into more durable, institutional . . . channels."[105] In Calles's case, the loss of momentum came with the multiple crises of 1926–1927, when his government overextended itself and made the ill-advised decision to confront the Catholic Church at the worst possible moment.

In addition, the Calles presidency was a product of its own historical context. Calles centralized political power and suppressed dissent at a time when fourteen years of revolution and civil war made political stability a paramount objective in the minds of many Mexicans. His methods resembled those of other populists, leaders who believed in the guiding role of the state in education, economic development, and social reform. Although Calles could not remake Mexico in the image of the United States or Germany, he was the first revolutionary president to carry out a concerted reform program designed to maximize the country's agricultural and industrial production, to put Mexicans on an equal legal footing with foreign residents, and to attempt to promote patriotic sentiments that would unify the nation. If he represents the ruthless character of the revolutionary leadership, Calles also deserves credit for promoting the institutionalization of the revolution, a process that ultimately reined in the generals in favor of a civilian bureaucracy.

CHAPTER SIX

Jefe Máximo of the Revolution

> I could be well mov'd, if I were as you
> If I could pray to move, prayers would move me
> But I am constant as the northern star
> Of whose true-fix'd and resting quality
> There is no fellow in the firmament.
> The skies are painted with unnumb'red sparks
> They are all fire and everyone doth shine
> But there's but one in all doth hold his place
>
> —Shakespeare, *The Tragedy of Julius Caesar,*
> act 3, scene 1

In the afternoon of July 17, 1928, Obregón attended a lavish luncheon in his honor in the La Bombilla restaurant in San Angel, Mexico City. While waiters refilled wine glasses and brought one sumptuous course after another, a young artist named José de León Toral made rounds drawing caricatures of the guests. An emaciated young man, Toral gave off the air of the poor artist honored to be in the company of such eminent men. At last, he approached Obregón and asked him whether he would like to see his artwork. When the president-elect consented, Toral pumped five bullets into his head. The dying caudillo slumped in his chair, setting off pandemonium in the restaurant and in the national political scene.[1]

Obregón's assassination made Calles the new "northern star" of Mexican politics. The death of the caudillo gave the president an opportunity to restructure politics on the national level. In 1929, the inauguration of the Partido Nacional Revolucionario (PNR, or National Revolutionary Party) marked the beginning of a long era in which a ruling party dominated politics. Therefore, Obregón's assassination amounted to a milestone in political history as well. As political scientist Arnaldo Córdova has stated hyperbolically, Obregón's death was the "most decisive event in the political development of [Mexico] in the postrevolutionary era."[2]

Calles's influence was never greater than in the years following Obregón's death. Three leaders—Emilio Portes Gil, Pascual Ortiz Rubio, and Abelardo Rodríguez—served relatively brief terms as president in a political system in which Calles remained the power behind the scenes, and a fourth, Lázaro Cárdenas, initially followed Calles's lead as well. For seven years, government officials, foreign diplomats, and entrepreneurs trekked to Calles's whereabouts for consultation, often bypassing these presidents altogether. With reason, historians have called these years the Maximato, the time in which Calles informally ruled over the country as *Jefe Máximo*. Popular lore even dubbed the presidents of this era the *peleles* (puppets).

However, the Jefe Máximo was not quite as powerful as most historians have imagined.[3] To this day, a summary judgment remains difficult in light of the fact that his influence rested primarily on "opinions" offered in the course of informal conversations with other politicians. Yet the available documentation reveals a complex interplay between Calles and other political agents such as the presidents, leading PNR officials, and the mass political base of the party. Rather than a dictator who imposed major policy decisions on weak puppet presidents, the Jefe Máximo was the arbiter of political life. Through an intricate alliance system that included members of the national government, legislators, the party leadership, and state governors, he undermined politicians he considered either incompetent leaders or unwanted rivals. He was also capable of exerting decisive influence in the executive branch, elections, and congressional debates. But he neither shaped the terms of those debates nor did he centralize decision making in his own hands. In particular, interim Presidents Portes Gil and Rodríguez made their own mark as political leaders. Even more importantly, the PNR was not strong enough to mediate conflict at the regional level. In deteriorating health, Calles tended to political matters only intermittently and satisfied himself with the role of a kingmaker who enjoyed veto power. Instead of a machine that methodically defended Calles's power, the Maximato was a prolonged political stalemate that contained the elements of its own undoing.

Calles and the Beginnings of the PNR

Obregón's assassination touched off a wild wave of speculation. Based on interrogations under torture of Toral and other suspects, Calles concluded that Catholic radicals bent on avenging the campaign against the church had perpetrated the crime.[4] Although Toral claimed to have acted on his own initiative, he formed part of a Catholic opposition group. An introverted mystic, he was an admirer of the martyred Father Pro. He had also engaged in secret gatherings of Catholic dissidents led by Concepción Acevedo y de la Llata, better known as Madre Conchita, the Mother Superior of the Espíritu Santo convent. But the word on the street implicated the government, and Obregonistas such as PNA (Partido Nacional Agrarista) leader Soto y Gama blamed Morones, whose name had been stained with blood ever since the 1924 assassination of Senator Field Jurado. A few opponents of the regime accused Calles of masterminding or at least tolerating the plot, pointing to the fact that he stood to gain much from the disappearance of the last caudillo.[5] A few people suspected the followers of Serrano and Gómez, who might have desired to seek retribution for the assassinations of their leaders less than one year before. After almost eighty years, the circumstances of Obregón's murder have yet to be fully elucidated.[6]

The weeks following July 17, 1928, ushered in the most unsettled time in Calles's presidency. Most significantly, there was no heir apparent, as the office of vice president had been abolished in the 1917 Constitution. Obregón's death threatened to provoke a revolt of his supporters in case someone close to Morones or other rivals of the slain caudillo emerged as the choice to replace him as Calles's successor. Further, new complications loomed on the Cristero front. The assassination of Obregón interrupted Ambassador Morrow's efforts to mediate the church-state conflict through the offices of a U.S. priest. In the absence of a solution to the conflict, the Catholic Church continued its boycott of religious services, and the Cristero rebellion continued into its third year.[7]

Calles's response to the assassination displayed a degree of flexibility that had often been missing in the previous two years. His immediate reaction was a call for unity among the revolutionaries. As he reportedly told his friend Luis León, "This time they really screwed us! We will need to unite to resist the force of reaction."[8] As the president knew, the first order of business was to placate the angry Obregonistas who demanded retribution. Aware of the rumors that implicated his government, he stepped aside and allowed the Obregonistas to vent their anger at Morones and the CROM (Confederación Regional Obrera Mexicana). He also gave them a great degree of control over the criminal investigation. Upon their urging, he replaced the Callista police chief in charge of the investigation with an Obregonista.[9] Finally, in perhaps his greatest overture toward the Obregonistas, he dismissed his loyal ally Morones from the Consejo de Ministros.[10]

Calles then turned to the problem of the presidential succession. Many of Calles's closest advisers, including Morones and, reportedly, Ambassador Morrow, urged him to remain in office until new elections could be held, or even to serve another full term as president.[11] At first glance, continuing in office appeared the best option. Compared to Obregón's questionable tactics of pushing a constitutional amendment through Congress that allowed him to run for a second term, an emergency extension of Calles's tenure appeared a far lesser infringement on the principle of no reelection. However, there were good reasons to step down on November 30, 1928, as stipulated. Soto y Gama and other PNA leaders loyal to Obregón suspected Calles of having played a role in the assassination attempt. In addition, Calles had reason to fear that he might be the next target, as Toral's bullets had ironically struck down a leader who—unlike Calles and Morones—desired a negotiated solution to the church-state conflict. Finally, how could Calles expect the military to step aside from politics if he (himself a *divisionario*) mocked the constitution by remaining in office? Both proponents and opponents of a term extension looked forward to September 1, when the president was to give his last annual *informe*, or state-of-the-nation address.[12]

The *informe* settled the issue in a shrewd gambit that amounted to Calles's finest moment as a political leader. The president began his speech by praising Obregón's role as a leader of the revolution, and he noted that the progress achieved during his own administration primarily followed the initiatives of his predecessor. Yet in obvious allusion to Obregón, he also blamed *caudillismo* for his country's ills. After this clever combination of praise for Obregón (which served as a sop for the Obregonistas) and criticism of caudillo rule (which drew the applause of the Antirreeleccionistas), Calles made his long-awaited announcement regarding the future. Under no circumstances, he proclaimed, would he serve as president again. Mexico, he stated, had entered the transition from a "country of one man" to a "nation of institutions and laws."[13] In one fell swoop, Calles had not only silenced those who had suspected his involvement in the murder, but he had also announced his opposition to the ambitions of the generals and ensured for himself a continuing political role behind the scenes. His blueprint was Obregón's powerful influence in the two years prior to his death. Calles knew that he could play a similar informal role behind an interim president who would lack the cachet that Obregón would have brought to the office.

Having thus dismissed the rumors that he would seek to prolong his term in office, Calles spelled out his plans during the remainder of the *informe*. He asked Congress to select an interim president until elections could be held to choose a successor. In addition, the president called for the creation of a party that combined all national and regional revolutionary parties so that political differences could be settled peacefully rather than by military conflict. Finally, he even welcomed the formation of a conservative opposition party as a means of co-opting the Catholics, who had insistently complained about their inability to press their agenda through legislative channels.[14] It is highly doubtful that Calles indeed desired a two-party system, which would have entailed the possibility of losing power to what he labeled the "reactionary" opposition. Instead, he likely envisioned a political system in which the ruling party dominated through electoral triumph, if possible, and fraud, if necessary. Calles's call for an opposition party hence served two purposes: to lure Catholics into the political system and to ensure U.S. diplomatic recognition of the next administration.[15]

The next step consisted of the selection of an interim president, a process that involved obtaining the support of Congress and at least the acquiescence of the military leadership. In both cases, Calles confronted resistance as well as thinly disguised personal ambitions. Although Calles's speech had won over many members of Congress, Ricardo Topete, the leader of the Obregonista faction in Congress, held secret meetings designed to elevate an enemy of Calles to the presidency. However, with the help of a variety of Obregonista deputies, senators, and governors, the president assembled a majority in Congress that ousted Topete from his leadership post.[16]

The military proved even more difficult to control. Since Obregón's assassination, some of the more ambitious generals had held regular meetings at the Hotel Regis with a view of choosing a presidential candidate. The group reportedly discussed three particular generals as leading contenders: the independent Juan Andreu Almazán, the Obregonista José Gonzalo Escobar, and the Callista Manuel Pérez Treviño. Of the three, Almazán enjoyed the greatest wealth and the best political and military connections.[17] Concerned that the generals practiced caudillo politics as usual, Calles convened thirty of them in Chapultepec Castle on September 4. During this meeting, he asserted that the candidacy of a military leader would lead to more political and military conflict. He exhorted the generals to stay out of the process of choosing an interim president and to remain in active service, which would render them ineligible for the elections for the constitutional presidency. Face-to-face with the president and Calles loyalists such as Saturnino Cedillo and Lázaro Cárdenas, those generals harboring secret plans for a coup declared their support of the government. Most importantly, the president gained the reluctant assent of the generals for nominating a civilian, in Calles's view the only hope for political stability. Beginning with Almazán, one general after another declared that they would not seek the presidency, and Escobar finally did the same. Almazán also enjoined his colleagues to leave the selection of the interim president up to Calles and Congress. It became clear during this meeting that most of the generals were tired of fighting and eager to enjoy the fruits of a spoils system that had brought them material comfort, and (in some cases) phenomenal wealth. The vast majority of them had much to lose from ongoing strife.[18]

Ultimately, the nomination for the interim presidency went to a compromise candidate. On September 25, 1928, the Chamber of Deputies chose Gobernación Secretary Emilio Portes Gil for a term beginning on December 1, 1928, and ending on March 1, 1930. Elections for the constitutional presidency, from which Portes Gil would be barred as a current officeholder, were slated for November 17, 1929. Portes Gil, who had joined Calles's Consejo de Ministros after Obregón's death, was the leader of a regional agrarian party and former governor of Tamaulipas. A civilian Obregonista, he was acceptable to a majority in Congress as well as the military. Portes Gil was by no means the ideal candidate as far as the president was concerned.[19] The nominee drew strength from his regional base in Tamaulipas, and his candidacy received support from Agraristas such as Soto y Gama and Aurelio Manrique, who had fallen out with Calles after Obregón's death. Thus, even if Portes Gil got the congressional nomination through Calles's influence, as most historians believe, the president's decision to support him rather than one of his own allies constituted an opportunistic reaction to the political lay of the land. In other words, Calles did not so much impose Portes Gil as he made a pragmatic choice that reflected the Obregonistas' strength in Congress.[20] As a result, Portes Gil approached his short presidential term with a great deal of independence from Calles. For example, Calles accepted the nominee's demand for restoration of an agrarian reform fund that had been deleted from the 1929 budget.[21]

With the question of the interim presidency settled, Calles moved toward the founding of a national ruling party, the PNR. In the late 1910s and early 1920s, the Partido Liberal Constitucionalista (PLC) had aspired to such a role, as did the Partido Nacional Cooperatista (PNC) in subsequent years. Both the PLC and the PNC, however, had ended up as vehicles of individual presidential ambitions rather than broad-based parties, and both had therefore disappeared under the Obregón-Calles political machine. Forging a durable national ruling party therefore required uniting the diverse political elements beyond individual ambitions. In particular, such a party would need to include the foremost groups in the revolutionary political elite. While the disappearance of Calles, Morones, and Obregón as presidential contenders finally made such an ambitious endeavor possible, the evolution of a mass-based party was a long-term process. It was not until the late 1930s that the party effectively incorporated the major agrarian and labor movements as well as the multitude of regional parties.[22]

Most immediately, the PNR needed an organizing committee and a candidate for the 1929 presidential elections. The planning for the new party began at Mexico City residence of Calles loyalist Luis L. León on November 21, 1928, only ten days before Portes Gil's inauguration. Both Calles and the president-designate attended the meeting, as did Aarón Sáenz and several regional strongmen, including Bartolomé García Correa (Yucatán), Pérez Treviño (Coahuila), and Tejeda (Veracruz). The meeting produced an organizing committee with Calles as its chair. At the meeting, Calles asked all those in attendance to remain in their respective political offices through November 21, 1929, which barred them from the presidency.[23] This maneuver appeared to clear the way for Sáenz, the former head of Obregón's presidential campaign and the only one present who did not hold political office at that time. In Calles's mind, Sáenz's candidacy would reconcile the Obregonistas to the existence of a civilian party structure. On December 2, a manifesto published in all major newspapers announced the formation of the PNR and invited all those loyal to the revolution to join the new party.[24]

Just three days later, Calles committed a political gaffe that sidelined him from further formal involvement in the party's creation. Sensing the need to shore up Laborista support at a moment when the nascent PNR did not include any elements from the CROM or its political wing, the PLM, he attended the ninth annual convention of the CROM in the Teatro Hidalgo in Mexico City. Just after Calles had given a conciliatory speech to the delegates, Morones launched a diatribe against Portes Gil. In particular, the CROM leader attacked the interim president for allowing the performance of a skit entitled "El desmoronamiento de Morones" (The Coming Apart of Morones).[25] To Portes Gil and his supporters, Calles was guilty by association. As a result, the former president resigned from the organizing committee. He announced that he would "retire absolutely and definitively from political life and return . . . to the condition of the most obscure citizen who no longer intends to be—nor ever will be again—a political factor in Mexico."[26] In the long run, however, Calles's gambit increased his ability to maneuver as a seemingly nonpartisan and impartial senior statesman. His choice of residence reflected his intention of staying close to the center of power: in December

1928, he moved into a new, expensively furbished house in Colonia Anzures, just north of Chapultepec Castle.[27] Hence the popular adage "*Esta es la casa del presidente/pero él que manda vive enfrente*" (This is the house of the president, but the one who rules lives over there).

Without Calles's participation, the organizing committee drafted a program and a set of statutes to be approved at the first PNR convention scheduled for March 1929 in the city of Querétaro, a symbolic choice as that city had also hosted the *Constituyente* of 1916–1917. Committee members also traveled throughout the nation to invite the existing parties to apply for PNR affiliation, a status that would allow those parties to send delegates to the Querétaro convention and, hence, wield influence in the choice of the next president. With Calles's informal backing, the organizing committee was successful in incorporating regional parties such as Garrido's Partido Radical Tabasqueño (Radical Tabascan Party), Portes Gil's Partido Socialista Fronterizo (Socialist Party of the Frontier), and the PSS (Partido Socialista del Sureste) of Yucatán founded by Felipe Carrillo Puerto. Notably absent was the PLM (Partido Laborista Mexicano), which had begun to lose influence after its leader Morones left the national government. Unlike the PNA, a purged and weakened version of which entered the PNR minus Soto y Gama and Manrique, the PLM remained intact as a party with a steadily dwindling membership. This process illustrated the top-down nature of the PNR. From the beginning, it was a party controlled and organized by the governing elite close to Calles. Significantly, neither Portes Gil nor presidential hopeful Sáenz had any further involvement with the organizing committee. Indeed, Calles envisioned a party separate from the executive branch, a parallel power structure by means of which Calles could weaken the authority of the president.[28]

Reflecting a desire to give broad appeal to the new party, the organizing committee crafted foundational documents that invoked the populist rhetoric of Calles's first years as president. As the draft program stated, "The PNR is the instrument of political action by means of which Mexico's great campesino and worker masses fight to keep the control of the public power in their hands; a control wrested from the landowning and privileged minorities through the great armed movement that began in 1910."[29] Or, in the words of the Declaration of Principles, "The PNR . . . will endeavor to improve the situation of the popular masses by enforcing Articles 123 and 27 of the constitution, as the party considers the working and campesino classes the most important elements of Mexican society."[30] This platform was successful in attracting the bulk of the PNA and PLM leadership to the new party.

In large part for that reason, Sáenz did not succeed in obtaining the PNR nomination at the Querétaro convention. Although Sáenz enjoyed the right political connections as Aco's brother-in-law and a partner of the Calles family in the ownership of the El Mante sugar complex, his political views constituted a liability. He stood on the right of the PNR, and his tenure as governor of Nuevo León had been marked by tax cuts, business deregulation, and other measures that favored the state's beer and steel industry. By the time of the convention, Sáenz and General Almazán worked in tandem to ensure control over government contracts for road building and other infrastructure improvements.[31] For those reasons, Portes Gil and other leaders close to agrarian and labor interests opposed Sáenz's candidacy. This opposition put Calles in a bind, as he had apparently assured Sáenz of his support. As a way out, the ex-president let PNR leaders know that he favored the presentation of two candidates at the convention to give the appearance of a democratic process. The second candidate turned out to be the ambassador to Brazil, Pascual Ortiz Rubio, an ex-general who had been out of the country on diplomatic service since 1923. Although a lack of available documentation precludes definitive conclusions on this matter, Ortiz Rubio was likely Calles's handpicked choice. In the end, Sáenz withdrew his candidacy, and Ortiz Rubio easily obtained the nomination.[32] Although Sáenz quickly proclaimed his loyalty to the party despite his defeat, the lasting legacy of the nomination battle was the formation of clientelist factions. In fact, as political scientist Luis Javier Garrido has demonstrated, the party was initially little more than a "confederation of caciques."[33] In this club that only imperfectly checked the ambitions of powerful generals, Calles's support for Ortiz Rubio had shown once again his astute sense of the political landscape.

The Querétaro convention marked the triumph of Calles's strategy to construct a new political system in which he enjoyed power behind the scenes. One of his most trusted allies, Coahuila governor Manuel Pérez Treviño, became president of the new party, and another Callista, Luis León, became secretary. Although Veracruz strongman Tejeda—an inveterate supporter of agrarian aims disappointed in the presidential choices—defected from the new party, other Callistas headed up regional parties within the PNR. In a symbolic move that indicated the true hierarchy within the new party, León assigned Calles the first membership card issued by the PNR.[34]

However, Calles's strategy immediately confronted a stern test. On March 3, 1929, the third day of the PNR convention, Pérez Treviño surprised the delegates with the news of a revolt headed by General José Gonzalo Escobar in Sonora. Under the banner of the "Plan of Hermosillo," a group of Obregonista generals called for the overthrow of the Portes Gil administration as a supposed instrument of Calles. The Plan of Hermosillo dubbed Calles the "Judas of the Mexican Revolution" and accused the former president of waging a corrupt and repressive campaign to impose his will on the republic.[35] The Escobar rebellion, which ultimately involved 28 percent of the Mexican army, was thus an essentially anti-Callista movement. As such, it lacked any ideological orientation. The Escobaristas included ancient enemies of Calles such as the Yaqui commander and former Maytorena ally Francisco Urbalejo, along with Obregonistas such as Escobar himself. The Escobar rebellion quickly seized the states of Sonora, Durango, Chihuahua, and Veracruz, among others, and it sought to enlist the help of the approximately twenty-five thousand Cristero guerrillas in central and western Mexico.[36]

Within three months, however, Calles and his allies had vanquished the Escobar Rebellion, which was hampered by the poor quality of its leadership and the ill-defined nature of its political goals. Since Amaro was recovering from a polo accident that cost him one of his eyes, Calles himself commanded the government troops as secretary of war. Calles's nomination paid immediate dividends, as Sáenz and Almazán remained loyal to the government despite their disappointment at the convention. At all times, Calles was well informed about rebel movements by means of intercepted letters and telegrams. He was able to strike quickly against the rebels after one of their leaders had made the mistake of inviting a Calles loyalist, General Abelardo Rodríguez, to join the uprising. Rodríguez's warning to Calles gave the government plenty of advance notice.[37] Bolstered by weapons and ammunition from the United States, government troops pushed back the Escobaristas. Focused on taking urban areas, the rebels were unable to coordinate a military strategy with the rural Cristeros, who preferred to keep their guerrilla war away from the cities. The end came in Sonora in late May, when Almazán and Cárdenas defeated the last redoubts of the rebellion. The third military revolt against the government since 1920, this rebellion eliminated many of the last recalcitrant *divisionarios*. It left Calles, who himself had used the military to come to power, disgusted with the military officers. In a speech on May 22, 1929, he admitted that the revolution had thus far failed in political terms, and he called for the elimination of the military from political life.[38]

The Escobar rebellion highlighted the need for the resolution of the Cristero rebellion, an uprising that had proven to be a far more intractable problem. The rebellion had diverted federal forces from central and western Mexico and allowed the Cristeros to go on the offensive. In May, a U.S. intelligence report counted eight thousand Cristeros in the core area of the rebellion, including five thousand in Jalisco.[39] After the defeat of the Escobaristas, Portes Gil combined an effort to bring the church to the negotiating table with a new military operation against the Cristeros. The president's diplomatic effort had begun as early as March 1929, when U.S. ambassador Morrow resumed the mediation efforts that had been interrupted by Obregón's assassination eight months before. He knew that the clergy desired to resume religious services under a face-saving compromise. In Portes Gil, the church found a president amenable to dialogue with Apostolic Delegate Leopoldo Ruiz y Flores. The president insisted that he would not amend the Calles Law that required the registration of priests, but he let it be known that he did not intend to destroy the Catholic Church. In May, Ruiz y Flores broke ranks with the Liga Nacional de la Defensa de la Libertad Religiosa and entered into negotiations with Portes Gil, with Calles and Morrow serving as informal advisers. Morrow even drafted position papers for both sides that served as the basis of discussions.[40] Meanwhile, the army dealt the Cristeros a crushing defeat in Jalisco, dispersing the rebels to neighboring states.[41]

This combination of diplomacy and military force finally brought the Cristero rebellion to an end. On June 21, Portes Gil and Ruiz y Flores announced an agreement that ended the church's self-imposed ban on religious services that had been in effect for almost three years. Although the anti-clerical laws remained on the books, church bells once again tolled over Mexico, and soon thereafter, the Cristeros put down their arms. The fact that the interim president had been able to find a solution where Calles had failed not only highlighted the benefit of the passage of time, which forced the Catholic bishops to come to terms with a revolutionary state they despised, but also Portes Gil's considerable negotiating skills.[42] Even though the agreement did not imply the conclusion of the church-state conflict, the end of the rebellion gave the government room to maneuver at a time when the military budget consumed a third of federal expenditures.[43]

The end of the Cristero rebellion marked the passage of a turbulent year in which Calles and his allies had reshaped the political landscape. The death of the last great caudillo had created a political vacuum that offered the threat of continual conflict but also the opportunity of incorporating the factious generals into a new political system that demanded their loyalty on the national level in exchange for giving them continued leverage in their regional fiefdoms. Since then, both the army and the CROM had ceased to be significant factors in national politics. Instead, a fledgling party had appeared as the country's most significant political institution, and Calles retained considerable influence behind the scenes. The question of just how powerful the ex-president would be in this new system, however, awaited a definitive answer over the next several years.

The Heyday of the Maximato

The test for this new political arrangement came in the second half of 1929—a period that coincided with an extended hiatus in Calles's political role. The trials and tribulations of the year since Obregón's murder had left Calles exhausted, and in July, he departed for Paris in order to tend to his health, and he did not return until five months later. His absence greatly strengthened Portes Gil's hand, and the president used it as an opportunity to step up a land distribution program that had languished during the previous few years. In all, Portes Gil distributed 2.5 million acres of land to more than one hundred thousand households, much of it while Calles was in Paris.[44]

The most significant political event during Calles's absence was the 1929 presidential campaign, an election that Calles had promised would be democratic and fair. In this campaign, PNR candidate Ortiz Rubio confronted José Vasconcelos, the former secretary of education and an opponent of Calles since the de la Huerta rebellion. A lawyer, Vasconcelos was far superior to Ortiz Rubio in terms of national recognition and intellect, and he represented a federalist, decentralizing, and Catholic strain of Mexican populism. He had joined Madero's movement in 1909, and he had spent most of the 1910s in the United States—the latter part as an exile from the Carranza administration. As head of the National University (UNAM) and the Education Secretariat, successively, his ideas had greatly influenced the urban middle class. Vasconcelos promoted the vision of the "cosmic race," the fusion of indigenous and Spanish elements in a Catholic and mestizo identity. He sought to unify the Latin American nations against the United States, which he despised as godless and materialistic. Vasconcelos's ideas had inspired populists such as the Peruvian Víctor Raúl Haya de la Torre, the founder of the populist Alianza Popular Revolucionaria Americana (APRA, or American Popular Revolutionary Alliance), who had met him during his stay in Mexico City in the summer of 1924. As a presidential candidate, Vasconcelos represented himself as a civilian nationalist who would rescue his country from the generals and the clutches of U.S. imperialism. He also highlighted his intellectual connections to the *indigenismo* movement with references to preconquest mythology. He portrayed himself as a "civilizing Quetzalcóatl," a priest-king who would triumph over the bloodthirsty Huitzilopochtli, the god of war in whose name the Aztec emperors had sacrificed thousands of people. Vasconcelos's candidacy garnered widespread support, particularly among university students.[45]

Vasconcelos's popularity forced the PNR to pull out all the stops to help its colorless and relatively unknown candidate. Ortiz Rubio's presidential bid therefore turned into a marathon to advertise the new party as the authentic heir of the revolution, and the campaign featured six months of almost non-stop travel by the candidate. In this endeavor, Ortiz Rubio held up Calles and the PNR as the defenders of the principles of the revolution. In Tulancingo, Hidalgo, he announced that "Calles and [Portes Gil] are consolidating the conquests of the revolution," and in nearby Necaxa, Puebla, he praised Calles as a "good, sincere man dedicated to the [Mexican] people."[46] This campaign tour, however, was not enough, and widespread fraud marred Ortiz Rubio's triumph on November 17, 1929, by the official count of more than 1.8 million votes to 106,000 for his opponent.[47] In large part, this lopsided tally could be attributed to the suppression of the Vasconcelos vote in urban areas. The use of brutal force played a role as well, as the killings of sixty Vasconcelistas in Topilejo on the road from Mexico City to Cuernavaca demonstrated.[48] Ortiz Rubio's triumph marked the true beginning of the Maximato, as the party (and Calles behind it) overshadowed the incoming president whom they had helped elect.

Beginning with the 1929 presidential campaign, the PNR propagated a set of unifying ideas about the revolution and, most importantly, a historical interpretation that made Calles the patriarch of the revolutionary process. This rewriting of history to suit the party's needs occurred through its newspaper, *El Nacional,* public speeches such as those given by Ortiz Rubio on his campaign tour, and newly constructed monuments. The key to Calles's place in this official PNR history was his position as the head of a "revolutionary family." In his September 1928 presentation to the military, Calles had first made reference to this term that would gain increasing importance as a unifying metaphor.[49] As families tend toward hierarchy rather than democracy, the notion of the revolutionary family also implied that dissent would not be tolerated. As we have seen, Ortiz Rubio's huge advantage in the official vote count of 1929 masked electoral fraud and violence. The PNR branded the Vasconcelistas as "reactionaries" and flung the same rhetoric at other opponents who decided to take their protests outside the official party channels.

It was in this capacity as the symbolic paterfamilias of the revolution that Calles became known as the "Jefe Máximo de la Revolución Mexicana." Curiously, the moniker was the work of one of his opponents, Soto y Gama, who coined the term in order to criticize Calles's authoritarianism. However, *El Nacional* editor Luis León soon thereafter redefined it to describe the former president's political significance. With good reason, Calles never used this term to refer to himself in order to avoid its dictatorial connotations. The label stuck, however, identifying Calles for better or for worse with the political system he had helped forge.[50] As Jefe Máximo, Calles enjoyed significant symbolic power. He met with members of the national government at his convenience, and at one point, the state governors even gave a banquet in his honor.[51] The most unique aspect of the Maximato lay in the complex relationship involving the president, the Jefe Máximo, the legislature, and the party. While other ruling parties in Latin America bolstered the power of an executive branch headed by a dictator who ruled the nation by means of force, the PNR formed part of a system of shared government in which it competed for power with the president and the Jefe Máximo.

The metaphor of the revolutionary family denoted not only the PNR but also an official version of the history of the revolution. The revolutionary family combined all those who had fought for the revolution, and particularly leaders such as Madero, Carranza, Obregón, Villa, and Zapata. Conveniently for Calles, all five of these leaders had died by assassination. The notion of a revolutionary family was a historical artifact that ignored the fact that the latter four of these heroes had fought and, in some cases, even killed one another. As the actual fighting grew more distant in time, the dead revolutionary heroes could serve a useful political purpose for the claim of the PNR to political supremacy. Exploiting the martyrdom (or sacrifice) of these leaders, the new ruling party combined Villa's and Zapata's agrarian aims with Carranza's and Obregón's economic nationalism and Madero's commitment to effective suffrage and political democracy. In party ideology, the road that had begun with Madero ended with Calles and the PNR. The dead heroes also allowed Calles to claim their legacy as the current head of the revolutionary family.[52]

The ultimate manifestation of this political symbolism came by means of two impressive monuments built during the mid-1930s: the Monumento a la Revolución and the Monumento al General Alvaro Obregón. These monuments to the fallen heroes promoted the PNR version of history that held that the revolution was unitary rather than a heterogeneous process made by conflicting forces. Built upon the unfinished structure of what Porfirio Díaz had hoped would be his new Legislative Palace, the Monumento a la Revolución served as the official memorial of the revolutionary family, eventually commemorating Madero, Zapata, Villa, Carranza, Calles, and Cárdenas.[53] Obregón, whom Sáenz called the "undefeated caudillo of the revolution," slain only when the bullets of an assassin "did in a few minutes what armies and weapons had not been able to accomplish in . . . long years of war," got his own memorial on the site of his death.[54] The Monumento Obregón contained a bronze likeness of the caudillo; a part of the original floor of the La Bombilla restaurant, complete with bullet holes; and (after 1943) Obregón's arm, which had been severed by a Villista grenade in 1915 and conserved by his private physician for twenty-eight years thereafter. Sáenz's dedication speech alluded to the three elements of the PNR— campesinos, workers, and the military—as mainstays of Obregón's support. As he stated, "in the place of your sacrifice, the Fatherland consecrates to your memory this reminder made into stone. In it are also figures that represent those who accompanied you in battle: the campesino, the worker, and the soldier."[55] Sáenz did not mention a fourth sector to which he himself belonged: the new class of landowners and industrialists that had gained power with the Constitutionalist triumph.[56] Just as Porfirio Díaz had glorified the late Benito Juárez to detract from his emerging dictatorship, so did the Callistas venerate Obregón in their bid to expand their political power.[57]

This political symbolism, however, could not hide the weakness of the new political arrangement and, in particular, that of incoming president Ortiz Rubio, who sought to build up a power base of his own before the Jefe Máximo returned from Paris. This attempt proved a mistake, as Portes Gil resisted all of Ortiz Rubio's efforts to build a political base. Upon Calles's return in December 1929, the partisans of the outgoing and the incoming president threatened to tear asunder the unity of the PNR. Portesgilistas and Ortizrubistas battled over control over Congress, a struggle that ended with a narrow victory for the former group and put an effective damper on Ortiz Rubio's power before he had even taken office. The congressional strife also highlighted Calles's prestige as the only leader capable of holding the nation together.[58] This period witnessed the rise of political operators such as Gonzalo N. Santos, who maintained close ties to both Calles's inner circle and the former Obregonistas and served as a crucial intermediary between the legislative and executive branches as well as between Calles and the governors. As a result of the influence of Santos and others, the congressional elections of 1930 put an anti-Ortiz Rubio coalition in control. The first Congress elected since Obregón's assassination, it was also the first in which most deputies and senators were loyal to Calles.[59]

The Ortiz Rubio presidency (March 1930–September 1932) was thus ill-fated from the beginning. In an ominous foreboding, the president was the target of an assassination attempt right after his inauguration on February 5, 1930. When the new president's Cadillac left the National Palace that afternoon, gunfire rang out. Of the six shots fired, one hit Ortiz Rubio's wife above the right ear and ricocheted to enter the president's right jawbone. The would-be assassin, twenty-three-year-old Daniel Flores, resisted all methods to make him talk, including torture and a faked shooting of his father. Nonetheless, public opinion implicated Gobernación Secretary Portes Gil (technically the next in line for the presidency) and, to a lesser degree,

Calles, who had become a default suspect for all politically motivated assassinations.[60] Whatever Flores's motives for the assassination attempt, the incident crippled Ortiz Rubio's resolve to be his own man as president. After his near death, he understandably became tentative and frightful, and his general health deteriorated.[61]

At no time did the Jefe Máximo wield greater informal political influence than during the Ortiz Rubio administration. Whereas Portes Gil had enjoyed a degree of independence from the Jefe Máximo, as witnessed by his revival of the land distribution program while Calles was in Paris, Ortiz Rubio found himself besieged by a constant political crisis that forced him to rely on the head of the revolutionary family. Not only was Congress in a state of upheaval, but his government also resembled a game of musical chairs. Calles, who usually weighed in with the forces arrayed against Ortiz Rubio, repeatedly made himself the peacemaker; during 1931 alone, he met twice with the Consejo de Ministros without the president. Three days after the second of these meetings on October 12, all four *divisionarios* in the Consejo—Almazán, Amaro, Cárdenas, and Rodríguez—resigned from their positions. This shakeup not only weakened Ortiz Rubio but also longtime Secretary of War Amaro. Many observers saw Calles's hand at work in Amaro's demotion to the directorship of the Colegio Militar, or Military College, a step that helped the Jefe Máximo assure himself of the loyalty of the only institution that could potentially threaten the dominance of the PNR.[62] Indeed, Calles served a third term as secretary of war, which seemed to corroborate the impression that the changes had been designed to get rid of Amaro.[63] In fact, however, Amaro had merely become a coincidental casualty in a larger power struggle that pitted Ortiz Rubio against the Jefe Máximo.[64] This power struggle also bore the marks of the personal ambitions of three *divisionarios* who had emerged as significant power brokers: future president Cárdenas, the conservative agrarian leader Cedillo, and eventual presidential candidate Almazán. Despite the shakeup, the political crisis continued.[65]

In August 1932, Ortiz Rubio's situation became untenable. When he had served long enough in office that his resignation would not trigger new elections under the constitution, Calles provoked Ortiz Rubio's fall over a hospital administration scandal that implicated the president's brother. The Jefe Máximo requested that no friend of his serve in the administration, a move that effectively blocked all prominent PNR politicos from service in the Consejo de Ministros. Ortiz Rubio then asked Puig, then chief officer of the Federal District, to draft his resignation letter. On September 4, 1932, the president resigned from office.[66] Calles's heavy hand gave rise to the apocryphal story (still repeated in a current textbook) that Ortiz Rubio opened the newspaper one morning to learn that he had resigned.[67] In any event, the ease with which the Jefe Máximo brought about the president's resignation represents the high-water mark of his influence in politics.

This political crisis, however, was not just the product of Calles's own manipulations. Ortiz Rubio's tenure had coincided with the worst years of the Great Depression, which followed the collapse of the stock market on Black Friday, October 29, 1929. The Great Depression led to mass bankruptcies and layoffs throughout the United States and Europe, drastically reducing demand for Mexican raw materials. It also caused the repatriation and deportation of more than one hundred thousand Mexicans and Chicanos in the United States, including thousands of U.S. citizens of Mexican descent. These displaced people swelled the ranks of the unemployed, which grew daily due to the lack of demand for Mexican exports. By 1930, Mexico, already hit by the slowdown of the late 1920s, experienced negative economic growth of 4 percent annually. The Depression was a daunting challenge for any government—one that decisively contributed to the defeat of U.S. President Herbert Hoover in the 1932 presidential elections and the rise of the Nazi Party in Germany. In Mexico, the crisis led to a plummeting of government revenue, already down 7 percent from the beginning of the Calles presidency. Between the first and last year of Ortiz Rubio's tenure, federal revenue dropped 25 percent in real terms. The crisis was exacerbated by the decline of the peso, a currency buttressed by the country's silver export. While worldwide deflation kept prices in check for those spending dollars, marks, and pounds, Mexicans experienced rising prices for imported goods.[68]

The Great Depression greatly deepened the chasm between the official party rhetoric and Calles's own, increasingly conservative political views. The economic crisis contributed to a steady drift to the right in the political persona of the Jefe Máximo, who increasingly leaned on Ambassador Morrow and U.S. investors in an effort to blunt the impact of the Depression. As presidential candidate, Calles had wrapped himself in the Zapatista banner and advocated land reform, and as president, he had confronted the United States in the oil controversy and over Nicaragua. The Jefe Máximo, on the other hand, opposed land reform and forged a cordial relationship with the U.S. government. Only in the areas of education and the religious conflict did his rhetoric still resemble the firebrand populism of the early to mid-1920s.[69]

Yet an analysis of the issue of land reform reveals that the Jefe Máximo did not make a unilateral decision to halt further distribution of land. By 1930, ongoing disputes about *ejido* land, declining productivity, and significant opposition to land reform in many states had convinced many other national politicians to back off the ambitious goal of returning land to the campesinos. That year, Agriculture Secretary, landowner, and Calles confidant Manuel Pérez Treviño seized upon a food crisis in which the volume of production had declined almost 25 percent as a pretext to halt further land distribution.[70] When Ortiz Rubio declared that further expropriations would be paid for in cash, this move effectively ended the Portesgilista effort to revive the land distribution program, as the government had no such cash. On June 23, 1930, a reporter overheard Calles remarking that the agrarian program was not working and that radical change was necessary. Although food production rebounded the following year, land reform—a significant pillar of the PNR program—languished for the remainder of the Ortiz Rubio administration.[71]

Regarding urban labor, neither Calles nor the PNR could afford to retrench from their promises. After years of relative complacency under Morones, industrial and mine workers once again took to the streets, demanding higher wages to make up for the loss in real income. In the north, the crisis of the mining sector and the influx of returnees from the United States produced a particularly acute situation. In Sonora, the crisis provoked a surge of xenophobia directed at the local Chinese population. When the state government took no steps to protect them, most of the Chinese left the country for fear for their lives. It was therefore not surprising that Ortiz Rubio's greatest achievement was the passage of the Ley Federal del Trabajo (Federal Labor Law) on August 28, 1931. This law expanded the purview of labor unions; it forced midsized firms to allow the establishment of unions; it codified the practice of asking foreign entrepreneurs to forsake the protection of their diplomatic representatives; and it established guidelines for the federal arbitration of labor disputes. Under Ortiz Rubio's direction, this law did not help workers to the extent that it promised, as the federal arbitration board declared most strikes "illicit" in view of the precarious economic situation. Nonetheless, the Labor Law would play an important role in the mass mobilization of the Cárdenas years and hence constituted a step toward the incorporation of the workers into the state.[72]

Calles and his family saw good times during these years. After the death of Natalia, Plutarco found solace with Leonor Llorente, a young employee of Yucatecan origins who worked in the posh Mexico City post office. Leonor was only twenty-three years old at the beginning of their relationship, and she married Calles on August 2, 1930, when she was three months pregnant. The couple had two sons: Plutarco José, known to the family as "Caco," born on January 15, 1931, and Leonardo Gilberto, or "Nanis," born on February 4, 1932.[73] Moreover, the Jefe Máximo's children from his first marriage followed promising careers. Beginning in 1931, his oldest son, Rodolfo, played a particularly important role in buttressing the Maximato by following in his father's footsteps as governor of Sonora. A year later, Calles's half-brother, Arturo M. Elías, began a term as governor of neighboring Baja California. In 1934, young Alfredo, who had settled down to work at the El Mante sugar venture owned by the Calleses and Sáenz after years of frittering away his future and his family's money, was elected a congressional deputy for the state of Tamaulipas.[74]

Rodolfo's tenure as governor of Sonora, however, shows the extent to which Calles and his family followed rather than directed the shifting political tides. Unlike his father, Rodolfo Calles pursued a modest land reform program in his native state as a part of an ambitious attempt to diversify an agricultural base hit hard by the Great Depression due to its vicinity to the United States. He opened up the former holdings of the Yaquis and the Compañía Constructora Richardson in southern Sonora for agricultural colonization, and he was particularly successful in promoting new irrigation projects that increased the amount of arable land in his state. Of course, Rodolfo Calles is also remembered as the governor who oversaw the disappearance of the Chinese community in Sonora.[75]

Perhaps the best indication that Calles was not an informal dictator as traditionally understood was the fact that he spent most of his time outside Mexico City, and much of it in remote locations such as Paris. As finance secretary, Calles spent several weeks in thermal water baths in Tehuacán. He also enjoyed staying at Aco's citrus hacienda in Nuevo León, and during the Rodríguez presidency, he vacationed for months at a time on the president's ranch in El Sauzal, Baja California, and at his daughter Alicia's beach cottage in El Tambor, Sinaloa.[76] Finally, Calles bought a property called Quinta Las Palmas in the city of Cuernavaca, fifty miles south of Mexico City. Located on what Calles critics knew as "Ali Baba Street" or "Street of the Millionaire Socialist," the house lay among a stretch of palatial homes inhabited by fellow politicos and wealthy entrepreneurs.[77] With its lush vegetation and warm climate, the ranch became his favorite residence when he needed to be near Mexico City. To be sure, party leaders, members of the Consejo de Ministros, and governors visited him in his vacation redoubts throughout Mexico. Just as Obregón had wielded influence by entertaining a procession of generals and politicians who came to Sonora to ask him for advice, so did Calles entertain a steady stream of visitors. Nonetheless, Calles could not keep close tabs on the political situation while outside the capital, and he was as unable to micromanage the political process as Obregón had during his own presidency.[78]

The travels of the Jefe Máximo were in large part due to his poor and deteriorating health. Calles had suffered from a rheumatic ailment since the siege of Naco in the winter of 1915, in which he had spent many nights outdoors in subfreezing temperatures. This painful illness, however, only constituted the beginning of a long physical decline. By 1922, the pain in his right leg had intensified, and Calles subsequently visited a variety of physicians in France, Germany, Mexico, and the United States to find a cure. While therapeutic treatments and rest relieved the pain, it came back whenever Calles returned to work, a pattern that led French and German physicians to suspect neurological and psychological causes. Over the years, severe intermittent colic and insomnia added to these symptoms. It was not until 1932 that Mexican doctors discovered the nature of Calles's illness: a combination of arthritis, atherosclerosis, and chronic intestinal disease caused by his poor diet. Together, the Jefe Máximo's ailments amounted to far more than results of the natural aging process, and the insomnia and the excruciating pain in his legs made Calles feel like an old man at only fifty-five years of age. For Calles, this illness amounted to yet another enemy, one that he confronted as stubbornly and futilely as he had the Cristeros. Instead of following his physician's recommendations that included a low-fat diet rich in grains, fruits, and vegetables, Calles persisted in eating meat, fish, and eggs along with the occasional tortilla and small amounts of juice. He defied his doctor's orders to give up coffee, alcohol, and tobacco, and he lay off his cognac and cigarettes only when the colic kept him awake at night. The Jefe Máximo's behavior typified his approach to both life and politics: a desire to get to the root of the problem paired with a lack of flexibility in the face of obstacles.[79] His health increasingly detracted from his attention to political issues.

Another great distraction was the health of Calles's second wife, Leonor. In the spring of 1932, she complained of a persistent headache. Initially misdiagnosed, the ailment turned out to be a brain tumor. In July, Leonor underwent surgery in Boston, but it was already too late to save her. On November 25, 1932, she died in Mexico City, leaving Calles a widower again.[80] Her death left her husband in a serious state of depression, and Calles's sojourns at El Sauzal and El Tambor constituted in part an effort to find refuge from his sorrow. In sum, Calles's health and state of mind constituted the Achilles heel of this powerful leader known to many Mexicans as the man of iron. Capable of inflicting great suffering on others, the Jefe Máximo was nevertheless a mere mortal with a fragile body, and his steely exterior masked a sensitive, caring, and somewhat hypochondriac psyche.[81]

The Maximato in Crisis

Thus, what later appeared like the sudden demise of the Maximato at the hands of President Lázaro Cárdenas and his followers constituted the culmination of a gradual process that began during the presidency of Abelardo Rodríguez (September 1932–December 1934). Indeed, the tenure of the third supposed *pelele* marked the beginning of the decline of the Maximato. Unlike Portes Gil and Ortiz Rubio, Rodríguez was one of Calles's friends and allies. With the possible exception of Sáenz, he had also profited personally from the revolution more than anyone else, having emerged as the wealthiest man in Baja California due to his control over the casinos, prostitution, and tourist industry in the border region.[82] His ascent had closely followed Calles's, and in 1931–1932, he had served as the Jefe Máximo's hit man in purging the army of Amaro followers before moving on to positions as secretary of industry, commerce, and labor, and finally, secretary of war. Rodríguez's political trajectory has led some historians to describe his time in power as the Maximato on autopilot, a time during which Calles enjoyed the luxury of having a trusted friend in office who would pursue his policies.[83] However, the Rodríguez presidency was a time of transition in which the power of the Jefe Máximo began to dim in favor of a new coalition led by the PNR presidential nominee Lázaro Cárdenas. Moreover, Rodríguez turned out to be more independent than Calles had imagined, using his mentor's extended absences from the capital to make his own mark. Behind a façade of paying continued homage to Calles, Rodríguez, Cárdenas, and other politicians increasingly found space to oppose the influence of the Jefe Máximo.[84]

The idea that Calles's behind-the-scenes rule continued unabated during the Rodríguez presidency rests primarily on the continued rituals to honor the Jefe Máximo practiced by both Mexican politicians and U.S. diplomats. On one of his trips to El Tambor, the entire Consejo de Ministros as well as several senators, deputies, and diplomats saw Calles off at the Buenavista train station. The Jefe Máximo undertook the long voyage aboard the presidential train, and the secretary of war accompanied him all the way to Guadalajara.[85] On another occasion, the new U.S. ambassador, Josephus Daniels, prepared to attend a luncheon given in honor of Calles in Cuernavaca with a letter written by President Franklin D. Roosevelt. As the letter—read by Foreign Relations Secretary Puig before Daniels's journey to Quinta Las Palmas—praised Calles for his work of institutionalization and reform, the president forbade members of his Consejo de Ministros to attend the luncheon.[86] Indeed, the power of the Maximato rested as much on an assumption shared widely by Mexican politicians and foreign diplomats as it did on the real power of the

Jefe Máximo. Not surprisingly, Rodríguez sought to install a different culture among his subordinates. In November 1932, one of his memoranda reminded the Consejo de Ministros of his sole authority over their actions, and ten months later, he wrote another missive stating that he, and not Calles, was vested with the executive power of the nation.[87] Rodríguez's orders indicate that he sought to break his subordinates' habit of consulting with Calles, and his desire to assume real authority as president. The repeated missives also show that the president was not altogether successful in attaining loyalty among his subordinates.

Helped by an improving economic climate, President Rodríguez pledged to renew the reform drive interrupted by the crisis of the Ortiz Rubio years. His government promulgated the Código Agrario, or Agrarian Code, a body of legislation that united the disparate legislation on agricultural matters. He also resumed Portes Gil's effort to distribute hacienda lands to campesinos. Influenced by the new economic theory of John Maynard Keynes, which argued for consumer-driven growth anchored by deficit spending in times of economic crisis, Rodríguez established a minimum wage indexed to the cost of living in each state. Finally, shortly before leaving office, the foundation of Petromex, a private company funded by a state subvention, created the first Mexican oil company large enough to compete with foreign investors and safeguard the meeting of domestic demand for oil.[88]

Over time, Rodríguez found out that he enjoyed far greater leverage than Ortiz Rubio. Much like Portes Gil, who had enjoyed political leeway when the Maximato was still under construction and Calles spent five months in Europe, the new president participated in a system of shared government in which Calles played a primary role within the party and Rodríguez ran the executive office.[89] Four months after Rodríguez had taken office, the U.S. military attaché observed that the president "is assuming more and more the responsibilities and decisions, which were formerly left to . . . Calles during the Ortiz Rubio administration."[90]

The case of Finance Minister Alberto Pani—who had worked closely with Calles going back to the Carranza administration—demonstrated that Rodríguez made a serious and at least partially successful effort to limit the Jefe Máximo's influence. In September 1933, Rodríguez's emphasis on Keynesian deficit spending (however modest given the situation of the treasury) clashed with Pani's belief in classical liberal economics and balancing the books. Moreover, Pani disagreed with the anticlericals in the Consejo de Ministros over state policy toward the church. Ordinarily, the president would have attempted to resolve the differences diplomatically. When Pani attempted to enlist Calles's help, however, Rodríguez asked for the finance minister's resignation. With Calles in Tehuacán, the president enjoyed the luxury of over-ruling the Jefe Máximo's plea for reconciliation, and he informed U.S. Ambassador Daniels that he was "no Ortiz Rubio."[91] To avoid an open conflict with Calles, Rodríguez appointed him Pani's successor, a post Calles held for six weeks before stepping aside in favor of a mutually agreeable replacement. It was the Jefe Máximo's final post in the government.[92]

Despite the president's efforts to free himself from the influence of the Jefe Máximo, Calles continued to make his influence felt in the Rodríguez administration and, above all, in the area of education. In 1933, Education Secretary Narciso Bassols, a radical within the PNR and a close ally of Calles's, called for "socialist education" in the public schools. As understood by Calles and Bassols, socialist education constituted an aggressive rejection of religious education rather than the imparting of ideas of social justice, let alone the dialectic materialism taught in Soviet schools. Instead of teaching Marx and Engels—and in great contrast to the lay education imparted in U.S. public schools and favored by Rodríguez—Bassols's curriculum confronted religious dogmas and sought to orient students toward a scientific view of the world. Influenced by eugenic thought, Bassols also unsuccessfully tried to introduce sex education as a way of reducing teenage pregnancies. Predictably, both socialist education and sex education produced an outcry from among the Catholic clergy as well as their parishioners. So strong were the protests against the new curriculum that Calles came to fear another revolt to oppose a public education openly hostile to the Catholic Church. Indeed, the controversy came on the heels of deteriorating church-state relations after Pope Pius XI issued the encyclical "Acerba Animi" that bitterly attacked the Mexican government.[93] In Veracruz, Tejeda limited the number of priests to one per 100,000 inhabitants, and in Tabasco, Governor Garrido's "Red Shirts" staged public burnings of crucifixes and other religious imagery. In May 1934, as tempers flared, Calles retreated. During that month, Bassols resigned from his post after withdrawing the proposal for sex education from the primary and secondary school curriculum. Having been moved up to Gobernación Secretary, Bassols lasted only for a few weeks before a challenge to Rodríguez's authority similar to the one that had cost Pani his job forced him to resign from that post as well.[94]

The debate over socialist education, however, raged on, and the former schoolteacher Calles remained as radical on this issue as ever. As he announced in Guadalajara on July 20, 1934, "the revolution is not over. . . . It is necessary to enter into a new period, one I would call the period of the psychological revolution. We have to enter and take possession of the conscience of children and youths, because they belong and should belong to the revolution. . . . [The revolution must] uproot the prejudices and form the new national soul."[95] As a result of this speech and ongoing efforts in Congress to amend Article 3 of the constitution to require socialist education, a second Cristero rebellion broke out in the fall of 1934. A far cry from the original rebellion, this second uprising by adherents of the Catholic Church nevertheless brought new bloodshed.

One of the issues most important to Calles personally, the ongoing debate about public education highlighted the relative weakness of the state more generally and the Jefe Máximo specifically to affect the implementation of programmatic statements at the regional and local levels. As Mary Kay Vaughan has demonstrated, the implementation of socialist education obeyed local and regional political dynamics rather than the dictates of national-level policy. In some areas, teachers as well as local authorities ignored the mandates from above in view of stiff popular opposition; in other regions, they far exceeded the directives from Mexico City.[96] Hence, the Maximato (as well as the Cardenista state that succeeded it) fell far short in its efforts to transform popular political consciousness. The revolutionary state remained unable to claim the political loyalty of its subjects, and it could only make incremental gains in its efforts to displace local and regionalist loyalties.

Calles had a similar experience with his efforts to centralize the new political system. Between 1932 and 1934, the Jefe Máximo sponsored two important initiatives: extending the idea of no reelection to the legislative branch, and eliminating the parties and organizations that made up the PNR. Since the former idea directly challenged the prerogatives of top party leaders who represented the party in Congress, it encountered considerable opposition among PNR deputies and senators. At an extraordinary party convention in the city of Aguascalientes, the delegates rejected Calles's plan. Nonetheless, the party ultimately bowed to the combination of popular pressure and the Jefe Máximo's wishes, and in March 1933, Congress amended the constitution to forbid consecutive reelection at the federal and state levels. This measure strengthened the party by preventing congressional seats from becoming sinecures of powerful bosses. In December of that year, the second national convention of the PNR in Querétaro ratified Calles's proposal to dissolve the constituent organizations of the party—organizations that, as Calles believed, threatened the unity of the party. The disappearance of the parties and organizations that had once banded together to form the new ruling party had equivocal results. On the one hand, the reorganization strengthened the PNR, which boasted 1.3 million members by April 1934; on the other hand, these regional parties "colonized" the national PNR, which found itself unable to enforce its directives at the state level.[97]

The Querétaro convention had an even more important task before itself. Elections to choose a president for the next six years were slated for July 1934, and the PNR needed to nominate a candidate. By the summer of 1933, two generals loyal to Calles had risen to the top: Manuel Pérez Treviño and Lázaro Cárdenas. Of the two, the Coahuilan Pérez Treviño more closely resembled Calles's political views, and he had been mentioned as a possible candidate for interim president after the assassination of Obregón. A veteran Obregonista, former president of the PNR, and a significant player in bringing about the downfall of Ortiz Rubio, Pérez Treviño appeared to enjoy the inside track for the nomination. Rodríguez, however, loathed the Coahuilan, as Pérez Treviño had once been the boyfriend of the president's wife, and inclined himself toward the alternative. A native of Jiquilpan, Michoacán, Cárdenas appeared as unlikely to break away from Calles's influence as Pérez Treviño did. In 1915, Cárdenas had joined Calles and the Constitutionalists after serving in the battalion of Juan Cabral, who had just gone into exile in the United States tired of years of bloodshed. During the Obregón presidency, Cárdenas first distinguished himself as an able chief of military operations in the Isthmus of Tehuantepec, a strategically sensitive area where opposition movements had abounded since the days of Félix Díaz. As governor of Michoacán, one of the leading food-producing states, he had carried out an ambitious land reform program that targeted the state's large haciendas, a policy that contrasted with Calles's reluctance to make further land distributions. During the Maximato, he had held various positions in the Consejo de Ministros.[98]

Although most indications favored Pérez Treviño, Calles threw his weight behind Cárdenas several months before the convention. Even before statewide PNR meetings in August 1933, his support of Cárdenas made the nomination of the next candidate a fait accompli. The reasons for Calles's decision remain a subject of debate among historians, but his choice constituted more evidence that he followed rather than directed political currents within the party. Whether he supported Cárdenas following the advice of his son Rodolfo and politicians such as Gonzalo N. Santos, as some evidence suggests, whether he decided on a candidate with excellent ties to labor and campesino organizations to defuse the mounting popular protests of his era, or whether he realized that Pérez Treviño faced insurmountable opposition, he gauged the sentiment in the party and acted accordingly.[99]

Calles believed that he could continue his informal role even with Cárdenas in office. In particular, he judged the candidate's relative youth an asset to him, as Cárdenas was only thirty-eight years old when he was nominated. Moreover, the Jefe Máximo suggested that the party draft a six-year plan to ensure continuity of policy. He sought to install none other than Pérez Treviño as chair of the committee in charge of writing a plan that would be binding on Cárdenas as the presidential nominee of the PNR. Beside the rhetoric promoting the plan as a way to place programmatic objectives ahead of individual ambitions was an effort to minimize any temptations on the part of a candidate known for his agrarian sympathies to overstep the boundaries of what the Jefe Máximo considered an acceptable commitment to reform. In the end, however, Calles failed on both fronts, as a Rodríguez loyalist headed the committee, and supporters of land reform within the PNR amended the original draft in a direction more acceptable to Cárdenas.[100] Bolstered by the new plan, Rodríguez—although hardly a radical within the PNR—used it as his guiding program during his last year in office. Likewise, it is plausible to assume that Calles stoked the fires of the church-state conflict in order to force both Rodríguez and Cárdenas to rely on his tested crisis management.

In response to these maneuvers by Calles, Cárdenas embarked on the greatest presidential campaign tour witnessed thus far in Mexico. Between December 1933 and July 1934, he visited every state and every territory, stopping in both rural and urban areas to give campaign speeches and to become acquainted with the people over whom he was to rule. Unlike Calles, Cárdenas relished the opportunity to meet ordinary Mexicans and to listen to their concerns. During the campaign, his ability to connect with people from a variety of social backgrounds on a personal level provided evidence of a charismatic personality that could renegotiate the terms that bound him to the party and Calles. As Cárdenas was running practically unopposed—a testament to the incipient strength of the PNR machine—the purpose of this tour was to build an independent political base. Although the candidate gave every indication that he would continue to respect Calles's authority, he was even more determined than Rodríguez to avoid becoming another Ortiz Rubio. The campaign constituted the first step to building a national personality cult that ultimately made Cárdenas the "magical man" of Mexico.[101]

Whatever the case may be, a personal encounter with Cárdenas soon convinced Calles that the candidate might one day pose a threat to him. Briefly after obtaining the PNR nomination, Cárdenas visited the Jefe Máximo at his daughter Alicia's beach cottage at El Tambor, Sinaloa. Although the presidential candidate showed due deference to his mentor during this visit, he showed off his independence when he refused to join Calles at his favorite bathing spot on the Pacific Ocean, choosing instead to jump into the water several hundred yards away in the company of one of his friends. In the Mexican political culture, this seemingly insignificant event held great import, and according to historian Enrique Krauze, Calles did not forget the slight.[102] From that point on, Calles kept a careful watch for signs of excessive independence by the PNR nominee, but he knew he could not reverse the process that led to Cárdenas's election.

Nonetheless, upon the closure of the second Querétaro convention, few participants imagined that Cárdenas would put an end to the Maximato. He had the reputation of being a die-hard Calles loyalist, and the Jefe Máximo considered him his political son. Both in public and in correspondence, Cárdenas had treated Calles with almost filial deference. Whether this posture amounted to genuine allegiance or shrewd tactics, he had benefited from his close association with Calles, and the Jefe Máximo's support of his presidential candidacy constituted the ultimate seal of approval. Upon Cárdenas's inauguration on December 1, 1934, the Maximato hence began its seventh year, and Calles fully expected to retain his informal role in both the PNR and the national government.

As Jefe Máximo, Calles played a crucial behind-the-scenes role. After Obregón's assassination, he shrewdly maneuvered himself into a position of arbiter of national political life. Read only six weeks after Obregón's death, his final presidential *informe* appeared to the public a statesmanlike gambit in which the president gave up an opportunity to prolong his term in office for the greater good of the nation, and it earned Calles the support of most of the Obregonistas. In fact, however, this gambit paved the way for the creation of a ruling party dominated by Calles and his allies. Over the next six years, the Jefe Máximo of the Mexican Revolution exerted informal authority in three different arenas: the PNR itself, and, hence, Congress; the Consejo de Ministros; and—to a lesser extent—the state governorships, most of which were held by PNR members as well. As head of the revolutionary family, a powerful metaphor in the service of a growing personality cult, the Jefe Máximo played a prominent informal role. Presidents, members of the Consejo de Ministros, governors, and diplomats often consulted with Calles directly, and no one interested in his political survival ever confronted him. The Jefe Máximo and his family also did well economically, expanding their holdings into successful agribusinesses managed by Rodolfo, Aco, and Alfredo as well as Alicia's husband, Jorge Almada.

A unique political system at a time when authoritarian regimes arose in the rest of Latin America in response to the Great Depression, the Maximato was a system of shared governance in constant crisis rather than a dictatorship. Calles's relative lack of popularity compared to other authoritarian leaders of his time, and the fact that he exerted his influence from behind the scenes, prevented the type of exclusive personality cult that enabled leaders such as Italy's Benito Mussolini to stay in power indefinitely and rule by fiat. The man of steel was Mexico's "Mr. No," a political arbiter strong enough to topple potential rivals and prevent any legislation he did not agree with. Unlike the dictators of his time, however, he did not set the direction of government policy, nor could he stand in the way of presidential candidates such as Cárdenas who enjoyed widespread popular support. Even more importantly, neither he nor any other politician at the national level asserted effective control over the countryside. Mexico remained a relatively weak state throughout the 1930s, and the negotiation of its power remained fiercely contested.[103] As political scientist Jeffrey Rubin noted, "State formation in the 1930s involved particular, localized and changing forms of resistance and accommodation."[104]

In this weak state, Calles's power rested on a different type of personality cult, one embedded in memory of other, more popular revolutionary leaders who had died as political martyrs. Never a hero of the masses, the Jefe Máximo, whose brooding, austere public persona did not endear him to most Mexicans, claimed the diverse legacies of Madero, Zapata, Carranza, Villa, and Obregón as his own. It was the historical artifact of the revolutionary family that afforded Calles the opportunity to claim political allegiance beyond his term as president, and it was his status as the most prominent survivor of the revolution that had made him Jefe Máximo. His frequent consultations with political notables therefore amounted to political rituals rather than command performances. The Jefe Máximo did not hold court in distant locales such as El Sauzal, El Tambor, and Tehuacán just to prove his mettle, as Enrique Krauze has argued, and one would be hard pressed to concur with Krauze's conclusion that Calles "moved the pieces of the national chessboard from his hideouts."[105] Instead, Calles fled the capital primarily for reasons of health and personal enjoyment, and his consultations with other politicians, most of whom essentially shared his own political orientation, obeyed mutual expectations of benefit. Quite often, personal business matters rather than political issues dominated the agenda at those meetings. On some occasions, Calles even tired of his sycophantic visitors, who desired to have their own agendas legitimized by his approval.[106]

The popular level, of course, was another matter. For most Mexicans, the Maximato was a period of economic crisis and social stagnation, a time in which the government paid mere lip service to the redemption of workers and campesinos. As the Jefe Máximo, Calles received his share of the blame for the failings of the revolution: the slow pace of land reform, the persistence of corruption and repression, and the failed emergence of a national, independent labor movement. From the bottom up, the PNR and the state over which it ruled appeared like a club of generals and career bureaucrats who monopolized power at the exclusion of workers and campesinos. As the foremost politician in both state and party, Calles became the target of increasing criticism as the PNR failed to fulfill its lofty promises of economic growth and social justice.

Finally, Calles's role in the Maximato waxed and waned with the exigencies of the moment, the ability of the sitting president to negotiate some radius of action, and the Jefe Máximo's health. The first supposed *pelele*, Portes Gil, enjoyed a power base of his own among the campesinos of Tamaulipas. Portes Gil was also able to take advantage of Calles's lengthy stay in Paris— a city too far away for even the most devoted Callista to visit on a regular basis. Without a doubt, it was during the Ortiz Rubio presidency that Calles enjoyed his greatest influence on the everyday workings of the government. Nevertheless, although Calles systematically weakened the president and ultimately brought about his resignation, he had to share power with Ortiz Rubio, the PNR leadership, and influential generals such as Almazán, Cárdenas, and Cedillo, not to mention Amaro. Due to Calles's declining health, his own private wealth, and astute political maneuvering of his own, President Rodríguez was able to reclaim a significant degree of political power for his office. Historian Tzvi Medin's notion of the period 1928–1934 as a "presidential Minimato" is therefore more accurate for the Ortiz Rubio government than for the other two administrations.[107]

Indeed, as the Rodríguez presidency illustrated, one important key to the Maximato lay in Calles's ability to exploit economic crisis and social unrest in order to sustain a perpetual political crisis that resulted in a high turnover in the Consejo de Ministros and the leadership posts of the PNR. Absent this crisis, which allowed him to use political differences and personal animosities among the governing elite for his own benefit, the scales of power shifted away from the Jefe Máximo. During the Ortiz Rubio presidency, his strategy of dividing the political leadership against itself rested in large part on the fiscal difficulties of the Mexican state and the constant challenges to both federal and state authorities by campesinos and workers unhappy with the broken promises of the revolution. Once the state's financial situation improved in the Rodríguez administration, the president enjoyed a greater degree of leeway of addressing his country's social problems and, hence, reducing his dependence on Calles.

The Rodríguez presidency therefore marked the beginning of a period of transition to a political landscape without Calles. Without detracting from Cárdenas's considerable political acumen, this analysis of the Jefe Máximo's role in Mexican politics demonstrates that Cárdenas came to power at an auspicious time for a challenge to the Maximato. In December 1934, Calles was a tired and sick man older than his years, a survivor of a turbulent quarter-century rather than a visionary to lead the country into the future. Many Mexicans were ready for him to fade into the twilight.

CHAPTER SEVEN

In the Twilight

Calles is a corrupt crook, and everything he did was only for his convenience, but Cárdenas is a Bolshevik by conviction.

—A Catholic proprietor, quoted in Knight (1994)

On June 12, 1935, the Mexico City daily *El Universal* roused its readership
with the headline "Sensational Declarations of General Plutarco Elías
Calles." Six weeks before, the Jefe Máximo had returned to Mexico City after undergoing gall bladder surgery in a Los Angeles hospital in January, followed by months of recuperating in El Tambor.[1] In early June, he had met
with seven senators at his ranch Santa Bárbara, an old hacienda located near
the village of Ixtapaluca east of Mexico City. At the meeting, Calles issued
"guidance" to the senators on how to handle the developing split among the
PNR into left-wing and right-wing factions. Calles's private remarks made
the papers the next day, and they amounted to a blistering attack on the direction his country had taken during his absence. Without criticizing President Cárdenas directly, the Jefe Máximo declared, "We have to confront the
wave of egotism that is sweeping the country." He deplored the "constant
strikes that have rocked the nation for six months. The labor organizations
are showing in many cases examples of a lack of gratitude. The strikes hurt
capital much less than they do the government, because they close the door
to prosperity. In this fashion, they constantly obstruct the good intentions
and the tireless work of the president."[2]

Cárdenas, however, let it be known that he did not need the Jefe Máximo's advice, much less his paternalistic concern. He immediately asked for the resignation of his entire Consejo de Ministros and put together a team much less likely to defer to Calles, who had helped pick Cárdenas's first cabinet. Soon thereafter, most former Callistas in Congress pledged their allegiance to Cárdenas. Those who did not lost their leadership positions in the legislature and in the party.[3]

The events of June 1935 augured Calles's effective retirement from politics. Although he retained a vivid interest in the arena to which he had dedicated more than twenty years, Calles was little more than an observer of the political scene during the decade he had left to live. His break with Cárdenas robbed him of his remaining political influence. Calles spent the years 1936–1941 in exile in San Diego, incensed at the direction the revolution had taken under his erstwhile protégé but increasingly resigned to his retirement. In March 1941, he returned to Mexico City to spend most of his last four years attending to private and business matters.

The Break with Cárdenas

When Cárdenas took office on December 1, 1934, it appeared that the revolution had lost momentum. Millions of campesinos remained without land of their own. With the labor movement splintered into thousands of small local and regional organizations, the Maximato had kept a tight hold on labor activism, outlawing strikes that threatened economic growth in the Jefe Máximo's opinion. Thus, a new industrial class had emerged as the winners of the revolution: a class of native capitalists that had taken advantage of the political reshuffling to establish itself at the center of economic development in a close alliance with foreign investors. The era when Calles had supported wholesale unionization and appropriated the Zapatista program of land reform appeared as if it had taken place eons earlier. Indeed, many of those who had once supported Calles—whether Agraristas such as Soto y Gama or the U.S. intellectual Beals—had noted that he had led Mexico into the Thermidor of its revolution. During the past fourteen years, a new bourgeoisie had emerged triumphant over the lower classes in whose name the revolution had been fought. In 1934, the revolution appeared mere rhetoric in the face of years of economic crisis and government repression.

Not surprisingly, popular organizations challenged the established order throughout many states in the republic. Agrarian protest raged in Veracruz and several other states, often accompanied by violence. Led by the Marxist Vicente Lombardo Toledano, the Confederación General de Obreros y

Campesinos Mexicanos (CGOCM, or General Confederation of Mexican Workers and Campesinos) broke with the CROM and made radical demands for social change while purposefully avoiding the close relationship with the Jefe Máximo that had characterized Morones's union. Strikes exponentially increased in number during the Rodríguez administration: in 1934, the government counted 202 registered strikes, up from 13 in 1932, and unregistered (wildcat) strikes far exceeded that number.[4] In May 1934, the workers of El Aguila Mexican Petroleum Co. in southern Veracruz began the most significant one of these strikes, one that ended only with President Rodríguez's arbitration. Favorable to the oil workers' demands for higher salaries, Rodríguez's award caused a ripple effect throughout the largely foreign-owned oil industry. Finally, students held the country's largest and oldest university, the Universidad Autónoma Nacional de México, in constant turmoil.

Worker and student radicalism followed the signs of the times. In Europe as well as the Americas, the 1930s witnessed the rise of radical ideologies, whether right-wing totalitarianism or communism. After the Great Depression, Western capitalism appeared in crisis, and radicals persuasively argued for a fundamental transformation of society in favor of the patronage of the state. The three-sided conflict among right-wing totalitarianism, communism, and liberal democracy captivated many Mexicans. The country witnessed the same political polarization that contributed to the emergence of the Nazi dictatorship in Germany, the Spanish Civil War, and the Estado Nôvo in Brazil. In particular, communist ideas gained strength among industrial workers in the hard-hit export sector, especially oil workers, miners, and railroad workers, and European fascism decisively influenced the formation of the right-wing Catholic Sinarquista movement later on in the Cárdenas administration.[5]

Although Cárdenas was not a communist, he stood on the left wing of the PNR, and he was sympathetic to the plight of campesinos and workers. The new president displayed a genuine concern for the poor. Cárdenas was the first president who had grown up with the revolution, fighting his first battles in early 1913 at the age of seventeen. A member of a generation known as the "cubs of the Revolution," he grasped the motives that drove people to armed revolution better than his predecessors, and he acted to fulfill the basic needs of his followers. As governor of Michoacán between 1928 and 1932, he had parceled out more than 140,000 acres of land—more than his predecessors combined during the previous ten years.[6] As the native of a state that was a hotbed of the Cristero rebellion, he also enjoyed a far better grasp on the attitude of rural people from "Old Mexico" than his mentor. Indeed, his ability to listen constituted his greatest strength, and he had taken advantage of the opportunity to meet Mexicans from all walks of life during his extended campaign tour. Cárdenas's political persona was in many ways the opposite of Calles's: he governed through compromise, and he paid attention to personal relationships. In the opinion of former Education Secretary Narciso Bassols, Cárdenas "had political instinct at the tip of his fingers."[7] On the other hand, Bassols believed that his willingness to delegate important decisions to subordinates also masked an intellect shallow in comparison to Calles's analytical mind. His personal convictions aside, a degree of opportunism also influenced Cárdenas's decisions. He realized even before coming to power that his political survival depended on revitalizing the revolution by legitimating his regime with popular support. Such widespread support only came to those who responded to the grievances of the two large groups of the population—campesinos and workers—that had been excluded from power despite the PNR's claim to represent their interests.

While Calles remained in El Tambor, Cárdenas took the first symbolic steps toward a new political culture that highlighted communication between the president and his subjects. He announced that every Mexican was allowed to send one telegram to the presidential office free of charge from state-owned telegraph offices between noon and 1 PM each day. Tens of thousands took advantage of this opportunity. Similarly, Cárdenas refused to wear a coat and tie at most official functions, and he cut his salary in half. Finally, rather than living on Chapultepec Hill, he remained in a house on the nearby Rancho La Hormiga where Calles had lived as secretary of *gobernación* in the early 1920s. Known as Los Pinos, this property has remained the official residence of Mexican presidents to the present day. To make the change permanent, Cárdenas turned Chapultepec Castle into a museum of national history.[8]

The new president then moved to rid himself of Calles's influence in more substantive ways. In particular, he targeted the army, never a mainstay of Callista support. Cárdenas cultivated junior officers from his own generation by increasing their pay and giving them educational opportunities. Even more importantly, he rotated regional military chiefs (*jefes de operaciones militares*) allied with Calles away from their home bases and replaced them with his own loyalists. He also installed one of his confidants as head of the PNR (Partido Nacional Revolucionario), and he sent the potential rival Pérez Treviño to Spain on a diplomatic mission.[9]

Meanwhile, Cárdenas kept a solicitous tone in his letters to the Jefe Máximo, whom he had always regarded as his mentor. In April 1935, he even sent Bassols to El Tambor to consult with Calles about monetary policy. However, the relationship between the two generals was already strained. Calles brusquely sent Bassols back to Mexico City after a short conference.[10] According to U.S. consular reports, the Jefe Máximo may even have considered an armed movement against Cárdenas from U.S. soil as early as January 1935.[11]

Cárdenas's most important strategy in confronting Calles, however, consisted of giving free rein to organized labor. The exponential increase of strikes in the Rodríguez era had already shown that the Maximato could no longer keep a lid on social discontent. It had also demonstrated the weakening of the CROM, which had hitherto blocked many strikes through its hold on national and regional arbitration boards. Faced with the choice between repressing labor and using it for his own purposes, Cárdenas allowed the unleashing of a wave of strikes throughout Mexico with a view of eventually incorporating the workers into his own clientelist relationships. In particular, two groups of workers repressed during the Calles years—oil and railroad workers—took center stage during the strikes of the first half of 1935. In total, the country witnessed approximately twelve hundred strikes involving companies such as the national railroads, the El Aguila and Huasteca oil companies, and the telecommunications sector in the capital. Cárdenas not only allowed these strikes to proceed, but he also lent his support to the workers, stating that they had "always suffered injustices, disregard, and privations."[12] He also attacked capitalists for ignoring the "human dignity of the workers."[13] After years of stagnation, Cárdenas therefore revived revolutionary populism and took it to a new level. In his inaugural speech, he had promised a government responsive to the needs of the less fortunate, and he began to deliver by freeing labor from its shackles and revitalizing the land reform program.

Yet Cárdenas by no means invented populism in Mexico as political scientist Jorge Basurto has argued.[14] As we have seen, Cardenismo was an evolution of Callista authoritarian populism; its reliance on mass mobilization masked the use of strong-arm tactics to assert the power of the central government. The emphasis on public education, the campaign against alcoholism, the belief that the state had an important role to play in the economy, the quest to centralize power in the ruling party, and a paternalistic attitude toward allies and political opponents alike all constituted elements of continuity from Callismo to Cardenismo. Although Cárdenas's personal rapport with ordinary Mexicans contrasted with Calles's stern posture, the two men shared Rousseau's exhortation to politicians to implement the public interest, however defined. However much Cárdenas strained to convince ordinary Mexicans that he listened to their concerns, he was just as convinced as his former mentor that he knew what was good for "the people."

As an example, Cárdenas promised to implement women's suffrage on the national level, only to retreat from this idea in 1939 for fear that the new, Catholic-backed Partido de Acción Nacional (PAN, or National Action Party) would find widespread support among rural women.

This basic similarity in political philosophy made the clash between Calles and Cárdenas all the more inevitable. Despite his weakened health, Calles did not tolerate Cárdenas's left-wing populism—and especially his reliance on popular mass movements. Alarmed at his former protégé's support for labor radicalism, he hoped that his loyalists in the Cárdenas administration would keep the president in check. The most important one of these allies was his son Rodolfo, but other Callistas in the Consejo de Ministros included Sáenz, Garrido Canabal, and Abraham Ayala González, Calles's private physician and the husband of his private secretary. In particular, Garrido was to contain agrarian radicalism and ensure that the Cárdenas administration pursued the one radical initiative in which Calles remained vividly interested: the campaign against the Catholic Church. Throughout Garrido's six-month tenure as secretary of agriculture, his Red Shirts from Tabasco terrorized parishioners in Mexico City and even killed some of them in a melee outside a church in the suburb of Coyoacán. In response, former Villista general Nicolás Rodríguez organized a fascist *Camisas Doradas*, or "Gold Shirt," movement.[15] The clash between the Callista, left-wing "Red Shirts" and the anti-Callista, right-wing "Gold Shirts" showed the political complexity on the eve of the showdown between the president and the Jefe Máximo. Personal allegiances played as much of a role as ideology.

During Calles's long absence from December 1934 to May 1935, Cárdenas gradually strengthened his hand vis-à-vis the Jefe Máximo. The president could not only count on the newly appointed *jefes de operaciones* but also on his own allies in the Consejo de Ministros, including his mentor, former Michoacán governor Francisco Múgica, and former president Emilio Portes Gil, who had fallen out with Calles during the Ortiz Rubio administration. Indeed, most of these allies belonged to the president's own generation: the average age of his cabinet was forty.[16] Most importantly, as a result of the cynical political games of the Maximato, Calles enjoyed only soft support in Congress. By June 1935, Congress was already divided into Callista and Cardenista wings, and many Callista senators and deputies had adopted a wait-and-see attitude. These politicians stood at the sidelines in anticipation of the conflict between the president and the Jefe Máximo, ready to embrace the winner. Many of these erstwhile Callistas would conveniently jump ship to become, in the words of historian Alan Knight, "skin-deep and tactical" Cardenistas.[17] Another group, those politicians who had lost ground during the Calles years, at least initially backed Cárdenas as the anti-Calles.[18] Last but not least, the U.S. ambassador was firmly in Cárdenas's camp. Just as Dwight Morrow had helped prop up Calles in the late 1920s, Josephus Daniels remained true to his roots as a Wilsonian Democrat in desiring constitutional rule, that is, effective government by the elected president without the interference of the Jefe Máximo.[19]

Calles's public criticism of organized labor in June 1935 therefore constituted a major tactical error. His attack on the right to strike demonstrated that the Jefe Máximo had lost touch with the political reality. When Calles exhorted all Mexicans to abandon strikes he considered useless, he rallied labor leaders around Cárdenas. Counterproductive to his efforts to remain a political force during Cárdenas's tenure, his comments raise the question of how a wily, sophisticated politician such as Calles could commit such a serious error of judgment.

Although historians will never know for sure, the memoirs of the politicians involved in this affair offer some clues that indicate that Calles may have walked into a trap designed by his conservative supporters. One of these supporters, Ezequiel Padilla, the Mexico City senator and ardent Callista who issued the Jefe Máximo's declarations to the press, claimed in a 1956 interview with historian John W. F. Dulles that he had attempted to discourage the Jefe Máximo from a public challenge to Cárdenas. As Padilla recalled, Calles insisted on the publication of his remarks in the Mexico City newspapers.[20] However, Portes Gil claimed in his memoirs that he and Cárdenas resolved to prevent the publication of Calles's remarks in order to prevent discord within the revolutionary family. According to Portes Gil, he failed to locate Padilla even after strenuous efforts, insinuating that the senator may have avoided contact with him so the publication might go forward unimpeded.[21] It is therefore quite possible that Cárdenas opponents such as Padilla had the statements published in a desire to bring about a conflict similar to the one that had toppled Ortiz Rubio less than three years before this incident. Whatever the case may be, either Calles or someone close to him misread the political reality. As tens of thousands rallied in support of Cárdenas, Calles understood that the end of his informal role had arrived. On June 19, 1935, only a week after the interview, he flew off to Sinaloa aboard a small plane after informing new PNR president Portes Gil that he considered his political career finished.[22]

The Maximato fell with swift suddenness. The day of Calles's departure, the resignation of the entire Consejo de Ministros eliminated the Callista mainstays from the executive branch. In the new cabinet, Cárdenas replaced Garrido with General Saturnino Cedillo, a conservative opposed to Calles's and Garrido's anticlericalism. Múgica took Rodolfo Calles's job as secretary of communications, and Sáenz lost his position to another Cárdenas loyalist. With the military already under Cárdenas's control, the reshuffling of the cabinet set the stage for the almost total triumph of the Cardenistas in Congress, as dozens of Callista senators and deputies either resigned or joined the president's side. The new Congress then took the Cardenista triumph to the state level. Thus, Aco Elías Calles lost his opportunity to become governor of Nuevo León following a highly contested and fraudulent election.[23] At the same time, an anti-Garrido expedition seized the state government in Tabasco, undercutting one of the Jefe Máximo's most valuable allies, and Cárdenas removed the remaining Calles supporters from positions of authority in the military.[24] The lack of violence during the showdown, and the relative ease with which Cárdenas imposed himself as the real ruler, provided evidence that the Maximato had been much weaker than it appeared.

Cárdenas's decisive action left Calles without viable options. The leadership of Congress, the party, and the army had deserted him, and only among the state governors did Calles continue to enjoy majority support. The former Jefe Máximo therefore decided to leave Mexico to await the passing of the storm set off by his injudicious remarks and to give the opposition to Cárdenas time to regroup. From Sinaloa, he traveled to San Diego, where he made further critical statements about Cárdenas's government. In an October 1935 letter to Pérez Treviño, the man whom he had passed over in favor of Cárdenas for the 1934 presidential nomination, he wrote that the president and his associates "clearly and openly attempt[ed] to transform our constitutional government toward communism."[25] The following month, Cárdenas reportedly asked Calles to remain in the United States indefinitely for the sake of political stability. In light of his poor health and out of concern that his own property might be expropriated if he refused, Calles initially agreed to the president's request.[26]

On December 13, 1935, however, Calles returned to Mexico City in the company of Morones. At the time, Cárdenas was ill and running a high fever, and the national university was under siege by left-wing students who had taken over several buildings of the university. In an announcement kept from the press by the government, Calles announced that he had returned to defend himself against the slander to which he had been subject over the past six months. He also took full responsibility for the course of the revolution from his inauguration as president through June 15, 1935.[27] The large entourage of unrepentant Callistas at the airport, a throng of one thousand people that included Amaro, Luis León, and more than twenty members of Congress, indicated that Calles had far more in mind than launching a rhetorical defense of his actions. U.S. military intelligence reported preparations for a coup against Cárdenas, and according to historian Carlos Macías, Calles "thought that he still enjoyed the support of the majority of the political class."[28] Indeed, twenty-one states remained under Callista governors, and four powerful generals—Amaro, Almazán, Cedillo, and Rodríguez—regretted their decision to side with the president in June. On December 17, Calles alluded to the formation of a rival political party, the Partido Constitucionalista Revolucionario (Constitutionalist Revolutionary Party) by allies such as León and former Guanajuato governor Melchor Ortega. Following a warning by telegram, Calles did not announce his own intentions to join the party. When he found out that Cárdenas had a copy of the telegram, he knew that he was under strict surveillance.[29]

The specter of an opposition party gave the Cardenistas the pretext for removing all remaining vestiges of the Maximato at the national and state levels. This step followed the same authoritarian script that Calles had used during his time in power. The PNR declared Calles's expulsion on the grounds that the former Jefe Máximo was involved in the formation of another political party. Without following due procedure, Congress expelled all those deputies and senators who had met Calles at his arrival at the airport. On December 18, the senate ordered Morones's arrest upon the discovery of fifty-seven rifles and ten thousand cartridges in his residence. Congress also declared the disappearance of powers in several states ruled by Callista governors—a pretext for federal intervention. In Sonora, for example, the Cardenistas elevated a Calles nemesis to power, the conservative Mayo general and Escobarista veteran Román Yocupicio Valenzuela. Leaders like the devout Catholic Yocupicio demonstrated the mixed nature of Cárdenas's grand coalition. The president had defeated Calles with the help of two networks: the leaders of new, mass-based campesino and worker organizations, and the political casualties of the Maximato who were eager to reclaim a role in post-Callista Mexico. The rule of the conservative Yocupicio, who stemmed the advance of organized labor and refused to implement the socialist education project, proved a peculiar result of Cárdenas's reliance on the latter network. The transition from the Maximato to Cardenismo therefore did not usher in a uniformly progressive movement. Instead, Cárdenas recognized the utility of a broad-based coalition for removing the Jefe Máximo.[30]

Nonetheless, Calles's return drove the government further into an alliance with campesinos and workers. Cárdenas received thousands of telegrams demanding the incarceration or expulsion of the former Jefe Máximo. On December 22, 1935, the president gave a fiery speech to eighty thousand workers during a rally organized for the express purpose of condemning Calles's return. He announced that "a passionate group stir[red] up the country for personal goals" against an administration in compliance with its mandate to govern according to the constitution. Cárdenas rejected the imputations of the Callistas that his government was communist, pointing to the peaceful, gradual nature of his reforms and to the existence of a democratic process that could repudiate his policies in the presidential elections of 1940. Only in the last sentence of his speech did he mention Calles by name, reassuring his audience that the former strongman offered no threat to his government and could hence remain in Mexico.[31]

Over the next four months, Calles's presence in the capital contributed to consolidating the Cardenista coalition, which in turn allowed the president to embark on an ambitious program of land reform and unionization. In late February 1936, the CGOCM and a smaller union merged to form the Confederación de Trabajadores Mexicanos (CTM, or Mexican Workers' Confederation) under the leadership of Lombardo. The union, which counted almost one million members by 1937, enjoyed Cárdenas's patronage much like Calles had protected the CROM. The CTM, however, was far more ideologically focused than the CROM had been, advocating the expropriation of private property as a means of redeeming the workers. Indeed, Cárdenas expropriated a total of 49 million acres during his presidency, or four times as much as all his predecessors combined, targeting the very structure of the commercial hacienda that had thus far eluded land reform. He placed most of this land in the possession of the communal *ejido* rather than in the hands of small landowners as Calles would have preferred. As part of the land reform, the Cardenistas went after the landholdings of prominent Callistas. In the cotton-growing Laguna region of Coahuila, the government nationalized not only the lands of foreign investors but also that of Pérez Treviño. In neighboring Tamaulipas, the government went after the Compañía Azucarera El Mante, a sugar-producing agribusiness of 38,000 acres in which the Calles and Sáenz families were the principal investors. The proceedings ultimately resulted in the expropriation of the estate.[32] In late January 1936, 250 campesino women from the neighborhood invaded Santa Bárbara, the country estate near Mexico City that Calles had recently acquired as his private residence, and demanded its conversion into a women's school. Although the actions of the women obeyed no command other than their own, Calles regarded Cárdenas as the force behind this attack.[33] Consequently, he asked for and received his discharge from the army.[34]

Not surprisingly, Calles viewed popular mobilization with alarm from his retirement at Santa Bárbara. In early April 1936, he received a surprise visit from the famed historian José C. Valadés, who would go on to write path-breaking histories of the Reforma and the Porfiriato. Reminded by his visitor that he once favored "socialism," Calles said—in reference to Cárdenas allies such as CGOCM leader Lombardo—that the socialist state he favored was not "the communist state. I have always believed in the necessity of state protection for the weak classes. . . . But there is a great difference between the intervention of the state on behalf of an equitable distribution of surplus value, and the dictatorship of the state with its interference in all aspects of . . . moral and material life." "I once knew," he asserted, "a different General Cárdenas who was a revolutionary rather than a demagogue; and a man of action rather than a boundless agitator."[35]

Shortly thereafter, Cárdenas decided to drive his former mentor into exile after all. The president feared that Calles could still count on many supporters, especially in the military. As long as Calles remained in the country, his supporters caused trouble for the government, and rumors abounded that the former Jefe Máximo was planning a coup d'état.[36] Moreover, demands for Calles's expulsion reached a fever pitch in April 1936 after a sabotage attempt interrupted rail communications between Mexico City and Veracruz. Although the authors and motives of this attempt remain shrouded in mystery, many Mexicans considered Calles a suspect. On April 9, 1936, Cárdenas therefore gave the order to expel Calles "to avoid disturbing the work of institutions" dedicated to furthering "the meaning of our social struggle."[37] It was the final act in the showdown between the two political leaders.

Hotel California

About 11 PM that night, a van and several cars pulled up the driveway of Santa Bárbara. Ten officers clambered out and rang the bell of the house, in search of the owner of the country estate. They found Calles in bed reading Adolf Hitler's *Mein Kampf*. Sick with the flu and clad in blue and white pajamas, the former Jefe Máximo shook his head in amazement as General Rafael Navarro Cortina, the district commander who had replaced a Callista less than a year before, read him the order giving him a choice between arrest and leaving the country. For a man familiar with the Mexican justice system, the choice was easy. The leader who had been known as the Jefe Máximo of the Mexican Revolution had only a few hours to gather some of his most important belongings. Before noon of April 10, he was aboard a small airplane with fellow deportees and friends León, Morones, and Ortega, heading north to Brownsville, Texas.[38] The next day, Calles was in exile in California, immigration formalities cleared for him courtesy of the help of Ambassador Daniels.[39] After a short stay in Los

On the way to exile
From left: three military officers, General Rafael Navarro Cortina, Rodolfo Elías Calles Chacón, Plutarco Elías Calles, and Alfredo Elías Calles Chacón
Source: FAPEC.

Angeles, he moved in with his daughter Hortensia, then in San Diego due to her daughter's recent enrollment in a Catholic school near that city. From a small house that lacked the comfort of his country estates, he was left to ponder how a man whom he had handpicked as president could have shaken off his tutelage. History had passed him by.

Only recently have newly catalogued documents available in the Calles archive allowed researchers to answer two persistent questions that have surrounded the five years he spent in San Diego. First, how did the old strongman view events in Mexico and the world, and particularly the unfolding three-sided conflict among the two great totalitarian ideologies and the democracies of Europe? Second, did Calles use his exile, as other leaders living abroad have done, to plot against the Cárdenas government or otherwise influence Mexican politics? An examination of Calles's personal correspondence reveals that the Jefe Máximo definitively retired from politics following his flight into exile, and that he found the Mexican political scene increasingly distasteful. Despite his unwillingness to step back into the limelight, however, Calles supported or at least sympathized with a number of schemes to remove Cárdenas from power.

In conceptual terms, Calles's exile tests political scientist Yosse Shain's notion that political exile is characterized by "the moving frontier of loyalty."[40] According to Shain, political exiles construct a discourse in which they represent themselves as authentic patriots and justify their departure or expulsion from their homeland by repositioning loyalty to the nation as opposition to the government.[41] If Calles had followed this pattern, he would have presented himself as a viable alternative to Cárdenas. In the words of historians Ingrid Fey and Karen Racine, he would have displayed "exilic behavior" that featured an "intensified awareness of personal and collective identity" and attachment to the home country.[42] Having tired of the political struggle, however, Calles followed a slightly different pattern. Although the so-called iron man was only fifty-eight years old at the time of his deportation, his steely exterior belied poor health, and his persistent ailments made a return to a political career impossible.[43] In addition, even though Calles never saw his exile as a permanent condition, he came to display characteristics of the adaptation to an expatriate existence.[44] In this case, the effort to adapt to a new environment was accompanied by a process of transculturation in which Calles viewed Mexican politics through the larger optic of world affairs. In his letters to political allies, friends, and family, Calles saw himself as the member of the international disillusioned left that—in its desperation—turned to the right for inspiration and political solutions. While Mexico always remained the point of reference, the struggle between left and right in Europe commanded much of his attention by the time Hitler's armies overran Poland in September 1939.

Free from all compunction, Calles stepped up his public criticism of Cárdenas once he had established himself in the United States. "I do not agree with the government of . . . General Cárdenas," he stated in a newspaper interview, "because he is trying to establish communism in Mexico with his radical policy, using methods of agitation and demagogism [sic], loosening the popular discipline and driving the laborers to misery."[45] In a June 1936 speech at an AFL convention in Tulsa, Oklahoma, Calles drew a sharp contrast between what he called "rational socialism," his term for state intervention in an essentially capitalist and secular society, and Cardenista "false socialism": the desire to organize agricultural and industrial production in state-run cooperatives.[46] In an essay published in the magazine *Today,* he portrayed his position as the middle road between the swings of the pendulum of the 1930s toward "leftist" extremes in Mexico and Soviet Russia and "rightist" extremes in Nazi Germany.[47]

In Calles's view, evidence of left-wing extremism included Cárdenas's alliance with the CTM labor union and what he saw as the unbridled expropriation of private property. As he told the AFL, he opposed Cárdenas's effort to achieve the unity of the workers by government fiat. "The unification of the workers," he stated, "needs to be their own work; they should not be manipulated by the government."[48] He also likened the land reform program to that of Soviet Russia and portrayed the *ejido* as a gigantic mistake that would diminish agricultural production and keep the campesinos in perpetual misery.[49] Both viewpoints were consistent with Calles's opinion since the beginning of the revolution, but it is ironic that the former Jefe Máximo belatedly realized the pitfalls of a state-supported labor union such as the CTM or Morones's CROM of the 1920s. From his vantage point, of course, Calles would have never admitted that the CTM accomplished more for workers in the Cárdenas period than the CROM in the preceding ten years.

Calles's rants from his exile, however, went far beyond such attacks on Cardenismo and entailed a frontal assault on Mexican politics in general. Life in the United States showed him a different style of politics, which contributed to judging the politicians of his own country in unforgiving terms: "I know the political landscape of [my] country . . . [and] it has always been the same," he wrote to his eldest daughter, Hortensia, then in Mexico City. "The friends of today are the enemies of tomorrow; ardent admirers become scathing critics; what they affirm today, they will deny tomorrow; Liberals turn into Conservatives and vice versa; and the fanatical Communists of today will be the recalcitrant Fascists of tomorrow."[50] With these words, Calles not only described other Mexican politicians but also his own trajectory from a revolutionary governor calling for "land and books for all" to the Jefe Máximo who feared the destabilizing potential of mass-based campesino and workers' movements. His remarks thus wrote a fitting epitaph to his career, and they reveal his profound disillusionment with Mexican politics as well as his adaptation to a very different political culture.

Disgusted with politics, Calles settled into a quiet life. Shortly after his arrival, he enjoyed a rare stroke of luck. During a visit of the 1936 World's Fair held in San Diego, his son-in-law, Jorge Almada, bought a ticket to a lottery. The ticket won the grand prize, the Casa del Tempo—a model house with ultramodern amenities such as a dishwasher that had been one of the sensations unveiled during the fair. The prosperous owner of a sugar mill in Sinaloa, Almada allowed his father-in-law to live in the house free of charge. Installed at 1212 Upas Street on the edge of beautiful Balboa Park, from where Calles could distinctly hear the roar of lions and other animals in the San Diego Zoo, the Casa del Tempo was the perfect residence for Calles to spend his years in exile. It was smaller than his residence in Cuernavaca but large enough to accommodate members of his family who came to visit.[51] From his new house, Calles ventured out of town in a late-model Buick to visit nearby farms, or he walked through the extensive green spaces of the park. Calles's favorite summer spot was a beach cottage in Del Mar, California, eighteen miles north of San Diego, where he spent three months a year in the company of his relatives to devote himself to swimming, his favorite hobby. Although the exile, in Enrique Krauze's words, "accentuated his character traits of gravity, melancholy, and stoicism," Calles enjoyed his Southern California surroundings.[52] He never learned much English, leaving it to his secretary, Jorge Castellanos, and his daughter Hortensia to negotiate his interactions with Anglo-Americans. Calles also never got used to the early lunch hour in the United States, and he complained about his kitchen help until Hortensia finally procured a Mexican maid who would prepare his main meal of the day around 3 PM. But as the years passed, he enjoyed the peaceful atmosphere of his exile after twenty-three years of virtually nonstop action. As a leader from a border state, he admired the efficient government, strong economy, and technological progress of the United States.[53]

Once acclimated to his new surroundings, Calles no longer gave interviews or speeches regarding Mexican politics. He was bitter about what he viewed as Cárdenas's betrayal, and he also desired to minimize Cardenista efforts to expropriate property belonging to his family. Aside from efforts to clear his name from suspected conspiracies during his rule that might affect his place in the history books, he refused to discuss Mexican politics in public.[54] As Portes Gil later related, his erstwhile friends began to desert him once the magnetism of political power no longer surrounded him.[55] Particularly notable in the Calles archive is the lack of any written correspondence with Morones. Calles did keep in touch with fellow detainees León and Ortega, both of whom moved back to Mexico within the next year, and he even mended fences with fierce political rivals such as José Vasconcelos, also exiled in the United States. For his part, Calles declined a 1937 invitation by Cárdenas to return under the president's blanket amnesty decree for political exiles. As he saw it, he had not committed deeds that would force him to seek amnesty from Cárdenas.[56]

Had Calles followed up on the president's invitation, he might have been able to look past the radical slogans of the multitudes demonstrating in the streets to realize that Cárdenas improved rather than overthrew the Callista system, and he might even have witnessed a glimpse of his own populist past. Indeed, the inclusive nature of the Cardenista coalition pushed the president to the political center as his term went on. Although the new politics of the masses manifested popular participation in Cardenista reforms, neither the expropriation of hacienda land nor the state's support for workers challenged the capitalist nature of economic development.[57] Just like Calles, Cárdenas advocated state-mediated capitalism and sought to exercise control over the mass movements that supported him. Beginning in 1937, he transformed the PNR into a new party, the Partido de la Revolución Mexicana (PRM, or Party of the Mexican Revolution), which constrained both labor and campesinos by vertically integrating their official organization into its structure.[58] This party consummated the process of centralization that Calles had set in motion and vanquished the ambitions of regional caciques.[59] Widely considered the apex of Cardenista nationalism, the expropriation of the foreign-owned oil industry on March 18, 1938, fit the same mold. Cárdenas took the step to nationalize the oil companies only after they had defied a court order favorable to the demands of the workers. Calles, however, saw it differently. As he wrote to Amaro, the oil expropriation was the "least thought out, most illegal, and most aggressive act of the Communistoid regime presided over by the most imbecile ruler that Mexico has ever had," a part of the "frightening moral and material disaster" created by the Cárdenas regime. Calles believed (wrongly, as it turned out) that the united front of the oil companies would ultimately force the government to return their property.[60] Although Calles's anger at Cárdenas lingered throughout his exile, he thus gradually became alien to the Mexican political landscape.

Calles's ruminations on world affairs, and particularly Falange Spain and Nazi Germany, are equally intriguing as his thoughts on Mexican politics. After 1937, Calles increasingly sympathized with these and other European right-wing movements. His interest in right-wing totalitarianism stemmed from his idea that these three movements responded to situations similar to those he saw in Mexico in the 1930s—anarchy, rampant strikes, demagoguery, and incapable political leadership. In each case, he believed, the exclusion of the bourgeoisie from national political power led to a strong backlash that, while not quite to the liking of Calles, was ultimately preferable to the leftist anarchy that he believed Cárdenas had created in Mexico.[61] Thus, Calles's letters on the subject of Falange Spain and Nazi Germany do not support the assertion of Carlos Macías that the ideology of the former Jefe Máximo was marked by an abstract belief in liberal democracy.[62] Based on an isolated source directed to a U.S. audience, Macías's view contradicts Calles's voluminous correspondence with Ortega and others—correspondence not available in his edited collection of Calles's letters.[63]

In Calles's mind, Spain in particular imparted an important object lesson in how the failures of the left enabled the right to triumph. The letters of the old strongman to Ortega reveal a gradual shift in his thinking away from the pendulum of two evil extremes toward his acceptance of the triumph of the Falange forces under Generalísimo Francisco Franco. As president and Jefe

Máximo, Calles had befriended Spanish socialists such as Luis Araquistáin, who admired the Mexican Revolution and the man who led it.[64] Over time, however, Calles's sympathies shifted to the right. In the summer of 1937, Calles wrote to Ortega that Spanish fascism and communism were "equally arbitrary."[65] Engaged in a fratricidal war, he maintained, Spain lost hundreds of thousands of men to the global, impersonal struggle between radical ideologies. Lost in the process, he believed, were the interests of the Spanish nation, sold down the river by dishonest politicians of democratic European powers such as Britain and France.[66] As thousands of Spanish Republicans sought refuge in Mexico, Calles began to gravitate toward Franco. These left-leaning refugees from Falange terror not only espoused an ideology Calles disliked, but they also immediately became staunch Cárdenas supporters upon their arrival.[67] As Calles recognized the strength of left-wing solidarity across nations, he began to imagine a common international response against these leftists. Or, one might say, he held his nose with one hand while holding out the other hand to the Falangists.

Calles's opinion on Nazi Germany also underwent considerable change during his exile. Upon his arrival in San Diego, he had expressed criticism of Hitler's "intolerance and violence," although he explained away Nazi repression as a response to the "excesses" of the German left.[68] The diplomatic and military successes of Germany in the remainder of the 1930s, however, produced unguarded admiration in Calles. In an October 1939 letter to León, the old strongman likened the Führer to the greatest statesmen of all times. Just five weeks after the German armies had invaded and occupied Poland, Calles labeled as a "peace offering" Hitler's appeal to the Western allies to accept his newest conquest as a fait accompli. He called Hitler's speech "the best crafted . . . and most significant . . . historical document produced in our times."[69] He admired the "magnificent" organization of the German military and Hitler's resolve to avenge what he saw as past injustices perpetrated against the German people.[70] In April 1940, the blitzkrieg in Scandinavia was nothing more than a preemptive strike, one that the British would have carried out if the Nazis had not. One month later, Calles even justified the German attack against Belgium, Holland, and France—which Ortega had criticized—as a necessary part of Germany's war strategy. Fascinated with the war, he followed its progress on a large radio.[71]

Although he lived in one of them, Calles did not expound much on his views on the Western democracies that opposed Hitler and Franco. As we have seen, Calles's attraction to the United States was based on pragmatic considerations of the advantages of capitalism, discipline, and efficiency rather than his host country's form of government. In fact, the old strongman scarcely commented on U.S. politics in his letters, even though he witnessed—and approved of—the presidency of Franklin D. Roosevelt, one of the most charismatic and dynamic politicians in the history of the United States. From his comments about Britain and France in the course of the war, however, one can deduce that he viewed the Western democracies as bickering, clumsy systems incapable of confronting the wily dictators of their day.[72]

Finally, he viewed Soviet Russia as the paradise of the demagogues surrounding Cárdenas. Not surprisingly, Soviet communism met with Calles's stern condemnation. While the old strongman viewed Hitler's and Franco's annihilation of opponents as at least partially justified—especially as regarded their communist enemies—he regarded Joseph Stalin's purges as the worst form of government barbarism. Whereas Hitler's attacks on Germany's neighbors had been actions of self-defense, the Soviet invasion of Finland was evidence of "criminal conduct."[73] Calles considered Stalin's claim that he governed on behalf of the proletarians the worst aspect of his rule. In his opinion, the workers did not need a politician to guide them, let alone someone like Stalin.[74]

These ruminations are the thoughts of a former strongman resigned to the end of his political career rather than evidence of plans to mount a comeback during or after the Cárdenas regime. For all his errors and misjudging of politics in Mexico and elsewhere, Calles remained a pragmatist who had come to understand that his time in power had passed. After the first few months, his exile was therefore not so much an effort to move the frontiers of loyalty away from Cárdenas but the beginning of his final life phase.

Indeed, despite the undeniable fact that the old strongman desired the overthrow of Cárdenas, little evidence exists that Calles made a concerted effort to achieve either this end or to alter the outcome of the hotly contested 1940 elections held to replace Cárdenas. If Calles ever entertained thoughts of plotting insurrection from the United States, the surveillance measures of the Cárdenas administration made the idea difficult to carry out. On Cárdenas's orders, at least three Mexican secret service agents were stationed near the Casa del Tempo to report on all comings and goings, and U.S. military intelligence was looking on as well. Over the years, the agents reported little of interest and did not find evidence of plots against the Mexican government. The Cárdenas administration also placed Calles's friends and family under a close watch.[75]

As Calles was aware of the surveillance under which Cárdenas had placed him, however, the agents' failure to uncover suspicious activities does not necessarily mean that the former Jefe Máximo kept quiet. In a recent work, historian Carlos Silva Cáceres cites Calles's support for an opposition party, the Partido Revolucionario Anti-Comunista (PRAC, or Revolutionary Anti-Communist Party).[76] Historian Steve Niblo also lists Calles as a supporter of presidential candidate Juan Andreu Almazán.[77] Finally, according to historian Friedrich Schuler, Calles presented a memorandum in late 1940 to a representative of the Spanish Falange that contained plans for an armed insurrection in northern Mexico.[78] Judging from the available documentary evidence, however, such attempts to influence Mexican politics were feeble and haphazard. The PRAC, for example, received a monthly subsidy of 150 dollars from Calles—a pittance compared to the tens of thousands of dollars paid to the party by the oil companies.[79] Further, although Calles's letters to Ortega reveal his preference for Almazán, the former Jefe Máximo maintained connections throughout his exile with the corrupt cacique of Puebla, General Maximino Avila Camacho, who was the brother of the winner of the 1940 vote, General Manuel Avila Camacho.[80] He was thus not so much pro-Almazán or anti-Avila Camacho as he was opposed to the continued influence of the Cárdenas faction. Of the three contestants, Calles opposed only Francisco Múgica, a Cárdenas ally who had no real shot at winning the elections. In the larger picture, these plans did not amount to a campaign of subversion waged from his exile. Calles did not have much money to give to Amaro and Almazán, and the memorandum cited by Schuler may well have been a ploy to goad the Falange into planning an operation of their own. In fact, Calles occasionally boasted to whomever would listen that he still commanded significant loyalty, and that a revolt would soon sweep away the Cárdenas regime.[81] However, neither Mexican nor U.S. government records contain any substantive evidence of Calles's plans to support such a revolt.

Calles's relative passivity begs the question why Cárdenas had exiled him in the first place. Most importantly, Calles in Mexico was a living symbol of the opposition to Cárdenas within the revolutionary movement. Although Calles was exhausted and tired, other strongmen such as Almazán, Amaro, Cedillo, and Rodríguez were not. Several of Cárdenas's predecessors, Calles included, had confronted rebellions on a national scale. Exiling Calles had sent a strong message that twenty-five years of armed revolution and rebellion lay in the past. Cedillo ultimately did not heed this message and rose up against Cárdenas in 1937. Within six weeks, however, the army had crushed his revolt. The president might also have overestimated Calles's ability to continue opposing him after his retirement. Finally, the exile struck a preemptive blow against any future attempts of a political comeback. We will never know whether a Calles at Santa Bárbara would have proven as harmless as he appeared in his exile in California.

The Quick and the Dead

Calles did not seriously consider returning to Mexico while Cárdenas was president. The election of Avila Camacho in July 1940, however, changed the equation, as the outgoing president made it clear that he would not seek to construct a Maximato of his own under his successor's nominal leadership. After Avila Camacho took office on December 1, 1940, the new president toned down the radical rhetoric of the previous administration. The change in tone indicated that Avila Camacho would pursue a moderate program, including tight control over the mass organizations of the PRM such as the CTM and the Consejo Nacional Campesino (CNC, or National Campesino Council).[82]

The change at the top paved the way for Calles's return. According to Macías, the president initiated discussions through Tencha's husband, Fernando Torreblanca; Caco, by contrast, claims that it was the president-elect's brother Maximino who approached Calles with the idea of returning after the expiration of Cárdenas's term. Once the idea had taken root in Calles's mind, his son-in-law sold the Casa del Tempo in order to free up liquidity to save his sugar estate from impending ruin. As Calles awaited the most propitious time to return to Mexico, he moved into a small house at 5182 Bedford Drive. The previous summer, his small sons Caco and Nanis, who had lived with their father for some of the time he was exiled, had enrolled in military academies in California.[83]

In May 1941, Calles returned to Mexico City after an absence of almost five years. This time, he arrived by car, which did not give his friends and supporters any opportunity to organize a welcoming reception similar to the one that had greeted Calles at the airport in December 1935. He bought a home in one of Mexico City's most modern neighborhoods, Lomas de Chapultepec, located in the hills to the west of the park. While that house was being remodeled, he moved into Hortensia's and Fernando Torreblanca's house at Guadalajara 104 in the Colonia Condesa, one mile east of Chapultepec, where his archive is located today.[84]

Calles soon found that Mexico had not changed much for the better beyond the retirement of Cárdenas. As he wrote to Alicia in 1942, "This metropolitan life that I am leading is too sterile."[85] Pointing to both internal and global factors, he blamed the prevailing conditions in Mexico for his lack of activity. In clear reference to the *ejido* that he continued to oppose, he lambasted the government for failing to give "protection, guarantees, and stimulus" to the countryside. Amidst the economic boom, he correctly perceived the wartime scarcity of raw materials as a problem, anticipating the inflation that would diminish the real earnings of workers and employees later in the decade. The situation would only change, he believed, when someone came along "in this country who will put our house in order."[86]

In a grumpy mood, Calles was not fair in his judgment. Much as he had ignored Cárdenas's turn to the right beginning in 1938, he initially did not realize that Avila Camacho pursued policies similar to some of his own initatives. Most significantly, the last general to occupy the presidential chair concluded the demobilization of the army begun under Obregón and Calles and advanced under Cárdenas. After the civil wars of the 1920s, the agitation of the 1930s, and the hotly contested 1940 elections, he presided over a new phase of political stability not seen since the days of Porfirio Díaz. Although Avila Camacho still distributed more hacienda land than Calles would have liked—12.5 million acres in all—his commitment to land reform was a far cry from that of the Cardenistas. In a return to Callista patterns, the president gave most of this land to smallholders, and he emphasized large-scale irrigation projects.[87] The country was moving forward into the industrial age, in partnership with the United States, with pliant labor and campesino movements that depended on the government for their voice in the political process. In contrast to Calles's prediction, the U.S. government finally acquiesced in the oil expropriation upon the 1941 signing of an agreement that provided for the payment of an indemnity and a Mexican alliance with the United States. Perhaps Avila Camacho's greatest difference from Calles was his appeasement of the church. A military leader who had displayed kindness toward the Cristeros in the late 1920s, the president publicly announced that he was "a believer," thus definitively putting an end to the conflict between the church and the revolutionary state.[88]

The exigencies of world politics soon forced Calles to embrace his fatherland regardless of his misgivings about Mexican politics. As hostilities between Mexico and Germany became increasingly likely following the U.S. entry into World War II after the Japanese attack on Pearl Harbor, his fascist sympathies waned. In May 1942, Avila Camacho declared war on Nazi Germany following the German sinking of two Mexican merchant ships. The state of war not only buried the remnants of what Calles had lambasted as Cardenista radicalism, but it also encouraged political enemies to bury the hatchet.

In this context, Calles did his part to foster an atmosphere of national unity. On Independence Day, September 15, 1942, he joined five other living ex-presidents (de la Huerta, Portes Gil, Ortiz Rubio, Rodríguez, Cárdenas) and Avila Camacho on Mexico City's main square, the Zócalo, for an impressive demonstration of national unity. Flanked by Cárdenas and Calles,

A demonstration of national unity
From left: Pascual Ortiz Rubio, Abelardo L. Rodríguez, Plutarco Elías Calles, Manuel Avila Camacho, Lázaro Cárdenas, Emilio Portes Gil
Source: FAPEC.

the president declared a truce on the political conflicts of the past decades. For Calles, the occasion of meeting Cárdenas as well as his former close friend de la Huerta was awkward indeed. According to the Mexico City press, Calles did not exchange a personal word with either Cárdenas or de la Huerta. Before the ceremony, an icy silence had prevailed among the six leaders until they found themselves before a locked door that the groundskeeper had forgot to open—an error that finally produced some levity and smiles. Cárdenas, however, painted a different picture of the ceremony in his diary, noting that Calles had greeted him with "nobility" that day. Likewise, Calles's daughter Alicia recalled that courtesy had prevailed between Cárdenas and her father.[89]

Whatever the case, Calles turned his back on the political landscape of his country after this sole public appearance. His appearance alongside the other presidents had completed his public rehabilitation, and shortly thereafter, the Senate reinstated him to the army at the rank of General de División.[90] To demonstrate the evenhanded nature of his policy of reconciliation, Avila

Camacho awarded the same rank to José María Maytorena, former governor of Sonora and Calles's enemy in the war between the factions of 1914–1915, "for the services which he rendered to the Revolution in which he lost his personal fortune."[91] As people familiar with the history of Sonora knew, the decline of Maytorena's fortune had been the work of none other than Calles and Obregón, and Maytorena had never served in the military.

As in exile, Calles henceforth tended to the business affairs of his family. The conflict with Cárdenas had diminished the family patrimony, especially upon the expropriation of El Mante. Fortunately for the Calles family, Aco's hacienda, Soledad de la Mota, emerged unscathed despite persistent worries that it, too, might be parceled out to campesinos, and the Mexican government in 1944 paid a modest indemnity for El Mante. Elsewhere, however, the family noted the effects of its removal from political power. Rodolfo owned a car dealership in Ciudad Obregón, Sonora, and his brother-in-law Jorge Almada battled bankruptcy on his sugar estate near Navolato, Sinaloa.[92] Calles's personal fortune in the last years of his life did not measure up to that of other generals who had become rich through the revolution, such as the multimillionaires Abelardo Rodríguez and Aarón Sáenz. His last will of January 31, 1945, listed 2,589,484.10 pesos in assets, or approximately 600,000 dollars.[93]

Just as in San Diego, Calles also found time to focus on his personal life. He spent his day with his family, gardening, golfing, and taking long walks. His Mexico City house was not only home to Caco and Nanis, who both returned to live with their father after a few years in U.S. military academies, but also to another son, Manuel Elías Calles Ruiz, the product of a fleeting liaison with Amanda Ruiz in Agua Prieta. Calles's decision to take in Manuelito spoke to his self-image as a responsible paterfamilias who—unlike his own father—took care of his own.[94] While his family often tied him to Mexico City, he also enjoyed spending time on his ranch in Cuernavaca. In serious disrepair after his five-year absence, the ranch required a variety of tasks of him that reminded him of his meanderings through a variety of professions during his early adulthood. He refurbished the ranch, he grew grapes and other fruit in its orchard, and he even opened a small dry goods store "to maintain contact with the people," as Caco reported.[95] Each June 28, the Club Verde, an association of women from Mexico City's upper classes, threw him a party on the occasion of his *onomástico* (saint's day) in Cuernavaca. To prepare for those occasions, Calles spent the previous day cooking Sonoran-style beef barbeque.[96]

The annual celebration of his saint's day points to an essential irony. A leader who had personified the revolutionary campaign against the Catholic

Church and who had not attended the church wedding of his favorite daughter amidst intensive media coverage proved more compromising when no one was looking. For example, in 1925, Calles served as *padrino* (godfather) to one of his grandchildren.[97] Caco (Plutarco José, Leonor's eldest son) was baptized in a Catholic church, and Calles and his family actively patronized Catholic educational institutions. For example, both Caco and Calles's granddaughter Norma attended Catholic schools near San Diego.[98] Calles most trusted religious institutions in the area of health, an issue that constantly reminded him of the random and uncontrollable nature of human existence. Natalia had been treated at a Lutheran hospital in Los Angeles for her final illness, and in 1935, Plutarco had his gall bladder removed in a Catholic hospital in that same city.

Important for an analysis of his last years, Calles therefore made a distinction between the practice of the Catholic faith, which he despised, and religiosity and spirituality in general. As his health deteriorated, he sought out cures that involved psychosomatic and faith-based healing. The earliest and most spectacular instance of this quest for supernatural intervention in his health was Calles's visit to a *curandero* (faith healer) known as El Niño Fidencio. At the height of the Cristero rebellion, Calles was suffering from a serious skin ailment when he heard reports of Fidencio's healing powers. On February 8, 1928, he took the presidential train to the small northern town of Espinazo, Nuevo León, where thousands had congregated to seek Fidencio's help. Upon his return to Mexico City, the president protected the *curandero* from his recent legislation that forbade the practice of popular medicine.[99]

During his last years, Calles's interest in spiritual healing took a new form, as the man who had once declared war on organized Catholicism in Mexico dedicated one night per week to spiritist séances and conversations with the dead. In July 1941, Calles joined the Círculo de Investigaciones Metapsíquicas de México (Circle of Metapsychic Research in Mexico), a spiritist group founded in 1939 by the former senator Rafael Alvarez y Alvarez. Later renamed Instituto Mexicano de Investigaciones Psíquicas (IMIS, or Mexican Institute of Psychic Research), this group followed in the tracks of earlier Mexican spiritists such as the original member of the revolutionary family, Francisco I. Madero.[100] Like spiritualism, spiritism entails the belief that the spirit is eternal. What is unique to spiritism is the notion that the living can communicate with the spirits of the dead or with those of other living people across great distances. Spiritists profess faith in a Supreme Being and espouse not only the idea of life after death but also that of reincarnation. The spiritists with whom Calles associated formed part of a worldwide community that followed Allan Kardec's *The Book of Spirits*, a book from 1860s France containing advice on how the living can enter into communication with the departed. They saw their faith as a mixture of science, religion, and philosophy that formed the essence of every major school of thought and religion.[101]

Calles attended his first séance at IMIS on July 9, 1941, at the invitation of a close friend and exilee, General José María Tapia, because he wanted to expose spiritism as a hoax. At that initial session, he reportedly witnessed an apparition amidst the group. According to the minutes of that session, the apparition approached and caressed him.[102] From that point on, Calles was sold on spiritism, which appealed to him as a substitute religion that encouraged its practitioners' faith in an afterlife without subjecting them to the orthodoxy and hierarchy of the Catholic Church. Moreover, the group's most important guiding spirit in the *más allá*, the afterworld, was a nineteenth-century physician named Enrique del Castillo who gave the group practical advice about their physical and mental health. "The recommendations of the maestro," wrote Calles to his son Rodolfo, "are full of wisdom, . . . and I hope they will prolong my life."[103] Of course, Calles's track record in heeding advice regarding his health was not good, and it is not likely that he changed his unhealthy lifestyle as a result of the séances.

Once Calles had joined the circle, IMIS attracted an increasing number of political notables. Calles immediately emerged as the focal point of the group, which sometimes congregated at his house in Cuernavaca. He also became one of the group's most regular and devoted attendees. Over the years, dozens of prominent *políticos* attended the sessions, including old allies and rivals such as Almazán, Morones, and Valenzuela, as well as Foreign Secretary Ezequiel Padilla and Secretario de Gobernación and future president Miguel Alemán Valdés. Politically, the group shared Calles's dislike of Cardenismo. Women participated as well, though seldom without familial ties to the men in the group; among others, Alicia, Ernestina, and Hortensia attended sessions, as did Alfredo's wife, Elena. Calles also brought Rodolfo into the spiritist circle. From 1942 to 1946, Rodolfo attended a few IMIS sessions in Mexico City, but ordinarily "communicated" with Maestro Castillo and the group through intense meditation from his home in Ciudad Obregón. On occasion, the famous Nicaraguan poet Rubén Darío appeared to him as well as his father.[104]

As his conversations with the dead reflected some of Calles's innermost thoughts, the minutes of the spiritist sessions offer a glimpse into his reflections on an eventful life that was approaching its end. One time, these reflections arrived through the medium of the fellow Guaymense Carlos E. Randall, one of Calles's enemies during the war between the factions. Randall had served as the last Conventionist governor of Sonora in the fall of 1915 while Carranza had already invested Calles with the Constitutionalist governorship, and he had died in exile shortly after supporting the Escobar rebellion of 1929. Addressing himself to Calles, Randall's spirit lamented the fact that politics had enveloped his destiny. "I am leaving," the minutes quote the spirit as saying, ". . . with the advice not to remember your political past. It is not worth worrying about a world like ours full of barbarians [in the original: Kaffirs]. Devote your last years to leading a comfortable life."[105] The spirit also exhorted Calles to write his memoirs to inform his country of its errors. These errors, of course, resided in Cardenista policies. "That Agrarian Law and that Labor Law [are] two knives that are killing the nation. . . . Let those work the land who are able, those who are willing, and [let these farmers have] the acreage that they can manage. . . . The Ley de Trabajo should have been named Law for the Encouragement of Vagrancy."[106] Of course, the errors were also Calles's, as the two laws dated from the Ortiz Rubio and Rodríguez administrations, respectively. The spiritist minutes also reveal what the rest of the circle thought of Calles. As Castillo's spirit reportedly said, "Plutarco Elías Calles was and continues to be a patriot. He has never been as well prepared as he is now. Day by day, the hour draws near in which our poor and unfortunate fatherland will turn to his experience and wisdom. No one could help the fatherland better than this man of strong character, perfected by his years, without selfishness and vanity."[107]

Strikingly, Calles's spiritist experiences seem not to have involved departed women of his own family. The minutes of the IMIS do not contain evidence that Calles conversed with his two deceased wives. Instead, he claimed spiritist contacts only with his father and dead political leaders, as well as with his living son Rodolfo across a distance. This absence of women from his ideations illustrates that Calles considered them relatively unimportant as far as his personal voyage was concerned. The one exception was his daughter Tencha, who had played the role of First Lady during her mother's last years and remained Calles's principal confidante up to his death.

It was Tencha and the rest of his family that was with him when his body finally failed him after decades of self-inflicted abuse. On October 13, 1945, doctors at Mexico City's Sanatorio Cowdray performed surgery to correct a blocked bile duct, an extremely painful condition for someone who had lived ten years without a gall bladder. Doctors also attempted to remove adhesions that had formed around the intestines. Although the procedure involved considerable risk, Calles had consented to it to rid himself of persistent severe colic caused by the excretion of bile into his abdominal cavity.[108] Initially, the operation appeared to have been successful. Five days after the operation, however, Calles developed circulatory complications. He died at 2:40 PM on the following day, October 19, 1945, surrounded by his family circle. His death certificate lists as causes of death the blocked bile duct and a mesenteric thrombosis, a blood clot in an artery close to the intestine. Just like the baptismal certificate many years earlier, the death certificate listed the wrong age, listing it at sixty-seven rather than sixty-eight years.[109]

Not surprisingly, the funeral at the secular Panteón Civil de Dolores on October 20 was a state affair. Inaugurated in 1880 as the country's final resting place for illustrious politicians, intellectuals, and artists, this secular cemetery located inside Chapultepec Park is the property of the Mexican government. Among the graves of other celebrities, it contains those of two other former presidents, photographer Tina Modotti, muralists José Clemente Orozco, Diego Rivera, and David Alfaro Siqueiros, and writer Octavio Paz. Befitting this setting, much of Mexico's political class, including President Avila Camacho, attended the ceremony, where Luis León gave an inspiring eulogy. As León reminded his audience, Calles's "unbreakable energy and his character of steel were forged in the Revolution."[110]

To Rodolfo, however, his father had now entered the realm of the spirits, from where he continued to communicate with him over the next three months, giving him advice on his health and his career. The minutes of the October 25 session might well have captured Calles's attitude toward death in his last days: "I am sometimes sad, but I am consoled by the fact that I no longer feel the pain that tormented me in my last days. It is necessary for you to forget my death, and not to comment on the cause of my leave-taking. All suppositions are useless. It was destiny that marked my end."[111]

After losing his struggle with Cárdenas for the control of the party and the direction of the revolution, Calles spent the last nine years of his life retired from politics. In San Diego and in Mexico City, he observed a turbulent world that had passed him by. The Jefe Máximo watched from afar while Cárdenas refashioned the PNR through the shrewd use of mass political mobilization. Unlike other Latin American exiles like Fidel Castro and Domingo Sarmiento, who left their countries as young men eager to return triumphant, Calles's fall from power coincided with a physical and emotional exhaustion that made a return to prominence impossible.

In the few years he had left to live upon returning to Mexico, Calles therefore communed with the quick and the dead rather than seeking his ultimate vindication by a return to politics. His embrace of spiritism was a way for a nonbeliever in Mexico's dominant religion, Roman Catholicism, to cope with his own mortality and to reflect on the legacy of his career. Unlike other important figures such as Madero, Zapata, Carranza, Villa, and Obregón, Calles's death came peacefully, marking the very progress in the political stability of his country that he had desired. Rather than riddled by bullets, Calles died in a hospital bed.

Epilogue

On October 19, 1971, Plutarco Elías Calles Chacón, also known as "Aco" among his family, prepared to read the eulogy at the annual anniversary commemoration of his father's death. Rather than at the leafy Panteón de Dolores in Chapultepec, the ceremony was to take place at the stern Monumento a la Revolución. His father's remains had been transferred to the monument two years before.[1] Exemplifying the ironies surrounding the metaphor of the revolutionary family, the transfer had united Calles with four martyred revolutionary heroes enshrined in the monument: Madero, Zapata, Carranza, and Villa. The latter three leaders had at one time or another numbered among Calles's enemies, and Carranza had ordered Zapata's death. As Aco knew, the ironies did not stop there. For the past year, the Monumento a la Revolución had also been the final resting place for the remains of Lázaro Cárdenas. The man who had thwarted the Jefe Máximo had died on October 19, 1970, exactly twenty-five years after Calles's death. The occasion, then, was a political minefield for the younger Plutarco. He was certain to encounter opposition if he used the occasion to revisit the break between the two leaders to defend his father's position. After all, the other speaker at the ceremony was Cárdenas's son, Cuauhtémoc, a loyal defender of his father's legacy who would go on to challenge the PRI (Partido Revolucionario Institucional) when it turned to neoliberal policies in the 1980s and 1990s.

Aco instead endeavored to unite in death what life had divided. He pointed to the factional conflict that had claimed the lives of the revolutionary martyrs in the monument as a natural, if regrettable, outcome of successful social revolutions. The younger Plutarco paid homage to each of the martyrs includ-ing Obregón, whose remains—except for his severed arm exhibited in the Monumento al General Alvaro Obregón in San Angel—lay a thousand miles away in Huatabampo, Sonora. He then pointed to his father as the one who ended the cycle of violence between Madero's uprising of 1910 and the Esco-bar Rebellion in 1929. In particular, Aco highlighted his father's *informe* of 1928 as the turning point in the road to political stability and the unification of the revolution. His father's words, the younger Plutarco argued, led to "the formation of our party, its development and evolution; it has guaranteed Mex-ico a democratic, institutional life that has achieved political stability; . . . thus establishing a base for the development and economic progress of Mexico founded increasingly on social justice."[2] Finally, he drew continuities from Calles to Cárdenas, pointing out that the latter expropriated the oil industry under a law promulgated during the Calles presidency. "Nothing is more ap-propriate," Aco exclaimed, "than to unite in this ceremony . . . the memory of two great men of the Revolution: Plutarco Elías Calles and Lázaro Cárdenas."[3]

Following Aco's lead, recent decades have witnessed a reconsideration of both Calles and Cárdenas within the PRI, which owes its existence primarily to those two leaders. In particular, the debt crisis of 1982 forced the PRI-led Mexican government to devalue the peso and carry out an austerity program that drastically cut government spending, including many social programs such as subsidized food and housing. Disenchanted with his party's turn to the right, Cuauhtémoc Cárdenas broke ranks and launched an opposition presidential bid in the 1988 elections. Upon the desertion of the younger Cárdenas and his supporters, the PRI nomination fell to the neoliberal tech-nocrat Carlos Salinas de Gortari, who promoted Calles as a model for the path he intended to follow as president. As Salinas proclaimed in Her-mosillo, "With vision and strength, Calles built our institutions of political and economic development, and he gave the country what we might call the first modernizing push of the revolutionary history of Mexico."[4] Upon Sali-nas's election, the PRI stressed its political debt to Calles. On the occasion of the forty-fifth anniversary of Calles's death on October 19, 1990, the party unveiled a bust of the former Jefe Máximo in front of its headquarters. The speaker at the ceremony, Commerce Secretary Andrés Caso Lombardo, lauded both Calles and Salinas as great modernizers.[5] As another example of this trend, Calles—who as president had created the Banco de México—finally found his way onto bank notes. In 1991, when the dollar reached an all-time high of 3,300 pesos, the devaluation forced the bank to issue a 100,000 peso bill. The following year, the Mexican government introduced the Nuevo Peso, or New Peso, and 100-peso bills with the same motif re-

Front side of "Calles" 100,000-peso bill (1991)

placed the old 100,000-peso notes. The timing was ironic, as Calles had founded the Banco de México in an effort to end the financial instability that had marked the previous two decades.[6]

Aco's eulogy pointed to the fundamental difficulty in evaluating the career of a leader overshadowed by the highly popular man who ended his political role. It is a commonplace in Mexican historiography to credit Cárdenas, along with Zapata and Villa one of the most beloved figures of the revolution, with the principal achievements of the era of consolidation (1920–1940). To quote a recent scholarly work, Cárdenas "carried out vast programs to achieve goals written into the Constitution of 1917. He remodeled and strengthened the multiclass party his predecessor had founded. He eased the powerful Mexican army out of its preeminent role in politics. His outstanding qualities were deep concern for the campesinos and workers, plus steady pursuit of constructive reforms."[7] Cárdenas gets much credit here that is due his predecessors; for example, he only put the finishing touches on the weakening of the army's political role begun under Obregón, Calles, and long-time Secretary of War Amaro. The "steady pursuit of constructive reforms" applies equally to Calles until economic crisis, the Cristero Rebellion, and the threat of U.S. intervention stifled his government in late 1926, and both leaders centralized authority. As historian Lyle Brown put it, both

Reverse side of "Calles" new 100-peso bill (1992)

"Calles and Cárdenas were pragmatic politicians with distinct styles of leadership that served them well in a political environment where assassination and rebellion were ever-present dangers. To presidents of the post-1940 period . . . they bequeathed a political machine . . . to monopolize power."[8]

This study has portrayed Calles as an authoritarian populist who defied easy characterization. Before the crisis of 1926, his political persona represented five out of Alan Knight's elements of the revolution: anticlericalism, economic nationalism, labor reform, patriotism, and developmentalism, defined by Knight as an effort to "remake Mexican society, to eliminate social vices and instill social virtues."[9] A sixth element—agrarianism—initially formed part of Calles's political program as well. Most dramatically displayed in his election-year appeal to Zapata's friends and family at the tomb of the slain hero, this element was conspicuously absent from Calles the Jefe Máximo. By that time, Calles's populist rhetoric had faded, and he had given up on economic nationalism and labor reform as well, leaving only anticlericalism and developmentalism as enduring traits of his political agenda. The remaining two elements, political liberalism and *indigenismo*, were never a part of Calles's political philosophy, if one discounts his timid support for Maderismo.[10] Not surprisingly, these elements featured prominently in the anti-Calles campaign of José Vasconcelos in 1929.

Calles's political formation began during his search for professional opportunity in Sonora, a period that lasted the unusually long period of thirty-four years, or exactly half of his life. In his quest to restore himself and his family to the social standing that his notable forebears had known, Calles meandered aimlessly through a variety of avocations. These meanderings, however, introduced Calles to the principal regions of his native state as well as to many of the most significant social groups and political players. He grew up poor in the household of his uncle, who adopted him after his mother had died and his father had abandoned him. His teachers imprinted the positivist thought of the Porfirian era on his mind, which held that politics consisted of administration rather than a democratic contest, and that Mexico needed to emulate the societies of Western Europe and the United States in order to be successful. After receiving the equivalent of a ninth-grade education, Calles enhanced these foundations by reading and writing, and he served as a schoolteacher in Hermosillo and Guaymas. He lost interest in this relatively low-paid work, however, and tried his hand at hotel management, until the hotel he administered burned down to the ground. Calles then followed his relatives to the northeast of the state, where he dedicated himself to farming, before giving up the hardscrabble life in the arid border region to manage a flour mill. In that capacity, he held a variety of positions in local politics, but tired of his position amidst the nasty fights for land and water in an unforgiving environment. When the flour mill failed, he therefore went back to Guaymas to open an export/import business. In Guaymas, he joined the revolutionary movement of Madero, under the local leadership of Maytorena, who was elected governor upon the triumph of the revolution in 1911.

Calles's next peregrination—back to the northeast after the failure of the business in Guaymas—proved exceptionally fortuitous and constituted the first turning point of his career. Shortly after arriving in Agua Prieta, Maytorena appointed Calles to the position of comisario in a strategically important border town that soon thereafter witnessed clashes between government forces and Orozquista rebels. Calles, who had no military background, recruited a small volunteer army to defend the established order, and thus became a revolutionary commander. The Orozquistas proved to be only the vanguard of further trouble, as Huerta's assassination of Madero pitted the Sonoran state government against the might of the federal army. Although Calles did not distinguish himself in battle against the Federales, both Maytorena and Obregón, the caudillo of Sonora's volunteer forces, recognized him as an important player in the northeast of the state. After Obregón's departure to fight Huerta in central Mexico, Calles became the point man in the Sonoran theater of the war between the Constitutionalists of Carranza and Obregón and the Conventionists of Villa and Zapata. He again picked the winning side, as Obregón's forces annihilated Villa's great army. Calles and the other Constitutionalists held their own in Sonora, digging themselves in with their backs to the U.S. border at Naco and Agua Prieta. After neither Maytorena nor his ally Villa could dislodge the Constitutionalists from their well-defended redoubts, Calles went on the offensive and, with Obregón's help, claimed Sonora for Carranza's new government. During these chaotic years, in which he had adroitly picked the winner at each turn, Calles found out his true calling as a politician. He also realized that revolutionary mobilization had raised expectations among workers and campesinos, and he developed a populist program that appealed to them.

Beginning in August 1915, when Carranza appointed him as military governor of Sonora, Calles applied this populist program to his native state as a dress rehearsal of the reforms he would later attempt at the national level. Even before the end of hostilities with the Conventionists, he outlawed alcohol and gambling. After the defeat of Villa, Calles drastically increased expenditures for public education and introduced new production taxes for the copper mining companies to pay for his education program. Together with de la Huerta, who served as governor from May 1916 to Calles's election as constitutional governor in June 1917, he also helped organized labor, particularly in the large copper mines. The formation of the Cámara Obrera led to a host of progressive legislation that provided workers with sick leave, vacation and overtime pay, compensation in case of injury, and a maximum workday of eight hours. Finally, the governor undertook a modest land redistribution program, providing landless veterans of the war between the factions with the property seized from his enemies. All of these reforms provided building blocks for the new national constitution, promulgated in February 1917 as the only constitution in the entire world that safeguarded the interests of workers and campesinos. He also waged a repressive campaign against his political enemies, enforcing his campaign against drinking and gambling by draconian measures despite Carranza's and Obregón's efforts to stop him. Further demonstrating a proclivity for drastic steps, he expelled Catholic priests from the state. Calles even took the field against the Yaquis in two futile campaigns in the spring of 1916 and the summer of the following year.

In the second major turning point of his career, Calles became a member of the national government in September 1919, and the focus of his life shifted from Sonora to Mexico City. As secretary of commerce, industry, and labor under Carranza; as secretary of war under de la Huerta; and as secretary of *gobernación* under Obregón, he soon acquired a reputation as one of the leading radicals in the government. He formed part of the Sonoran Triangle together with de la Huerta and Obregón, a constellation dominated by the latter due to his alliances with military and agrarian leaders. Calles therefore turned to CROM leader Morones to build a political base of his own, focused on organized labor, but he found little support among the Obregonistas. However, two strategic marriages strengthened his own ties to Obregón: Tencha's marriage to the caudillo's private secretary, Fernando Torreblanca, and Aco's marriage to Aarón Sáenz's sister, Elisa. In the fall of 1923, the Sonoran Triangle disintegrated, and Calles jettisoned his friendship with de la Huerta in order to reach the presidency. When Obregón decided to support Calles as his successor, a coalition nominally headed by de la Huerta rose up in rebellion. The government's narrow victory in this conflict appeared to leave Calles as a fatally weak incoming president, unpopular and propped up only by Obregón's armed forces.

Nonetheless, Calles's tenure as president was much more constructive, especially in his first two years, than observers would have expected. Calles and his advisers took advantage of increasing demand for exports to put the country's financial system on a more solid footing. Examples of this effort included the foundation of the Banco de México, the establishment of a rural credit system for campesinos, and the renegotiation of the foreign debt. Despite his dependence on Obregón, the new president and his allies also forged ahead with a comprehensive reform program that included new checks and balances on the military, an ambitious education program, as well as Petroleum and Alien Land Laws that precipitated a crisis with the U.S. government. Shrewdly playing on U.S. public opinion, Calles emerged victorious from this standoff, albeit at the price of important concessions to U.S. entrepreneurs. Finally, the president pushed through the Calles Law, which codified the anticlerical provisions of the constitution. This law, however, led to a wholesale strike by the Catholic Church that shut down virtually all religious services for three years, and it decisively contributed to the devastating Cristero rebellion that claimed thousands of lives, destroyed the country's primary grain-producing region, and—combined with a serious economic downturn—deprived the government of the funds needed to continue the reform program. The crisis of 1926 provided yet another important turning point, as Calles jettisoned most of his populist rhetoric soon afterward. He thus appeared to lose political significance: toward the end of his term, Obregón overshadowed Calles yet again, succeeding in his bid for a second term after the bloody elimination of his chief political rivals, Serrano and Gómez.

On July 17, 1928, however, it was Obregón himself who was assassinated. Gone was the caudillo who had sponsored Calles's emergence as a politician at the state and national levels, and who had held sway over most of the country's remaining military warlords. Calles's September 1, 1928, speech, in which he announced his intention to retire from politics and to dedicate himself to a process of institutionalization that would end the age of caudillos, was a master stroke that allowed the outgoing president to play a major role in the restructuring of the national political landscape. Even before leaving office, Calles helped his allies found a ruling party, the Partido Nacional Revolucionario, which under different names dominated national politics for the next seventy-one years. While he left the presidency to other, weaker politicians such as Portes Gil, Ortiz Rubio, and Rodríguez, Calles became the supreme chief of the Mexican Revolution. For the next six and a half years, the Jefe Máximo was at the center of political life, shaping many of the most important decisions of the party and the federal government. Yet Calles was less dominant than previous researchers have assumed, and his deteriorating health forced him to spend a lot of time in remote locales. During the Maximato, he became increasingly conservative, and education and anticlericalism constituted the only areas in which he continued his reform fervor. By the time of the Rodríguez administration (1932–1934), Calles was reduced to virtual veto power, and the major initiatives he launched, such as the formulation of a six-year plan for the party, ended up producing results he found undesirable.

It was not surprising, then, that Cárdenas, the fourth president he had handpicked, freed himself from the shackles of the Jefe Máximo in what constituted the end of Calles's political career. The relative ease with which Cárdenas asserted his authority not only demonstrated the new president's considerable political acumen, but it also put an end to a slow and inevitable process. The Jefe Máximo had increasingly lost touch with his country over the years, and he was left with few friends during his exile in San Diego. Realizing the slim odds of a challenge to Cárdenas and heeding his deteriorating health, Calles retired from politics and launched only feeble attempts to influence events in Mexico. After his return, he turned inward, seeking comfort in his family circle and in a practice of spiritism that promised an opportunity to commune with the dead. He looked back on a long career as one of most significant architects of the new state that emerged from decades of violence. Through both reform and repression, Calles had left his mark on modern Mexico.

Abbreviations Used in Notes

AGN	Archivo General de la Nación, Mexico City
AHGES	Archivo Histórico General del Estado de Sonora, Hermosillo
AHSRE	Archivo Histórico de la Secretaría de Relaciones Exteriores, Mexico City
APEC	FAPEC, Archivo Plutarco Elías Calles
ASDN	Archivo de la Secretaría de la Defensa Nacional, Mexico City
AVC	Centro de Estudios de la Historia de México, Condumex, Mexico City, Archivo Venustiano Carranza
BNAH	Biblioteca Nacional de Antropología e Historia
DHS	BNAH, Archivo Histórico en Micropelícula, 59: Documentos para la historia de Sonora
FAO	FAPEC, Archivo Fernando Torreblanca, Fondo Alvaro Obregón
FAPEC	Fondo Fideicomiso Archivos Plutarco Elías Calles y Fernando Torreblanca, Mexico City
FEC	FAPEC, Archivo Plutarco Elías Calles, Fondo Plutarco Elías Calles
FFT	FAPEC, Archivo Fernando Torreblanco, Fondo Fernando Torreblanca
FO	PRO, Foreign Office
FP	FAPEC, APEC, Fondo Presidentes
FPEC	FAPEC, Archivo Fernando Torreblanca, Fondo Plutarco Elías Calles

LC   AGN, Fondo Presidentes, Lázaro Cárdenas del Río
LCMSS   Library of Congress, Washington, D.C., Manuscript Division
MID   NA, RG 165: Records of the War Department General and
            Special Staffs, Military Intelligence Division Correspon-
            dence
NA   National Archives, College Park, Maryland
PAAA   Politisches Archiv, Auswärtiges Amt, Berlin
PHO   Programa de Historia Oral, BNAH
PRO   Public Record Office, London

Notes

Notes to Introduction

1. Leticia Mayer, "El proceso de recuperación simbólica de cuatro héroes de la revolución mexicana de 1910 a través de la prensa nacional," *Historia Mexicana* 178 (October 1995): 363–71.

2. *El Demócrata*, April 11, 1924.

3. *El Demócrata*, April 11, 1924.

4. Archivo General de la Nación (hereafter AGN), Fondo Presidentes, Lázaro Cárdenas del Río (hereafter LC), 546.2/10.

5. Holland D. Watkins, "Plutarco Elias Calles: El Jefe Maximo of Mexico," PhD diss., Texas Technological College, 1968; James C. Brown, "Consolidation of the Mexican Revolution under Calles, 1924–1928: Politics, Modernization, and the Roots of the Revolutionary National Party," PhD diss., University of New Mexico, 1979; Carl H. Marcoux, "Plutarco Elías Calles and the Partido Nacional Revolucionario: Mexican National and Regional Politics in 1928 and 1929," PhD diss., University of California at Riverside, 1994; and Edward M. Farmer, "Plutarco Elías Calles and the Revolutionary Government in Sonora, Mexico, 1915–1919," PhD diss., Cambridge University, 1997.

As an example for the relative lack of attention the Calles period has received in the English-language historical literature, a recent 270-page synthesis of the Mexican Revolution devotes a grand total of eighteen pages to the decade covering the Calles presidency and Maximato. Michael J. Gonzales, *The Mexican Revolution, 1910–1940* (Albuquerque: University of New Mexico Press, 2002).

6. For example, Fernando Medina Ruiz, *Calles: Un destino melancólico* (Mexico City: Editorial Jus, 1960), a Catholic polemic; Ricardo Zevada, *Calles presidente*

(Mexico City: Editorial Nuestro Tiempo, 1971), a study focused on the Calles presidency; Enrique Krauze, *Reformar desde el origen: Plutarco Elías Calles* (Mexico City: Fondo de Cultura Económica, 1987), a biographical essay; and Carlos Silva Cáceres, *Plutarco Elías Calles* (Mexico City: Editorial Planeta, 2002), a synthesis based on secondary sources. The biography using the Calles archive that became available in the 1980s is Carlos Macías Richard, *Vida y temperamento: Plutarco Elías Calles, 1877–1920* (Mexico City: Fondo Archivos Plutarco Elías Calles (FAPEC) and Fondo de Cultura Económica, 1995). Macías's unpublished dissertation covers the years 1920–1945 as well, but it only examines Calles's family history and personal linkages of those years; Carlos Macías Richard, "La fuerza del destino: Una biografía de Plutarco Elías Calles, 1877–1945," doctoral diss., El Colegio de México, 1994.

7. Alan Knight, *The Mexican Revolution* (Cambridge: Cambridge University Press, 1986), 2:218.

8. Alistair Hennessy, "Latin America," in *Populism: Its Meanings and National Characteristics*, edited by Ghiṭa Ionescu and Ernest Gellner (London: Weidenfeld and Nicolson, 1969), 28–47. Hennessy ignores the trajectory of Mexican urban populism, focusing entirely on Cardenismo and its promotion of land reform.

9. Jean-Jacques Rousseau, *The Social Contract and the First and Second Discourses*, edited by Susan Dunn (New Haven, CT: Yale University Press, 2002), 180.

10. Margaret Canovan, *Populism* (London: Longman, 1981); Alan Knight, "Populism and Neo-Populism in Latin America, Especially Mexico," *Journal of Latin American Studies* 30, no. 2 (1998): 226.

11. For authoritarian populism, see Robert H. Dix, "Populism: Authoritarian and Democratic," *Latin American Research Review* 20, no. 2 (1985): 29–52; Kristin Harper, "Revolutionary Tabasco in the Time of Tomás Garrido Canabal, 1923–1935: A Mexican House Divided," PhD diss., University of Massachusetts at Amherst, 2004, 8–9.

12. Torcuato di Tella, "Populism and Reform in Latin America," in *Obstacles to Change in Latin America*, edited by Claudio Veliz (Oxford: Oxford University Press, 1965), 47–74. See also chapter 5.

13. Michael L. Conniff, ed., *Latin American Populism in Comparative Perspective* (Albuquerque: University of New Mexico Press, 1982); and Michael L. Conniff, ed., *Populism in Latin America* (Tuscaloosa: University of Alabama Press, 1999).

14. Djed Bórquez (pseud.), *Hombres de México: Calles* (Mexico City: A. Botas, 1925).

15. Francis McCullagh, *Red Mexico: A Reign of Terror in America* (New York: Carrier, 1928). For a later assessment by an eyewitness, see Graham Greene, *The Lawless Roads: A Mexican Journey* (London: Longman, Green, 1939).

16. See, for example, Roberto Guzmán Esparza, *Memorias de don Adolfo de la Huerta, según su propio dictado* (Mexico City: Ediciones Guzmán, 1957).

17. Amado Cháverri Matamoros and Clodoveo Valenzuela, *El verdadero Calles* (Mexico City: Editorial Patria, 1929); and Luciano Kubli, *Calles y su gobierno: Ensayo biográfico* (Mexico City: n.p., 1931).

18. See the interview with Cardenista labor leader Vicente Lombardo Toledano in James W. Wilkie and Edna Monzón de Wilkie, *México visto en el siglo XX: Entrevistas de historia oral* (Mexico City: Instituto Mexicano de Investigaciones Económicas, 1969), 307–11.

19. Ramón Puente, *Hombres de la Revolución: Calles* (Mexico City: Fondo de Cultura Económica, 1994 [1933]), 9.

20. Carleton Beals, *Glass Houses: Ten Years of Free-Lancing* (Philadelphia: Lippincott, 1938), 57.

21. Frank Tannenbaum, *Mexico: The Struggle for Peace and Bread* (New York: Knopf, 1950), 69–70.

22. Michael C. Meyer, William L. Sherman, and Susan M. Deeds, *The Course of Mexican History*, 7th ed. (New York: Oxford University Press, 2003), 570.

23. See Arnaldo Córdova, *La ideología de la revolución mexicana: La formación del nuevo régimen* (Mexico City: Ediciones Era, 1972); Adolfo Gilly, *La revolución interrumpida: Una guerra campesina por la tierra y el poder* (Mexico City: Ediciones el Caballito, 1971); and Jean Meyer, "Revolution and Reconstruction in the 1920s," *Mexico since Independence*, ed. Leslie Bethell (Cambridge: Cambridge University Press, 1991), 201–40.

With regard to Cárdenas, see Alicia Hernández Chávez, *Historia de la revolución mexicana, periodo 1934–1940: La mecánica cardenista* (Mexico City: Colegio de México, 1979). For a recent critique of the revisionist paradigm in the case of Cardenismo, see Alan Knight, "Cardenismo: Juggernaut or Jalopy," *Journal of Latin American Studies* 26 (1994): 73–107.

More recently, regional and cultural historians have challenged the notion of a Leviathan state that forced popular movements into submission, and they have revealed the vitality of popular resistance against the state in the field of popular culture. See, for example, Christopher R. Boyer, *Becoming Campesinos: Politics, Identity, and Agrarian Struggle in Postrevolutionary Michoacán, 1920–1935* (Stanford, CA: Stanford University Press, 2003); and Mary Kay Vaughan, *Cultural Politics in Revolution: Teachers, Peasants, and Schools in Mexico, 1930–1940* (Tucson: University of Arizona Press, 1998), and the work reviewed in Mary Kay Vaughan, "Cultural Approaches to Peasant Politics in the Mexican Revolution," Stephen Haber, "Anything Goes: Mexico's 'New' Cultural History," and Claudio Lomnitz, "Barbarians at the Gate? A Few Remarks on the Politics of the 'New Cultural History of Mexico,'" *Hispanic American Historical Review* 79, no. 2 (1999): 269–305, 309–30, 367–85.

24. Macías, *Vida y temperamento;* Farmer, *Calles;* Martha Beatriz Loyo Camacho, *Joaquín Amaro y el proceso de institucionalización del ejército mexicano, 1917–1931* (Mexico City: UNAM, 2003).

25. Ignacio Almada Bay, "La conexión Yocupicio: Soberanía estatal, tradición cívico-liberal y resistencia al reemplazo de las lealtades en Sonora, 1913–1939," doctoral dissertation, El Colegio de México, 1993; Pedro Castro Martínez, *Adolfo de la Huerta: La integridad como arma de la revolución* (Mexico City: Siglo XXI Editores, 1998);, Pedro Castro Martínez, *Soto y Gama: Genio y figura* (Mexico City: Universidad

Autónoma Metropolitana, 2002); Pedro Castro Martínez, A la sombra de un caudillo: vida y muerte del general Francisco R. Serrano (Mexico City: Plaza y Janés, 2005). Almada also uses the term "authoritarian populist" to refer to Calles.

26. Claudio Lomnitz, Deep Mexico, Silent Mexico: An Anthropology of Nationalism (Minneapolis: University of Minnesota Press, 2001), 217.

27. Robert L. Miller, Researching Life Stories and Family Histories (London: Sage, 2000), 1–20.

Notes to Chapter One

1. Roberto Guzmán Esparza, Memorias de don Adolfo de la Huerta, según su propio dictado (Mexico City: Ediciones Guzmán, 1957), 15–16.

2. Interview with Plutarco Elías Calles Llorente, Mexico City, May 31, 2004.

3. Fideicomiso Archivos Plutarco Elías Calles y Fernando Torreblanca (hereafter FAPEC), Archivo Fernando Torreblanca, Fondo Plutarco Elías Calles (hereafter FPEC), serie 010901, exp. 42, inv. 677, "Elías Calles, Plutarco. Fe de bautismo," Iglesia Parroquial de Guaymas, libro de bautismos, p. 125, December 23, 1878; Biblioteca Nacional de Antropología e Historia, Mexico City (hereafter cited as BNAH), Programa de Historia Oral (hereafter cited as PHO), 4/45, Eugenia Meyer, interview with Alicia Calles de Almada, Mexico City, June 4, 1975.

4. Carlos Macías Richard, Vida y temperamento: Plutarco Elías Calles, 1877–1920 (Mexico City: FAPEC and Fondo de Cultura Económica, 1995), 43–44.

5. Enrique Krauze, Reformar desde el origen: Plutarco Elías Calles (Mexico City: Fondo de Cultura Económica, 1987), 12; Michael C. Monteón, "The Child Is Father of the Man: Personality and Politics in Revolutionary Mexico," Journal of Iberian and Latin American Studies 10, no. 1 (2004): 43–61.

6. Ignacio Almada Bay, "Alvaro Obregón Salido: Nuevos datos y nuevas interpretaciones," www.colson.edu.mx/historia/ialmada/inherm-obreg%F3n.pdf (accessed November 21, 2005), 11, 18–23.

7. Ignacio Almada Bay, Breve historia de Sonora (Mexico City: Fideicomiso Historia de las Américas, 2000), 128–29.

8. Quoted in Héctor Aguilar Camín, La frontera nómada: Sonora y la revolución mexicana (Mexico City: Siglo XXI Editores, 1977), 9.

9. Miguel Tinker Salas, In the Shadow of the Eagles: Sonora and the Transformation of the Border during the Porfiriato (Berkeley: University of California Press, 1997), 3–4.

10. FAPEC, Archivo Plutarco Elías Calles, Fondo Plutarco Elías Calles (hereafter FEC), serie 0202, exp. 64, inv. 919 "Espinoza, Tomás D.," Calles to Espinoza, Hermosillo, December 31, 1917.

11. Cited in Macías, Vida y temperamento, 27.

12. Lesley B. Simpson, Many Mexicos, 4th rev. ed. (Berkeley: University of California Press, 1967).

13. Stuart F. Voss, On the Periphery of Nineteenth-Century Mexico: Sonora and Sinaloa, 1810–1877 (Tucson: University of Arizona Press, 1982), especially 46–47.

14. Aguilar Camín, *La frontera nómada*. See also Barry Carr, "Las peculiaridades del norte mexicano: Ensayo de interpretación," *Historia Mexicana* 22, no. 3 (January 1973): 320–46.

15. Evelyn Hu-DeHart, *Missionaries, Miners, and Indians: Spanish Contact with the Yaqui Nation of Northwestern New Spain, 1533–1820* (Tucson: University of Arizona Press, 1981); Cynthia Radding, *Wandering Peoples: Colonialism, Ethnic Spaces, and Ecological Frontiers in Northwest Mexico, 1700–1850* (Durham, NC: Duke University Press, 1997).

16. Evelyn Hu-DeHart, *Yaqui Resistance and Survival: The Struggle for Land and Autonomy, 1821–1910* (Madison: University of Wisconsin Press, 1984), 18–93.

17. Tinker, *In the Shadow*, 8–14; Voss, *On the Periphery*, 237–56.

18. Ramón Eduardo Ruiz, *The People of Sonora and Yankee Capitalists* (Tucson: University of Arizona Press, 1988), 198–99.

19. Ignacio Almada Bay, "La patria chica antes que la justicia: Indagación sobre el papel del estado de Sonora en la lucha contra el gobierno de Huerta," www.colson .edu.mx/historia/ialmada/inherm-huertismo.pdf (accessed November 21, 2005), 11.

20. Fernando Medina Ruiz, *Calles: Un destino melancólico* (Mexico City: Editorial Jus, 1960), 11–15; Aguilar Camín, *Frontera nómada*, 180.

21. Most recently, a historical novel: Ralph M. Goldman, *The Mentor and the Protégé: The Story of Presidents Calles and Cárdenas* (n.p.: Xlibris, 2003).

22. In Mexican usage, the term "turco" could denote anyone of Middle Eastern descent.

23. Macías, *Vida y temperamento*, 19–31; Voss, *On the Periphery*, 148–60.

24. Krauze, *Reformar desde el origen*, 8.

25. Macías, *Vida y temperamento*, 35–38.

26. Ramón Puente, *Hombres de la Revolución: Calles* (Mexico City: Fondo de Cultura Económica, 1994 [1933]), 13.

27. PHO/4/45, interview with Alicia Calles, June 5, 1975.

28. Macías, *Vida y temperamento*, 36–38.

29. Puente, *Calles*, 13–15.

30. Mary Kay Vaughan, *The State, Education, and Social Class in Mexico, 1880–1924* (DeKalb: Northern Illinois University Press, 1982), 42, 64.

31. Archivo Histórico General del Estado de Sonora, Hermosillo (hereafter AHGES), vol. 855, "Instrucción Pública Hermosillo," Eduardo Castañeda to Secretario del Estado, June 4, 1884.

32. Puente, *Calles*, 14.

33. AHGES, vol. 855, "Instrucción Pública, Hermosillo," Segunda Escuela Municipal de Niños, "Estado nominal de los alumnos que concurrieron a este establecimiento en el prepasado mes de septiembre de 1884 con las faltas de asistencia, aplicación, y conducta."

34. Macías, *Vida y temperamento*, 49.

35. Macías, *Vida y temperamento*, 44–50.

36. AHGES, vol. 870, "Instrucción Pública, Hermosillo."

1. AHGES, vol. 899, "Distrito de Hermosillo: Exámenes generales y premios"; Macías, *Vida y temperamento*, 50–53.

38. Paul H. Garner, *Porfirio Díaz* (London: Longman, 2001).

39. Tinker, *In the Shadow*, 79–100.

40. Friedrich Katz, *The Secret War in Mexico: Europe, the United States, and the Mexican Revolution* (Chicago: University of Chicago Press, 1981), 9.

41. Tinker, *In the Shadow*, 14–16; Voss, *On the Periphery*, 277–87.

42. David M. Pletcher, "The Development of Railroads in Sonora," *Inter-American Economic Affairs* 1, no. 4 (March 1948): 3–45; John Coatsworth, *Growth against Development: The Economic Impact of Railroads in Porfirian Mexico* (DeKalb: Northern Illinois University Press, 1981), 38–41; Tinker Salas, *In the Shadow*, 127–48.

43. Hu-DeHart, *Yaqui Resistance and Survival*, 94–154.

44. John Kenneth Turner, *Barbarous Mexico* (New York: Cassell, 1912), 6–15; Hu-DeHart, *Yaqui Resistance and Survival*, 163–96.

45. Edward M. Farmer, "Plutarco Elías Calles and the Revolutionary Government in Sonora, Mexico, 1915–1919," PhD diss., Cambridge University, 1997, 75–77.

46. Michael J. Gonzales, "United States Copper Companies, the State, and Labour Conflict in Mexico, 1900–1910," *Journal of Latin American Studies* 26 (October 1994): 655–59.

47. Vaughan, *State, Education, and Social Class*, 42.

48. David Pletcher, cited in Ruiz, *People of Sonora*, 20.

49. Vaughan, *State, Education, and Social Class*, 17–20.

50. Enrique Krauze, *Mexico: Biography of Power*, trans. Hank Heifetz (New York: Harper Collins, 1997), 405.

51. Krauze, *Reformar desde el origen*, 11.

52. Charles Hale, *The Transformation of Liberalism in Late Nineteenth-Century Mexico* (Princeton, NJ: Princeton University Press, 1989); and W. Dirk Raat, *El positivismo durante el porfiriato* (Mexico City: El Colegio de México, 1975).

53. William H. Beezley, *Judas at the Jockey Club and Other Episodes of Porfirian Mexico* (Lincoln: University of Nebraska Press, 1987), 6.

54. W. Dirk Raat, "Ideas and Society in Don Porfirio's Mexico," *The Americas* 30, no. 1 (July 1973): 32–53.

55. Quoted in Holland D. Watkins, "Plutarco Elias Calles: El Jefe Maximo of Mexico," PhD diss., Texas Technological College, 1968, 5.

56. PHO/4/45, interview with Alicia Calles, June 5, 1975.

57. Puente, *Calles*, 9.

58. FPEC, serie 010901, exp. 31, inv. 666, "Elías Calles, familia," Hermosillo, August 9, 1897.

59. Roderic A. Camp, *Mexican Political Biographies, 1884–1935* (Austin: University of Texas Press, 1991), 74–75; *Diccionario Porrúa de historia, biografía y geografía de México*, 6th ed. (Mexico City: Editorial Porrúa, 1995), 2:1173; Aguilar Camín, *Frontera nómada*, 181.

60. Macías, *Vida y temperamento*.

61. AHGES, vol. 934, "Instrucción pública."

62. AHGES, vol. 924, "Escuela de varones No. 1," vol. 936; "Carta de nombramiento del gobernador a Plutarco Calles," October 7, 1897.

63. Quoted in Krauze, *Reformar desde el origen*, 14.

64. Quoted in Krauze, *Reformar desde el origen*, 14.

65. Macías, *Vida y temperamento*, 67–77.

66. AHGES, vol. 856, "Escuela de varones No. 2," Nov. 1899.

67. "Acta de matrimonio," Guaymas, August 24, 1899, FPEC, serie 010901, exp. 31, inv. 666, "Elías Calles, familia;" and birth certificates in same file.

68. Macías, *Vida y temperamento*, 91–92.

69. Macías, *Vida y temperamento*, 89–91, 94–95; Medina, *Un destino melancólico*, 28–29.

70. Macías, *Vida y temperamento*, 98–101.

71. Robert H. Holden, *Mexico and the Survey of Public Lands, 1876–1911: The Management of Modernization* (DeKalb: Northern Illinois University Press, 1994).

72. Macías, *Vida y temperamento*, 101–2.

73. Linda B. Hall, *Alvaro Obregón: Power and Revolution in Mexico, 1911–1920* (College Station: Texas A&M University Press, 1981), 16.

74. FPEC, serie 010901, exp. 65, inv. 700, "Elías Lucero, Rafael," Calles to Elías Lucero, Santa Rosa, January 28, 1904; Macías, *Vida y temperamento*, 103–8; Farmer, "Plutarco Elías Calles," 114–15.

75. Macías, *Vida y temperamento*, 108–13; Aguilar Camín, *Frontera nómada*, 182.

76. Macías, *Vida y temperamento*, 121. This passage avoids the abbreviation PLM for the Floresmagonista Party in order to avoid confusion with the Partido Laborista Mexicano of the 1920s, which will be more significant in this book.

77. Antonio G. Rivera, *La revolución en Sonora* (Hermosillo: Gobierno de Sonora, 1981), 169; James D. Cockcroft, *Intellectual Precursors of the Mexican Revolution, 1900–1913* (Austin: University of Texas Press, 1968).

78. Gonzales, "United States Copper Companies," 667–72.

79. Unless otherwise indicated, all biographical information on figures outside the Elías Calles family comes from *Diccionario Porrúa*.

80. Almada Bay, "Alvaro Obregón," 13; AHGES, vol. 2430, Ignacio Elías to Secretario de Estado, Arizpe, September 28, 1908.

81. AHGES, vol. 2185, Distrito de Arizpe.

82. AHGES, vol. 2418, "Acusaciones contra autoridades," Distrito de Arizpe, Calles et al. to Prefecto, Distrito de Arizpe, October 18, 1909.

83. Gregorio Mora, "Sonora al filo de la tormenta: Desilusión con el porfiriato, 1900–1911," *The Revolutionary Process in Mexico: Essays on Political and Social Change, 1880–1940*, edited by Jaime E. Rodríguez (Los Angeles: UCLA Latin American Center Publications, 1990), 77.

84. AHGES, vol. 2418, "Acusaciones contra autoridades," Distrito de Arizpe, Calles and others to Prefecto, Distrito de Arizpe, October 18, 1909; Macías, *Vida y temperamento*, 116–27; Ruiz, *People of Sonora*, 243–46.

85. Ruiz, *People of Sonora*, 243.

86. Ruiz, *People of Sonora*, 232; Tinker Salas, *In the Shadow*, 134–37.

87. Rivera, *La revolución en Sonora*, 111–16.

88. Susan M. Deeds, "José María Maytorena and the Mexican Revolution in Sonora (Part 1)," *Arizona and the West* 18, no. 1 (1976): 24.

89. Almada Bay, *Breve historia de Sonora*, 130–31.

90. Aguilar Camín, *Frontera nómada*, 77–86.

91. Francisco I. Madero, *La sucesión presidencial: El Partido Nacional Democrático* [1909] (Mexico City: Secretaría de Hacienda, 1960).

92. Guzmán Esparza, *Memorias*, 18–19.

93. Rivera, *La revolución en Sonora*, 161–64; Macías, *Vida y temperamento*, 129; Guzmán Esparza, *Memorias*, 18–19.

94. Ruiz, *People of Sonora*, 228.

95. Deeds, "Maytorena (Part 1)," 26–27.

96. Ruiz, *People of Sonora*, 228–43.

97. Alan Knight, *The Mexican Revolution* (Cambridge: Cambridge University Press, 1986), 1:193–97.

98. William H. Beezley, *Insurgent Governor: Abraham González of Chihuahua* (Lincoln: University of Nebraska Press, 1973), 55–114.

99. Walter Moore, "Adolfo de la Huerta: His Political Role in Sonora, 1906–1920," PhD diss., University of California, San Diego, 1982, 65–69; Macías, *Vida y temperamento*, 132–34.

100. Krauze, *Reformar desde el origen*; Monteón, "The Child Is Father of the Man."

Notes to Chapter Two

1. National Archives, Washington (hereafter cited as NA), RG 165: Records of the War Department General and Special Staffs, Military Intelligence Division Correspondence (hereafter cited as MID), box 1940, 8534–1, Emil Engel to Army War College Division, Douglas, AZ, April 21, 1914; Carlos Macías Richard, *Vida y temperamento: Plutarco Elías Calles, 1877–1920* (Mexico City: FAPEC and Fondo de Cultura Económica, 1995), 136–37.

2. NA, MID, box 1940, 8534–1, Engel to Army War College Division, Douglas, AZ, April 21, 1914.

3. AHGES, vol. 2673 "Nombramientos 1912," Secretario del Estado to Benjamín Hill, Hermosillo, September 5, 1911.

4. Héctor Aguilar Camín, *La frontera nómada: Sonora y la Revolución Mexicana* (Mexico City: Siglo Veintiuno Editores, 1977), 184; Roberto Guzmán Esparza, *Memorias de don Adolfo de la Huerta, según su propio dictado* (Mexico City: Ediciones Guzmán, 1957), 24.

5. Guzmán Esparza, *Memorias*, 24–25.

6. Aguilar Camín, *Frontera nómada*, 327. In the Spanish original, *broker fronterizo*.

7. Macías, *Vida y temperamento*, 140–41.

8. NA, MID, box 1941, 8534–145, O. M. Bigelow to Commanding General, Douglas, AZ, November 21, 1916.

9. AHGES vol. 2765, Distrito de Arizpe, "Tranquilidad pública (1911)," Calles to Maytorena, Agua Prieta, September 7, 1911.

10. AHGES, vol. 2777, "Acusaciones contra autoridades," vol. 2659, "Bandos de policía," and vol. 2689 "Instrucción pública;" NA, MID, box 1940, 8534–1, Engel to Army War College Division, Douglas, AZ, April 21, 1914; Alan Knight, *The Mexican Revolution* (Cambridge: Cambridge University Press, 1986), 1:444.

11. Fernando Medina Ruiz, *Calles: Un destino melancólico* (Mexico City: Editorial Jus, 1960), 31.

12. Knight, *Mexican Revolution*, 228–46.

13. William H. Beezley, "Madero, the 'Unknown' President and His Political Failure to Organize Rural Mexico," in *Essays on the Mexican Revolution: Revisionist Views of the Leaders*, edited by George Wolfskill and Douglas W. Richmond (Austin: University of Texas Press, 1979), 1–24. On León de la Barra, see Peter V. N. Henderson, *In the Absence of Don Porfirio: Francisco León de la Barra and the Mexican Revolution* (Wilmington, DE: Scholarly Resources, 2000).

14. Peter V. N. Henderson, "Un gobernador maderista: José María Maytorena y la Revolución en Sonora," *Historia Mexicana* 51, no. 1 (2001): 151–86; NA, Record Group 59: General Records of the Department of State (hereafter RG 59), 812.00/5751, Frederick Simpich to Secretary of State, Nogales, December 23, 1912; BNAH, Archivo Histórico en Micropelícula, 59: Documentos para la historia de Sonora (hereafter DHS), reel 9, "Informe presentado por el C. José María Maytorena, Gobernador Constitucional del Estado de Sonora, ante la XXIII Legislatura de la misma," September 23, 1912.

15. Knight, *Mexican Revolution* 1:257–388.

16. Aguilar Camín, *Frontera nómada*, 210–11.

17. Susan M. Deeds, "José María Maytorena and the Mexican Revolution in Sonora (Part 1)," *Arizona and the West* 18, no. 1 (1976): 30.

18. Aguilar Camín, *Frontera nómada*, 173–75.

19. Macías, *Vida y temperamento*, 144–45.

20. AHGES, vol. 2765, Distrito de Arizpe, "Tranquilidad pública (1911)," Calles to Maytorena, Agua Prieta, December 15, 1911.

21. Michael C. Meyer, *Mexican Rebel: Pascual Orozco and the Mexican Revolution, 1910–1915* (Lincoln: University of Nebraska Press, 1967), 52–93; Knight, *Mexican Revolution*, 1:290–329.

22. DHS, reel 9, Maytorena, "Informe," September 23, 1912.

23. NA, RG 59, 812.00/4278 and 4496, Louis Hostetter to Secretary of State, Hermosillo, June 15 and July 21, 1912.

24. AHGES, vol. 2777, "Acusaciones contra autoridades 1912"; Macías, *Vida y temperamento*, 147–51; Deeds, "Maytorena (Part I)," 37; Ramón Eduardo Ruiz, *The People of Sonora and Yankee Capitalists* (Tucson: University of Arizona Press, 1988), 232.

25. AHGES, vol. 2886, Distrito de Arizpe, "Tranquilidad pública (1912)," Calles to Maytorena, Agua Prieta, May 22, 1912.

26. Macías, *Vida y temperamento*, 151–54.

27. Macías, *Vida y temperamento*, 151–54; Alvaro Obregón, *Ocho mil kilómetros en campaña*, 2nd ed. (Mexico City: Fondo de Cultura Económica, 1959), 12–20; Aguilar Camín, *Frontera nómada*, chap. 5.

28. Linda B. Hall, *Alvaro Obregón: Power and Revolution in Mexico, 1911–1920* (College Station: Texas A&M University Press, 1981), 19–24.

29. Quoted in Enrique Krauze, *Reformar desde el origen: Plutarco Elías Calles* (Mexico City: Fondo de Cultura Económica, 1987), 44.

30. Quoted in Enrique Krauze, *El vértigo de la victoria: Alvaro Obregón* (Mexico City: Fondo de Cultura Económica, 1987), 65.

31. Deeds, "Maytorena (Part I)," 39–40.

32. Michael C. Meyer, *Huerta: A Political Portrait* (Lincoln: University of Nebraska Press, 1972), 53–67.

33. NA, RG 59, 812.00/6313 and 6474, Bowman to Secretary of State, Nogales, February 21, 1913, and Hostetter to Secretary of State, Hermosillo, February 28, 1913; Knight, *Mexican Revolution*, 2:16.

34. DHS, reel 9, José María Maytorena, "Informe del gobernador de Sonora sobre el golpe de estado de febrero de 1913 y hechos posteriores" (hereafter Informe); NA, RG 59, 812.00/6434, Hostetter to Secretary of State, Hermosillo, February 22, 1913; Susan M. Deeds, "José María Maytorena and the Mexican Revolution in Sonora (Part 2)," *Arizona and the West* 18, no. 1 (1976): 127.

35. Deeds, "Maytorena (Part II)," 128–29.

36. Quoted in Knight, *Mexican Revolution*, 2:16.

37. DHS, reel 9, Maytorena, "Informe."

38. Plutarco Elías Calles, *Pensamiento político y social: Antología, 1913–1936*, edited by Carlos Macías Richard (Mexico City: Fondo de Cultura Económica, 1988), 28–31.

39. NA, MID, box 1940, 8534–4, Engel to Army War College Division, Douglas, April 22, 1914.

40. Douglas Richmond, *Venustiano Carranza's Nationalist Struggle, 1893–1920* (Lincoln: University of Nebraska Press, 1983), 1–44.

41. William H. Beezley, *Insurgent Governor: Abraham González of Chihuahua* (Lincoln: University of Nebraska Press, 1973), 156–62.

42. DHS, reel 9, "Convención de Monclova."

43. John Womack, *Zapata and the Mexican Revolution* (New York: Knopf, 1968).

44. Alfredo Breceda, *México revolucionario, 1913–1917* (Madrid: Tipografía Artística, 1920–1941), 2:195.

45. NA, RG 59, 812.00/6928, Calles to Campos, February 28, 1913, in FBI report, Douglas, AZ.

46. FPEC, serie 010100, exp. 1, inv. 1, "Teniente Coronel de las Fuerzas del Estado de Sonora," "Acta de nombramiento," Ignacio L. Pesqueira, March 1, 1913.

47. Macías, *Vida y temperamento*, 173–74. For the critique, see Brígido Caro, *Plutarco Elías Calles, dictador bolcheviki de México: Episodios de la revolución mexicana desde 1910 al 1924* (Los Angeles: n.p. 1924), 13–18.

48. Guzmán Esparza, *Memorias*, 54–63; Obregón, *Ocho mil kilómetros*, 40–54.

49. Macías, *Vida y temperamento*, 165.

50. NA, MID, box 1940, 8534–22, J. A. Ryan to Department Engineer, Southern Department, Douglas, April 19, 1915; box 1940, 8534–67, M. O. Bigelow to same, April 15, 1916.

51. Michael J. Gonzales, "U.S. Copper Companies, the Mine Workers' Movement, and the Mexican Revolution, 1910–1920," *Hispanic American Historical Review* 76.3 (1996): 512.

52. Deeds, "Mayorena (Part II)," 133; NA, RG 59, 812.00/7760, Sam Bliss, "Border Report," Fort Sam Houston, May 31, 1913.

53. Edward M. Farmer, "Plutarco Elías Calles and the Revolutionary Government in Sonora, Mexico, 1915–1919," PhD diss., Cambridge University, 1997, 138–39.

54. Knight, *Mexican Revolution*, 2:29.

55. Obregón, *Ocho mil kilómetros*, 54–79.

56. Deeds, "Mayorena (Part I)," 31–36; see also earlier discussion in this chapter.

57. Aguilar Camín, *Frontera nómada*, 360–63; Macías, *Vida y temperamento*, 168–69; Knight, *Mexican Revolution*, 2:28.

58. Maytorena, Decreto No. 9, DHS, reel 9.

59. Aguilar Camín, *Frontera nómada*, 365.

60. Richmond, *Venustiano Carranza*, 48–49.

61. Quoted in Friedrich Katz, *The Secret War in Mexico: Europe, the United States, and the Mexican Revolution* (Chicago: University of Chicago Press, 1981), 133–34.

62. Meyer, *Huerta*.

63. Aguilar Camín, *Frontera nómada*, 381–82; Macías, *Vida y temperamento*, 170–71; Knight, *Mexican Revolution*, 2:29.

64. According to Miguel Alessio Robles, quoted in Farmer, "Calles," 144.

65. Archivo de la Secretaría de Defensa Nacional, Mexico City (hereafter ASDN), Archivo de Cancelados, XI/III/1–44, vol. 1, p. 29, Calles, "hoja de servicios," May 25, 1918; Obregón, *Ocho mil kilómetros*, 105; Aguilar Camín, *Frontera nómada*, 378–83.

66. Aguilar Camín, *Frontera nómada*, 392.

67. AHGES vol. 2997, "Quejas por despojo," Maytorena to Secretario de Gobernación (of Carranza government), Cd. Juárez, Chih., April 7, 1914.

68. Centro de Estudios de la Historia de México, Condumex, Mexico City, Archivo Venustiano Carranza (hereafter cited as AVC), carpeta 7, leg. 861, Decreto, Carranza, March 1914.

69. FAPEC, Archivo Plutarco Elías Calles, Fondo Presidentes (hereafter FP), serie 0201, gav. 83, exp. 2, inv. 711, "Elías Calles, Plutarco (Corl.) 1914," Carranza to Calles, Cd. Juárez, May 30, 1914; DHS, reel 9, "Telegramas de los Generales P. Elías Calles y Salvador Alvarado al Primer Jefe del Ejército Constitucionalista, Venustiano

Carranza"; ASDN, Archivo de Cancelados, XI/III/1–44, vol. 1, p. 49, Calles, "hoja de servicios," April 14, 1920; Macías, *Vida y temperamento*, 172–75; Deeds, "Maytorena (Part II)," 140.

70. AVC, carpeta 10, leg. 987, Carlos Plank to de la Huerta, Agua Prieta, July 2, 1914; Deeds, "Maytorena (Part II)," 140–41.

71. Knight, *Mexican Revolution*, 2:26.

72. Mariano Azuela, *Los de abajo: Novela de la Revolución Mexicana* [1915] (Mexico City: Ediciones Botas, 1941).

73. Knight, *Mexican Revolution*, 2:219.

74. Ernesto Laclau considered such elite appropriation of popular grievances an essential characteristic trait of populist rhetoric. See Ernesto Laclau, *Politics and Ideology in Marxist Theory: Marxism, Fascism, Populism* (London: Humanities Press, 1977), 173.

75. Breceda, *México revolucionario*, 2:195.

76. Quoted in Knight, *Mexican Revolution*, 2:219.

77. NA, MID, box 1940, 8534–3, Engel to Army War College Division, Douglas, April 22, 1914; Archivo Histórico de la Secretaría de Relaciones Exteriores, Mexico City, (hereafter AHSRE), L-E-776, Arturo M. Elías to Secretaría de Relaciones Exteriores, El Paso, TX, Mexico, July 8, 13, and 17, 1914.

78. Cited in Robert E. Quirk, *The Mexican Revolution, 1914–1915: The Convention of Aguascalientes* (Bloomington: Indiana University Press, 1960), 138.

79. Friedrich Katz, *The Life and Times of Pancho Villa* (Stanford, CA: Stanford University Press, 1998), 330–38.

80. Knight, *Mexican Revolution*, vol. 2.

81. Ignacio Almada Bay, *Breve historia de Sonora* (Mexico City: Fideicomiso Historia de las Américas, 2000), 137.

82. Obregón, *Ocho mil kilómetros*, 169–75.

83. Katz, *Pancho Villa*, 364–67, DHS, reel 9, "Manifiesto de don José María Maytorena," September 23, 1914.

84. Quirk, *Mexican Revolution, 1914–1915*; Hall, *Obregón*, 76–94.

85. ASDN, Archivo de Cancelados, XI/III/1–44, vol. 1, p. 17, Official Mayor to Calles, September 22, 1914; Plutarco Elías Calles, *Informe relativo al sitio de Naco, 1914–1915* (Mexico City: Talleres Gráficos de la Nación, 1932).

86. Knight, *Mexican Revolution*, 2:278.

87. AVC, carpeta 111, leg. 12750, "Acuerdo" January 1, 1915, enclosed in Benjamín Hill to Carranza, March 17, 1915; FP, serie 0201, gav. 83, exp. 3, inv. 712, "Elías Calles, Plutarco (Gral.) 1915," Calles to Carranza, Agua Prieta, January 20, 1915, and Carranza to Calles, Veracruz, February 2, 1915.

88. FPEC, serie 010100, exp. 2, inv. 2, "General Brigadier," "Acta de nombramiento," Venustiano Carranza, October 18, 1914.

89. Aguilar Camín, *Frontera nómada*, 411.

90. Holland D. Watkins, "Plutarco Elias Calles: El Jefe Maximo of Mexico," PhD diss., Texas Technological College, 1968, 17.

91. NA, MID, box 1940, 8534–22, J. A. Ryan to Department Engineer, Southern Department, Douglas, April 19, 1915.

92. Aguilar Camín, *Frontera nómada*, 416–18; ASDN, Archivo de Cancelados, XI/III/1–44, vol. 1, p. 30, Calles, "hoja de servicios," May 25, 1918.

93. Plutarco Elías Calles, *Partes oficiales de la campaña de Sonora* (Mexico City: Talleres Gráficos de la Nación, 1932), 1–62; NA, RG 59, 812.00/15822, Hostetter to Department of State, Hermosillo, August 9, 1915.

94. Richmond, *Venustiano Carranza*, 68–76.

95. John M. Hart, "The Mexican Revolution, 1910–1920," *The Oxford History of Mexico*, edited by Michael C. Meyer and William H. Beezley (Oxford: Oxford University Press, 2000), 451–57.

96. ASDN, Archivo de Cancelados, XI/III/1–44, vol. 1, p. 30, Calles, "hoja de servicios," May 25, 1918.

97. Aguilar Camín, *Frontera nómada*, 418.

98. AHGES, vol. 3046, Plutarco Elías Calles, "Al valiente pueblo de Sonora," September 24, 1915.

99. NA, MID, box 1940, 8534–33, Ryan to Army War College Division, Douglas, August 12, 1915; Calles, *Partes oficiales*.

100. FPEC, serie 010100, exp. 3, inv. 3, "General de Brigada," "Acta de nombramiento," Venustiano Carranza, September 22, 1915.

Notes to Chapter Three

1. NA, MID, box 1943, 8536–241, Louis L. Van Schaick, "Weekly Border Report," Nogales, AZ, May 19, 1917.

2. NA, MID, box 1943, 8536–241, Louis L. Van Schaick, "Weekly Border Report," Nogales, AZ, May 19, 1917.

3. NA, MID, box 1943, 8536–241, Louis L. Van Schaick, "Weekly Border Report," Nogales, AZ, May 19, 1917.

4. Adrian A. Bantjes, *As If Jesus Walked on Earth: Cardenismo, Sonora, and the Mexican Revolution* (Wilmington, DE: Scholarly Resources, 1998), 3.

5. Ignacio Almada Bay, *Breve historia de Sonora*. Mexico City: Fideicomiso Historia de las Américas, 2000, 138; see also Ignacio Almada Bay, "La conexión Yocupicio: Soberanía estatal, tradición cívico-liberal y resistencia al reemplazo de las lealtades en Sonora, 1913–1939," doctoral diss., El Colegio de México, 1993.

6. See also Edward M. Farmer, "Plutarco Elías Calles and the Revolutionary Government in Sonora, Mexico, 1915–1919," PhD diss., Cambridge University, 1997.

7. Cynthia Radding de Murrieta, "El triunfo constitucionalista y las reformas en la región, 1913–1919," in *Historia General de Sonora, vol. 4: Sonora moderno, 1880–1929* (Hermosillo: Gobierno del Estado de Sonora, 1997), 265–66.

8. Héctor Aguilar Camín, "The Relevant Tradition: Sonoran Leaders in the Revolution," in *Caudillo and Peasant in the Mexican Revolution*, edited by D. A. Brading (Cambridge: Cambridge University Press, 1980), 92–123.

. Linda B. Hall, *Alvaro Obregón: Power and Revolution in Mexico, 1911–1920* (College Station: Texas A&M University Press, 1981), 134–46.

10. Plutarco Elías Calles, *Decretos, circulares y demás disposiciones dictadas por el C. Gobernador y Comandante Militar del Estado de Sonora, General Plutarco Elías Calles, durante el año de 1915* (Hermosillo: Imprenta de Gobierno, 1915), 3.

11. Calles, *Decretos 1915*, 3–9.

12. Calles, *Decretos 1915*, 11–12.

13. AVC, carpeta 55, leg. 6240, Andrés García to Carranza, El Paso, October 19, 1915. García encloses a press clipping with his remarks to the *El Paso Times*.

14. Farmer, "Plutarco Elías Calles," 185, n. 24, and 195.

15. FEC, serie 0202, gav. 85, exp. 64, inv. 919, "Espinoza, Tomás D.," Calles to Espinoza, Hermosillo, December 31, 1917.

16. FEC, serie 0202, gav. 85, exp. 85, inv. 940, "Iturbe, Ramón F.," Calles to Iturbe, Nogales, August 18, 1917, and Iturbe to Calles, Culiacán, August 19, 1917.

17. Calles, *Decretos 1915*, 11–12.

18. Alan Knight, *The Mexican Revolution*, 2 vols. (Cambridge: Cambridge University Press, 1986), 2:462.

19. AVC, telegramas, Carranza to Calles, Colima, February 19, 1916.

20. AHGES, vol. 3072, and Calles, *Decretos 1915*, 15–17.

21. Carlos Macías Richard, *Vida y temperamento: Plutarco Elías Calles, 1877–1920* (Mexico City: FAPEC and Fondo de Cultura Económica, 1995), 190–92.

22. Plutarco Elías Calles, *Decretos, circulares y demás disposiciones dictadas por el C. Gobernador y Comandante Militar del Estado de Sonora, General Plutarco Elías Calles, durante el año de 1916* (Hermosillo: Imprenta de Gobierno, 1916), 51–57 and 86–87.

23. Gilbert M. Joseph, *Revolution from Without: Yucatán, Mexico, and the United States, 1880–1924* (Cambridge: Cambridge University Press, 1982), 134.

24. Joseph, *Revolution from Without*, 125–30; Ben Fallaw, "Dry Law, Wet Politics: Drinking and Prohibition in Post-Revolutionary Yucatán, 1915–1935," *Latin American Research Review* 37, no. 2 (2002): 37–64.

25. Farmer, "Plutarco Elías Calles," 182.

26. Calles, *Decretos 1915*, 20–34.

27. Calles, *Decretos 1915*, 34–41.

28. Calles, *Decretos 1915*, 20.

29. Calles, *Decretos 1915*, 19–21, 41–45, 47–48.

30. "Ley de Egresos," *Boletín oficial: órgano del gobierno constitucionalista de Sonora*, IV, no. 2–6 (January 13–27, 1917).

31. Farmer, "Plutarco Elías Calles," 339.

32. Calles, *Decretos 1915*, 45–46.

33. Robert H. Murray, trans. and ed., *Mexico before the World: Public Documents and Addresses of Plutarco Elías Calles* (New York: Academy Press, 1927), 217.

34. Calles, *Decretos 1915*, 45–46.

35. Murray, *Mexico*, 217.

36. *Boletín oficial*, IV, no. 2 (January 13, 1917): 2, "Ley de Egresos."

37. Engracia Loyo, *Las escuelas J. Cruz Gálvez: Fundación y primeros años, Boletín No. 40* (Mexico City: Fideicomiso Archivos Plutarco Elías Calles y Fernando Torreblanca, 2002).

38. Farmer, "Plutarco Elías Calles," 238–41; Calles, *Decretos 1915*, 54.

39. Calles, *Decretos 1916*, 68–69; Farmer, "Plutarco Elías Calles," 242–43.

40. AVC, carpeta 66, leg. 7323, A. Ruiz to Carranza, n.p., January 30, 1916.

41. Calles, *Decretos 1915*, 18–19.

42. Calles, *Decretos 1916*, 59–61.

43. Calles, *Decretos 1916*, 62–64.

44. Calles, *Decretos 1916*, 62–64.

45. Macías, *Vida y temperamento*, 200–202.

46. AHGES, vol. 3129, Calles to Moreno, Hermosillo, March 19, 1916.

47. Farmer, "Plutarco Elías Calles," 204.

48. Calles, *Decretos 1916*, 95–98.

49. Friedrich Katz, *The Life and Times of Pancho Villa* (Stanford, CA: Stanford University Press, 1998), 560–66.

50. Katz, *Pancho Villa*, 566–614; Joseph A. Stout Jr., *Border Conflict: Villistas, Carrancistas, and the Punitive Expedition, 1915–1920* (Fort Worth: Texas Christian University Press, 1999).

51. ASDN, Archivo de Cancelados, exp. XI/III/1–44, vol. 1, p. 69, Obregón to Enrique Estrada, Querétaro, March 28, 1916.

52. NA, MID, box 1940, 8534/80, 84, and 134, Bigelow to Hetrick, Douglas, AZ, May 19, 1916; Commanding Officer to Commanding General, Douglas, May 20, 1916, and Bigelow to Commanding General, Douglas, September 12, 1916; NA, RG 59, 812/18420 and 19458, Hostetter to Secretary of State, Hermosillo, June 7, 1916, and border report, Douglas, September 16, 1916.

53. ASDN, Archivo de Cancelados, exp. XI/III/1–44, vol. 1, pp. 93 and 96, Cándido Aguilar to Obregón Querétaro, July 28, 1916, and Calles to Obregón, Empalme, August 3, 1916.

54. Roberto Guzmán Esparza, *Memorias de don Adolfo de la Huerta, según su propio dictado* (Mexico City: Ediciones Guzmán, 1957), 109–13.

55. Farmer, "Plutarco Elías Calles," 151.

56. AVC, carpeta 145, leg. 16751, Carranza, "Decreto," n.d. [1916].

57. AHGES, vol. 3132, de la Huerta, "Informe," May 19, 1917.

58. NA, MID, box 1940, 8534–50, Bigelow to Commanding Officer, 1st Cavalry, Douglas, April 4, 1916.

59. NA, MID, box 1940, 8534–84, Commanding officer to Commanding General, Southern Department, Douglas, May 20, 1916.

60. Héctor Aguilar Camín, *La frontera nómada: Sonora y la Revolución Mexicana* (Mexico City: Siglo Veintiuno Editores, 1977), 430–36.

61. AHGES, vol. 3132, de la Huerta, "Informe," May 19, 1917.

62. FP, serie 0202, gav. 83, exp. 2, inv. 719, "Elías Calles, Plutarco (Gral.) 1918," Calles to de la Huerta, Hermosillo, August 9, 1918.

63. See the extended discussion in chapter 6; see also Pedro Castro, *Adolfo de la Huerta y la Revolución Mexicana*, 12.

64. Friedrich Katz, *The Secret War in Mexico: Europe, the United States, and the Mexican Revolution* (Chicago: University of Chicago Press, 1981), 306–14.

65. Mark T. Gilderhus, *Diplomacy and Revolution: U.S.-Mexican Relations under Wilson and Carranza* (Tucson: University of Arizona Press, 1977), 40–46.

66. Alan Knight, *U.S.-Mexican Relations, 1910–1940: An Interpretation* (San Diego: Center for U.S.-Mexican Studies, University of California, San Diego, 1987), especially 25–27.

67. For Carranza's foreign policy, see Douglas Richmond, *Venustiano Carranza's Nationalist Struggle, 1893–1920* (Lincoln: University of Nebraska Press, 1983), 189–219.

68. ASDN, Archivo de Cancelados, exp. XI/III/1–44, vol. 1, p. 75, Obregón to Jesús Acuña, Querétaro, April 6, 1916.

69. NA, MID, box 1941, 8534–138, Bigelow to Commanding General, Douglas, October 2, 1916.

70. *Boletín oficial: Órgano del gobierno constgitucionalista de Sonora* (Hermosillo: n.p.), III, no. 3 (July 15, 1916): 2.

71. The decree can be found in Guzmán Esparza, *Adolfo de la Huerta*, 117–22.

72. For versions of these decrees codified as state law in 1918, see FPEC, serie 010201, exp. 2, inv. 38, "Elías Calles, Plutarco (Gral. Gob.)," leg. 3.

73. Farmer, "Plutarco Elías Calles," 260.

74. Peter H. Smith, "La política dentro de la Revolución: El congreso constituyente de 1916–1917," *Historia Mexicana* 22, no. 4 (April 1973): 363–95; and E. Victor Niemeyer Jr., *Revolution at Querétaro: The Mexican Constitutional Convention of 1916–1917* (Austin: University of Texas Press, 1974).

75. NA, MID, box 1941, 8534–140, Bigelow to Commanding General, Douglas, October 5, 1916.

76. Macías, *Vida y temperamento*, 263–69.

77. ASDN, Archivo de Cancelados, XI/III/1–44, vol. 1, pp. 105–7, Calles to Obregón, Empalme, Son., October 21, 1916, and Obregón to Calles, Mexico City, October 24, 1916.

78. NA, MID, box 2163, 9700–42, Commanding General to Chief of Staff, Nogales, AZ, October 30, 1916.

79. NA, MID, box 1943, 8536–156, Knabenshue, "Weekly Border Report," Nogales, January 20, 1917.

80. NA, MID, box 1943, 8536–241, Van Schaick, "Weekly Border Report," Nogales, May 19, 1917.

81. Farmer, "Plutarco Elías Calles," 264–80.

82. Quoted in Linda B. Hall and Don M. Coerver, *Revolution on the Border: The United States and Mexico, 1910–1920* (Albuquerque: University of New Mexico Press, 1988), 39.

83. Hall and Coerver, *Revolution on the Border*, 39–40.

84. NA, MID, box 1941, 8534–160 and 161, enclosures in Fred J. Wright to Commanding Officer, Douglas, June 25, 1917, and Weekly Report, June 19, 1917; Gonzales, *Mexican Revolution*, 176.

85. Farmer, "Plutarco Elías Calles," 280–301.

86. NA, RG 59, 812.00/21282 and 21312, Lawton to Secretary of State, Hermosillo, September 12, 1917, and border report, Nogales, September 29, 1917.

87. Edward Farmer, *Un nacionalismo pragmático: El gobierno callista en Sonora y el capital extranjero, Boletín 31* (Mexico City: Fideicomiso Archivos Plutarco Elías Calles y Fernando Torreblanca, 1999), 8–9.

88. ASDN, Archivo de Cancelados, XI/III/1–44, vol. 1, p. 114, J. A. Castro to Calles, Mexico City, August 4, 1917.

89. NA, MID, van Schaick, "Weekly Border Report," Nogales, June 2, 1917, 8536–242.

90. FP, serie 0201, gav. 83, exp. 4, inv. 713, "Elías Calles, Plutarco (Gral.) 1917," Calles to Carranza, Hermosillo, October 6, 1917, and Carranza to Calles, Mexico City, October 18, 1917.

91. Quoted in NA, MID, box 1944, 8536/280/1.

92. Caro, *Plutarco Elías Calles, dictador bolsheviki*, 95; FP, serie 0202, gav. 83, exp. 2, inv. 718, "Elías Calles, Plutarco (Gral.), 1918," Calles to de la Huerta, Hermosillo, July 27, 1918.

93. Farmer, "Plutarco Elías Calles," 205–8; FPEC, serie 010201, exp. 2, inv. 38, "Elías Calles, Plutarco (Gral. Gob.)," "Ley que fija el número de ministros de cultos religiosos que deberán ejercer su ministerio en el Estado," April 24, 1919.

94. Evelyn Hu-DeHart, "La comunidad china en el desarrollo de Sonora," in *Historia general de Sonora, vol. 4: Sonora moderno, 1880–1929* (Hermosillo: Gobierno del Estado de Sonora, 1997), 197.

95. Evelyn Hu-DeHart, "From Immigrant Minority to Racial Minority: The Chinese of Mexico, 1876–1930," paper presented at the Tenth Congreso de Historiadores, Ft. Worth, TX, November 1999, 1.

96. Hu-DeHart, "From Immigrant Minority to Racial Minority," 1.

97. Quoted in Farmer, "Plutarco Elías Calles," 198.

98. FPEC, serie 010203, exp. 1, inv. 40, "Soriano, Cesáreo, G," circular, Cesáreo Soriano, December 4, 1917.

99. FEC, serie 0204, gav. 86, exp. 56, inv. 1082, Calles to Nicolás Burgos, Hermosillo, January 2, 1918.

100. FP, serie 0201, gav. 83, exp. 4, inv. 713, "Elías Calles, Plutarco (Gral.) 1917," Calles to Carranza, Hermosillo, October 22, 1917; NA, MID, box 1444, 8536–297, Joel A. Lipscomb to Southern Department, Nogales, February 8, 1918; Charles H. Harris III and Louis R. Sadler, "The Witzke Affair: German Intrigue on the Mexican Border, 1917–1918," *Military Review* 59 (1979): 41.

101. Katz, *Secret War in Mexico*, 431.

102. United States Senate, *Investigations of Mexican Affairs: Preliminary report and hearings of the Committee on foreign relations, United States Senate, pursuant to S. res.*

106, directing the Committee on foreign relations to investigate the matter of outrages on citizens of the United States in Mexico (Washington, DC: Government Printing Office, 1920), 1:460; German military attaché to Auswärtiges Amt, Madrid, July 8, 1918, Politisches Archiv, Auswärtiges Amt, Berlin, Germany (hereafter cited as PAAA), R 16917.

103. See NA, MID, file 10541–367 and 473.

104. FPEC, serie 010201, exp. 2, inv. 38, "Elías Calles, Plutarco (Gral. Gob.)," legs. 9–10.

105. Farmer, "Plutarco Elías Calles," 210–19.

106. Macías, *Vida y temperamento*, 269–71; FPEC, serie 011100, gav. 72, exp. 153, "Elías Calles Ruiz, Manuel."

107. Macías, *Vida y temperamento*, 255; on Calles's tenure as secretary of industry and commerce, see chapter 4.

108. The term comes from Carlos R. Martínez Assad, *Laboratorio de la revolución: el Tabasco garridista* (Mexico City: Siglo XXI, 1979).

Notes to Chapter Four

1. In the original, "fuera de México, todo es Cuauhtitlán."

2. Carlos Macías Richard, *Vida y temperamento: Plutarco Elías Calles, 1877–1920* (Mexico City: FAPEC and Fondo de Cultura Económica, 1995), 272.

3. Mary Kay Vaughan and Stephen E. Lewis, eds., *The Eagle and the Virgin: Nation and Cultural Revolution in Mexico, 1920–1940* (Durham, NC: Duke University Press, 2006), 11.

4. Ramón Puente, *Hombres de la Revolución: Calles* (Mexico City: Fondo de Cultura Económica, 1994 [1933]), 68.

5. Macías, *Vida y temperamento*, 260.

6. María del Carmen Collado Herrera, *Empresarios y políticos: Entre la Restauración y la Revolución* (Mexico City: Instituto Nacional de Estudios Históricos de la Revolución Mexicana, 1996).

7. See, for instance, Adolfo Gilly, *La revolución interrumpida: Una guerra campesina por la tierra y el poder* (Mexico City: Ediciones el Caballito, 1971).

8. Antonio Gramsci, *Selections from the Prison Notebooks*, edited and translated by Quintin Hoare and Geoffrey N. Smith (New York: International Publishers, 1971), 276.

9. José Alfredo Gómez Estrada, *Gobierno y casinos: El origen de la riqueza de Abelardo L. Rodríguez* (Mexicali: Universidad Autónoma de Baja California, 2002), 38–59; Eric M. Schantz, "From the Mexicali Rose to the Tijuana Brass: Vice Tours of the United States-Mexico Border, 1910–1965," PhD diss., University of California-Los Angeles, 2001, 149–243.

10. Friedrich Katz, *The Life and Times of Pancho Villa* (Stanford, CA: Stanford University Press, 1998), 706–15.

11. Nora Hamilton, *The Limits of State Autonomy: Post-Revolutionary Mexico* (Princeton, NJ: Princeton University Press, 1982), 63–66.

12. Héctor Aguilar Camín and Lorenzo Meyer, *In the Shadow of the Mexican Revolution: Contemporary Mexican History, 1910–1989*, translated by Luis Alberto Fierro (Austin: University of Texas Press, 1993), 71.

13. Alan Knight, *The Mexican Revolution*, 2 vols. (Cambridge: Cambridge University Press, 1986), 2:406–23; Stephen H. Haber, *Industry and Underdevelopment: The Industrialization of Mexico, 1890–1940* (Stanford, CA: Stanford University Press, 1989), 133–49.

14. Daniela Spenser, *The Impossible Triangle: Mexico, Soviet Russia, and the United States in the 1920s* (Durham, NC: Duke University Press, 1999), 51–58.

15. Carleton Beals, *Mexican Maze* (Philadelphia: Lippincott, 1931), 45.

16. Samuel Brunk, *Emiliano Zapata: Revolution and Betrayal in Mexico* (Albuquerque: University of New Mexico Press, 1995), 217–25.

17. Robert F. Smith, *The United States and Revolutionary Nationalism in Mexico, 1916–1932* (Chicago: University of Chicago Press, 1972), 128–32; Linda B. Hall, *Oil, Banks, and Politics: The United States and Postrevolutionary Mexico* (Austin: University of Texas Press, 1995), 36–48.

18. Alberto J. Pani, *Apuntes autobiográficos* (Mexico: Porrúa, 1950), 1:260–64.

19. FAPEC, Archivo Fernando Torreblanca, Fondo Alvaro Obregón (hereafter FAO), serie 030100, exp. C-1/89, inv. 1158, "Calles, Plutarco Elías (Gral.)," Calles to Obregón, Querétaro, October 12 and 14, 1919; FP, serie 0204, gav. 83, exp. 1, inv. 755, "Obregón, Alvaro, y Plutarco Elías Calles, 1915–1920"; Obregón to Calles, Nogales, October 18 and 19, 1919; de la Huerta to Calles, Hermosillo, October 14, 1919, in Elías Calles, *Correspondencia personal*, 1:27–28.

20. Daniela Spenser, *En el gabinete de Venustiano Carranza*, Boletín 30 (Mexico City: FAPEC, 1999), 11–15.

21. *El Universal*, November 25, 1919, in Elías Calles, *Pensamiento político y social*, 50–51.

22. Spenser, *En el gabinete de Venustiano Carranza*, 6–9.

23. FAPEC, Archivo Plutarco Elías Calles, Archivo Plutarco Elías Calles (hereafter APEC), gav. 45, exp.121, inv. 3179, "León, Luis L. (Ing.)," Calles to León, Mexico City, October 20, 1919, and León to Calles, Hermosillo, October 27, 1919. APEC forms part of a larger archive by the same name.

24. AHGES, vol. 2648, Distrito de Arizpe, exp. Ejidos de Fronteras (1897).

25. FPEC, serie 010100, exp. 5, inv. 5, "Secretario de Industria, Comercio y Trabajo," Calles to Secretario de Gobernación, Mexico City, February 1, 1920.

26. Calles to de la Huerta, Mexico City, February 1, 1920, in Elías Calles, *Correspondencia personal*, 1:39.

27. Macías, *Vida y temperamento*, 294.

28. DHS, reel 10, de la Huerta to Carranza, Hermosillo, March 30 and April 4, 1920, and Carranza to de la Huerta, Mexico City, April 2, 1920.

29. DHS, reel 10, Calles to Diéguez, Nogales, April 8, 1920.

30. DHS, reel 10, "Al pueblo mexicano," April 9, 1920, DHS; Castro, *Adolfo de la Huerta*, 31–35; FPEC, serie 010100, exp. 6, inv. 6, "Comandante Militar del Estado," de la Huerta to Calles, April 10, 1920.

31. Pedro Castro Martínez, *De la Huerta y Calles: Los límites políticos de la amistad,* Boletín 23 (Mexico City: FAPEC, 1996), 9.

32. John W. F. Dulles, *Yesterday in Mexico: A Chronicle of the Revolution, 1919–1936* (Austin: University of Texas Press, 1961), 36–48.

33. Pedro Castro Martínez, *La muerte de Carranza: Dudas y certezas,* Boletín 34 (Mexico City: FAPEC, 2000), 13.

34. FPEC, serie 010100, exp. 7, inv. 7, "Secretario de Estado y del Despacho de Guerra y Marina," and exp. 8, inv. 8, "General de División," "Acta de nombramiento como Secretario de Estado y del Despacho de Guerra y Marina por Adolfo de la Huerta, Presidente Substituto," June 1, 1920, and "Acta de nombramiento como General de División por Adolfo de la Huerta, Presidente Substituto," November 23, 1920.

35. Martín Luis Guzmán, *La sombra del caudillo* (Madrid: Espasa-Calpe, 1930), 280.

36. Guzmán, *La sombra del caudillo,* 78.

37. "Informe confidencial," U.S. Embassy, June 3, 1923, *Boletín del Archivo General de la Nación* (tercera serie), III, no. 4 (October 1979), 13.

38. Puente, *Calles,* 74.

39. PHO/4/45, interview with Alicia Calles, July 4, 1975.

40. Puente, *Calles,* 81.

41. FAO, serie 030400, exp. 387, inv. 2403, "De la Huerta, Adolfo," Obregón to de la Huerta, Nogales, July 17 and 18, 1920, and Culiacán, Sin., July 23, 1920; de la Huerta to Obregón, Mexico City, July 17 and 19, 1920.

42. Castro, *Adolfo de la Huerta: La integridad como arma de la revolución,* 45–107; FAO, serie 030400, exp. C-7 y E-03/104, inv. 2120, "Calles, Plutarco Elías (Gral.)," Calles to Obregón, Mexico City, July 2 and 6, 1920.

43. Martha Beatriz Loyo Camacho, *Joaquín Amaro y el proceso de institucionalización del ejército mexicano, 1917–1931* (Mexico City: UNAM, 2003), 65–67.

44. Loyo Camacho, *Joaquín Amaro;* NA, MID, 10640–2308/1, Scott Israel to Assistant Chief of Staff for Military Intelligence, Nogales, AZ, July 19, 1920.

45. Abelardo L. Rodríguez, *Autobiografía* (Mexico City: n.p., 1962), 101–5; APEC, gav. 66, exp. 189, inv. 5010, "Rodríguez, Abelardo L.," leg. 2/11, "Informe que rinde el C. General Abelardo L. Rodríguez . . . ," February 15, 1922; Gómez Estrada, *Gobierno y casinos,* 38–63. Rodríguez hailed from the hamlet of San José de Guaymas in the vicinity of the district capital.

46. Pedro Castro Martínez, *Soto y Gama: Genio y figura* (Mexico City: Universidad Autónoma Metropolitana, 2002), 11–63.

47. Natalia Chacón to Plutarco Elías Calles, Hermosillo, January 26, 1919, November [n.d.] 1919, December [n.d.] 1919, and January 6, 1920; Mexico City, September 16, 1921 and February 18, 1924, in Elías Calles, *Correspondencia personal,* 1:408–11, 415–17, 419.

48. NA, MID, box 1661, 2657-G-547, G-2 report, Mexico City, March 2, 1925.

49. Macías, *Vida y temperamento,* 272–78.

50. APEC, gav. 15, exp. 120, inv. 976, "Compañía Azucarera de El Mante, S.A.," leg. 1/16; Carlos Macías Richard, "La fuerza del destino: Una biografía de Plutarco Elías Calles, 1877–1945," doctoral diss., El Colegio de México, 1994, 285–87.

51. Macías, "Fuerza del destino," 289.

52. APEC, gav. 27, exp. 60, inv. 1726, "Elías Calles Chacón, Alfredo."

53. David C. Bailey, "Obregón: Mexico's Accommodating President," in *Essays on the Mexican Revolution: Revisionist Views of the Leaders*, edited by George Wolfskill and Douglas W. Richmond (Austin: University of Texas Press, 1979), 82.

54. Timothy J. Henderson, *The Worm in the Wheat: Rosalie Evans and Agrarian Struggle in the Puebla-Tlaxcala Valley of Mexico, 1906–1927* (Durham, NC: Duke University Press, 1998), 117–92.

55. Gilbert M. Joseph and Daniel Nugent, eds., *Everyday Forms of State Formation: Revolution and the Negotiation of Rule in Modern Mexico* (Durham, NC: Duke University Press, 1994).

56. Mary Kay Vaughan, *The State, Education, and Social Class in Mexico, 1880–1924* (DeKalb: Northern Illinois University Press, 1982), 239–66; Helen Delpar, *The Enormous Vogue of Things Mexican: Cultural Relations between the United States and Mexico* (Tuscaloosa: University of Alabama Press, 1992); Henry C. Schmidt, *The Roots of "Lo Mexicano": Self and Society in Mexican Thought, 1900–1934* (College Station: Texas A&M University Press, 1978), 97–116.

57. Vaughan and Lewis, *Eagle and the Virgin*, 2–16; Alan Knight, "Racism, Revolution, and *Indigenismo*: Mexico, 1910–1940," in *The Idea of Race in Latin America, 1870–1940*, edited by Richard Graham (Austin: University of Texas Press, 1990)," 71–113.

58. *El Universal*, January 1, 1922.

59. Dudley Ankerson, *Agrarian Warlord: Saturnino Cedillo and the Mexican Revolution in San Luis Potosí* (DeKalb: Northern Illinois University Press, 1984), 92–114.

60. APEC, gav. 66, exp. 189, inv. 5010, "Rodríguez, Abelardo L.," leg. 2/11, "Informe que rinde el C. General Abelardo L. Rodríguez . . . ," February 15, 1922.

61. Gómez Estrada, *Gobierno y casinos*, 143–60; Schantz, "From the Mexicali Rose," 415–16.

62. Heather Fowler-Salamini, *Agrarian Radicalism in Veracruz, 1920–1938* (Lincoln: University of Nebraska Press, 1971), especially 39; Andrew G. Wood, *Revolution in the Street: Women, Workers, and Urban Protest in Veracruz, 1870–1927* (Wilmington, DE: Scholarly Resources, 2001), 51–63.

63. Quoted in Aguilar Camín and Meyer, *In the Shadow*, 80.

64. Quoted in Enrique Krauze, *El vértigo de la victoria: Alvaro Obregón* (Mexico City: Fondo de Cultura Económica, 1987), 62–63.

65. Joseph A. Stout Jr., "General Plutarco Elías Calles, Colonel Francisco M. Delgado, and the Servicio Confidencial, 1914–1930," paper presented at the Eleventh Reunión de Historiadores Mexicanos, Estadounidenses y Canadienses, Monterrey, October 2003.

66. Dulles, *Yesterday in Mexico*, 110, 377.

67. Georgette José Valenzuela, *La campaña presidencial de 1923–1924 en México* (Mexico City: Instituto Nacional de Estudios Históricos de la Revolución Mexicana, 1998), 11.

68. José Valenzuela, *La campaña presidencial.*

69. Camile Nick Buford, "A Biography of Luis N. Morones, Mexican Labor and Political Leader," PhD diss., Louisiana State University, 1972, 6–47.

70. Buford, "A Biography of Luis N. Morones."

71. "Discurso pronunciado en la Tercera Convención de la Confederación Panamericana del Trabajo," January 20, 1921, in Elías Calles, *Pensamiento político y social*, 53.

72. Dulles, *Yesterday in Mexico*, 129–31.

73. Gilbert M. Joseph, *Revolution from Without: Yucatán, Mexico, and the United States, 1880–1924* (Cambridge: Cambridge University Press, 1982), 188–95.

74. "Discurso," February 20, 1921, in Elías Calles, *Pensamiento político y social*, 55–56.

75. "Discurso," Feb. 27, 1921, in Elías Calles, *Pensamiento político y social*, 57–59.

76. Dulles, *Yesterday in Mexico*, 174–75.

77. FAPEC, Archivo Fernando Torreblanca, Fondo Fernando Torreblanca (hereafter FFT), serie 010203, exp. 5/6, leg. 2, "Convenio de la Huerta-Lamont," de la Huerta to Obregón, New York, June 13, 1922, and Obregón to de la Huerta, Mexico, June 14, 1922; Hall, *Oil, Banks, and Politics*, 95–100.

78. Correspondence between Calles and Gompers, and Calles and Haberman, Macías, *Correspondencia personal*, 2:31–45.

79. Katz, *Pancho Villa*, 765–66.

80. Quoted in Brígido Caro, *Plutarco Elías Calles, dictador bolcheviki de México: Episodios de la revolución mexicana desde 1910 al 1924* (Los Angeles: n.p., 1924), 13.

81. Katz, *Pancho Villa*, 772–82; Loyo Camacho, *Joaquín Amaro*, 107–8; Ignacio A. Richkarday, *60 años en la vida de México* (Mexico City: n.p., 1963), 2:25–86.

82. Pedro Castro Martínez, *Adolfo de la Huerta y la Revolución Mexicana* (Mexico City: Instituto Nacional de Estudios Históricos de la Revolución Mexicana, 1992), 89.

83. Carlos R. Martínez Assad, *Laboratorio de la revolución: El Tabasco garridista* (Mexico City: Siglo XXI, 1979).

84. Plutarco Elías Calles, *Pensamiento político y social: Antología, 1913–1936*, edited by Carlos Macías Richard (Mexico City: FAPEC and Fondo de Cultura Económica, 1988, 69–71).

85. Elías Calles, *Pensamiento político y social*, 78.

86. Elías Calles, *Pensamiento político y social*, 72–73.

87. Loyo Camacho, *Joaquín Amaro*, 105–6; Georgette José Valenzuela, *El relevo del caudillo: De cómo y por qué Calles fue candidato presidencial* (Mexico City: El Caballito, 1982).

88. FPEC, serie 011000, gav. 70, exp. 226, "Vasconcelos, José."

89. Ankerson, *Agrarian Warlord*, 105–8.

90. Castro, *Adolfo de la Huerta*, 93–95; APEC, exp. 56, inv. 1379, "De la Huerta, Adolfo," leg. 8 and 9, de la Huerta to Calles, Mexico City, September 25, 1923; Calles to de la Huerta, Monterrey, September 25, 1923; Obregón to Calles, Mexico City, September 27, 1923.

91. Castro, *Adolfo de la Huerta*, 98; Dulles, *Yesterday in Mexico*, 194–204.

92. NA, MID, box 1660, 2657-G-432/38, George Russell, G-2 Report, Mexico City, December 29, 1923; Castro, *Adolfo de la Huerta*, 121.

93. Alonso Capetillo, *La rebelión sin cabeza: Génesis y desarrollo del movimiento delahuertista* (Mexico City: Botas, 1925).

94. Enrique Plasencia de la Parra, *Escenarios y personajes de la rebelión delahuertista* (Mexico City: Miguel Porrúa, 1998).

95. APEC, gav. 12, exp. 25, inv. 830, t. 7/7, "Carrillo Puerto, Felipe," Calles to Obregón and Morones, Mexico City, January 4, 1924.

96. NA, MID, box 1660, 2657-G-432/14, George Russell, G-2 Report, Mexico City, December 8, 1923; Edwin Lieuwen, *Mexican Militarism: The Political Rise and Fall of the Revolutionary Army, 1910–1940* (Albuquerque: University of New Mexico Press, 1968), 76.

97. Castro, *Adolfo de la Huerta*, 209–44; NA, MID, box 1661, 2657-G-432/60, "Weekly Survey of Mexican Revolutionary Situation, February 1, 1924."

98. Elías Calles, *Pensamiento político y social*, 85–87.

99. Elías Calles, *Pensamiento político y social*, 85–87.

100. José Valenzuela, *La campaña presidencial*, 93.

101. Elías Calles, *Pensamiento político y social*, 97.

102. Elías Calles, *Pensamiento político y social*, 95.

103. Elías Calles, *Pensamiento político y social*, 130.

104. Dulles, *Yesterday in Mexico*, 265.

Notes to Chapter Five

1. *Excélsior*, August 16, 1924.

2. Cited in Stefan Rinke, *"Der letzte freie Kontinent": Deutsche Lateinamerikapolitik im Zeichen transnationaler Beziehungen, 1918–1933* (Stuttgart: Heinz, 1996), 192.

3. FPEC, serie 010602, Presidente Electo de la República Mexicana: Alemania; clippings from German newspapers in FPEC, serie 010701, Hemeroteca; Georgette José Valenzuela, "El viaje de Plutarco Elías Calles como presidente electo por Europa y Estados Unidos," *Revista Mexicana de Sociología* 57, no. 3 (1995): 191–210. For the parallels between Latin American populism and European social democracy, see also Torcuato Di Tella, "Populism and Reform in Latin America," in *Obstacles to Change in Latin America*, edited by Claudio Veliz (Oxford: Oxford University Press, 1965), 47–53.

4. *El Universal*, November 1, 1924.

5. *El Demócrata*, December 1, 1924.

6. Alberto J. Pani, *Apuntes autobiográficos*, 2 vols. (Mexico: Porrúa, 1950), 2:63–71.

7. José Guadalupe Zuno, *Reminiscencias de una vida,* 2nd ed. (Guadalajara: Biblioteca de autores jalisciences modernos, 1973), 149–53.

8. NA, MID, box 1661, 2657-G-547/1, G-2 report, Mexico City, January 28, 1925.

9. Hans Werner Tobler, "Peasants and the Shaping of the Revolutionary State, 1910–1940," *Riot, Rebellion, and Revolution: Rural Social Conflict in Mexico,* edited by Friedrich Katz (Princeton, NJ: Princeton University Press, 1988), 497–503.

10. Camile Nick Buford, "A Biography of Luis N. Morones, Mexican Labor and Political Leader," PhD diss., Louisiana State University, 1972, 79–80. Buford only cites secondary sources in support of his assertion that such a pact existed.

11. Stephen H. Haber, *Industry and Underdevelopment: The Industrialization of Mexico, 1890–1940* (Stanford, CA: Stanford University Press, 1989), 151.

12. Buford, "Morones," 98.

13. John Gunther, quoted in Buford, "Morones," 110.

14. Katherine Anne Porter, *Flowering Judas and Other Stories* (New York: Harcourt, Brace, and Co., 1935), 139–60. For an analysis of this and other images of Morones, see Gregory Crider, "Labor's Hero and Labor's Gangster: A Cultural Biography of Luis Napoleón Morones," paper presented at the meeting of the Southeast Council of Latin American Studies, Santo Domingo, 2004.

15. Marjorie R. Clark, *Organized Labor in Mexico* (Chapel Hill: University of North Carolina Press, 1934), 177.

16. Lorenzo Meyer, *Mexico and the United States in the Oil Controversy, 1917–1942,* translated by Lidia Lozano (Austin: University of Texas Press, 1972), 8, 107–14.

17. Carleton Beals, *Glass Houses: Ten Years of Free-Lancing* (Philadelphia: Lippincott, 1938), 339.

18. NA, RG 59, 711.12/546a, Kellogg, declaration to the press, June 12, 1925. For the joint authorship of the declaration, see Robert F. Smith, *The United States and Revolutionary Nationalism in Mexico, 1916–1932* (Chicago: University of Chicago Press, 1972), 234.

19. James J. Horn, "El embajador Sheffield contra el presidente Calles," *Historia Mexicana* 20, no. 2 (October 1970): 265–84; and James J. Horn, "U.S. Diplomacy and the Specter of 'Bolshevism' in Mexico (1924–1927)," *The Americas* 32, no. 1 (July 1975): 32–33.

20. Yale University Library, James R. Sheffield Papers (hereafter Sheffield Papers), series I, box 5, folder 49, Sheffield to Nicholas Murray Butler, Mexico City, November 17, 1925.

21. Sheffield Papers, series I, box 5, folder 50, Sheffield to William Lyon Phelps, Mexico City, May 7, 1926.

22. Daniela Spenser, *The Impossible Triangle: Mexico, Soviet Russia, and the United States in the 1920s* (Durham, NC: Duke University Press, 1999), 79–82.

23. *Excélsior,* June 15, 1925.

24. APEC, gav. 18 bis, exp. 28, "Declaraciones del general Calles," Calles to Herbert Bayard Swope, Mexico City, June 18, 1925.

25. The law and congressional debate can be found in Archivo General de la Nación, *Boletín del Archivo General de la Nación*, vol. 24/25 *La legislación petrolera en México, 1887–1927* (Mexico City: Archivo General de la Nación, 1983).

26. John W. F. Dulles, *Yesterday in Mexico: A Chronicle of the Revolution, 1919–1936* (Austin: University of Texas Press, 1961), 282–85.

27. Nacional Financiera, *Statistics on the Mexican Economy* (Mexico City: Nacional Financiera, 1977), 350.

28. Pani, *Apuntes autobiográficos*, 2:47–53.

29. Enrique Krauze, Jean Meyer, and Cayetano Reyes, *Historia de la Revolución Mexicana, 1924–1928: La reconstrucción económica* (Mexico City: Colegio de México, 1977), 83–84.

30. Martha Beatriz Loyo Camacho, *Joaquín Amaro y el proceso de institucionalización del ejército mexicano, 1917–1931* (Mexico City: UNAM, 2003), 123–49.

31. Loyo Camacho, *Joaquín Amaro*, 123–49.

32. Edwin Lieuwen, *Mexican Militarism: The Political Rise and Fall of the Revolutionary Army, 1910–1940* (Albuquerque: University of New Mexico Press, 1968), 85–95.

33. Krauze, Meyer, and Reyes, *Historia de la Revolución Mexicana*, 98–107.

34. Pedro Salmerón Sanginés, *Aarón Sáenz Garza: Militar, diplomático, político, empresario* (Mexico City: Editorial Porrúa, 2001), 25–103.

35. Haber, *Industry and Underdevelopment*, 139–44.

36. Mira Wilkins and Frank E. Hill, *American Business Abroad: Ford on Six Continents* (Detroit, MI: Wayne State University Press, 1964), 147.

37. Dulles, *Yesterday in Mexico*, 282–87.

38. Romana Falcón, "Charisma, Tradition, and Caciquismo: Revolution in San Luis Potosí," in *Riot, Rebellion, and Revolution: Rural Social Conflict in Mexico*, edited by Friedrich Katz (Princeton, NJ: Princeton University Press, 1988), 439–47.

39. Tobler, "Peasants and the Shaping of the Revolutionary State," 497–504.

40. Plutarco Elías Calles, *Pensamiento político y social: Antología, 1913–1936*, edited by Carlos Macías Richard (Mexico City: FAPEC and Fondo de Cultura Económica, 1988), 188.

41. Mary Kay Vaughan, *The State, Education, and Social Class in Mexico, 1880–1924* (DeKalb: Northern Illinois University Press, 1982), 279.

42. Mary Kay Vaughan, *Cultural Politics in Revolution: Teachers, Peasants, and Schools in Mexico, 1930–1940* (Tucson: University of Arizona Press, 1998), especially 3–30.

43. Katherine E. Bliss, *Compromised Positions: Prostitution, Public Health, and Gender Politics in Revolutionary Mexico City* (University Park: Pennsylvania State University Press, 2001), 1–5.

44. Jean Meyer, Enrique Krauze, and Cayetano Reyes, *Historia de la Revolución Mexicana, 1924–1928: Estado y sociedad con Calles* (Mexico City: Colegio de México, 1977), 157–66; Spenser, *The Impossible Triangle*, 103–6.

45. Krauze, *Reformar desde el origen*, 12.

46. Enrique Krauze, *Reformar desde el origen: Plutarco Elías Calles* (Mexico City: Fondo de Cultura Económica, 1987); Carlos Macías Richard, *Vida y temperamento: Plutarco Elías Calles, 1877–1920* (Mexico City: FAPEC and Fondo de Cultura Económica, 1995); Michael C. Monteón, "The Child Is Father of the Man: Personality and Politics in Revolutionary Mexico," *Journal of Iberian and Latin American Studies* 10, no. 1 (2004): 43–61; Ignacio Almada Bay, "La conexión Yocupicio: Soberanía estatal, tradición cívico-liberal y resistencia al reemplazo de las lealtades en Sonora, 1913–1939," doctoral diss., El Colegio de México, 1993.

47. For nineteenth-century Liberals and the church, see Charles A. Hale, *Mexican Liberalism in the Age of Mora, 1821–1853* (New Haven, CT: Yale University Press, 1968).

48. Robert E. Quirk, *The Mexican Revolution and the Catholic Church, 1910–1929* (Bloomington: Indiana University Press, 1973).

49. NA, MID, box 1664, 2657-G-616/2, Edward Davis, G-2 Report, Mexico City, February 23, 1926.

50. Elías Calles, *Pensamiento político y social*, 122.

51. Salmerón Sanginés, *Aarón Sáenz Garza*, 25–28.

52. Roger D. Gouran, "A Study of Two Attempts by President Plutarco Elías Calles to Establish a National Church in Mexico," MA thesis, Portland State University, 1995, 100–11.

53. David C. Bailey, *Viva Cristo Rey: The Cristero Rebellion and the Church-State Conflict in Mexico* (Austin: University of Texas Press, 1974), 53.

54. APEC, exp. 5, "Obregón, Alvaro" leg. 13/13, inv. 4038, Obregón to Calles, Navojoa, Sonora, April 7, 1925.

55. PHO/1/25, Alicia O. de Bonfil and Eugenia Meyer, interview with Rafael F. Muñoz, Mexico City, July 15, 1970; *El Universal*, February 4, 1926; Dwight W. Morrow Papers (microfilmed), series X, reel 17, Morrow, "Memorandum of conversation with Lic. Mestre" (hereafter Mestre memorandum), March 8, 1929, Amherst College Library.

56. NA, MID, box 1664, 2657-G-616/9, G-2 reports.

57. Quoted in Enrique Krauze, *Mexico: Biography of Power*, translated by Hank Heifetz (New York: Harper Collins, 1997), 421.

58. APEC, gav. 3, exp. 147, "Arzobispos," "Entrevista del presidente Calles con los obispos Leopoldo Ruiz y Pascual Díaz," August 21, 1926.

59. Mestre memorandum.

60. Jennie Purnell, *Popular Movements and State Formation in Revolutionary Mexico: The Agraristas and Cristeros of Michoacán* (Durham, NC: Duke University Press, 1999).

61. Jean Meyer, *The Cristero Rebellion: The Mexican People between Church and State, 1926–1929*, translated by Richard Southern (Cambridge: Cambridge University Press, 1976), 48–200.

62. Nacional Financiera, *Statistics on the Mexican Economy*, 23 and 351.

63. Haber, *Industry and Underdevelopment*, 150–56; Richard Tardanico, "State Dependency and Nationalism: Revolutionary Mexico, 1924–1928," *Comparative Studies in Society and History* 24, no. 3 (July 1982): 416–17.

64. Nacional Financiera, *Statistics on the Mexican Economy*, 385.

65. AHSRE, 39–9–9, Fernández de Regata to Secretary, Managua, October 2, 1924; NA, RG 59, 817.00/3244, White to Secretary of State, Managua, December 8, 1924.

66. NA, RG 59, 817.00/3318, Eberhardt to Secretary of State, Managua, September 5, 1925.

67. Jürgen Buchenau, *In the Shadow of the Giant: The Making of Mexico's Central America Policy, 1876–1930* (Tuscaloosa: University of Alabama Press, 1996), 165–74.

68. *New York Times*, December 9, 1926.

69. Spenser, *The Impossible Triangle*, 106–12.

70. Library of Congress, Washington, D.C., Manuscript Division (hereafter LCMSS), Frank B. Kellogg Papers, reel 24, frames 141–159, Kellogg, "Bolshevik Aims and Policies in Mexico and Latin America."

71. Buchenau, *In the Shadow of the Giant*, 175.

72. *Excélsior*, January 9, 1927.

73. John A. Britton, "Propaganda, Property, and the Image of Stability: The Mexican Government and the U.S. Print Media, 1921–1929," *South Eastern Latin Americanist* 19 (March 1988): 12–16; APEC, gav. 21, exp. 54, "Elías, Arturo M.," 45–47, Arturo M. Elías to Soledad González, New York, January 14, 1926.

74. Mauricio Tenorio Trillo, "The Cosmopolitan Mexican Summer, 1920–1949," *Latin American Research Review* 32, no. 2 (1997): 224–40.

75. PHO/4/3, Eugenia Meyer, interview with Gruening, Oaxtepec, Morelos, November 4, 1969.

76. B. Traven, *Land des Frühlings* (Berlin: Büchergilde Gutenberg, 1928), 18.

77. *New York Times*, January 13, 1927; *Excélsior*, January 15, 1927.

78. James J. Horn, "Did the United States Plan an Invasion of Mexico in 1927?" *Journal of Inter-American Studies and World Affairs* 15, no. 4 (November 1973): 454–71.

79. APEC Anexo, exp. 747, report by 10-B, February 2, 1927.

80. Emilio Portes Gil, *Autobiografía de la Revolución Mexicana: Un tratado de interpretación histórica* (Mexico City: Instituto Mexicano de Cultura, 1964), 397.

81. Richard A. Melzer, "Dwight Morrow's Role in the Mexican Revolution: Good Neighbor or Meddling Yankee?" PhD diss., University of New Mexico, 1979, 120–27.

82. PHO/4/45, interview with Alicia Calles, July 4, 1975.

83. FPEC, serie 010901, exp. 31, inv. 666, "Elías Calles, Familia," Acta Registro Civil, Mexico City, August 27, 1927; interview with Norma Torreblanca Elías Calles, Mexico City, June 1, 2004; PHO/4/45, interview with Alicia Calles, June 5, 1975.

84. The cartoon can be found in Meyer, Krauze, and Reyes, *Historia de la Revolución Mexicana*, 125.

85. PHO/1/20, Daniel Cazes, interview with Luis Sánchez Pontón, Mexico City, April 1961.

86. Meyer, Krauze, and Reyes, *Historia de la Revolución Mexicana*, 123–50.

87. Greene, *The Power and the Glory* (New York: Viking Press, 1946).

88. Meyer, Krauze, and Reyes, *Historia de la Revolución Mexicana*, 123–50.

89. NA, MID, box 1665, 2657-G-622/2, Edward Davis, G-2 report, Mexico City, April 23, 1926.

90. APEC (Anexo), exp. 672, "Alexander Weddell, cónsul general americano en México, Abril 1926 (Reporte)," 55–56, "Acuerdo privado provisional entre el General de División Alvaro Obregón, por sus propios derechos, y el señor Arturo de Saracho como representante del Sr. Luis N. Morones," Cajeme, Son., February 10, 1926."

91. NA, MID, box 1665, 2657-G-622/4, Edward Davis, G-2 report, Mexico City, August 19, 1926.

92. Pedro Castro Martínez, *Soto y Gama: Genio y figura* (Mexico City: Universidad Autónoma Metropolitana, 2002), 72–76.

93. NA, MID, box 1665, 2657-G-622/2 and 6, Edward Davis, G-2 reports, Mexico City, April 23 and October 29, 1926.

94. NA, RG 59, 711.12/856, Sheffield to Kellogg, Mexico City, January 5, 1927.

95. Rafael Loyola Díaz, *La crisis Obregón-Calles y el estado mexicano*, 3rd ed. (Mexico City: Siglo XXI Editores, 1987), 20–22.

96. Quoted in Meyer, Krauze, and Reyes, *Historia de la Revolución Mexicana*, 124.

97. Enrique Krauze, *El vértigo de la victoria: Alvaro Obregón* (Mexico City: Fondo de Cultura Económica, 1987), 109–10.

98. For a biography of Serrano, see Pedro Castro Martínez, *A la sombra de un caudillo: Vida y muerte del general Francisco R. Serrano* (Mexico City: Plaza y Janés, 2005).

99. Obregón speech, June 25, 1927, in Alvaro Obregón, *Discursos del General Alvaro Obregón* (Mexico City: Dirección General de Educación Militar, 1932) 2:36–59; various speeches during June, July, and August 1927, Obregón, *Discursos del General Alvaro Obregón*.

100. FAO, serie 050100, exp. 41, inv. 4836, "Obregón, Alvaro (Gral.): Discurso," speech in Morelia, Michoacán, August 8, 1927.

101. NA, MID, box 1665, 2657-G-622/22, Harold Thompson, G-2 report, Mexico City, October 5, 1927; Castro, *A la sombra de un caudillo*, 173–228.

102. Meyer, Krauze, and Reyes, *Historia de la Revolución Mexicana*, 139–42.

103. Dulles, *Yesterday in Mexico*, 358.

104. Speech in Orizaba, Veracruz, April 20, 1928, in Obregón, *Discursos*, 2:382.

105. Alan Knight, "Populism and Neo-Populism in Latin America, especially Mexico," *Journal of Latin American Studies* 30, no. 2 (1998), 231.

Notes to Chapter Six

1. *Excélsior*, July 18, 1928.

2. Arnaldo Córdova, *La Revolución en crisis: La aventura del maximato* (Mexico City: Cal y Arena, 1995), 23.

3. See John W. Sherman, *The Mexican Right* (Westport, CT: Praeger, 1997), 18–19; Lorenzo Meyer, Rafael Segovia, and Alejandra Lajous, *Historia de la Revolución Mexicana, 1928–1934: Los inicios de la institucionalización* (Mexico City: Colegio de México, 1978); and Lorenzo Meyer, *Historia de la Revolución Mexicana, 1928–1934: El conflicto social y los gobiernos del maximato* (Mexico City: Colegio de México, 1978); Tzvi Medín, *El minimato presidencial: Historia política del Maximato* (Mexico City: Ediciones Era, 1982); and Rafael Loyola Díaz, *La crisis Obregón-Calles y el estado mexicano*, 3rd ed. (Mexico City: Siglo XXI Editores, 1987). For the argument that *jefe máximo* Calles was weaker than previously imagined, see also Córdova, *La Revolución en crisis*.

4. FAO, serie 060100, exp. 2, inv. 5046, "Elías Calles, Plutarco (Gral.). Discurso," Plutarco Elías Calles, "A la nación," July 18, 1928.

5. *New York Times,* July 22, 1928.

6. See Enrique Krauze, *El vértigo de la victoria: Alvaro Obregón* (Mexico City: Fondo de Cultura Económica, 1987), 205. Even Vasconcelos, a devout Catholic in his later years, came to concur with the official version, albeit not without elevating Toral to hero status. José Vasconcelos, *El proconsulado* (Mexico City: Ediciones Botas, 1939), 22–23.

7. Medín, *El minimato presidencial,* 29–30.

8. Luis L. León, *Crónica del poder: En los recuerdos de un político en el México revolucionario* (Mexico City: Fondo de Cultura Económica, 1987), 272.

9. Carl H. Marcoux, "Plutarco Elías Calles and the Partido Nacional Revolucionario: Mexican National and Regional Politics in 1928 and 1929," PhD diss., University of California at Riverside, 1994, 116.

10. Meyer, Segovia, and Lajous, *Historia de la Revolución Mexicana,* 18.

11. FPEC, serie 011400, exp. 20, "Homenajes 1964," eulogy by Luis L. León, October 19, 1964.

12. John W. F. Dulles, *Yesterday in Mexico: A Chronicle of the Revolution, 1919–1936* (Austin: University of Texas Press, 1961), 379–83.

13. "Informe de gobierno del 10. de septiembre de 1928," in Plutarco Elías Calles, *Declaraciones y discursos políticos* (Mexico City: Cuadernos de causa, 1979), 167–68.

14. Elías Calles, *Declaraciones y discursos políticos.*

15. Marcoux, "Plutarco Elías Calles and the Partido Nacional Revolucionario," 132–33.

16. Loyola Díaz, *La crisis Obregón-Calles,* 111–12.

17. Froylán C. Manjarrez, *La jornada institucional* (Mexico City: Talleres Gráficos de la Nación, 1930), 1:24.

18. FFT, serie 010213, gav. 45, exp. 26, inv. 1093, vol. 1, "Junta de los generales."

19. NA, MID, box 1665, 2657-G-657/5, Robert Halpin, G-2 report, Mexico City, October 30, 1928.

20. Meyer, Segovia, and Lajous, *Historia de la Revolución Mexicana,* 27–28. In his memoirs, Portes Gil claims that Calles played a passive role in his selection. Emilio Portes Gil, *Quince años de política mexicana,* 2nd ed. (Mexico City: Ediciones Botas, 1941), 29–30.

21. Alejandra Lajous, *Los orígenes del partido único en México* (Mexico City: UNAM, 1979), 394.

22. Luis Javier Garrido, *El Partido de la Revolución Institucionalizada: La formación del nuevo estado en México (1928–1945)* (Mexico City: Siglo XXI Editores, 1982), 103–232.

23. León, *Crónica del poder*, 294–96.

24. *El Universal*, December 2, 1928.

25. *Excélsior*, December 6, 1928; Plutarco Elías Calles, *Pensamiento político y social: Antología, 1913–1936*, edited by Carlos Macías Richard (Mexico City: FAPEC and Fondo de Cultura Económica, 1988), 280–81.

26. *El Universal*, December 8, 1928. The text can also be found in APEC, gav. 21, exp. 28, "Declaraciones del General Plutarco Elías Calles."

27. FPEC, serie 010901, exp. 23, inv. 658, "Casa de Anzures. Menaje de casa."

28. Garrido, *El Partido de la Revolución Institucionalizada*, 99–102.

29. FPEC, serie 010801, exp. 6, inv. 393, "Programa de Trabajo del PNR," vol. 1.

30. Quoted in Meyer, Segovia, and Lajous, *Historia de la Revolución Mexicana*, 47.

31. Alex M. Saragoza, *The Monterrey Elite and the Mexican State, 1880–1940* (Austin: University of Texas Press, 1988), 120–25.

32. Meyer, Segovia, and Lajous, *Historia de la Revolución Mexicana*, 59–63.

33. Garrido, *El Partido de la Revolución Institucionalizada*, 103.

34. FPEC, serie 010100, exp. 12, inv. 12, Luis León to Calles, July 24, 1929.

35. Quoted in Lajous, *Los orígenes del partido único*, 55.

36. NA, MID, box 1665, 2657-G-657/8 and 11, G-2 reports, Mexico City, February 21 and March 5, 1929.

37. FPEC, serie 010802, exp. 1, inv. 395, "Rebelión Escobarista."

38. Elías Calles, *Pensamiento político y social*, 286–92.

39. NA, MID, box 1664, 2657-G-616/26, Gordon Johnston, G-2 report, May 8, 1929.

40. Morrow papers, series X, reel 17, Morrow, draft statements for Ruiz and Portes Gil, May 11 and June 13, 1929.

41. NA, MID, box 1664, 2657-G-616/30, Gordon Johnston, G-2 report, June 25, 1929.

42. NA, MID, box 1664, 2657-G-616/31, Gordon Johnston, G-2 report, July 3, 1929; David C. Bailey, *Viva Cristo Rey: The Cristero Rebellion and the Church-State Conflict in Mexico* (Austin: University of Texas Press, 1974), 255.

43. Nacional Financiera, *Statistics on the Mexican Economy* (Mexico City: Nacional Financiera, 1977), 358.

44. Dulles, *Yesterday in Mexico*, 479.

45. John Skirius, *José Vasconcelos y la cruzada de 1929* (Mexico City: Siglo XXI, 1978).

46. APEC, gav. 58, exp. 51, inv. 4239, "Ortiz Rubio, Pascual (Ing.)," vol. 1.

47. Garrido, *El Partido de la Revolución Institucionalizada*, 110.

48. Alfonso Taracena, *Los vasconcelistas sacrificados en Topilejo* (Mexico City: Editora Librera, 1958).

49. FFT, serie 010213, gav. 45, exp. 26, inv. 1093, vol. 1, "Junta de los generales."

50. This attribution of the origin of the term is Abelardo Rodríguez's, in Dulles, *Yesterday in Mexico*, 673.

51. *Excélsior*, October 31, 1931.

52. For a discussion of this concept, see Thomas Benjamin, *La Revolución: Mexico's Great Revolution in Memory, Myth, and History* (Austin: University of Texas Press, 2000), 76–110; and Ilene V. O'Malley, *The Myth of the Revolution: Hero Cults and the Institutionalization of the Mexican State, 1920–1940* (New York: Greenwood Press, 1986).

53. Although the monument was not inaugurated until 1938, Calles and Pani submitted the original plan in January 1933. Benjamin, *La Revolución*, 127–33; FPEC, serie 010804, exp. 67, inv. 509, "Monumento a la Revolución," Calles and Alberto Pani, "El Monumento a la Revolución," January 13, 1933.

54. FAO, serie 060400, gav. 33, exp. 2, inv. 5129, "Discurso pronunciado por el Lic. Aarón Sáenz," Monterrey, N. L., July 17, 1929.

55. FAO, serie 060400, gav. 33, exp. 8, inv. 5135, Aarón Sáenz, "Discurso pronunciado en la solemne inauguración del monumento erigido a la memoria del señor General Alvaro Obregón, 17 de julio de 1935."

56. Jürgen Buchenau, "The Arm and Body of the Revolution: Remembering Mexico's Last Caudillo, Alvaro Obregón," in Lyman Johnson, ed., *Death, Dismemberment, and Memory: Body Politics in Latin America* (Albuquerque: University of New Mexico Press, 2004), 179–206.

57. For the Porfirian promotion of the "Juárez myth," see Charles Weeks, *The Juárez Myth in Mexico* (Tuscaloosa: University of Alabama Press, 1987), 29–53.

58. Meyer, Segovia, and Lajous, *Historia de la Revolución Mexicana*, 105–45.

59. Gonzalo N. Santos, *Memorias*, 4th ed. (Mexico City: Grijalbo, 1986), 389–511.

60. Dulles, *Yesterday in Mexico*, 481–87; Pascual Ortiz Rubio, *Memorias, 1925–1928* (Morelia: Universidad Michoacana de San Nicolás, 1981), 215.

61. NA, MID, box 1664, 2657-G-605/328, Robert G. Cummings, G-2 Report, Mexico City, September 13, 1932.

62. NA, MID, box 1664, 2657-G-605/302, Robert G. Cummings, G-2 Report, Mexico City.

63. FPEC, serie 010100, exp. 13, inv. 13, "Secretario de Estado Encargado del Despacho de Guerra y Marina," acta de nombramiento, Pascual Ortiz Rubio.

64. Martha Beatriz Loyo Camacho, *Joaquín Amaro y el proceso de institucionalización del ejército mexicano, 1917–1931* (Mexico City: UNAM, 2003), 173–76.

65. NA, MID, box 1664, 2657-G-605/314, G-2 report, Mexico City, December 31, 1931.

66. Dulles, *Yesterday in Mexico*, 533–40; NA, MID, box 1664, 2657-G-605/329, Robert E. Cummings, G-2 Report, Mexico City, September 5, 1932.

67. Michael C. Meyer, William L. Sherman, and Susan M. Deeds, *The Course of Mexican History*, 7th rev. ed. (New York: Oxford University Press, 2003), 570. Another recent textbook correctly points out that this story is a "joke" or "legend";

Douglas W. Richmond, *The Mexican Nation: Historical Continuity and Modern Change* (Upper Saddle River, NJ: Prentice Hall, 2002), 271.

68. Stephen H. Haber, *Industry and Underdevelopment: The Industrialization of Mexico, 1890–1940* (Stanford, CA: Stanford University Press, 1989), 149–70; Nacional Financiera, *Statistics on the Mexican Economy*, 351.

69. Interview with Portes Gil in James W. Wilkie and Edna Monzón de Wilkie, *México visto en el siglo XX: Entrevistas de historia oral* (Mexico City: Instituto Mexicano de Investigaciones Económicas, 1969), 540–41; James W. Wilkie, *The Mexican Revolution: Federal Expenditure and Social Change since 1910* (Berkeley: University of California Press, 1970), 66–67.

70. Nacional Financiera, *Statistics on the Mexican Economy*, 107.

71. NA, MID, box 1662, 2657-G-561/10–12, Gordon Johnston, G-2 reports, Mexico City, February 21 and June 6, 1930, and "Memorandum on the Mexican Agrarian Situation," September 30, 1930.

72. Meyer, *Historia de la Revolución Mexicana, 1928–1934*, 148–54.

73. FPEC, serie 010901, exp. 31, inv. 666, "Elías Calles, Familia," acta de matrimonio, August 2, 1930; birth certificates, Plutarco José Elías Calles Llorente, January 15, 1931, and Leonardo Gilberto Elías Calles Llorente, February 4, 1932.

74. APEC, gav. 27, exp. 60, inv. 1726, "Elías Calles Chacón, Alfredo." Alfredo's unpaid debt would plague his family for years to come.

75. José Carlos Ramírez, Ricardo León, and Oscar Conde, "La estrategia económica de los callistas," *Historia General de Sonora* 5:65–78.

76. APEC, gav. 66, exp. 189, inv. 5010, Calles to Rodríguez, El Sauzal, B.C., March 29, 1933.

77. For these terms, see Josephus Daniels, *Shirt-Sleeve Diplomat* (Chapel Hill: University of North Carolina Press, 1947), 60.

78. See last section of chapter 5.

79. FPEC, serie 010901, exp. 40, inv. 625, "Elías Calles, Plutarco (Gral.). Datos clínicos," and exp. 46, inv. 681, "Elías Calles, Plutarco (Gral.). Reportes Médicos."

80. FPEC, serie 010901, exp. 32, inv. 667, "Elías Calles, Leonor. Datos clínicos."

81. Interviews with Plutarco Elías Calles Llorente, Mexico City, May 31, 2004; and Norma Torreblanca Elías Calles, Mexico City, June 1, 2004.

82. José Alfredo Gómez Estrada, *Gobierno y casinos: El origen de la riqueza de Abelardo L. Rodríguez* (Mexicali: Universidad Autónoma de Baja California, 2002); Pedro Salmerón Sanginés, *Aarón Sáenz Garza: Militar, diplomático, político, empresario* (Mexico City: Editorial Porrúa, 2001).

83. See, for example, Meyer, Segovia, and Lajous, *Historia de la Revolución Mexicana*, 158–87.

84. See also Barbara A. Kuzio, "President Abelardo Rodríguez (1932–34): From Maximato to Cardenismo," MA thesis, Portland State University, 1996. Kuzio's thesis is based only on U.S. archival sources.

85. NA, RG 59, 812.00/30040, Daniels to Secretary of State, April 17, 1934.

86. Daniels, *Shirt-Sleeve Diplomat*, 52–54.

87. Francisco J. Gaxiola, *El Presidente Rodríguez (1932–1934)* (Mexico City: Editorial Cultura, 1938), 94–96, 120.

88. Meyer, Segovia, and Lajous, *Historia de la Revolución Mexicana*, 163–65.

89. Dulles, *Yesterday in Mexico*, 573.

90. NA, RG 59, 812.00/29828, Robert Cummings, G-2 Report, January 1933.

91. NA, RG 59, 812.00/29926, Daniels to Secretary of State, September 29, 1933.

92. FPEC, serie 010100, exp. 14, inv. 14, "Secretario de Estado Encargado del Despacho de Hacienda y Crédito Público," Abelardo Rodríguez, "Acta de Nombramiento," September 29, 1932.

93. A Spanish translation of the encyclical can be found in FPEC, serie 010806, exp. 44, inv. 624, "Papa Pío XI."

94. Dulles, *Yesterday in Mexico*, 560–61.

95. Quoted in Meyer, Segovia, and Lajous, *Historia de la Revolución Mexicana*, 178.

96. Mary Kay Vaughan, *Cultural Politics in Revolution* (Tucson: University of Arizona Press, 1998), 77–136.

97. Meyer, Segovia, and Lajous, *Historia de la Revolución Mexicana*, 184–87; Garrido, *El Partido de la Revolución Institucionalizada*, 158–59.

98. For Cárdenas's early career, see Enrique Krauze, *Mexico: Biography of Power*, translated by Hank Heifetz (New York: Harper Collins, 1997), 438–54; and Enrique Guerra Manzo, "La gubernatura de Lázaro Cárdenas en Michoacán (1928–1932): Una vía agrarista moderada," *Secuencia* 45 (September 1999): 131.

99. Arnaldo Córdova, *La política de masas del cardenismo* (Mexico City: Ediciones Era, 1974), 16–36.

100. Garrido, *El Partido de la Revolución Institucionalizada*, 156–57.

101. Victoriano Anguiano Equíhua, *Lázaro Cárdenas: Su feudo y la política nacional* (Mexico City: Editorial Eréndira, 1951), 29.

102. Krauze, *Reformar desde el origen*, 131–33.

103. Nora Hamilton, *The Limits of State Authority: Post-Revolutionary Mexico* (Princeton, NJ: Princeton University Press, 1982), 67–103.

104. Jeffrey Rubin, *Decentering the Regime: Ethnicity, Radicalism, and Democracy in Juchitán, Mexico* (Durham, NC: Duke University Press, 1997), 12. See also the essays in Gilbert M. Joseph and Daniel Nugent, eds., *Everyday Forms of State Formation: Revolution and the Negotiation of Rule in Mexico* (Durham, NC: Duke University Press, 1994).

105. Enrique Krauze, *Reformar desde el origen: Plutarco Elías Calles* (Mexico City: Fondo de Cultura Económica, 1987), 115–17.

106. PHO/4/45, interview with Alicia Calles, July 3, 1975.

107. Medín, *El minimato presidencial*.

Notes to Chapter Seven

1. FPEC, serie 010901, exp. 44, inv. 679, "Elías Calles, Plutarco (Gral.). Operación vesícula," Fernando Torreblanca to Alicia Elías Calles de Almada, Los Angeles, January 15, 1935.

2. *El Universal,* June 12, 1935.

3. John W. F. Dulles, *Yesterday in Mexico: A Chronicle of the Revolution, 1919–1936* (Austin: University of Texas Press, 1961), 640–46.

4. Alicia Hernández Chávez, *Historia de la Revolución Mexicana, periodo 1934–1940: La mecánica cardenista* (Mexico City: Colegio de México, 1979), 140.

5. Friedrich E. Schuler, *Mexico between Hitler and Roosevelt: Mexican Foreign Relations in the Age of Lázaro Cárdenas, 1934–1940* (Albuquerque: University of New Mexico Press, 1998), especially 33–61.

6. Enrique Krauze, *Mexico: Biography of Power,* translated by Hank Heifetz (New York: Harper Collins, 1997), 451.

7. Quoted in Michael J. Gonzales, *The Mexican Revolution, 1910–1940* (Albuquerque: University of New Mexico Press, 2002), 229.

8. Luis González, *Historia de la Revolución Mexicana, periodo 1934–1940: Los días del presidente Cárdenas* (Mexico City: Colegio de México, 1981), 13.

9. Hernández Chávez, *Historia de la Revolución Mexicana, periodo 1934–1940,* 44–46.

10. APEC, gav. 12, exp. 206, inv. 280, "Cárdenas, Lázaro (Gral.)," Cárdenas to Calles, Mexico City, Apr. 17 and 23, 1935; Calles to Cárdenas, El Tambor, Sin., April 24, 1935.

11. NA, MID 2657-G-768/15, A. F. Yepis to Daniels, Guaymas, Jan. 15; and Guy W. Ray to Secretary of State, Guaymas, March 15, 1935.

12. Quoted in Dulles, *Yesterday in Mexico,* 630.

13. Enrique Krauze, *Reformar desde el origen: Plutarco Elías Calles* (Mexico City: Fondo de Cultura Económica, 1987), 134.

14. Jorge Basurto, "Populism in Mexico: From Cárdenas to Cuauhtémoc," in Michael L. Conniff, ed., *Latin American Populism in Comparative Perspective* (Albuquerque: University of New Mexico Press, 1982), 75–96.

15. Dulles, *Yesterday in Mexico,* 621–29.

16. González, *Historia de la Revolución Mexicana, periodo 1934–1940,* 12.

17. Alan Knight, "Cardenismo: Juggernaut or Jalopy," *Journal of Latin American Studies* 24 (1994): 79.

18. Knight, "Cardenismo," 79–81.

19. E. David Cronon, *Josephus Daniels in Mexico* (Madison: University of Wisconsin Press, 1960).

20. Dulles, *Yesterday in Mexico,* 636–39.

21. Emilio Portes Gil, *Quince años de política mexicana,* 2nd ed. (Mexico City: Ediciones Botas, 1941), 497–98; and Emilio Portes Gil, *Autobiografía de la Revolución Mexicana: Un tratado de interpretación histórica* (Mexico City: Instituto Mexicano de Cultura, 1964), 692–93. The two versions are virtually identical.

22. Portes Gil, *Autobiografía de la Revolución Mexicana,* 699–700.

23. Hernández Chávez, *La mecánica cardenista,* 57–75.

24. NA, MID 2657-G-768/22, G-2 report, H. E. Marshburn, Military Attaché, U.S. Embassy, Mexico City, August 2, 1935.

25. FPEC, gav. 70, exp. "Pérez Treviño, Manuel," Calles to Pérez Treviño, San Diego, October 29, 1935.

26. NA, MID 2657-G-768/36, G-2 report, H. E. Marshburn, Mexico City, December 5, 1935.

27. NA, MID 2657-G-768/50, enclosed in G-2 report, H. E. Marshburn, Mexico City, December 16, 1935.

28. NA, MID 2657-G-768/50, enclosed in G-2 report, H. E. Marshburn, Mexico City, December 16, 1935.; Carlos Macías Richard, "La fuerza del destino: Una biografía de Plutarco Elías Calles, 1877–1945," doctoral diss., El Colegio de México, 1994, 383.

29. NA, MID 2657-G-768/50 and 53, G-2 reports, H. E. Marshburn, Mexico City, December 16 and 20, 1935; Plutarco Elías Calles, *Correspondencia personal, 1919–1945*, edited by Carlos Macías Richard (Mexico City: FAPEC and Fondo de Cultura Económica, 1991–1993), 1:318–19.

30. NA, MID 2657-G-768/50, 52, and 53, G-2 reports, H. E. Marshburn, Mexico City, December 17 and 20, 1935; Josephus Daniels, *Shirt Sleeve Diplomat* (Chapel Hill: University of North Carolina Press, 1947), 62; Adrian A. Bantjes, *As If Jesus Walked on Earth: Cardenismo, Sonora, and the Mexican Revolution* (Wilmington, DE: Scholarly Resources, 1998), 23–122; Knight, "Cardenismo: Juggernaut or Jalopy," 79–80, 103.

31. APEC, gav. 12, exp. 206, inv. 280, Cárdenas speech, December 22, 1935.

32. APEC, gav. 15, exp. 120, inv. 976, "Compañía Azucarera El Mante," Calles to Aarón Sáenz, Mexico City, March 17, 1936; Macías, "Fuerza del destino," 400.

33. Jocelyn Olcott, *Revolutionary Women in Postrevolutionary Mexico* (Durham, NC: Duke University Press, 2005), 1–2.

34. AGN, LC, 404.1/1134; ASDN, Archivo de Cancelados, XI/III/1–44, vol. 8, no. 1092, Blas Corral Martínez to various, Mexico City, April 1, 1936.

35. FPEC, serie 011000, gav. 70, exp. 225, "Valadés, José C.," Valadés, "Entrevista con el Gral. Plutarco Elías Calles, expresidente de México."

36. NA, RG 165, NA, MID 2657-G-657/173, Lt. Col. F. B. Mallon to Assistant Chief of Staff, Ft. Sam Houston, February 18, 1936.

37. NA, RG 165, NA, MID 2657-G-768/88, G-2 report, H. E. Marshburn, Mexico City, April 10, 1936; AGN, LC, "Orden de expulsión," file 546.2/10.

38. NA, MID 2657-G-768/88, G-2 report, H. E. Marshburn, Mexico City, April 10, 1936; George Lynn, "Mexico's Exile," *Today*, July 19, 1936, 6–8. Calles's version of these events is available in FPEC, serie 011000, gav. 69, exp. 45, "Declaraciones," William G. Cayce, "Mexico—Communism or Calles?"

39. Daniels, *Shirt-Sleeve Diplomat*, 62–65.

40. Yosse Shain, *The Frontier of Loyalty: Political Exiles in the Age of the Nation State* (Middletown, CT: Wesleyan University Press, 1989), 153.

41. Shain, *The Frontier of Loyalty*, 153.

42. "Introduction," in *Strange Pilgrimages: Exile, Travel, and National Identity in Latin America, 1800–1990s*, edited by Ingrid E. Fey and Karen Racine (Wilmington, DE: Scholarly Resources, 2000), 15.

43. Krauze, *Biography of Power*, 434.

44. For a discussion of adaptation as the first step of the immigrant journey, see José C. Moya, *Cousins and Strangers: Spanish Immigrants in Buenos Aires, 1850–1930* (Berkeley: University of California Press, 1998), 6.

45. FPEC, serie 011000, gav. 69, exp. 45, "Declaraciones," William G. Cayce, "Mexico—Communism or Calles?"

46. FPEC, serie 011000, gav. 69, exp. 45, "Declaraciones," "Address Given by General Plutarco Elías Calles in the City of Tulsa, Oklahoma, on the First Day of June, 1936."

47. FPEC, serie 011000, gav. 69, exp. 45, "Declaraciones," Calles, "The Law of the Pendulum: From Radical Impulsiveness to Reactionary Intransigence."

48. FPEC, serie 011000, gav. 69, exp. 45, "Declaraciones," "Address Given by General Plutarco Elías Calles in the City of Tulsa, Oklahoma, on the First Day of June, 1936."

49. FPEC, serie 011000, gav. 69, exp. 45, "Declaraciones," "Address Given by General Plutarco Elías Calles in the City of Tulsa, Oklahoma, on the First Day of June, 1936."

50. Calles to Hortensia Calles de Torreblanca, San Diego, September 15, 1936, Elías Calles, *Correspondencia personal*, 1:443–44.

51. Interview with Norma Torreblanca de Mereles, Mexico City, June 1, 2004.

52. Krauze, *Reformar desde el origen*, 144.

53. Interview with Norma Torreblanca de Mereles, Mexico City, June 1, 2004.

54. FPEC, serie 011000, gav. 70, exp. 179, "Rodríguez, Abelardo," Calles to Rodríguez, November 30, 1936.

55. Portes Gil, *Autobiografía de la Revolución Mexicana*, 703.

56. FPEC, serie 011000, gav. 70, exp. 226, "Vasconcelos, José," Vasconcelos to Calles, Nogales, AZ, August 17, 1939; Martha Beatriz Loyo Camacho, "Plutarco Elías Calles desde su exilio," *Boletín* 45 (Mexico City: Archivo Fideicomiso Plutarco Elías Calles y Fernando Torreblanca, 2004), 13–15.

57. Knight, "Cardenismo: Juggernaut or Jalopy," 73–107.

58. NA, MID, box 1662, 2657-G-555/49, G-2 report, April 5, 1938.

59. For a case study of political centralization from the PNR to the PRM in Chihuahua, see Mark Wasserman, *Persistent Oligarchs: Elites and Politics in Chihuahua, Mexico, 1910–1940* (Durham, NC: Duke University Press, 1993), 50–67.

60. FPEC, serie 011000, gav. 69, exp. 6, "Amaro, Joaquín (Gral.)," Calles to Amaro, San Diego, July 2, 1938.

61. FPEC, gav. 69, exp. 45, "Declaraciones," Calles, "The Law of the Pendulum: From Radical Impulsiveness to Reactionary Intransigence."

62. Macías, "Fuerza del destino," 395.

63. Elías Calles, *Correspondencia personal, 1919–1945*, 1:442–70.

64. Luis Araquistáin, *La revolución mejicana: Sus orígenes, sus hombres, su obra* (Madrid: Editorial España, 1930), 151–68.

65. FPEC, serie 011000, gav. 69, exp. 117, "León, Luis L.," Calles to León, San Diego, June 22, 1937.

66. FPEC, serie 011000, gav. 69, exp. 117, "León, Luis L.," Calles to León, San Diego, June 22, 1937.

67. FPEC, serie 011000, gav. 70, exp. 145, "Ortega, Melchor," Calles to Ortega, San Diego, Apr. 18, 1939.

68. FPEC, serie 011000, gav. 69, exp. 45, "Declaraciones," Calles, "The Law of the Pendulum."

69. FPEC, serie 011000, gav. 69, exp. 117, "León, Luis L.," Calles to León, San Diego, Oct. 7, 1939.

70. FPEC, serie 011000, gav. 69, exp. 117, "León, Luis L.," Calles to León, San Diego, Oct. 7, 1939.

71. FPEC, serie 011000, gav. 70, exp. 145, "Ortega, Melchor," Calles to Ortega, San Diego, Apr. 18 and May 22, 1940; interview with Norma Torreblanca de Mereles, Mexico City, June 1, 2004.

72. FPEC, serie 011000, gav. 70, exp. 145, "Ortega, Melchor," Calles to Ortega, San Diego, August 30, 1939.

73. FPEC, serie 011000, gav. 70, exp. 145, "Ortega, Melchor," Calles to Ortega, San Diego, December 9, 1939.

74. FPEC, serie 011000, gav. 70, exp. 145, "Ortega, Melchor," Calles to Ortega, San Diego, December 9, 1939.

75. AGN, Archivo Particular Lázaro Cárdenas, reel 15–22.

76. Carlos Silva Cáceres, *Plutarco Elías Calles* (Mexico City: Editorial Planeta, 2002), 144–45.

77. Stephen R. Niblo, *Mexico in the 1940s: Modernity, Politics, and Corruption* (Wilmington, DE: Scholarly Resources, 1999), 86.

78. Schuler, *Mexico between Hitler and Roosevelt*, 7–8, 186–87.

79. FPEC, serie 011000, gav. 69, exp. 6, inv. 1208, "Amaro, Joaquín (Gral.)," Calles to Amaro, San Diego, October 10, 1939; Martha Beatriz Loyo Camacho, "El Partido Revolucionario Anti Comunista en las elecciones de 1940," *Estudios de Historia Moderna y Contemporánea de México* 23 (January 2002): 145–60.

80. FPEC, serie 011000, gav. 70, exp. 145, "Ortega, Melchor," Calles to Ortega, San Diego, March 17, 1940; FPEC, serie 011000, gav. 69, exp. "Avila Camacho, Maximino."

81. NA, MID 2657-G-657/323, H. R. Oldfield to Assistant Chief of Staff, San Francisco, October 11, 1938.

82. FPEC, serie 011000, gav. 70, exp. 216, "Torreblanca, Fernando," Fernando Torreblanca to Calles, December 31, 1940 and January 11, 1941, and Calles to Torreblanca, January 14, 1941.

83. Macías, "La fuerza del destino," 408; interview with Plutarco Elías Calles Llorente, Mexico City, May 31, 2004.

84. FPEC, serie 011100, gav. 71, exp. 64, "Casa Juan de Acuña #130."

85. FPEC, serie 011100, gav. 72, exp. 146, "Elías Calles de Almada, Alicia," Plutarco Elías Calles to Alicia Elías Calles de Almada, Mexico City, March 23, 1942.

86. FPEC, serie 011100, gav. 72, exp. 146, "Elías Calles de Almada, Alicia," Plutarco Elías Calles to Alicia Elías Calles de Almada, Mexico City, March 23, 1942.

87. Krauze, Biography of Power, 516.

88. Niblo, Mexico in the 1940s, chapter 1.

89. FPEC, serie 011100, gav. 71, exp. 95, "Comité Director de Acercamiento Nacional," Rodríguez to Calles, Mexico City, August 15, 1942; press clippings in FPEC, serie 011100, gav. 72, exp. 264, "Prensa;" Cárdenas, Obras 2:191; PHO/4/45, interview with Alicia Almada de Calles, July 4, 1975.

90. ASDN, Archivo de Cancelados, XI/III/1–44, vol. 8, no. 1934, Ramón Rodríguez to Calles, Mexico City, April 1, 1943.

91. Susan M. Deeds, "José María Maytorena and the Mexican Revolution in Sonora (Part 2)," Arizona and the West 18, no. 1 (1976): 147–48.

92. FPEC, serie 011100, gav. 72, exp. 145, "Elías Calles Chacón, Rodolfo," especially Rodolfo Elías Calles Chacón to Plutarco Elías Calles, Navolato, May 8, 1943, and Plutarco to Rodolfo, Mexico City, January 16, 1944.

93. FPEC, serie 011303, exp. 28, "Inventario"; exp. 31, "Testamento."

94. FPEC, serie 011100, gav. 72, exp. 152, "Escuela Niños"; and exp. 153, "Elías Calles Ruiz, Manuel."

95. FPEC, serie 011100, gav. 72, exp. 145, "Elías Calles Chacón, Rodolfo"; Interview with Plutarco Elías Calles Llorente, Mexico City, May 31, 2004.

96. Interview with Plutarco Elías Calles Llorente, Mexico City, May 31, 2004.

97. FPEC, serie 010901, exp. 57, inv. 692, "Elías Calles Lacy, Natalia."

98. FPEC, serie 010901, exp. 57, inv. 692, "Elías Calles Lacy, Natalia"; interview with Norma Torreblanca de Mereles, Mexico City, June 1, 2004; FPEC, serie 010901, exp. 59, inv. 694, "Elías Calles Llorente, Plutarco José."

99. El Universal, Nov. 17, 1958, "Memorias del General Juan Andreu Almazán"; Antonio N. Zavaleta, "El Niño Fidencio and the Fidencistas," in Sects, Cults and Spiritual Communities: A Sociological Analysis, edited by William W. Zellner and Marc Petrowski (Westport, CT: Praeger, 1998), 103. I am grateful to Timothy Henderson for the Almazán reference.

100. Una ventana al mundo invisible: Protocolos del IMIS (Mexico City: Ediciones Antorcha, 1960); Marcela Gomezharper de Treviño, "La parapsicología en México," at www.alipsi.com.ar/publicaciones_articulo.asp?id_articulo=32 (accessed July 2, 2004).

101. Allan Kardec, Le livre des esprits: contenant les principes de la doctrine spirite sur l'immortalité de l'âme, la nature des esprits et leurs rapports avec les hommes, les lois morales, la vie présente, la vie future et l'avenir de l'humanité: selon l'enseignement donné par les esprits supérieurs à l'aide de divers médiums, 15th ed. (Paris: Didier et Cie, 1867).

102. Interview with Plutarco Elías Calles Llorente, Mexico City, May 31, 2004; Ventana al mundo invisible, 105–6.

103. FPEC, serie 011100, gav. 72, exp. 145, "Elías Calles Chacón, Rodolfo," Calles to Rodolfo Elías Calles Chacón, Cuernavaca, April 29, 1944.

104. FPEC, serie 011100, gav. 71, exp. 86, "Castillo, Enrique del. Mtro. Sesiones espiritistas," minutes, February 15, 1944; *Ventana al mundo invisible*, 81–85.

105. FPEC, serie 011100, gav. 71, exp. 86, "Castillo, Enrique del. Mtro. Sesiones espiritistas," "Sesión en que trabajaron el Sr. Rodolfo Elías Calles y su Sra., en Cuernavaca, Morelos, el 28 de septiembre de 1944."

106. FPEC, serie 011100, gav. 71, exp. 86, "Castillo, Enrique del. Mtro. Sesiones espiritistas," "Sesión en que trabajaron el Sr. Rodolfo Elías Calles y su Sra., en Cuernavaca, Morelos, el 28 de septiembre de 1944."

107. Quoted in Krauze, *Biography of Power*, 436–37.

108. FPEC, serie 011100, gav. 71, exp. 134, "Elías Calles, Plutarco (Gral.) Enfermedades"; Fernando Torreblanca to Rodolfo Elías Calles Chacón, Mexico City, October 11, 1945; FPEC, serie 011100, gav. 71, exp. 128, "Elías Calles, Alicia Sáenz de," Plutarco Elías Calles to Elisa Sáenz de Elías Calles, Mexico City, January 4, 1945.

109. FPEC, serie 011200, exp. 1, "Acta de defunción del Gral. Plutarco Elías Calles"; and exp. 15, "Prensa La Nación."

110. FPEC, serie 011400, exp. 1, "Homenajes 1945," León, "Elogio del Gral. Plutarco Elías Calles."

111. FPEC, serie 011100, gav. 71, exp. 86, "Castillo, Enrique del. Mtro. Sesiones espiritistas," Rodolfo Elías Calles, minutes, October 25, 1945.

Notes to the Epilogue

1. Thomas Benjamin, *La Revolución: Mexico's Great Revolution as Memory, Myth, and History* (Austin: University of Texas Press, 2000), 134. This move had been authorized as early as 1946; FPEC, serie 011400, exp. 2, "Homenajes 1946," Manuel Avila Camacho, "Decreto que dispone . . . ," *Diario Oficial*, November 1, 1946.

2. FPEC, serie 010400, "Homenajes 1971," Plutarco Elías Calles Chacón, "Discurso."

3. FPEC, serie 010400, "Homenajes 1971," Plutarco Elías Calles Chacón, "Discurso."

4. Quoted in Antonio Ruibal Corella, *Calles, hombre de su tiempo* (n.p., 1987), iv.

5. FPEC, serie 010400, exp. 46, "Homenajes 1990."

6. On June 18, 1992, the central bank introduced a new currency, the nuevo peso, equivalent to 1,000 old pesos. For the next four years, Calles graced the new 100 peso notes.

7. Michael L. Conniff, *Populism in Latin America* (Tuscaloosa: University of Alabama Press, 1999), 11.

8. Lyle C. Brown, "The Calles-Cárdenas Connection," in *Twentieth-Century Mexico*, edited by W. Dirk Raat and William H. Beezley (Lincoln: University of Nebraska Press, 1986), 158.

9. Alan Knight, "The Ideology of the Mexican Revolution, 1910–1940," *Estudios Interdisciplinarios de América Latina y el Caribe* 8, no. 1 (1997): 95.

10. Knight, "Ideology of the Mexican Revolution," 88 and passim.

Bibliography

Archives

Mexico

Archivo de la Secretaría de la Defensa Nacional, Mexico City
    Archivo de Cancelados
Archivo General de la Nación, Mexico City
    Fondo Lázaro Cárdenas
    Fondo Presidentes
        Lázaro Cárdenas
        Manuel Avila Camacho
        Obregón-Calles
Archivo Histórico General del Estado de Sonora, Hermosillo
Biblioteca Nacional de Antropología e Historia, Mexico City
    Archivo Histórico en Micropelícula
        Documentos para la Historia de Sonora
    Programa de Historia Oral
Centro de Estudios de la Historia de México CONDUMEX, Mexico City
    Archivo Venustiano Carranza
Fideicomiso Archivos Plutarco Elías Calles y Fernando Torreblanca
    Archivo Fernando Torreblanca
        Fondo Plutarco Elías Calles
        Fondo Presidentes
    Archivo Plutarco Elías Calles
        Fondo Archivo Plutarco Elías Calles
        Fondo Archivo Plutarco Elías Calles Anexo

Archivo Luis Morones
Secretaría de Relaciones Exteriores, Mexico City. Archivo Histórico

United States
Amherst College Library, Amherst, MA
  Dwight Morrow Papers
Library of Congress, Washington, D.C., Manuscript Division
  Henry P. Fletcher Papers
  Frank B. Kellogg Papers
National Archives, Washington, D.C., and College Park, MD
  RG 59: General Records of the Department of State
  RG 84: Foreign Post Records of the Department of State
  RG 165: Records of the Army General and Special Staffs. Military Intelligence
    Division
University of North Carolina, Chapel Hill
  Southern Historical Collection
    Josephus Daniels Papers
Yale University Library
  James R. Sheffield Papers

Interviews

Elías Calles Llorente, Plutarco José. May 31, 2004
Torreblanca Elías Calles de Mereles, Norma. June 1, 2004

Newspapers

El Demócrata, Mexico City
El Nacional, Mexico City
El Universal, Mexico City
Excelsior, Mexico City

Published Primary Sources

Anguiano Equíhua, Victoriano. *Lázaro Cárdenas: Su feudo y la política nacional*. Mexico City: Editorial Eréndira, 1951.
Archivo General de la Nación. *Boletín del Archivo General de la Nación*. Mexico City: Archivo General de la Nación, 1977.
Azuela, Mariano. *Los de abajo: Novela de la Revolución Mexicana* [1915]. Mexico City: Ediciones Botas, 1941.
Beals, Carleton. *Glass Houses: Ten Years of Free-Lancing*. Philadelphia: Lippincott, 1938.

———. *Mexican Maze*. Philadelphia: Lippincott, 1931.

Boletín oficial: Órgano del gobierno constitucionalista de Sonora. Hermosillo: n.p., 1916–1917.

Bórquez, Djed [pseud.]. *Hombres de México: Calles*. Mexico City: A. Botas, 1925.

Breceda, Alfredo. *México revolucionario, 1913–1917*. 2 vols. Madrid: Tipografía Artística, 1920–1941.

Brenner, Anita, and George R. Leighton. *The Wind That Swept Mexico*. New York: Harper, 1943.

Caro, Brígido. *Plutarco Elías Calles, dictador bolcheviki de México: Episodios de la revolución mexicana desde 1910 al 1924*. Los Angeles: n.p., 1924.

Cháverri Matamoros, Amado, and Clodoveo Valenzuela. *El verdadero Calles*. Mexico City: Editorial Patria, 1929.

Coolidge, Calvin. *Conditions in Nicaragua: Message from the President of the United States Transmitting to the Congress of the United States the Conditions and the Action of the Government in the Present Disturbances in Nicaragua*. Washington, DC: Government Printing Office, 1927.

Daniels, Josephus. *Shirt-Sleeve Diplomat*. Chapel Hill: University of North Carolina Press, 1947.

Elías Calles, Plutarco. *Correspondencia personal, 1919–1945*. Ed. Carlos Macías Richard. 2 vols. Mexico City: FAPEC and Fondo de Cultura Económica, 1991–1993.

———. *Declaraciones y discursos políticos*. Mexico City: Cuadernos de causa, 1979.

———. *Decretos, circulares y demás disposiciones dictadas por el C. Gobernador y Comandante Militar del Estado de Sonora, General Plutarco Elías Calles, durante el año de 1915*. Hermosillo: Imprenta de Gobierno, 1915.

———. *Decretos, circulares y demás disposiciones dictadas por el C. Gobernador y Comandante Militar del Estado de Sonora, General Plutarco Elías Calles, durante el año de 1916*. Hermosillo: Imprenta de Gobierno, 1916.

———. *Informe relativo al sitio de Naco, 1914–1915*. Mexico City: Talleres Gráficos de la Nación, 1932.

———. *Partes oficiales de la campaña de Sonora*. Mexico City: Talleres Gráficos de la Nación, 1932.

———. *Pensamiento político y social: Antología, 1913–1936*. Ed. Carlos Macías Richard. Mexico City: FAPEC and Fondo de Cultura Económica, 1988.

Foreign Relations of the United States. Washington, DC: Government Printing Office, various dates.

Gaxiola, Francisco J. *El Presidente Rodríguez (1932–1934)*. Mexico City: Editorial Cultura, 1938.

Goldman, Ralph M. *The Mentor and the Protégé: The Story of Presidents Calles and Cárdenas*. n.p.: Xlibris, 2003.

González y González, Luis, ed. *Los Presidentes de México ante la nación*. 4 vols. Mexico City: Cámara de Diputados, 1966.

Greene, Graham. *The Lawless Roads: A Mexican Journey*. London: Longmans, Green, 1939.

————. *The Power and the Glory*. New York: Viking Press, 1946.

Guzmán, Martín Luis. *La sombra del caudillo*. Madrid: Espasa-Calpe, 1930.

Guzmán Esparza, Roberto. *Memorias de don Adolfo de la Huerta, según su propio dictado*. Mexico City: Ediciones Guzmán, 1957.

Kardec, Allan. *Le livre des esprits: contenant les principes de la doctrine spirite sur l'immortalité de l'âme, la nature des esprits et leurs rapports avec les hommes, les lois morales, la vie présente, la vie future et l'avenir de l'humanité: selon l'enseignement donné par les esprits supérieurs à l'aide de divers médiums*. 15th ed. Paris: Didier, 1867.

León, Luis L. *Crónica del poder: En los recuerdos de un político en el México revolucionario*. Mexico City: Fondo de Cultura Económica, 1987.

Madero, Francisco I. *La sucesión presidencial: El Partido Nacional Democrático* [1909]. Mexico City: Secretaría de Hacienda, 1960.

Manjarrez, Froylán C. *La jornada institucional*. 2 vols. Mexico City: Talleres Gráficos de la Nación, 1930.

McCullagh, Francis. *Red Mexico: A Reign of Terror in America*. New York: Carrier, 1928.

Murray, Robert H., trans. and ed. *Mexico before the World: Public Documents and Addresses of Plutarco Elías Calles*. New York: Academy Press, 1927.

Nacional Financiera. *Statistics on the Mexican Economy*. Mexico City: Nacional Financiera, 1977.

Obregón, Alvaro. *Discursos del General Alvaro Obregón*. 2 vols. Mexico City: Dirección General de Educación Militar, 1932.

————. *Ocho mil kilómetros en campaña*. 2nd ed. Mexico City: Fondo de Cultura Económica, 1959.

Ortiz Rubio, Pascual. *Memorias, 1925–1928*. Morelia: Universidad Michoacana de San Nicolás, 1981.

Pani, Alberto J. *Apuntes autobiográficos*. 2 vols. Mexico: Porrúa, 1950.

Porter, Katherine Anne. *Flowering Judas and Other Stories*. New York: Harcourt, Brace, 1935.

Portes Gil, Emilio. *Autobiografía de la Revolución Mexicana: Un tratado de interpretación histórica*. Mexico City: Instituto Mexicano de Cultura, 1964.

————. *Quince años de política mexicana*. 2nd ed. Mexico City: Ediciones Botas, 1941.

Richkarday, Ignacio A. *60 años en la vida de México*. Mexico City, 1963.

Rodríguez, Abelardo L. *Autobiografía*. Mexico City, 1962.

Rousseau, Jean-Jacques. *The Social Contract and the First and Second Discourses*. Ed. Susan Dunn. New Haven, CT: Yale University Press, 2002.

Santos, Gonzalo N. *Memorias*. 4th ed. Mexico City: Grijalbo, 1986.

Taracena, Alfonso. *Los vasconcelistas sacrificados en Topilejo*. Mexico City: Editora Librera, 1958.

Traven, B. *Land des Frühlings*. Berlin: Büchergilde Gutenberg, 1928.

Turner, John Kenneth. *Barbarous Mexico*. New York: Cassell, 1912.

Una ventana al mundo invisible: protocolos del IMIS. Mexico City: Ediciones Antorcha, 1960.

United States Senate. *Investigations of Mexican Affairs: Preliminary report and hearings of the Committee on foreign relations, United States Senate, pursuant to S. res. 106, directing the Committee on foreign relations to investigate the matter of outrages on citizens of the United States in Mexico*. 5 vols. Washington, DC: Government Printing Office, 1920.

Vasconcelos, José. *El desastre: Tercera parte de Ulises Criollo*. Mexico City: Acción Moderna Mercantil, 1938.

———. *El proconsulado*. Mexico City: Ediciones Botas, 1939.

Wilkie, James W., and Edna Monzón de Wilkie. *México visto en el siglo XX: Entrevistas de historia oral*. Mexico City: Instituto Mexicano de Investigaciones Económicas, 1969.

Zuno, José Guadalupe. *Reminiscencias de una vida*. 2nd ed. Guadalajara: Biblioteca de autores jalisciences modernos, 1973.

Secondary Literature

Aguilar Camín, Héctor. *La frontera nómada: Sonora y la Revolución Mexicana*. Mexico City: Siglo XXI Editores, 1977.

———. "The Relevant Tradition: Sonoran Leaders in the Revolution." In *Caudillo and Peasant in the Mexican Revolution*. Ed. D. A. Brading, 92–123. Cambridge: Cambridge University Press, 1980.

Aguilar Camín, Héctor, and Lorenzo Meyer. *In the Shadow of the Mexican Revolution: Contemporary Mexican History, 1910–1989*. Trans. Luis Alberto Fierro. Austin: University of Texas Press, 1993.

Almada Bay, Ignacio. *Breve historia de Sonora*. Mexico City: Fideicomiso Historia de las Américas, 2000.

———. "La conexión Yocupicio: Soberanía estatal, tradición cívico-liberal y resistencia al reemplazo de las lealtades en Sonora, 1913–1939." Doctoral diss., El Colegio de México, 1993.

Anderson, Benedict. *Imagined Communities: Reflections on the Spread of Nationalism*. London: Verso, 1983.

Ankerson, Dudley. *Agrarian Warlord: Saturnino Cedillo and the Mexican Revolution in San Luis Potosí*. DeKalb: Northern Illinois University Press, 1984.

Asturias, Miguel Angel. *El señor presidente*. New York: Atheneum, 1964.

Bailey, David C. "Obregón: Mexico's Accommodating President." In *Essays on the Mexican Revolution: Revisionist Views of the Leaders*. Ed. George Wolfskill and Douglas W. Richmond, 81–99. Austin: University of Texas Press, 1979.

———. *Viva Cristo Rey: The Cristero Rebellion and the Church-State Conflict in Mexico*. Austin: University of Texas Press, 1974.

Bantjes, Adrian A. *As If Jesus Walked on Earth: Cardenismo, Sonora, and the Mexican Revolution*. Wilmington, DE: Scholarly Resources, 1998.

Bazant, Jan. "From Independence to the Liberal Republic, 1821–1867." In *Mexico since Independence*. Ed. Leslie Bethell. Cambridge: Cambridge University Press, 1991.

Beelen, George D. "The Harding Administration and Mexico: Diplomacy by Economic Persuasion." *Americas* 41, no. 2 (October 1984): 177–89.

Beezley, William H. *Insurgent Governor: Abraham González of Chihuahua*. Lincoln: University of Nebraska Press, 1973.

———. *Judas at the Jockey Club and Other Episodes of Porfirian Mexico*. Lincoln: University of Nebraska Press, 1987.

———. "Madero, the 'Unknown' President and His Political Failure to Organize Rural Mexico." In *Essays on the Mexican Revolution: Revisionist Views of the Leaders*. Ed. George Wolfskill and Douglas W. Richmond, 1–24. Austin: University of Texas Press, 1979.

Benjamin, Thomas. *La Revolución: Mexico's Great Revolution as Memory, Myth, and History*. Austin: University of Texas Press, 2000.

———. *A Rich Land, a Poor People: Politics and Society in Modern Chiapas*. Albuquerque: University of New Mexico Press, 1989.

Bliss, Katherine E. *Compromised Positions: Prostitution, Public Health, and Gender Politics in Revolutionary Mexico City*. University Park: Pennsylvania State University Press, 2001.

Boyer, Christopher R. *Becoming Campesinos: Politics, Identity, and Agrarian Struggle in Postrevolutionary Michoacán, 1920–1935*. Stanford, CA: Stanford University Press, 2003.

Britton, John A. *Carleton Beals: A Radical Journalist in Latin America*. Albuquerque: University of New Mexico Press, 1987.

———. "Propaganda, Property, and the Image of Stability: The Mexican Government and the U.S. Print Media, 1921–1929." *South Eastern Latin Americanist* 19 (March 1988): 5–28.

Brown, James C. "Consolidation of the Mexican Revolution under Calles, 1924–1928: Politics, Modernization, and the Roots of the Revolutionary National Party." PhD diss., University of New Mexico, 1979.

Brown, Lyle C. "The Calles-Cárdenas Connection." In *Twentieth-Century Mexico*. Ed. W. Dirk Raat and William H. Beezley, 146–58. Lincoln: University of Nebraska Press, 1986.

Brunk, Samuel. *Emiliano Zapata: Revolution and Betrayal in Mexico*. Albuquerque: University of New Mexico Press, 1995.

Buchenau, Jürgen. "The Arm and Body of the Revolution: Remembering Mexico's Last Caudillo, Alvaro Obregón." In *Death, Dismemberment, and Memory: Body Politics in Latin America*. Ed. Lyman Johnson, 179–206. Albuquerque: University of New Mexico Press, 2004.

———. *Calles y el movimiento liberal en Nicaragua*. Boletín 9. Mexico: Fideicomiso Archivos Plutarco Elías Calles y Fernando Torreblanca, 1992.

———. *In the Shadow of the Giant: The Making of Mexico's Central America Policy, 1876–1930*. Tuscaloosa: University of Alabama Press, 1996.

———. "Small Numbers, Great Impact: Mexico and Its Immigrants." *Journal of American Ethnic History* 20, no. 3 (2001): 23–49.

Buford, Camile Nick. "A Biography of Luis N. Morones, Mexican Labor and Political Leader." PhD diss., Louisiana State University, 1972.

Camp, Roderic A. *Intellectuals and the State in Twentieth-Century Mexico*. Austin: University of Texas Press, 1985.

———. *Mexican Political Biographies, 1884–1935*. Austin: University of Texas Press, 1991.

Canovan, Margaret. *Populism*. London: Longman, 1981.

Capetillo, Alonso. *La rebelión sin cabeza: Génesis y desarrollo del movimiento delahuertista*. Mexico City: Botas, 1925.

Carr, Barry. "Las peculiaridades del norte mexicano: Ensayo de interpretación." *Historia Mexicana* 22, no. 3 (January 1973): 320–46.

Castro Martínez, Pedro. *Adolfo de la Huerta: La integridad como arma de la revolución*. Mexico City: Siglo XXI Editores, 1998.

———. *Adolfo de la Huerta y la Revolución Mexicana*. Mexico City: Instituto Nacional de Estudios Históricos de la Revolución Mexicana, 1992.

———. *A la sombra de un caudillo: Vida y muerte del general Francisco R. Serrano*. Mexico City: Plaza y Janés, 2005.

———. *De la Huerta y Calles: Los límites políticos de la amistad, Boletín 23*. Mexico City: FAPEC, 1996.

———. *La muerte de Carranza: Dudas y certezas. Boletín 34*. Mexico City: FAPEC, 2000.

———. *Soto y Gama: Genio y figura*. Mexico City: Universidad Autónoma Metropolitana, 2002.

Clark, Marjorie R. *Organized Labor in Mexico*. Chapel Hill: University of North Carolina Press, 1934.

Coatsworth, John. *Growth against Development: The Economic Impact of Railroads in Porfirian Mexico*. DeKalb: Northern Illinois University Press, 1981.

Cockcroft, James D. *Intellectual Precursors of the Mexican Revolution, 1900–1913*. Austin: University of Texas Press, 1968.

Collado Herrera, María del Carmen. *Empresarios y políticos: Entre la Restauración y la Revolución*. Mexico City: Instituto Nacional de Estudios Históricos de la Revolución Mexicana, 1996.

Conniff, Michael L., ed. *Latin American Populism in Comparative Perspective*. Albuquerque: University of New Mexico Press, 1982.

———. *Populism in Latin America*. Tuscaloosa: University of Alabama Press, 1999.

Córdova, Arnaldo. *La ideología de la revolución mexicana: La formación del nuevo régimen*. Mexico City: Ediciones Era, 1973.

———. *La política de masas del cardenismo*. Mexico City: Ediciones Era, 1974.

———. *La Revolución en crisis: La aventura del maximato*. Mexico City: Cal y Arena, 1995.

Cosío Villegas, Daniel, ed. *Historia moderna de México*. 9 vols. Mexico City: Editorial Hermes, 1956–1973.

Crider, Gregory. "Labor's Hero and Labor's Gangster: A Cultural Biography of Luis Napoleón Morones." Paper presented at the meeting of the Southeast Council of Latin American Studies, Santo Domingo, 2004.

Cronon, E. David. *Josephus Daniels in Mexico*. Madison: University of Wisconsin Press, 1960.

Cumberland, Charles C. *Mexican Revolution: Genesis under Madero*. Austin: University of Texas Press, 1952.

Deeds, Susan M. "José María Maytorena and the Mexican Revolution in Sonora (Part 1)." *Arizona and the West* 18, no. 1 (1976).

———. "José María Maytorena and the Mexican Revolution in Sonora (Part 2)." *Arizona and the West* 18, no. 1 (1976).

Delpar, Helen. *The Enormous Vogue of Things Mexican: Cultural Relations between the United States and Mexico*. Tuscaloosa: University of Alabama Press, 1992.

Diccionario Porrúa de historia, biografía y geografía de México. 6th ed. Mexico City: Editorial Porrúa, 1995.

Di Tella, Torcuato. "Populism and Reform in Latin America." In *Obstacles to Change in Latin America*. Ed. Claudio Veliz, 47–74. Oxford: Oxford University Press, 1965.

Dix, Robert H. "Populism: Authoritarian and Democratic." *Latin American Research Review* 20, no. 2 (1985): 29–52.

Dulles, John W. F. *Yesterday in Mexico: A Chronicle of the Revolution, 1919–1936*. Austin: University of Texas Press, 1961.

Falcón, Romana. "Charisma, Tradition, and Caciquismo: Revolution in San Luis Potosí." In *Riot, Rebellion, and Revolution: Rural Social Conflict in Mexico*. Ed. Friedrich Katz. Princeton, NJ: Princeton University Press, 1988.

Fallaw, Ben. "Dry Law, Wet Politics: Drinking and Prohibition in Post-Revolutionary Yucatán, 1915–1935." *Latin American Research Review* 37, no. 2 (2002): 37–64.

Farmer, Edward M. *Un nacionalismo pragmático: El gobierno callista en Sonora y el capital extranjero, Boletín 31*. Mexico City: Fideicomiso Archivos Plutarco Elías Calles y Fernando Torreblanca, 1999.

———. "Plutarco Elías Calles and the Revolutionary Government in Sonora, Mexico, 1915–1919." PhD diss., Cambridge University, 1997.

Fey, Ingrid E., and Karen Racine, eds. *Strange Pilgrimages: Exile, Travel, and National Identity in Latin America, 1800–1990s*. Wilmington, DE: Scholarly Resources, 2000.

Fowler-Salamini, Heather. *Agrarian Radicalism in Veracruz, 1920–1938*. Lincoln: University of Nebraska Press, 1971.

Garner, Paul H. *Porfirio Díaz*. London: Longman, 2001.

Garrido, Luis Javier. *El Partido de la Revolución Institucionalizada: La formación del nuevo estado en México (1928–1945)*. Mexico City: Siglo XXI Editores, 1982.

Gilderhus, Mark T. *Diplomacy and Revolution: U.S.-Mexican Relations under Wilson and Carranza*. Tucson: University of Arizona Press, 1977.

Gilly, Adolfo. *La revolución interrumpida: Una guerra campesina por la tierra y el poder*. Mexico City: Ediciones el Caballito, 1971.

Gómez Estrada, José Alfredo. *Gobierno y casinos: El origen de la riqueza de Abelardo L. Rodríguez*. Mexicali: Universidad Autónoma de Baja California, 2002.

Gonzales, Michael J. *The Mexican Revolution, 1910–1940*. Albuquerque: University of New Mexico Press, 2002.

———. "United States Copper Companies, the State, and Labour Conflict in Mexico, 1900–1910." *Journal of Latin American Studies* 26 (October 1994): 655–59.

———. "U.S. Copper Companies, the Mine Workers' Movement, and the Mexican Revolution, 1910–1920. *Hispanic American Historical Review* 76, no. 3 (1996): 503–34.

González Navarro, Moisés. "Las ideas raciales de los científicos." *Historia Mexicana* 37, no. 4 (April 1988): 565–84.

González, Luis. *Historia de la Revolución Mexicana, periodo 1934–1940: Los días del presidente Cárdenas*. Mexico City: Colegio de México, 1981.

Gouran, Roger D. "A Study of Two Attempts by President Plutarco Elías Calles to Establish a National Church in Mexico." MA thesis, Portland State University, 1995.

Gramsci, Antonio. *Selections from the Prison Notebooks*. Ed. and trans. Quintin Hoare and Geoffrey N. Smith. New York: International Publishers, 1971.

Guerra Manzo, Enrique. "La gubernatura de Lázaro Cárdenas en Michoacán (1928–1932): Una vía agrarista moderada." *Secuencia* 45 (September 1999).

———. *Industry and Underdevelopment: The Industrialization of Mexico, 1880–1940*. Stanford, CA: Stanford University Press, 1989.

Haber, Stephen. "Anything Goes: Mexico's 'New' Cultural History." *Hispanic American Historical Review* 79, no. 2 (1999): 309–30.

———. *Industry and Underdevelopment: The Industrialization of Mexico, 1890–1940*. Stanford, CA: Stanford University Press, 1989.

Hale, Charles A. *Mexican Liberalism in the Age of Mora, 1821–1853*. New Haven, CT: Yale University Press, 1968.

———. *The Transformation of Mexican Liberalism in the Late Nineteenth Century*. Princeton, NJ: University of Princeton Press, 1989.

Hall, Linda B. *Alvaro Obregón: Power and Revolution in Mexico, 1911–1920*. College Station: Texas A&M University Press, 1981.

———. *Oil, Banks, and Politics: The United States and Postrevolutionary Mexico*. Austin: University of Texas Press, 1995.

Hall, Linda B., and Don M. Coerver. *Revolution on the Border: The United States and Mexico, 1910–1920*. Albuquerque: University of New Mexico Press, 1988.

Hamilton, Nora. *The Limits of State Autonomy: Post-Revolutionary Mexico*. Princeton, NJ: Princeton University Press, 1982.

Harper, Kristin. "Revolutionary Tabasco in the Time of Tomás Garrido Canabal, 1923–1935: A Mexican House Divided." PhD diss., University of Massachusetts at Amherst, 2004.

Harris, Charles H., and Louis R. Sadler. "The Witzke Affair: German Intrigue on the Mexican Border, 1917–18." *Military Review* 59 (1979): 36–46.

Hart, John M. "The Mexican Revolution, 1910–1920." *The Oxford History of Mexico*. Ed. Michael C. Meyer and William H. Beezley, 435–66. Oxford: Oxford University Press, 2000.

———. *Revolutionary Mexico: The Coming and Process of the Mexican Revolution*. 2nd ed. Berkeley: University of California Press, 1997.

Henderson, Peter V. N. "Un gobernador maderista: José María Maytorena y la Revolución en Sonora." *Historia Mexicana* 51, no. 1 (2001): 151–86.

———. *In the Absence of Don Porfirio: Francisco León de la Barra and the Mexican Revolution*. Wilmington, DE: Scholarly Resources, 2000.

Henderson, Timothy J. *The Worm in the Wheat: Rosalie Evans and Agrarian Struggle in the Puebla-Tlaxcala Valley of Mexico, 1906–1927*. Durham, NC: Duke University Press, 1998.

Hennessy, Alistair. "Latin America." In *Populism: Its Meanings and National Characteristics*. Ed. Ghiṭa Ionescu and Ernest Gellner, 28–47. London: Weidenfeld and Nicolson, 1969.

Hernández Chávez, Alicia. *Historia de la Revolución Mexicana, periodo 1934–1940: La mecánica cardenista*. Mexico City: Colegio de México, 1979.

Holden, Robert H. *Mexico and the Survey of Public Lands, 1876–1911: The Management of Modernization*. DeKalb: Northern Illinois University Press, 1994.

Horn, James J. "Did the United States Plan an Invasion of Mexico in 1927?" *Journal of Inter-American Studies and World Affairs* 15, no. 4 (November 1973): 454–71.

———. "El embajador Sheffield contra el presidente Calles." *Historia Mexicana* 20, no. 2 (October 1970): 265–84.

———. "U.S. Diplomacy and the 'Specter of Bolshevism' in Mexico (1924–27)." *Americas* 32, no. 1 (July 1975): 31–45.

Hu-DeHart, Evelyn. "La comunidad china en el desarrollo de Sonora." In *Historia general de Sonora, vol. 4: Sonora moderno, 1880–1929*. Hermosillo: Gobierno del Estado de Sonora, 1997.

———. "From Immigrant Minority to Racial Minority: The Chinese of Mexico, 1876–1930." Paper presented at the Tenth Congreso de Historiadores, Ft. Worth, TX, November 1999.

———. *Missionaries, Miners, and Indians: Spanish Contact with the Yaqui Nation of Northwestern New Spain, 1533–1820*. Tucson: University of Arizona Press, 1981.

———. *Yaqui Resistance and Survival: The Struggle for Land and Autonomy, 1821–1910*. Madison: University of Wisconsin Press, 1984.

José Valenzuela, Georgette E. *La campaña presidencial de 1923–1924 en México*. Mexico City: Instituto Nacional de Estudios Históricos de la Revolución Mexicana, 1998.

———. *El relevo del caudillo: De cómo y por qué Calles fue candidato presidencial* (Mexico City: El Caballito, 1982).

———. "El viaje de Plutarco Elías Calles como presidente electo por Europa y Estados Unidos." *Revista Mexicana de Sociología* 57, no. 3 (1995): 191–210.

Joseph, Gilbert M. *Revolution from Without: Yucatán, Mexico, and the United States, 1880–1924*. Cambridge: Cambridge University Press, 1982.

Joseph, Gilbert M., and Daniel Nugent, eds. *Everyday Forms of State Formation: Revolution and the Negotiation of Rule in Mexico*. Durham, NC: Duke University Press, 1994.

Katz, Friedrich. "Liberal Republic and Porfiriato." *Mexico since Independence*. Ed. Leslie Bethell, 49–124. Cambridge: Cambridge University Press, 1991.

———. *The Life and Times of Pancho Villa*. Stanford, CA: Stanford University Press, 1998.

———. *The Secret War in Mexico: Europe, the United States, and the Mexican Revolution*. Chicago: University of Chicago Press, 1981.

Knight, Alan. "Cardenismo: Juggernaut or Jalopy." *Journal of Latin American Studies* 26 (1994): 73–107.

———. "The Ideology of the Mexican Revolution, 1910–1940." *Estudios Interdisciplinarios de América Latina y el Caribe* 8, no. 1 (1997): 77–110.

———. *The Mexican Revolution*. 2 vols. Cambridge: Cambridge University Press, 1986.

———. "Peasants into Patriots: Thoughts on the Making of the Mexican Nation." *Mexican Studies/Estudios Mexicanos* 10, no. 1 (1994): 135–61.

———. "Popular Culture and the Revolutionary State in Mexico, 1910–1940." *Hispanic American Historical Review* 74, no. 3 (1994): 395–444.

———. "Populism and Neo-Populism in Latin America, Especially Mexico." *Journal of Latin American Studies* 30, no. 2 (1998): 223–48.

———. "Racism, Revolution, and *Indigenismo*: Mexico, 1910–1940." *The Idea of Race in Latin America, 1870–1940*. Ed. Richard Graham, 71–113. Austin: University of Texas Press, 1990.

———. "Revolutionary Process, Recalcitrant People: Mexico, 1910–1940." *The Revolutionary Process in Mexico: Essays on Political and Social Change, 1880–1940*. Ed. Jaime Rodríguez O., 227–64. Los Angeles: UCLA Latin American Studies Center, 1990.

———. *U.S.-Mexican Relations, 1910–1940: An Interpretation*. San Diego: Center for U.S.-Mexican Studies, University of California, San Diego, 1987.

———. "The United States and the Mexican Peasantry, c. 1880–1940." In *Rural Revolt in Mexico: U.S. Intervention and the Domain of Subaltern Politics*. 2nd ed. Ed. Daniel Nugent, 25–63. Durham, NC: Duke University Press, 1998.

Krauze, Enrique. *Mexico: Biography of Power*. Trans. Hank Heifetz. New York: Harper Collins, 1997.

———. *Reformar desde el origen: Plutarco Elías Calles*. Mexico City: Fondo de Cultura Económica, 1987.

———. *El vértigo de la victoria: Alvaro Obregón*. Mexico City: Fondo de Cultura Económica, 1987.

Krauze, Enrique, Jean Meyer, and Cayetano Reyes. *Historia de la revolución mexicana: Periodo 1924–28: La reconstrucción económica*. Mexico City: El Colegio de México, 1977.

Kubli, Luciano. *Calles y su gobierno: Ensayo biográfico*. Mexico City, 1931.

Kuzio, Barbara A. "President Abelardo Rodríguez (1932–34): From Maximato to Cardenismo." MA thesis, Portland State University, 1996.

Laclau, Ernesto. *Politics and Ideology in Marxist Theory: Marxism, Fascism, Populism*. London: Humanities Press, 1977.

Lajous, Alejandra. *Los orígenes del partido único en México*. Mexico City: UNAM, 1979.

Lear, John. *Workers, Neighbors, and Citizens: The Revolution in Mexico City*. Lincoln: University of Nebraska Press, 2001.

Lieuwen, Edwin. *Mexican Militarism: The Political Rise and Fall of the Revolutionary Army, 1910–1940*. Albuquerque: University of New Mexico Press, 1968.

Lomnitz, Claudio. "Barbarians at the Gate? A Few Remarks on the Politics of the 'New Cultural History of Mexico.'" *Hispanic American Historical Review* 79, no. 2 (1999): 367–85.

———. *Deep Mexico, Silent Mexico: An Anthropology of Nationalism*. Minneapolis: University of Minnesota Press, 2001.

———. *Exits from the Labyrinth: Culture and Ideology in the Mexican National Space*. Berkeley: University of California Press, 1992.

Loyo, Engracia. *Las escuelas J. Cruz Gálvez: Fundación y primeros años*. Boletín 40. Mexico City: Fideicomiso Archivos Plutarco Elías Calles y Fernando Torreblanca, 2002.

Loyo Camacho, Martha Beatriz. *Joaquín Amaro y el proceso de institucionalización del ejército mexicano, 1917–1931*. Mexico City: UNAM, 2003.

———. "El Partido Revolucionario Anti Comunista en las elecciones de 1940." *Estudios de Historia Moderna y Contemporánea de México* 23 (January 2002): 145–60.

———. *Plutarco Elías Calles desde su exilio*. Boletín 45. Mexico City: Archivo Fideicomiso Plutarco Elías Calles y Fernando Torreblanca, 2004.

Loyola Díaz, Rafael. *La crisis Obregón-Calles y el estado mexicano*. 3rd ed. Mexico City: Siglo XXI Editores, 1987.

Macías Richard, Carlos. "La fuerza del destino: Una biografía de Plutarco Elías Calles, 1877–1945." Doctoral diss., El Colegio de México, 1994.

———. *Vida y temperamento: Plutarco Elías Calles, 1877–1920*. Mexico City: FAPEC and Fondo de Cultura Económica, 1995.

Marcoux, Carl H. "Plutarco Elías Calles and the Partido Nacional Revolucionario: Mexican National and Regional Politics in 1928 and 1929." PhD diss., University of California at Riverside, 1994.

Martínez Assad, Carlos R. *Laboratorio de la revolución: El Tabasco garridista*. Mexico City: Siglo XXI Editores, 1979.

Matute, Alvaro. *Historia de la revolución mexicana, 1917–1924: Las dificultades del nuevo estado*. Mexico City: Colegio de México, 1995.

Mayer, Leticia. "El proceso de recuperación simbólica de cuatro héroes de la revolución mexicana de 1910 a través de la prensa nacional." *Historia Mexicana* 178 (October 1995): 353–81.

McMullen, Christopher J. "Calles and the Diplomacy of Revolution: Mexican-American Relations, 1924–1928." PhD diss., Georgetown University, 1980.

Medín, Tzvi. *El minimato presidencial: Historia política del Maximato*. Mexico City: Ediciones Era, 1982.

Medina Ruiz, Fernando. *Calles: Un destino melancólico*. Mexico City: Editorial Jus, 1960.

Melzer, Richard A. "Dwight Morrow's Role in the Mexican Revolution: Good Neighbor or Meddling Yankee?" PhD diss., University of New Mexico, 1979.

Meyer, Jean. *The Cristero Rebellion: The Mexican People between Church and State, 1926–1929*. Trans. Richard Southern. Cambridge: Cambridge University Press, 1976.

———. "Mexico in the 1920s." In *Mexico Since Independence*. Ed. Leslie Bethell, 201–40. Cambridge: Cambridge University Press, 1991.

———. "Revolution and Reconstruction in the 1920s." In *Mexico since Independence*. Ed. Leslie Bethell. Cambridge: Cambridge University Press, 1991.

———. *La Révolution mexicaine*. Paris: Harmattan, 1973.

Meyer, Jean, Enrique Krauze, and Cayetano Reyes. *Historia de la Revolución Mexicana, 1924–1928: Estado y sociedad con Calles*. Mexico City: El Colegio de México, 1977.

Meyer, Lorenzo. *Historia de la Revolución Mexicana, 1928–1934: El conflicto social y los gobiernos del maximato*. Mexico City: Colegio de México, 1978.

———. *Mexico and the United States in the Oil Controversy, 1917–1942*. Trans. Lidia Lozano. Austin: University of Texas Press, 1972.

Meyer, Lorenzo, Rafael Segovia, and Alejandra Lajous. *Historia de la Revolución Mexicana, 1928–1934: Los inicios de la institucionalización*. Mexico City: Colegio de México, 1978.

Meyer, Michael C. *Huerta: A Political Portrait*. Lincoln: University of Nebraska Press, 1972.

———. *Mexican Rebel: Pascual Orozco and the Mexican Revolution, 1910–1915*. Lincoln: University of Nebraska Press, 1967.

Meyer, Michael C., William L. Sherman, and Susan M. Deeds. *The Course of Mexican History*. 7th rev. ed. New York: Oxford University Press, 2003.

Miller, Robert L. *Researching Life Stories and Family Histories*. London: Sage, 2000.

Monteón, Michael C. "The Child Is Father of the Man: Personality and Politics in Revolutionary Mexico." *Journal of Iberian and Latin American Studies* 10, no. 1 (2004): 43–61.

Moore, Walter. "Adolfo de la Huerta: His Political Role in Sonora, 1906–1920." PhD diss., University of California, San Diego, 1982.

Mora, Gregorio. "Sonora al filo de la tormenta: Desilusión con el porfiriato, 1900–1911." In *The Revolutionary Process in Mexico: Essays on Political and Social Change, 1880–1940*. Ed. Jaime E. Rodríguez, 57–80. Los Angeles: UCLA Latin American Center Publications, 1990.

Moya, José C. *Cousins and Strangers: Spanish Immigrants in Buenos Aires, 1850–1930*. Berkeley: University of California Press, 1998.

Niblo, Stephen R. *Mexico in the 1940s: Modernity, Politics, and Corruption*. Wilmington, DE: Scholarly Resources, 1999.

Niemeyer, E. Victor, Jr. *Revolution at Querétaro: The Mexican Constitutional Convention of 1916–1917*. Austin: University of Texas Press, 1974.

O'Malley, Ilene V. *The Myth of the Revolution: Hero Cults and the Institutionalization of the Mexican State, 1920–1940*. New York: Greenwood Press, 1986.

Olcott, Jocelyn. *Revolutionary Women in Postrevolutionary Mexico*. Durham, NC: Duke University Press, 2005.

Olliff, Donathon C. *Reforma Mexico and the United States: The Search for Alternatives to Annexation*. Tuscaloosa: University of Alabama Press, 1981.

Paz, Octavio. *The Labyrinth of Solitude*. Trans. Lysander Kemp. New York: Grove Press, 1985.

Piccato, Pablo. *City of Suspects: Crime in Mexico City, 1900–1931*. Durham, NC: Duke University Press, 2001.

Plasencia de la Parra, Enrique. *Escenarios y personajes de la rebelión delahuertista*. Mexico City: Miguel Porrúa, 1998.

Pletcher, David M. "The Development of Railroads in Sonora." *Inter-American Economic Affairs* 1, no. 4 (March 1948): 3–45.

———. *Rails, Mines, and Progress: Seven American Promoters in Mexico, 1867–1911*. Ithaca, NY: Cornell University Press, 1958.

Powell, Thomas G. *Mexico and the Spanish Civil War*. Albuquerque: University of New Mexico Press, 1980.

Puente, Ramón. *Hombres de la Revolución: Calles*. Mexico City: Fondo de Cultura Económica, 1994 [1933].

Purnell, Jennie. *Popular Movements and State Formation in Revolutionary Mexico: The Agraristas and Cristeros of Michoacán*. Durham, NC: Duke University Press, 1999.

Quirk, Robert E. *The Mexican Revolution, 1914–1915: The Convention of Aguascalientes*. Bloomington: Indiana University Press, 1960.

———. *The Mexican Revolution and the Catholic Church, 1910–1929*. Bloomington: Indiana University Press, 1973.

Raat, W. Dirk. "Ideas and Society in Don Porfirio's Mexico." *Americas* 30, no. 1 (July 1973): 32–53.

———. *El positivismo durante el porfiriato*. Mexico City: El Colegio de México, 1975.

Radding de Murrieta, Cynthia. "El triunfo constitucionalista y las reformas en la región, 1913–1919." In *Historia General de Sonora, vol. 4: Sonora moderno, 1880–1929*. Hermosillo: Gobierno del Estado de Sonora, 1997.

———. *Wandering Peoples: Colonialism, Ethnic Spaces, and Ecological Frontiers in Northwest Mexico, 1700–1850*. Durham, NC: Duke University Press, 1997.

Ramírez, José Carlos, Ricardo León, and Oscar Conde. "La estrategia económica de los callistas." *Historia General de Sonora*, 5:65–78.

Richmond, Douglas. *The Mexican Nation: Historical Continuity and Modern Change*. Upper Saddle River, NJ: Prentice Hall, 2002.

———. *Venustiano Carranza's Nationalist Struggle, 1893–1920*. Lincoln: University of Nebraska Press, 1983.

Rinke, Stefan. *"Der letzte freie Kontinent": Deutsche Lateinamerikapolitik im Zeichen transnationaler Beziehungen, 1918–1933*. 2 vols. Stuttgart: Verlag Hans Dieter Heinz, 1996.

Rivera, Antonio G. *La Revolución en Sonora*. Hermosillo: Gobierno de Sonora, 1981.

Ross, Stanley R. *Francisco I. Madero, Apostle of Mexican Democracy*. New York: Columbia University Press, 1955.

Rubin, Jeffrey. *Decentering the Regime: Ethnicity, Radicalism, and Democracy in Juchitán, Mexico*. Durham, NC.: Duke University Press, 1997.

Ruibal Corella, Antonio. *Calles, hombre de su tiempo*. N.p., 1987.

Ruiz, Ramón Eduardo. *The People of Sonora and Yankee Capitalists*. Tucson: University of Arizona Press, 1988.

Salmerón Sanginés, Pedro. *Aarón Sáenz Garza: Militar, diplomático, político, empresario*. Mexico City: Editorial Porrúa, 2001.

Saragoza, Alex. *The Monterrey Elite and the Mexican State, 1880–1940*. Austin: University of Texas Press, 1988.

———. "The Selling of Mexico: Tourism and the State." In *Fragments of a Golden Age: The Politics of Culture in Mexico since 1940*. Ed. Gilbert Joseph, Anne Rubenstein, and Eric Zolov, 91–115. Durham, NC: Duke University Press, 2001.

Schantz, Eric M. "From the Mexicali Rose to the Tijuana Brass: Vice Tours of the United Status-Mexico Border, 1910–1965." PhD diss., University of California-Los Angeles, 2001.

Schmidt, Arthur. "Making It Real Compared to What: Reconceptualizing Mexican History since 1940." In *Fragments of a Golden Age: The Politics of Culture in Mexico since 1940*. Ed. Gilbert Joseph, Anne Rubenstein, and Eric Zolov, 23–68. Durham, NC: Duke University Press, 2001.

Schmidt, Henry C. *The Roots of "Lo Mexicano": Self and Society in Mexican Thought, 1900–1934*. College Station: Texas A&M University Press, 1978.

Schuler, Friedrich E. *Mexico between Hitler and Roosevelt: Mexican Foreign Relations in the Age of Lázaro Cárdenas, 1934–1940*. Albuquerque: University of New Mexico Press, 1998.

Scott, James C. *Weapons of the Weak: Everyday Forms of Peasant Resistance*. New Haven, CT: Yale University Press, 1985.

Shain, Yosse. *The Frontier of Loyalty: Political Exiles in the Age of the Nation State*. Middletown, CT: Wesleyan University Press, 1989.

Sherman, John W. *The Mexican Right*. Westport, CT: Praeger, 1997.

Silva Cáceres, Carlos. *Plutarco Elías Calles*. Mexico City: Editorial Planeta, 2002.

Simpson, Lesley B. *Many Mexicos*. 4th rev. ed. Berkeley: University of California Press, 1967.

Skirius, John. *José Vasconcelos y la cruzada de 1929*. Mexico City: Siglo XXI Editores, 1978.

Smith, Peter H. "La política dentro de la Revolución: El congreso constituyente de 1916–1917." *Historia Mexicana* 22, no. 4 (April 1973): 363–95.

Smith, Robert F. *The United States and Revolutionary Nationalism in Mexico, 1916–1932.* Chicago: University of Chicago Press, 1972.

Spenser, Daniela. *The Impossible Triangle: Mexico, Soviet Russia, and the United States in the 1920s.* Durham, NC: Duke University Press, 1999.

———. *En el gabinete de Venustiano Carranza, Boletín 30.* Mexico City: FAPEC, 1999.

Stout, Joseph A., Jr. *Border Conflict: Villistas, Carrancistas, and the Punitive Expedition, 1915–1920.* Ft. Worth: Texas Christian University Press, 1999.

———. "General Plutarco Elías Calles, Colonel Francisco M. Delgado, and the Servicio Confidencial, 1914–1930." Paper presented at the Eleventh Reunión de Historiadores Mexicanos, Estadounidenses y Canadienses, Monterrey, October 2003.

Tannenbaum, Frank. *Mexico: The Struggle for Peace and Bread.* New York: Knopf, 1950.

Tardanico, Richard. "State Dependency and Nationalism: Revolutionary Mexico, 1924–1928." *Comparative Studies in Society and History* 24, no. 3 (July 1982): 400–23.

Tenorio Trillo, Mauricio. "The Cosmopolitan Mexican Summer, 1920–1949." *Latin American Research Review* 32, no. 2 (1997): 224–40.

———. *Mexico at the World's Fairs: Crafting a Modern Nation.* Berkeley: University of California Press, 1996.

Tinker Salas, Miguel. *In the Shadow of the Eagles: Sonora and the Transformation of the Border during the Porfiriato.* Berkeley: University of California Press, 1997.

Tobler, Hans Werner. "Peasants and the Shaping of the Revolutionary State, 1910–1940." In *Riot, Rebellion, and Revolution: Rural Social Conflict in Mexico.* Ed. Friedrich Katz, 487–518. Princeton, NJ: Princeton University Press, 1988.

Torres Ramírez, Blanca. *Historia de la Revolución Mexicana: México en la segunda guerra mundial.* Mexico City: Colegio de México, 1979.

Vaughan, Mary Kay. "Cultural Approaches to Peasant Politics in the Mexican Revolution." *Hispanic American Historical Review* 79, no. 2 (1999): 269–305.

———. *Cultural Politics in Revolution: Teachers, Peasants, and Schools in Mexico, 1930–1940.* Tucson: University of Arizona Press, 1998.

———. *The State, Education, and Social Class in Mexico, 1880–1924.* DeKalb: Northern Illinois University Press, 1982.

Vaughan, Mary Kay, and Stephen E. Lewis, eds. *The Eagle and the Virgin: Nation and Cultural Revolution in Mexico, 1920–1940.* Durham, NC: Duke University Press, 2006.

Voss, Stuart F. *On the Periphery of Nineteenth-Century Mexico: Sonora and Sinaloa, 1810–1877.* Tucson: University of Arizona Press, 1982.

Wasserman, Mark. *Persistent Oligarchs: Elites and Politics in Chihuahua, Mexico, 1910–1940.* Durham, NC: Duke University Press, 1993.

Watkins, Holland D. "Plutarco Elias Calles: El Jefe Maximo of Mexico." PhD diss., Texas Technological College, 1968.

Weeks, Charles. *The Juárez Myth in Mexico*. Tuscaloosa: University of Alabama Press, 1987.

Wilkie, James W. *The Mexican Revolution: Federal Expenditure and Social Change since 1910*. Berkeley: University of California Press, 1970.

Wilkins, Mira, and Frank E. Hill. *American Business Abroad: Ford on Six Continents*. Detroit, MI: Wayne State University Press, 1964.

Womack, John. *Zapata and the Mexican Revolution*. New York: Knopf, 1968.

——. "The Mexican Economy during the Revolution, 1910–1920: Historiography and Analysis." *Marxist Perspectives* 1 (1978): 80–123.

Wood, Andrew G. *Revolution in the Street: Women, Workers, and Urban Protest in Veracruz, 1870–1927*. Wilmington, DE: Scholarly Resources, 2001.

Zavaleta, Antonio N. "El Niño Fidencio and the *Fidencistas*." In *Sects, Cults and Spiritual Communities: A Sociological Analysis*. Ed. William W. Zellner and Marc Petrowski, 95–117. Westport, CT: Praeger, 1998.

Zevada, Ricardo. *Calles presidente*. Mexico City: Editorial Nuestro Tiempo, 1971.

Zogbaum, Heidi. *B. Traven: A Vision of Mexico*. Wilmington, DE: Scholarly Resources, 1992.

Sources on the Web

Almada Bay, Ignacio. "Alvaro Obregón Salido: Nuevos datos y nuevas interpretaciones." www.colson.edu.mx/historia/ialmada/inherm-obreg%F3n.pdf (accessed Nov. 21, 2005).

——. "La patria chica antes que la justicia: Indagación sobre el papel del estado de Sonora en la lucha contra el gobierno de Huerta." www.colson.edu.mx/historia/ialmada/inherm-huertismo.pdf (accessed Nov. 21, 2005).

Gomezharper de Treviño, Marcela. "La parapsicología en México." www.alipsi.com.ar/publicaciones_articulo.asp?id_articulo=32 (accessed July 2, 2004).

Index

Note: All of Calles's children are indexed under "E" for "Elías Calles" rather than under "C" for "Calles."

269

About the Author

Jürgen Buchenau is professor of history and director of Latin American studies at the University of North Carolina at Charlotte. He completed his undergraduate studies at the University of Cologne, Germany, and his MA and PhD in history at the University of North Carolina at Chapel Hill. His prior book-length publications include *In the Shadow of the Giant: The Making of Mexico's Central America Policy, 1876–1930* (1996), *Tools of Progress: A German Merchant Family in Mexico City, 1865–Present* (2004), and *Mexico OtherWise: Modern Mexico in the Eyes of Foreign Observers* (2005).

LATIN AMERICAN SILHOUETTES

Editors: William H. Beezley and Judith Ewell